A History
of Economic
Ideas

ROBERT LEKACHMAN

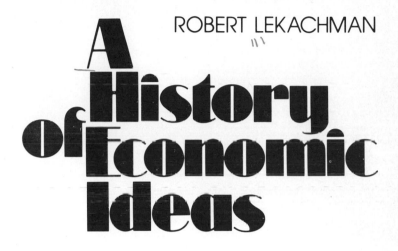

A History of Economic Ideas

McGRAW-HILL BOOK COMPANY

New York • St. Louis • San Francisco • Düsseldorf • Mexico • Montreal
Panama • Paris • São Paulo • Tokyo • Toronto

First McGraw-Hill Paperback Edition, 1976
23456789   MU   MU   7987

Library of Congress Cataloging in Publication Data

Lekachman, Robert.
   A history of economic ideas.

   Bibliography: p.
   Includes index.
   1. Economics—History. I. Title.
[HB75.L37   1976]   330'.09   76-14945
ISBN 0-07-037155-5

To Eva

Contents

PART III. MARGINALISTS AND OPPONENTS

PART IV. CONTEMPORARY ECONOMICS

Preface

Like any other substitute, a history of economic thought is inferior to the original. In this instance, "original" means nothing less than the best possible collection of significant, interesting, or, at happiest, significant *and* interesting writings of the men whose names are a roster of the landmarks in the development of economic ideas. Such a course is difficult, if only because not all economists write good English or fall into the hands of literate translators—an understatement of heroic dimensions. Few human beings can have written more abstrusely than Ricardo. Few philosophers could have split more hairs than Marx. Moreover, terminologies and literary conventions change so much that continual readjustment is the lot of the student who endeavors to follow the succession of names which flash across his intellectual horizon. It is much more than learning that in England "corn" means wheat and "maize" means corn and that a quarter is twenty-eight pounds. The student must grapple with strange problems and strange solutions as well as with strange language.

We cannot always do what is best. Libraries are restricted. Cheap, paper reprints of the economic classics do not cover the field. Worst of all, time is scant. Frequently, only a semester is available to cover the whole history of economic thought. With less excuse, even graduate schools occasionally profane the memory of their ancestors in this way. The justification for a

text in this subject is to be found in these unpleasant facts. But
if such a book is to be usable, it should not be so long as to defeat some of the reasons for its existence. Designed to save time,
summarize information, and compensate for inadequate libraries,
it should be short and selective. Both of these virtues, if none
other, I can claim for this book. In it, I have deliberately sought
to say enough about the major figures to give students a fighting
chance to carry away a coherent notion of each man's ideas.
This has meant extensive quotation. I do not apologize for this
practice, since the quotations act as a sample of each economist's
characteristic mode of expressing himself. The corollary of this
emphasis is ruthless pruning. Here my model has been Sir Alexander Gray, who boasted amiably of writing a history which
had omitted the most names, rather than the more compendious
volumes which serve justice by mentioning everybody.

I do not think that I have concealed either my preferences or
my prejudices. While I have endeavored to describe all important schools and movements, my own heart belongs to economists who were aware of the outside world and anxious to do
something sensible to improve it. In the nineteenth century, this
preference no doubt explains my indulgence toward the English
classical economists whose social tastes and practical remedies
are not necessarily my own. Would not every right-minded intellectual of the twentieth century have wished to be a Philosophical Radical in the nineteenth? In the twentieth century,
this preference dictates higher regard for Keynes than for the
paladins of the indifference curve, and for Pigou than for the
prophets of the new welfare economics.

This suggests what I hold to be true, that economics tries to
be a pure science at the peril of barrenness and intellectual
gamesmanship. Economics does its job best and commands most
respect when economists concern themselves with the problems
which afflict ordinary human beings. In the nineteenth century
these problems included the regrettable tendency of the poor to
multiply in number, soggy currencies, oppressive poverty, and
narrow agricultural resources. Smith, Ricardo, Malthus, and

Mill did their best to understand and meet these social perplexities, even though their remedies occasionally appear odd or even horrifying. Much in the same way, Keynes in this century attacked the disasters of depression and underemployment. Partly in penance for these unscientific leanings, I have included two long chapters on the marginalists and several shorter chapters on various aspects of technical economics.

What I have so far said suggests a last observation. The history of my subject naturally organizes itself for me around men and problems rather than concepts and doctrines. Although it is perfectly possible to write a valuable book which traces value, rent, wages, and profits through the centuries, I have centered my attention upon men rather than abstractions. Since men breathe and worry, I have tried to say something about what the major economists were like as people, what problems agitated them, and how they responded to them.

ROBERT LEKACHMAN

PART I

The Beginnings

Chapter 1

Greek and Roman Economics

THE ANCIENT WORLD

Frequently, historians of economic thought describe the economic notions of the ancient world with a certain amiable condescension composed in equal measure of scorn for their primitive characteristics and approval of their analytical prevision. By this approach, the historian of ideas runs the serious risk of parochialism, of arguing that since all history has struggled toward modern capitalism, and since economic theory is the explanation of contemporary capitalism, anything before our own time is imperfect as economic organization and incomplete at best as economic explanation. After all, it is undeniable that beside our sophisticated techniques the summary treatment of economic affairs by Plato and Aristotle appears sketchy and crude.

But we lose sight of the characteristic features of economic life in the fifth and fourth centuries before the Christian era if we leave it at that. Although the trading firm was not unknown in the ancient world, in the small city states of the period the representative unit of the economy was the household, the center of the productive economic activities we now handle through the market. Hence, Aristotle's emphasis upon the household envisaged a more important subject than that of consumption. Moreover, by far the bulk of activity in these states was agricultural. Fabrication of goods for sale and systematic trading of them by well-defined merchant classes, while important enough to merit serious discussion by contemporaries, were marginal and recent in the lives of these cities.

3

If free markets in commodities were rudimentary, free markets in labor scarcely existed. Although not all workers were slaves, and free men (the metics) carried on most trade, Plato and Aristotle took slavery for granted, defended it vigorously, and imagined no other basis of a civilized life. In place of our mobile worker, free to change jobs where his economic advantage dictates, there was the slave, fixed in abode and condition, sometimes a barbarian (as Greeks significantly termed the non-Greek), occasionally a fellow Hellene captured in war. The good life and the happy state of the philosophers rested squarely upon the menial labor of the bondsman. Naturally enough, Plato and Aristotle viewed his work with contempt. Manual labor was servile, suitable for the slave. Nor did the philosophers set much higher store upon moneymaking. The techniques of profit, said Plato, might "do us good, but we regard them as disagreeable; and no one would choose them for their own sakes, but only for the sake of some reward or result which flows from them."[1]

We see the economics of Plato and Aristotle somewhat differently when we realize that what they were discussing above all was the good life, the just state, and the happy man. Since they were persuaded that externals—money and what money bought—created neither happiness nor wisdom, their analysis of economic life was only a small part of their treatment of the whole life of man in society. Perhaps this is only another way of saying that their conception of what we somewhat largely call the social sciences was different from ours, although not necessarily inferior to it. Separating economics from sociology and concentrating upon the study of each as a subsystem, we rationally emphasize exchange relationships in which the proximate goals of all parties are monetary and the larger questions of life are put aside. Possibly because the world was young and everything seemed possible, Plato and Aristotle sought a unified science of society, the object which a few contemporary social students also wistfully pursue.[2] Their economics then were embedded in the

[1] Plato, *The Republic*, in *The Dialogues of Plato*, translated by Benjamin Jowett, Random House, 1937, Vol. I, p. 621.

[2] See, for example, Talcott Parsons' *The Social System*, Free Press, 1951, and his later *Economy and Society*, Free Press, 1956.

institutional arrangements of the time and shaped by the philosophical aims of the analyst.

Under the circumstances, it is all the more striking that even from the narrower viewpoint of contemporary economics, Plato and Aristotle saw so many of the key concepts of eighteenth- and nineteenth-century discussion. The distinction between use value and exchange value, the functions of money, and the division of labor are among the insights which Plato or Aristotle employed. Perhaps they seem better economists in the twentieth century, in which social students are becoming discontented with the severe specialization of their subjects, than they did in the nineteenth, when that specialization seemed the only road to scientific progress.[3]

There is a last preliminary observation to be made. Plato and Aristotle were Athenians, and Athens, as all the world came to know, was something special in Greece and the world. It was special partly because philosophy, art, and scientific speculation reached peaks there which were laboriously reclimbed only after many centuries had elapsed. It was special, also, because of the Athenian individualism, the tendency of the Greek to think and act for himself—always excepting the bulk of the population who were slaves. Plato and Aristotle wrote in the days of Athenian decline and, though their speculations were formulated within the context of Athenian democracy, they were critical of and even hostile to that democracy. The state may have made fewer demands upon the citizen in Athens than elsewhere in the ancient world, but it was Socrates who conceded its right, acting through his fellow citizens, to put him to death and who therefore refused to escape from the prison where he lay waiting for the hemlock. We can guess that this incident among much else led to Plato's celebrated recommendation for the rule of cities:

Until philosophers are kings, or the kings and princes of this world have the spirit and power of philosophy, and political greatness and wisdom meet in one, and those commoner natures who pursue either to the exclusion of the other are compelled to stand

[3] Extremely helpful on this subject is Karl Polanyi *et al.*, *Trade and Markets in the Early Empires*, Free Press, 1957, pp. 64–97.

aside, cities will never have rest from their evils—no, nor the human race, as I believe—and then only will this our state have a possibility of life and behold the light of day.[4]

PLATO (427–347 B.C.)

Plato's important economic ideas arose incidentally from his discussion of justice and the ideal state in the *Republic*. To an astonishing degree, his doctrine of the state depended upon the division of labor, and so did his conception of economic activity. Division of labor emerged from the natural differences among human beings, from the "diversities of nature among us which are adapted to different occupations."[5] He proceeded in the same passage to draw a utilitarian moral: ". . . all things are produced more plentifully and easily and of a better quality when one man does one thing which is natural to him and does it at the right time, and leaves other things." No doubt, if Plato's interest had been primarily in the expansion of output and the increase of efficiency, he would have gone on to make Adam Smith's point that, because division of labor became more complex as the market widened, it was, therefore, a good thing to widen the market. But Plato's angle of vision was different. The ideal state should be big enough to allow appropriate scope for the play of each man's natural talent. At the center of the state's appropriate concern was human improvement rather than increased output. And it was fairly obvious that Plato considered a quite small state adequate to his purpose. If the state were larger and strained to acquire still additional territory, the cause was likely to have been a degenerate taste for luxury which compelled a more complex division of labor but failed to improve the quality of human existence.

Three major occupational categories inhabited the ideal state: rulers, soldiers, and workers. Again Plato appealed to natural specialization, as in this exhortation:

---

[4] Plato, *op. cit.*, p. 737. Passage italicized in Jowett translation.
[5] *Ibid.*, p. 633.

Citizens . . . you are brothers, yet God has framed you differently. Some of you have the power of command, and in the composition of these he has mingled gold, wherefore also they have the greatest honour; others he has made of silver, to be auxiliaries; others again who are to be husbandmen and craftsmen he has composed of brass and iron; and the species will generally be preserved in the children. But as all are of the same original stock, a golden parent will sometimes have a silver son, or a silver parent a golden son.[6]

In this beautiful language, Plato described a caste system in which very little circulation of individuals was to be expected. His ranking was significant. Top position naturally went to the philosophers as rulers; a middle position to the auxiliaries or soldiers; and at the bottom of the pyramid were the farmers and the artisans.

This derogation of economic activity and economic goals was reinforced by Plato's description of ideal property arrangements for each class. Only the lowest, farmers and artisans, were allowed to work for profit and accumulate property. Rulers and auxiliaries should have neither homes nor property of their own. Only if this were true, could they be expected to pursue truth and justice, now free of base economic goals.

Aware of the sharpness of class conflict in Athens, Plato sought to minimize its extent and intensity by assigning appropriate goals to each group. The pursuit of money by the base would not arouse the envy of wise rulers any more than the prudent exercise of power by the latter would antagonize artisans and farmers. "Any city, however small, is in fact divided into two, one the city of the poor, the other of the rich; these are at war with one another."[7] Plato would have divided the city into three, but eliminated at the same time the causes of conflict, by dismissing money as a divisive force.

His argument against democracy was based upon his notion of the natural elite and the specialization of function. Ruling was a full-time job. It was disastrous to entrust government to men who spent the bulk of their days in commerce or agriculture.

[6] *Ibid.*, pp. 679–680.
[7] *Ibid.*, p. 685

But even if the husbandman devoted his full attention to governing, he would make but a poor job of it. Only a few, blessed by birth and nurtured by careful training, were capable of proper administration. The ideal state selected its rulers from the men of gold. More than that, it trained them and tested them before it entrusted authority to them. Never answered by Plato were the questions: Who tests the testers? Who selects the natural aristocrats? Who decides when a child born of silver parents is himself of gold?

ARISTOTLE (384–322 B.C.)

One of the pupils of Plato, Aristotle achieved unrivaled prestige, less perhaps in the ancient world than in medieval Europe, where he was frequently cited simply as the Philosopher. Encyclopedic in range, he wrote on economics as he did on other subjects, in the deliberate attempt to encompass all human knowledge. As followers of the films may know, Aristotle also, as tutor to Alexander the Great, had a direct opportunity to mold one of the world's great men. It illustrates the gap between life and philosophy to reflect how little Alexander's life was marked by the pursuit of that golden mean which his master preached. The *Politics* and the *Ethics* contain the bulk of Aristotle's economic comments. In tone, they are matter of fact and prosaic, in contrast to the poetry of Plato. Frequently Aristotle differed from Plato. Here we summarize his ideas on the state, property, value, and money.

THE STATE

The state, like the family and the village, "originates in the bare needs of life" and "continues in existence for the sake of a good life." Just as the state is a creation of nature, "man is by nature a political animal."[8] Because men naturally herd together, the state is possible.

[8] Aristotle, *Politics,* translated by Benjamin Jowett, Modern Library, 1942, p. 54.

Aristotle discussed systematically the various political arrangements logically conceivable: monarchy, aristocracy, and polity received qualified praise; their perversions—tyranny, oligarchy, and extreme democracy—were condemned. Further subdivision produced five forms of monarchy and four variants of democracy. The worst variant of the latter opened all offices to everybody. Unlike Plato, Aristotle was able to see merit in the participation of the masses (always realizing that he meant citizens, the minority; not slaves, the majority), for, as a common-sense proposition, the majority had the largest interest in events. But the participation had to be limited by law. Conditions were best in that state where the middle class was strong enough to control the rich on the one side and the poor on the other, for "a city ought to be composed, as far as possible, of equals and similars; and these are generally the middle classes. Wherefore the city which is composed of middle-class citizens is necessarily best constituted in respect of the elements of which we say the fabric of the state naturally consists."[9]

Only three classes should be eligible for citizenship: warriors, priests, and rulers. Each man should, at a different time in his life, act as warrior, priest, and ruler. Excluded from citizenship were merchants, husbandmen, and artisans. For "in the state which is best governed . . . the citizen must not lead the life of mechanics or tradesmen, for such a life is ignoble and inimical to virtue. Neither must they be husbandmen, since leisure is necessary both for the development of virtue and the performance of political duties."[10] It is worth remarking that leisure did not connote idle play, a principal meaning in today's usage. The intelligent man devoted his leisure to self-improvement, essentially by reading and discussion. Many moderns would prefer work to Aristotle's leisure.

There was in Aristotle a sense of the development of political institutions, of political process, absent from Plato, who wished to arrest change rather than to chart it. However, like his teacher,

9 *Ibid.*, p. 191.
10 *Ibid.*, p. 295.

Aristotle had nothing complimentary to say about those who pursued the actual economic life of the community. He even suggested that it might be best if the tillers of the soil were slaves chosen from an unspirited race.

PROPERTY

"Property is a part of the household, and the art of acquiring property is a part of the art of managing the household."[11] This definition is interesting both for what it included and what it excluded. Excluded were what we might call intangibles: money, securities, evidences of ownership, rather than the objects themselves. "Riches" were simply "the number of instruments to be used in a household or a state."[12] Obviously the definition was well adapted to the nearly self-sufficient households of the time. It could not be applied to capitalism.

The definition included slaves. Aristotle's views on slavery were in some respects like Plato's. Slavery was natural: ". . . that some should rule and others be ruled is a thing not only necessary but expedient; from the hour of their birth, some are marked out for subjection, others for rule."[13] But one contemporary feature of slavery made Aristotle uneasy. Undeniably, some slaves were slaves by law, not by birth: the misfortunes of their incessant quarrels had consigned numerous Greeks to slavery. But slavery by law was an evil, for "where the relation of master and slave between them is natural, they are friends and have a common interest, but where it rests merely on law and force the reverse is true."[14] Hence, Greeks should never enslave Greeks. However, at its best, the life of the slave improved both his existence and his master's. It was preferable to that of the artisan, because "the slave shares in his master's life; the artisan is less closely connected with him and only attains excellence in proportion as he becomes a slave. The meaner sort of mechanic

[11] *Ibid.*, p. 56.
[12] *Ibid.*, p. 56.
[13] *Ibid.*, p. 58.
[14] *Ibid.*, p. 62.

has a special and separate slavery; and whereas the slave exists by nature, not so the shoemaker or other artisan."[15]

In contrast to Plato, Aristotle favored private property and criticized communism. The pursuit of money might be a false aim, but life proceeded more smoothly when men had less occasion to quarrel, and each guarded his own. Here Aristotle appealed to men's strongest, not their highest, instincts. As he very practically put the matter, "Property should be in a certain sense common, but, as a general rule, private; for when everyone has a distinct interest, men will not complain of one another, and they will make more progress because everyone will be attending to his own business."[16] This was not a universal rule. Friends might customarily share their slaves, horses, and dogs. It would be best of all if property were private but its use were common, and "the special business of the legislator is to create in men this benevolent disposition."[17] But, as matters stood, men felt too great a pleasure in ownership, implanted by nature, to make experiments in communal ownership workable. Moreover, all the pleasures of liberality would be destroyed if there were no wealthy men capable of gratifying their finer feelings by gifts to the less fortunate. This last argument found a strange echo two millenia and more later in Malthus' population doctrine.

VALUE AND MONEY

Aristotle was responsible for one of economics' key distinctions, between value in exchange and value in use. The distinction appeared in this quotation, accompanied by a comparative judgment of the merits of the two modes: ". . . a shoe is used for wear and is used for exchange; both are uses of the shoe. He who gives a shoe in exchange for money or food to him who wants one, does indeed use the shoe as a shoe, but this is not its proper or primary purpose, for a shoe is not made to be an object of barter. The same may be said of all possessions. . . . retail

[15] *Ibid.*, p. 78.
[16] *Ibid.*, p. 88.
[17] *Ibid.*, p. 88.

trade is not a natural part of the art of getting wealth."[18] This preference for use over exchange ran through Aristotle's economic commentary. It was possible to get wealth through knowledge of livestock and husbandry. It was also possible to acquire wealth by the arts of commerce, the practice of usury, and service to another person for hire. The first two, partaking of household management, were "necessary and honourable, while that which consists in exchange is justly censured; for it is unnatural and a mode by which men gain from one another. The most hated sort, and with the greatest reason, is usury, which makes a gain out of money itself, and not from the natural object of it. For money was intended to be used in exchange, but not to increase at interest."[19]

Money was a convenient way of facilitating barter and expediting the development of retail trade. While exchange of the necessities of life "is not part of the wealth-getting art," it is "not contrary to nature" and "is needed for the satisfaction of men's natural wants."[20] Several of money's uses were implied here or elsewhere. Money was a medium of exchange. It was also a unit of account. Finally, Aristotle was able to see that money, by allowing a man to postpone consumption, acted as a store of value.

A natural question arises: If Aristotle saw so much, why did he not see still more? Especially, why did he not see that interest was a payment for the productive use of resources made available by one man to another? For Aristotle was vehement, as we have seen, against usury, and insistent that money was barren. Once more the question neglects history. In the circumstances of the time, loans were made to satisfy the urgent necessities of individuals. The man who made a loan added nothing to total output, as the unit of capital is now presumed to justify its reward. Rather, he transferred some of his surplus food and clothing to another person in greater need than himself. If he charged and collected interest, he could do so only by taking advantage of his

[18] *Ibid.*, p. 67.
[19] *Ibid.*, pp. 71–72.
[20] *Ibid.*, p. 67.

neighbor's plight. In such a society, it was not surprising that Aristotle, or even St. Thomas many centuries later, saw nothing but usurious oppression in the charging of interest.

Inevitably, therefore, what contributed directly to men's economic gratifications ranked high and what dealt largely in symbols rather than satisfactions ranked low. Hence such eulogies of household management as this one: ". . . household management attends more to men than to the acquisition of inanimate things, and to human excellence more than to the excellence of property which we call wealth, and to the virtue of freemen more than to the virtue of slaves."[21]

XENOPHON (c. 440–c. 355 B.C.)

Beside the two giants—Plato and Aristotle—Xenophon ranks very small, although the *Anabasis* is a classic of military adventure. He is interesting partly because he illustrated the diversity of Greek outlook on economic matters and partly because he suggested that the Chamber of Commerce spirit is as old as civilization. His work *On the Means of Improving the Revenue of the State of Athens*[22] was a prospectus, designed to attract outsiders, not a systematic economic treatise. In fact, what is most interesting in it is the complete absence of metaphysical or even ethical speculation. Here was a practical man, speaking through the ages, to other practical men.

He started by listing the natural advantages of Athens as a center of commerce and hence as a source of public revenue. Athens enjoyed a mild climate. Its soil was fertile. Rich fisheries surrounded it. It was blessed with stone and silver deposits ample in quantity and good in quality. A most important convenience was its naturally excellent port. All that Xenophon lacked was the illustrated brochure. With such advantages, the state was in an excellent position to attract foreigners. Foreigners should be wooed because they paid taxes and demanded no services. Xenophon put

[21] *Ibid.*, p. 75.
[22] See A. E. Monroe (ed.), *Early Economic Thought*, Harvard, 1924.

the point with characteristic bluntness: ". . . for that source of revenue appears to me to be one of the best, since strangers, while they maintain themselves, and confer great benefits on the states in which they live, receive no pensions from the public, but pay the tax imposed on aliens."[23]

Here was no nonsense about the natural inferiority of traders. Merchants and shipowners were highly valuable citizens because they brought wealth to the city. Therefore a sensible government made their life more pleasant. Disputes should be promptly and fairly adjudicated. The merchants themselves should be "honoured with seats of distinction on public occasions, and sometimes invited to entertainments."[24] Thus they can be flattered at no expense to the state.

Rubbing the observation in, Xenophon noted that "the more people settle among us, and visit us, the greater quantity of merchandise, it is evident, would be imported, exported, and sold, and the more gain would be secured, and tribute received."[25] This amounted to a fair enough anticipation of the mercantilist spirit. An armory of expedient devices for the encouragement of settlement amplified his recommendations: lodging houses for seamen and others for merchants, public houses of entertainment for visitors, erection of shops to be leased to retail merchants, and possibly the construction of galleys also to be rented to merchants.

Xenophon breathed the spirit of enterprise. Why not, he asked, lease public slaves for the operation of the silver mines? For it was impossible to have too much silver. When the state was prosperous, men bought beautiful arms, horses, and furniture. Their wives acquired clothing and ornaments. In time of distress, silver was still more desirable, for then it bought provisions and paid the wages of mercenaries. Here again the mercantilist analogy is inescapable. This student of Socrates displayed all the single-

[23] *Ibid.*, pp. 34–35.
[24] *Ibid.*, p. 36.
[25] *Ibid.*, p. 36.

mindedness and all the hard-headedness of an expert man of business.

ROMAN ECONOMICS

Through its many centuries of hegemony over the ancient world, Rome developed nothing new in the sphere of theoretical economics. Here, as in the remainder of her intellectual life, Rome followed Greece. Although the Romans waxed great in commerce and manufacture, the best that they could produce was the practical hint, the recipe for profit. There was much the same relation between their economic writings and economic analysis, as between the art of business management and the abstruse economic theory of the graduate school.

A glance at these maxims for greater profit will suffice. Cato (234–149 B.C.) in his *De Agri Cultura* exemplified the moral and economic outlook of the successful Roman landowner of the more intelligent stripe. Writing at a time when the great estates (*latifundia*) were swallowing smaller units, he neither denounced nor exalted them out of hand. He recommended instead a proper proportion between land and house. If the house were too luxurious, the owner would be tempted to idleness. If it were too mean, he would stay in the city. Successful management, Cato emphasized, always demanded frequent personal supervision. He assumed that the bulk of the workers were slaves, although at peak harvest periods some free laborers might have to be hired. Cato was free of nostalgia for small peasant holdings, the family farm of our day. What he described was commercial farming, farming for profit. Slaves were to be treated like oxen. When they became too old to work, they should be sold. One wonders who bought them. The best remedy for the ills of slaves was hard work.

Writing more than a century later, Cicero had even less to say. Like the Greeks, he looked down upon labor as producing moral and mental degradation. He considered the position of the freedman working for wages scarcely better than that of slaves. He envisaged a wage-earning class working side by side with slaves, treated, in justice, the way the slaves were treated. Adequate food and hard work were the complete prescription.

These were obviously the tag ends of Greek observation. The banal and the moralistic rested heavily upon Roman observations. The new spirit stirring in Rome was early Christianity. Its doctrines appealed to the poor, the humble, and the oppressed. In their teaching of the universal brotherhood of man, the sinfulness of slavery, and the desirability of universal sharing, Christian doctrines were profoundly revolutionary. They struck at the roots both of Roman social arrangements and Greek political and economic thought. We shall see in the next chapter what became of Christian economic ideas in the Middle Ages when the Church, dominant in Europe, had its chance to impose them upon Christendom.[26]

---

[26] A list of further readings for Part I appears on pp. 403–404.

Chapter 2

Medieval Economics

> There are some occupations which cannot be carried on
> without sin; for there are menial tasks which soil the body,
> such as cleaning sewers or chimneys, and others which stain
> the soul, like those now in question.
>
> *Nicole Oresme*

MEDIEVAL SOCIETY

It is customary to treat the five centuries from the eleventh to the sixteenth as one temporal unit, the Middle Ages. The period commenced with Charles the Great's precarious and temporary restoration of the Roman Empire. It ended at the threshold of Europe's expansion into the New World of North and South America. As a convenient abstraction, the Middle Ages have been romantically worshiped for towering religious and artistic achievement and viciously attacked for the poverty, brutality, and oppression which darkened the everyday lives of most men. As usual, both attitudes contain part of the truth and, as might be expected, in five centuries many changes occurred. Charles the Great's Europe was not St. Thomas Aquinas' Europe, more than two centuries later, nor yet St. Antonio's fifteenth-century scene. Towns slowly grew larger, their citizens acquired additional privileges, economic life became steadily more complex, and relations between King and townsman, townsman and noble, Church and King, all altered almost out of recognition.

All the same, some justification remains for summary treatment of this half millennium as one age. Although change undoubtedly marked the passage of the years, it was, by modern criteria, exceedingly majestic in its pace. Consider, as a single illustration, the increase of population. William the Conquerer's Domesday Book listed 325 habitable houses in Cambridge. In 1279, two centuries later, Cambridge boasted 534 dwellings. In other words, in this community, unusually favored by nature and pampered by authority though it was, an average of a house a year was erected. But Cambridge was fortunate: if it had expanded at more ordinary rates, in 1279 it would have possessed only 450 houses, erected at the rate of one every two years.[1] As it was with population, so it was in other human affairs. Peasants tilled the soil as their fathers and grandfathers had tilled it; they preserved their food and wove their clothing by ancient recipes. To follow tradition won social approval then, just as buying the latest model does its purchaser credit today.

Undoubtedly the towns were the center of change in the Middle Ages. In them congregated the boldest medieval spirits. Behind their fortifications, rebellious citizens resisted King and baron alike. Changes in technique and modes of trade naturally began here. Yet the spirit of the towns was also formally attached to the traditions of the past. The central institution of the town was the guild. Easily identifiable in the guild was a profoundly protective, conservative animus. By the fourteenth century there were three varieties of guilds. First of all, there was the mixture of the social and the religious sometimes to be seen in attenuated form in contemporary lodges or fraternal orders. Members ate and drank together; they also worshiped together, assisted the poor, and improved the town. These activities would not astonish a modern Rotarian, Lion, or Kiwanian. Earliest upon the scene was the merchant guild, whose strength was its monopoly of some salable commodity. Finally, there was the craft guild, whose members partially overlapped the merchant guilds. Unlike the latter, it classified its members by trade and matched each trade

---

[1] C. G. Coulton, *Medieval Panorama*, Meridian Books, 1955, p. 285. Originally published in 1938.

with a single guild. The guilds were a fascinating and perplexing mixture of trade-associationist protection of members, price and quality regulations in the interests of consumers, and declared hostility to strangers. Monopoly gave guild members preferred positions in dealing with their customers and staved off the competition of foreigners, who might be merchants as near as the next community. But it was alien alike to the ethos of the period and the guilds as institutions to use this monopoly to maximize the net revenue of the merchant—to employ anachronistically the terminology of nineteenth-century economics. Even more than in our day, consumers needed protection against monopoly. Their choices were fewer and they lacked almost entirely the modern option of leaving one community and moving to another.

Guild regulations sternly forbade forestalling and engrossing or regrating. The first prohibition defined the permissible limits of monopoly. By right, the guild monopolized the sale of the items its members traded in, but guild members were equal. Equality implied fair chances to purchase produce and merchandise at the same price. Therefore the individual merchant who grabbed on his own account the entire supply of an item—the fault of forestalling—was guilty not alone of oppressing his customers, but, worse, of violating the rules of his club. Similarly, the merchant who bought wholesale with the intention of selling retail—engrossing or regrating—also contravened the precepts of fair dealing. Nor was the merchant free to charge the price which his fancy dictated or market conditions permitted. St. Thomas directed him to charge a fair price and earn a moderate profit. Much complicated analysis accompanied St. Thomas' doctrine of fair price which elucidated this injunction. Moreover, the merchant was obliged to avoid deception and maintain quality. His duty to his fellow man took precedence over his own selfish advantage. Or should have done so.

Change was slow in the towns and still slower elsewhere partly because of the conception of life which emanated from the period's dominant social institution, the Church. In a secular age (imagine advising a medieval citizen to attend the church of his choice), it is difficult to imagine the spiritual and temporal position of the medieval Church. On the one hand, it was the source of spiritual solace in this world and eternal salvation in the next. On the other hand, it issued orders to sovereigns and nobles, and, as a worldly power, owned rich lands and collected from them enormous taxes and tithes. To be deprived of the right to share in the Church's life and receive its blessings was more than equivalent to the loss of citizenship in our time, for the second loss concerned this world only. But the Church was much more than a spiritual force: it was deeply interwoven with the most powerful institutions of the period. The Church collected rents, owned villeins or serfs (it was not always as a generous master), sold privileges to towns, and even occasionally loaned money. As this practice implies, its prosperity depended partly upon activities which it hesitated to support doctrinally.

Several aspects of its preaching concern us directly. Most important was the Church's emphasis upon the unity of life. All men's activities conduced either to salvation or perdition. Therefore the rules of ethics and right Christian conduct had to be observed as meticulously in the conduct of economic affairs as in any other sphere of human activity. In the opinion of a leading student,[2] not until well into the sixteenth century did economic activity become separated from the ordinary norms of personal conduct and subjected to rules of its own. If, as the quotation at the head of this chapter indicates, the medieval theorist viewed business activity with suspicion, it was because it was so dangerously easy to sin in buying and selling. The Middle Ages did not forget Aristotle's opinion that men's lust for gain was without limit. But avarice, just as much as lust, was a deadly sin. The Middle Ages could no more readily contemplate life organized around unlimited search for gain, than human existence obsessively centered upon fulfillment of the sexual instinct.

Nevertheless, if the individual were not to seek greedily the utmost gain his talents rendered plausible, surely he required com-

---

[2] R. H. Tawney, *Religion and the Rise of Capitalism*, Pelican, 1937, pp. 14 ff. First published in 1926.

pensating satisfaction. This the Church accorded him in the ideas of hierarchy and status. Tawney concluded that from the twelfth to the sixteenth century, society was persistently compared to the human body. Just as the human body was cunningly devised so that its parts supported each other and contributed to the efficiency of the organism, so were the various classes in society designed to comfort each other and advance the interests of the whole community. And, just as all parts of the body were important, so equally were all classes in society. As the human body had its head and its feet, the community had its leaders and its subordinates. The analogy implied that the good Christian should be content with the role in life in which he found himself. Effort to exchange that role for another diverted him from the true road to salvation, Christian pursuit of the tasks God had given him. Therefore, the serf should not aspire to freedom, the merchant to wealth, the artisan to the status of the merchant. Each had his own rules and the relative merits of each were also fixed. For the poor boy of talent, the only accepted way to rise was to enter the Church. But his new status died with him.

However, if each man was enjoined to stay where he was in life, he required assurance of the means to fall no lower as partial compensation for the hopes that he foreswore. As far as the merchant was concerned, the just price was a price which enabled him to maintain himself in the accustomed position of merchants in his community. The just reward that the artisan could ask for his labor would maintain him according to the traditions of his class, neither, according to these lights, enriching nor impoverishing him.

The characteristic teachings of the Church, then, regarded society as a group of classes, each with a different function, each sharing a common end. At the apex of the structure was the Church; at the summit of expectation was salvation; in every part of life was religion. Religion taught men not to take advantage of each other, since they were brothers. It taught them also to repress their economic appetites. How different was the spirit of capitalism. Smith described society as a mechanism which employed men's economic motives to fulfill society's economic needs. Far from deploring economic egotism, Adam Smith and his followers found in its play "God's providence."[3] Commercial expediency, not the teachings of the Church, was the guide to economic action. That pious Christian Samuel Johnson hazarded the opinion that men are seldom so innocently employed as in making money. The medieval Church could scarcely have agreed less.

How far this theory accorded with medieval practice, we shall shortly investigate. But as a body of doctrine, it was obviously much more closely attuned to the economic life of the period than to the more complicated economies of later times. It was true that the doctrine sought to regulate a multitude of individual transactions. However, these dealings were not related to each other in time and space through that intricate network of monetary and credit institutions essential to our own operations. No economic system could plausibly be inferred as we can infer one from the intricate interconnections among multitudinous transactions which are the glory of a modern economy. Since most people lived on the land and dealt little with money, since large-scale organization was rare, and since little mobility or competition marked the scene, analogies to modern capitalism are pointless.

Of course, medieval practice differed sharply from medieval teachings. When has it been otherwise in human history? Guild merchants did not always treat each other as brothers. They cheated customers on weight and quality, selling tainted meat, adulterated ale, and shoddy cloth. The records are full of cases of merchants fined, suspended from guild privileges, or even imprisoned for one breach or another. The steady scolding of engrossers and forestallers suffices to prove their existence. Moreover, even when the guild member lived at peace with his fellows of the town, he was quite ready to fall, frequently physically, upon the Christian merchants of other communities. The benevolence of the guild had a very short radius. Nor did lords always

[3] *Ibid.*, p. 19.

cherish the serfs on their lands. Where possible they interpreted traditional levies upon their villeins to their own advantage, added new ones where they could, and handled exceedingly roughly the persons of their inferiors.

Finally, the Church itself sometimes failed to enforce by example the standard it sought to impose on the souls in its care. For a priest to be ignorant was the common thing. All too frequently, he was so illiterate that he could not say Mass. Some priests maintained concubines. On occasion, priests stored grain in their churches and neglected the duties of religion in favor of the pursuits of commerce. Long before Trollope handled nineteenth-century pluralities in satirical novels, strong popes inveighed with scant success against clergymen who filled ten, twenty, or even more benefices, and performed the duties of none while collecting the emoluments of all. Chaucer's not always gentle, ironical treatment of monk, friar, and prioress in the *Canterbury Tales* revealed an educated view of the mortal failings of the immortal Church.

All of this was bad enough, but worse follows. Although usury was a deadly sin, monks all too often demanded pocket money from their superiors and used this money to lend at extortionate rates to the necessitous of their districts. The evidence suggests that they violated their vows of poverty as cheerfully as they breached the companion pledge of chastity. The papacy closed its eyes to usury among the nobles, dealt usuriously on its own account, and put usurers under its own protection. True, these transactions differed in spirit from the personal loans which Aquinas had in mind when he analyzed usury. Nevertheless, they violated the Church's own precepts. If the Church was rich, it was rich partly because it followed paths forbidden to others.

Is it then appropriate to conclude that the teachings of the Church were a massive piece of hypocrisy? Is it necessary to agree with Marxists who see in them only a cloak of ideology over the operations of primitive accumulation? Such a conclusion is obviously unfair. Ideals and practice never accord, not in twentieth-century capitalism any more than in thirteenth-century feudalism.

Yet, it is never unimportant to know what people profess, because belief influences practice. Men were too imperfect in the Middle Ages to pursue salvation with single-minded devotion. So was their Church. But the fact of the aim remains. Life was different in the Middle Ages because the Church in its best moments sought to make this existence a preparation for the next one.

ST. THOMAS AQUINAS (1225–1274)

St. Thomas' position in medieval thought bears comparison with Aristotle's in the ancient world. In the medieval world, only Aristotle himself was a rival. St. Thomas set out to examine human knowledge and place human action within God's commandments. The religious intention pervaded every page of the *Summa Theologica*. Nevertheless, Thomas believed that human reason was a divine instrument, designed to reveal truth. Hence his arguments were essentially rationalistic and he leaned heavily upon Aristotle as well as upon Christian sources. Like Aristotle's, his range was encyclopedic. His method was to start with a question, for example, whether a man might lawfully sell a thing for more than it was worth. He then stated the arguments for the proposition that he might. Following these arguments was a single quotation which, in deadly fashion, controverted them. Next, his own analysis stated the position which he considered consonant with good doctrine. He wound up each analysis with the destruction, one by one, of the arguments for the position which he opposed.

The writings of St. Thomas, an incredibly industrious man, extended over many volumes. Here we need consider only the two characteristic and outstanding economic doctrines of the period, just price and usury. Because St. Thomas' views had so much influence and also because his style of reasoning was common in the Middle Ages, we shall pursue these two doctrines quite closely.

JUST PRICE

Let us start with the question cited above. St. Thomas' answer was oblique. "It is wholly sinful to practise fraud for the express purpose of selling a thing for more than its just price, inasmuch as a man deceives his neighbor to his loss."[4] Buying and selling should benefit both parties and burden neither more than the other.

How high should the price be? It should equal the value of the object. ". . . whether the price exceeds the value of a thing or conversely, the equality required by justice is lacking. Consequently to sell dearer or to buy cheaper than a thing is worth is in itself unjust and unlawful."[5] Note that the buyer was enjoined from paying too little as much as the seller was urged not to charge too much. Aquinas immediately added a qualification to this conclusion. If a buyer needed an item badly, and if the seller were injured by parting with it, the price could fairly take into account the seller's loss. "Thus a thing may lawfully be sold for more than it is worth in itself, though not more than it is worth to its possessor."[6] If only one of the conditions were met and the seller felt no pain in parting with the greatly desired item, he had by the same token no warrant to charge more than the just price. However, he might be gracious about it: "He . . . who derives great advantage from something received from another, may of his own accord pay the seller something in addition. This is a matter of honor."[7] The good Christian does not take advantage of his neighbor's necessity. If his neighbor were an equally good Christian, his gratitude would induce a voluntary payment. Would the most scrupulous conscience, in turn, decline the gift? It is probably irrelevant, if not irreverent, to ask.

What, in fact, was the just price? It is "not absolutely definite, but depends rather upon a kind of estimate."[8] However, one thing was certain, if the discrepancy was great, restitution had to be made to the buyer. But then how great was "great"? Fifty percent? Twenty-five percent? One hundred percent? In the absence of cost accounting, just price was hard to determine. Nor did Thomas' discussion answer the question of how small excesses over the just price should be handled.

Next, St. Thomas asked whether a defect in the thing sold rendered the sale unlawful. If a seller knew of a defect in the item's substance, he committed fraud by selling it. The implied query centered upon the difference between substance and superficial attribute. The seller also committed fraud if he knowingly gave short measure. He committed fraud once more when he deceived the buyer about the quality of the object, for example, by "selling a broken-down animal as sound."[9] An honest dealer in horses must be difficult to find in any age. Suppose that the seller did not know of the defects in his merchandise. Then he was innocent of sin, but an obligation existed to make restitution to the buyer. Similarly, the buyer who got more than he bargained for was morally obliged to make restitution to the seller.

St. Thomas' next problem was whether a seller was bound to declare a defect in a thing sold. The answer was not simple. If the defects were concealed, the seller was obliged to point them out or the sale was "unlawful and fraudulent." But some defects were obvious. St. Thomas' illustration was a one-eyed horse. The seller made a deduction from the price. Therefore, he need not declare the defect to the buyer, lest the buyer feel emboldened to seek still an additional reduction. The reasoning was not crystalline, nor was the distinction between the concealed and the open defect entirely satisfactory, unless some undeclared standard of reasonable and prudent judgment were being invoked.

The final and not least important question was whether in trading it was unlawful to sell a thing for more than was paid for it. St. Thomas' answer deserves extended quotation because it illustrates his difficulties in fitting commercial activities into framework of Christian behavior:

Gain . . . which is the end of trading, though it does not logically involve anything honorable or necessary, does not logically involve anything sinful or contrary to virtue; hence there is no reason why gain may not be directed to some necessary or even honorable

[9] *Ibid.,* p. 58.

end . . . as when a man uses moderate gains acquired in trade for the support of his household, or even to help the needy; or even when a man devotes himself to trade for the public welfare, lest there be a lack of the things necessary for the life of the country; and seeks gain, not as an end, but as a reward for his efforts.[10]

The passage was full of meat. St. Thomas recognized that trade was necessary "for the life of the country." The pursuit of trade need not be sinful. Here St. Thomas went beyond the early teachings of the church fathers, who sweepingly condemned trade as sinful. But it was at best ethically neutral. Crucial to the judgment was the motive of the merchant. If he traded to support his household—the implication was, in its accustomed style—the result, while not ethically beneficial, did no injury. But it would be still better if the merchant traded to benefit the public or to solace the poor. In any case, the gain had to be moderate. The merchant had to control his avarice.

Moreover, trade was so vexatious an activity that St. Thomas advised priests to avoid its taint. Trade involved the mind too much in secular things. St. Thomas warned his readers of "the frequent sins of traders."[11] It was fairly plain that the merchant bore watching, and that the fastidious Christian chose some other work in life.

USURY

So much for just price. The second major economic topic St. Thomas analyzed was "the sin of Usury, which is committed in Loans." Was it sinful, St. Thomas asked, to receive usury for money lent? The reply was a sharp affirmative: ". . . to receive usury for money lent is, in itself, unjust, since it is a sale of what does not exist; whereby inequality obviously results."[12] Then followed a tight legal argument about the difference between the use of an object and the object itself. Thus a man might lawfully receive the rent from a house while retaining its ownership,

[10] *Ibid.*, p. 63.
[11] *Ibid.*, p. 64.
[12] *Ibid.*, p. 66.

for here it was possible to separate the use of the object from the object itself. Not so in the case of money. Exchange was the single, or, at least, the primary use of money. Therefore, money should be used and alienated at the same time. Implied was a restatement of Aristotle's judgment that money was barren. If it was barren, then charging for its use was unjust. But a house produced services, and it was appropriate to pay a rent for their enjoyment.

St. Thomas concluded his discussion of this question with a statement in reply to the argument that usury resulted from a free contract between lender and borrower: ". . . he who pays usury does not really do it voluntarily, but under some compulsion, for he needs to obtain the loan, and the one who has the money will not lend it without usury."[13] Here again St. Thomas dwelt in the world of the personal loan, designed to relieve immediate hardship, not in the universe of high finance, characteristic of the dealings of Kings and popes.

Closely related was another problem: whether it was lawful to ask any consideration other than money interest for money loaned. St. Thomas treated the procedure involved as an evasion of the prohibition against usury: ". . . anyone who, by tacit or explicit agreement, receives anything else, the price of which can be measured by money, is likewise guilty of sin."[14] Here St. Thomas prohibited payment in services or goods. But he did not think that the issue was completely settled, for the passage continued with the troublesome question of free gifts: "If, however, he receives something of this kind, not asking for it, and not according to any tacit or explicit obligation, but as a free gift, he does not sin."[15] Finally, St. Thomas pointed to the legitimacy of "things which are not measured by money . . . such as good will and love for the lender, or something similar."[16] It was something of a tribute to the realism of the analysis that these hopes came last.

[13] *Ibid.*, p. 69.
[14] *Ibid.*, p. 71.
[15] *Ibid.*, p. 72.
[16] *Ibid.*, p. 72.

As for the matter of compensation for loss incurred by giving up something which belonged to the seller, the judgment was guarded: "Compensation for loss . . . cannot be stipulated on the ground that the lender makes no profit on his money, because he should not sell what he does not yet possess, and which he may be prevented in various ways from getting."[17] In other words, the seller could not seek a higher price from one buyer on the ground that he might sell his commodity at an unlawfully high price to another customer.

Nor did St. Thomas allow credit sales as an evasion of the ban against usury. "If a man wishes to sell his goods for more than their just price, expecting the buyer to pay later, it is plainly a case of usury, because such waiting for payment has the character of a loan."[18] The reasoning was consistent. If money was barren, then delayed payment cost the seller nothing, for the money in his hands could produce nothing. The logic did not apparently extend to the next sentence of the passage: "If, however, a man wishes to deduct from the just price, in order to obtain the money sooner, he is not guilty of a sin of usury." If money was still barren, it is difficult to see why the seller should reduce his price in order to increase his supply of it at an earlier date.

Barrenness was the issue again in the two concluding questions. Was a man bound to restore anything that he might have made out of usurious gains? Oddly enough, St. Thomas' decision favored the recipient of monetary interest:

. . . if such things were extorted by usury . . . a man is not bound to make restitution beyond what he has received: because what is acquired by this means is not the fruit of such a thing but of human industry. . . .

Hence, if a man has extorted the house or the field of another by usury, he is bound to restore not only the house or field, but also the fruits obtained therefrom, because they are the fruits of things of which another is the owner . . .[19]

[17] Ibid., p. 73.
[18] Ibid., p. 73.
[19] Ibid., pp. 74–75.

Since money produced no fruit, money usuriously extorted had, of course, to be returned, but only that amount. The gains which apparently sprang from its employment were in reality the effects of human labor. On the other hand, if the usurer extorted a house, the house bore fruit and he therefore owed his victim house and fruits. Which seemed to suggest that the unjust man was better off to lend usurious gains (though he might incur a second charge of usury) than to extort them in goods. St. Thomas evidently did not advance to the complicated case of the man who collected money by usury and used the money to buy the house or field which produced fruit.

His last question asked whether it was lawful to borrow money upon usury. Was the borrower as well as the lender at fault? The answer was succinct: ". . . it is lawful to use the sin of another for a good end."[20] Therefore St. Thomas approved borrowing at usury if the money helped the borrower or someone else out of a difficulty. Here again he assumed that the borrower was driven by necessity to accept a disadvantageous bargain.

If usury and just price afforded fertile fields of endeavor for canon lawyers, the delicacy of the ideas and the difficulty of their application were explanation enough. Even in modern capitalism, the last traces of medieval habits of thought on these subjects have not disappeared. Otherwise, why do the states pass small-loan acts which put ceilings on interest rates charged in precisely the kind of transactions St. Thomas had in mind, the small loan to the needy individual? Why also does a price increase by a large industrial organization frequently arouse indignation? Surely some atavistic sense that injustice has been done must explain this otherwise inappropriate response. Yet justice in the individual transaction plays no role in the dominant versions of contemporary economic theory.

LATER MEDIEVAL THOUGHT

Though cast in old forms and constrained by binding precedents, medieval thought was not static. A century later than

[20] *Ibid.*, p. 76.

St. Thomas, Nicole Oresme (c. 1320–1382), while reaffirming much Thomist reasoning, shifted his emphasis interestingly, in a manner which reflected the increasing use and misuse of money.[21] Here is a striking passage which hints at the greater complexity of Oresme's fourteenth-century world: "There are three ways . . . in which one may make profit from money, aside from its natural use. The first of these is the art of exchange, the custody of or trafficking in money; the second is usury, and the third is the altering of money. The first is base, the second is bad; and the third is even worse."[22] In the century which elapsed between St. Thomas and Oresme, Kings and lesser rulers had increasingly discovered the charms of debasing their coinage. Oresme had to search for words strong enough to denounce this practice. The words that he did find shifted implicitly the emphasis from individual sin to social damage. He put it in this way:

. . . making a profit from the alteration of money is even worse than usury: the usurer gives his money to one who receives it voluntarily and who can use it to meet his urgent needs, and what he received is a matter of definite contract satisfactory to both; but the prince, by unnecessary altering of money, takes the property of his subjects against their will. . . . Since the gain made by a usurer is not so excessive or so generally harmful as this alteration, which is imposed upon the whole community, I say that it is not only like usury, but so tyrannical and fraudulent that I am uncertain whether it should be called violent theft or fraudulent exaction.[23]

Still a century later, St. Antonio modified austere Thomist doctrines of both just price and usury. On the first subject, his exposition emphasized the uncertainties surrounding the determination of just price. In view of these uncertainties, he held accidental lapses to be venial. Moreover, only when the excess over just price exceeded 50 percent need the seller reimburse the buyer. Lesser overcharges could be expiated by the giving of alms. Thus there came to be a range through which prices could lawfully vary. There was here also the suggestion of a more complex sys-

[21] See Nicole Oresme, *Traictié de la Premiere Invention des Monnoies* (written c. 1360) in Monroe, *op. cit.*
[22] *Ibid.*, p. 95.
[23] *Ibid.*, p. 96.

tem of market exchanges, a more frequent movement of prices, and still greater difficulties in adhering to the letter of the canonist rules.

Although St. Antonio continued to prohibit usury, it began to appear that only pure interest was illegal. In medieval circumstances, where risks were undeniably great and imputation difficult, the loopholes were probably large enough. A man might lawfully accept the profits of partnership, for his reward was presumably the fruits of honest labor. He might buy a rent charge or right to receive certain fixed amounts, because nature produced the fruits which occasioned the payment. To us it might appear that the individual had simply loaned at 5 or 6 percent interest a given sum of money. Moreover, the lender might properly seek compensation if a loan were repaid later than had been agreed. He could ask payment for a loss incurred or a gain foregone. He could purchase an annuity. These qualifications testified to St. Antonio's desperate effort to fit the new practices of ingenious businessmen into the framework of canon law. The number of liberalizing additions he was able to make said something for the flexibility of medieval thought.

There are no sharp breaks between periods, nor do modes of expression conveniently vanish when new things are said. Even into the sixteenth, seventeenth, and eighteenth centuries, many economic discussions employed the canonist categories. Tawney noted that in Bunyan's seventeenth-century *Pilgrim's Progress* Mr. Badman ground down the poor with usury and Baxter's *Christian Directory* (1673) was constructed in the style of a medieval summa. Undoubtedly the transition to capitalist modes of thought is properly located in the sixteenth and seventeenth centuries, but strong medieval influences can be identified in mercantilist thought. It was none other than the justices of Speenhamland who as late as 1795 in England blunderingly attempted to reproduce medieval justice by supporting wages and setting prices. The true compartmentalization of economic thought is a comparatively recent phenomenon. It has endured for a much shorter period than did the medieval Church's unified view of human behavior.

Chapter 3

Mercantilism

One of the hardest things to understand about mercantilism is the collection of meanings which have been imputed to the term. An indispensable first task is a work of identification.

THE CONCEPT

Although a Kingdom may be enriched by gifts received, or by purchases taken from some other Nations, yet these things are uncertain and of small consideration when they happen. The ordinary means therefore to encrease our wealth and treasure is by *Forraign Trade*, where wee must ever observe this rule; to sell more to strangers yearly than wee consume of theirs in value.

Thomas Mun

Mercantilism contrasted sharply both with medieval economic thought, its predecessor, and classical economic doctrine, its successor. It was very easy to identify official doctrine in the Middle Ages by simply consulting the writings of the Church philosophers. Not much was lost even by concentrating on only the greatest of them, St. Thomas Aquinas. Somewhat in the style of contemporary academicians, the medieval canonists were critics and commentators, not participants in the affairs they sought to understand and regulate. From the time of Adam Smith in the last quarter of the eighteenth century well into the nineteenth, the major figures of laissez-faire economics—Ricardo, Malthus, Nassau Senior, and the two Mills—can be identified with little disagreement. Despite many differences among themselves, these writers and their followers fathered a common theoretical doctrine, which explained the workings of the economy and implied a wide range of libertarian economic and social policies.

No such coherent body of principle was attached to the intellectual construct which we call mercantilism. Any effort to describe the phenomenon quickly leads to a struggle with the economic history and the practical policies of a great many European countries over at least three centuries, the sixteenth, the seventeenth, and the eighteenth. The men who took an interest in economic affairs were merchants and administrators, people engaged in the attainment of specific goals rather than in the creation of a general explanatory theory. Under the circumstances, it is not astonishing that, despite its considerable bulk, little mercantilist literature reached the level of coherent economic analysis and even that little concentrated upon restricted problems.

One of the disconcerting elements of the period is the number of writers, among them Locke, Hume, Cantillon, North, and Petty, who saw so much that their successors considered to be true. But with the possible exception of Cantillon, they achieved either the special insight into one part of the economic system, or, if they saw the whole truth, they wrote it small after the manner of David Hume. These sports came late in mercantilism's untidy history.

Because of the nature of its protagonists, an account of mercantilism talks as much about mercantilist acts as mercantilist ideas. The concept of mercantilism itself is inferred more from the economic policies of states than from the economic prescriptions of mercantilist pamphleteers.

Analysts of mercantilism have differed about its defining features. An interested enemy, Adam Smith, regarded it as a system of protection and a collection of mistaken views about money. In the nineteenth century, Schmoller, and in the twentieth, Heckscher, emphasized the state-building features of mercantilism, its concentrated effort to create unified national societies out of the jealously quarreling principalities of the time. Early in this century, Sombart argued that the key to the comprehension of mercantilism was the concept of power: mercantilists sought above all to enlarge their control over human beings and human actions. Agnosticism about these rival conceptions is possible, because they are largely either matters of emphasis or desperate attempts to create intellectual patterns out of factual anarchy. If we examine the leading characteristics of mercantilist thought and action, we can find support for each position, partly because mercantilist policies were frequently inconsistent, partly because the viewpoints often complement rather than contradict each other. Always we must remember that, in its glory, mercantilism was a battle against hampering medieval thought and practice. At its end, it merited Goethe's description in *Faust:*

> Old laws and rights, inherited
> From age to age, drag on and on
> Like some hereditary disease
> Steadily widening, growing worse.
> Wisdom turns nonsense, good deeds prove a curse,
> Your ancestors your doom!
> The native right that's born with us,
> For that, alas! no man makes room.[1]

In their efforts to construct the modern national state, mercantilist statesmen struggled against the universalism of the medieval age. The Church was the preëminent universal institution of the age, an organization which claimed as it right the homage of all Christians and, theoretically, whatever its practice, disregarded their geographical location. It took Luther and Calvin a long time to eradicate the idea that all men were brothers. And there were other pan-European ties. Latin was the universal language of literature and scholarship. When Erasmus raised his lone voice in behalf of tolerance, even as the Reformation was dividing Europe, any educated man could read what he had to say. It was a symbol of mercantilist success that vernacular tongues succeeded Latin, and that Luther, the separatist, vanquished Erasmus, the cosmopolitan. The institution of chivalry was a common bond

[1] Quoted by Eli Heckscher, *Mercantilism*, Macmillan, 1955, Vol. I, p. 457.

among warring knights, who were frequently more eager to win ransom than to destroy enemies. Roman law persisted and the international fairs gathered together merchants of all regions. To achieve their objectives, mercantilist statesmen were compelled seriously to weaken, where they did not destroy, social arrangements which had given the Middle Ages a sense of community, at best of European brotherhood, despite poverty, incessant quarrels, and physical barbarity.

The mercantilists had a second antagonist, the pervading particularism of the time. In the Middle Ages there was little between universal Christendom and the multitude of petty baronies, towns, and principalities, often at war with each other, and always inclined to hamper their neighbors' commerce with a thicket of local restrictions, inevitably deleterious to the claims of central authority. Mercantilists succeeded far better in destroying the universal Church than they did in abolishing local tolls, local systems of weights and measures, local tariffs, and multiple coinage arrangements. In an age of poor communications, town policy frequently proved stronger than national policy.

A modern need not be astonished. Even in today's national state, particular interests frequently encroach upon national interests. Although the United States is a relatively well-governed political unit, local businessmen raise tariffs on bicycles, prevent the sale of cheaper foreign equipment, and foster informal quotas against such competitive products as Japanese textiles. We still protect our own. Although the political unity of the national state has enlarged the number of persons whom we identify as our own, our instinct directs us to treat the foreigner as a medievalist might have treated the inhabitants of the next town.

The battle against particularism was not won by the mercantilists, even by such resolute shapers of policy as France's Colbert. Colbert's major triumph, the tariff of 1664, did indeed abolish some interprovincial tariffs. But it left untouched five-eighths of the country, and even Colbert could do nothing with highway and river tolls. Nevertheless, according to Heckscher, this tariff was one of the two outstanding victories for the mercantilist policy of unification. As we shall observe in the *Wealth of Nations*, English particularism still deserved vigorous polemic in 1776. Yet, as early as 1562, in the Statute of Artificers and Apprentices, Queen Elizabeth had struck a valiant blow for national policy. This famous statute, which lingered on less and less effectively into the nineteenth century, regulated labor and commerce, cities and countryside. It attempted to favor no special interest.

In England, only the nineteenth century finally dismantled the edifice of controls, local in application, against which mercantilists struggled. The victory belonged not to them but to the classicists who were their enemies. On the Continent, the final defeat of particularism came only when the French Revolution equalized taxes over the entire country, substituted departments for provinces and ended the inextricable confusion of provincial tools, standardized weights and measures, and abolished the guilds. Partly through conquest, mostly through emulation, the French example spread through most of Europe.

MERCANTILIST IDEAS

The quality of mercantilist thought can be glimpsed in the literature on money, the poor, the state, and the harmony of interests. Always, mercantilists of every persuasion esteemed money as a positive good. By money, they always meant the precious metals. Napoleon Bonaparte, a very late mercantilist, hoped to ruin England's economy by selling her goods produced on the Continent. No matter that Englishmen might have more food, even more munitions, to press their war against him. What counted was the drain upon their precious metals. This drain would destroy them. A much later group of mercantilists, the Daughters of the American Revolution, once compelled a special check on the quantity of gold stored at Fort Knox. They also considered the stock of gold a vital matter.

Why did the mercantilists value money or treasure? Among others, Edwin Cannan (and Adam Smith) distinguished between an early school of mercantilists, the bullionists, who regarded money itself as wealth, and a later school obsessed primarily with maintaining a proper balance of trade, an excess of exports over imports. This excess would lead to payments of gold and silver by foreigners. These payments would enlarge England's stock of precious metals. But it is dubious whether even the bullionists regarded money as important, rather than the purposes to which money could be put. What appeared to distinguish them from their more sophisticated successors was their reluctance to permit gold and silver to leave their country on any pretext, even that of ultimate advantage.

This distinction was cogently made by Thomas Mun, whose *England's Treasure by Forraign Trade*, probably written in 1630 though not published until the 1660's, was a leading mercantilist tract. Mun criticized the bullionist effort to prevent the export of gold and silver. An East India merchant himself with a direct interest in the free flow of the metals, he maintained that money, if exported to purchase raw materials, would return to the country in larger amounts after the raw materials had been converted into manufactures and reëxported. But whether Mun or a bullionist spoke, money was an important objective.

Was this no more than a quaint idiosyncracy, or did the reasoning conceal a logical point? Clearly, the second alternative is correct. Mercantilists wrote about states either at war with their neighbors, recovering from such wars, or about to plunge into another. With gold and silver, soldiers could be hired from other lands, goods could be purchased, and the means to prosecute a successful war expanded. As Cantillon remarked in the middle of the eighteenth century, a state could buy these goods even from its enemies, a condition which should suggest something of the relatively limited character of eighteenth-century warfare. In the garrison state there was nothing peculiar in the desire to keep one's assets liquid. The world of the mercantilists was narrow and suspicious. It remained for Adam Smith and his followers to reintroduce the cosmopolitan concept of mutual benefit from trade.

John Maynard Keynes advanced a much more conjectural defense of mercantilist policy. He argued that mercantilists instinctively grasped a long-run truth, that a gap between saving and investment tends to exist. Keynes credited mercantilists with the Keynesian corollary of this proposition: a plentiful supply of money lowers interest rates, promotes investment, and increases employment. Keynes read into mercantilism a great deal of contemporary monetary policy. Heckscher in a revised edition of his book took sharp issue with this reading of the period's history and thought.[2]

Writing in the middle of the eighteenth century, at mercantilism's close, David Hume, a perceptive man and friend of Adam Smith, strongly condemned the mercantilist conception of money. He was confident that money would always flow where it was wanted and needed. Here was a sample statement:

Here then we may learn the fallacy of the remark, often to be met with in historians, and even in common conversation, that any particular state is weak, though fertile, populous, and well cultivated, merely because it wants money. It appears that the want of money can never injure any state within itself: For men and commodities are the real strength of any community. It is the simple manner of living which here hurts the public, by confining the gold and silver to few hands, and preventing its universal diffusion and circulation. On the contrary, industry and refinements of all kinds incorporate it with the whole state, however small its quantity may be: They digest it into every vein, so to speak; and make it enter into every transaction and contract.[3]

None of which, be it said, helped the sovereign to raise funds speedily for his own purposes.

For mercantilist writers and their successors, ordinary laborers were termed the "poor." The label indicates the role attributed to the class. Such a late and comparatively sophisticated mercantilist as Sir James Steuart epitomized the common view of his time in his *An Inquiry into the Principles of Political Economy*

[2] *Ibid.*, Vol. II, pp. 340–358.
[3] David Hume, *Writings on Economics*, ed. by Eugene Rotwein, Nelson, 1955. p. 45.

(1767). In his judgment, the larger the state's population, the better off was the state. The logic of the postion was simple. More goods implied more people to produce them. Diminishing returns either from land or manufacture failed to qualify Steuart's conclusion. More goods led to greater exports. Combined with strict control over imports, larger exports implied that eminently desirable result, a favorable balance of trade and an influx of the precious metals.

But, Steuart and others hastened to add, larger population benefited the state only when people worked hard. Then only was Sir William Petty correct in saying that "fewness of people, is real poverty." But few mercantilists thought that it was easy to make the poor work hard. Author after author condemned them en masse as lazy, irresponsible, and prone to luxury and dissipation. It is startling to read that tea and sugar once ranked as luxuries. Here is a sample of the extravagances of the poor:

1; snuff-taking,
2; tea drinking,
3; ribbons, ruffles, silks,
4; dram drinking.

Have not extravagance in these articles contributed greatly to make labor and the servant's wages run so high. . . . From whence it follows a great loss of hands to our manufacturers and agriculture; extravagant high wages and great expense of labor, and obstruction and diminution of our trade at home and abroad.[4]

The agricultural expert and travel writer Arthur Young could restrain his vexation with difficulty: "The employment of women and children is drinking tea with white bread and butter twice a day; an extremity that may surely be called luxury in excess! No wonder rates are doubled."[5] The last sentence revealed one source of concern at any prospect of high wages. If higher wages induced less work and more drinking, the result was plain: dimin-

---

[4] Thomas Alcock, *Observations*, England, 1752, pp. 45 ff. Cited by Edgar Furniss, *The Position of the Laborer in a System of Nationalism*, Houghton Mifflin, 1920, p. 153.

[5] Furniss, *op. cit.*, p. 155.

ished exports and unemployment subsidized by the ratepayers. Hence the poor had to be compelled to work if they did not choose to work voluntarily, even if oppressive workhouse systems subjected them to something like the labor camps of the modern world.

Once more, mercantilist thought, however great its distance from the facts, was easy to follow. When workers consumed home-grown or home-processed goods, they diminished the supply available for export and affected the balance of trade unfavorably. But the case was worse still when England had to import such articles of consumption as tea and sugar and thus send valuable coin out of the country in order to support the luxury of the workers.

Many mercantilists esteemed workers much as they esteemed useful beasts of burden. The earlier they went to work, the better. A late but extreme example of the attitude occurred in William Temple's *Essay:*

> When these children are four years old, they shall be sent to the county workhouse and there taught to read two hours a day and be kept fully employed the rest of their time in any of the manufactures of the house which best suits their age, strength and capacity. If it be objected that at these early years, they cannot be made useful, I reply that at four years of age there are sturdy employments in which children can earn their living; but besides, there is considerable use in their being, somehow or other, constantly employed at least twelve hours in a day, whether they earn their living or not; for by these means we hope that the rising generation will be so habituated to constant employment that it would at length prove agreeable and entertaining to them.[6]

Twelve hours of labor at four years of age: in practice, not even the mercantilists could achieve so much. As Heckscher put it, mercantilists counted their inhabitants, they did not weigh their skills. Any notion of the superior productivity of the better-paid worker was far from their thoughts. A rich state implied poor inhabitants.

[6] *Ibid.,* pp. 114–115.

The last statements led to the mercantilist conception of the state. In the West, contemporary thought ascribes to the state the representation of the citizens who inhabit it. Hence, the state cannot be rich when most people are poor, because the nation's income is the sum of individuals' incomes. But the mercantilists measured not the national income but the national wealth. A major item of that wealth was the King's holdings of gold and silver. It was easy for them, therefore, to separate the interests of the state's residents from those of the state which governed them. Harder work and diminished rewards for the laboring poor increased the supply of gold and silver. When the poor consumed less, merchants exported more.

Whether the mercantilist statesman sought power, unification, or protection, these were desirable results. How could they be achieved? The mercantilists deployed an army of techniques, some of which will be discussed later. One generalization appears plausible: the state did not grow richer by permitting individuals freedom to pursue their individual interests. That true hero of the mercantilist drama, the statesman, had to control and direct all individual egotisms. As Sir James Steuart put it: "He who fits at the head of this operation, is called the statesman. I suppose him to be constantly awake, attentive to his employment, able and uncorrupted, tender in his love for the society that he governs, impartially just in his indulgence for every class of inhabitants, and disregardful of the interest of individuals, when that regard is inconsistent with the general welfare."[7] This was a good deal to ask of an imperfect human being. Perhaps, however, it attributed no more to the perfect statesman than some nineteenth-century economists attributed to their rational merchants and prudent industrialists. Steuart proceeded to distinguish the statesman still further from the common run of mortals:

The principle of self-interest will serve as a general key to this inquiry; and it may in one sense, be considered as the ruling principle of my subject, and may therefore be traced through the whole. This

[7] James Steuart, *An Inquiry into the Principles of Political Economy*, 1767,. Vol. I, p. 149.

is the main spring, and only motive which a statesman should make use of, to engage a free people to concur in the plans which lays down for their government.

I beg I may not here be understood to mean, that self-interest should conduct the statesman: by no means. Self-interest when considered with regard to him, is public spirit; and it can only be called self-interest, when it is applied to those who are to be governed by it.[8]

The first sentence almost startles by its superficial resemblance to the doctrine of Adam Smith and his disciples. But Steuart's drift was quite different: self-interest was what the statesman used to guide him in estimating the reactions of his fellow men. He could not allow self-interest free scope because he knew that disaster to the state would follow. He took men as they were. As Marshall said more than a century later, it is essential to enlist men's strongest as well as their highest motives. Mercantilist doctrine contained nothing otherworldly: it was a secular faith. Free of self-interest himself and unique in this respect, the statesman employed the self-interest of lesser men to achieve his own end, the aggrandizement of the state. The mercantilist confidence in the disinterestedness of the statesman represented the only romantic element in their hard-headed faith.

What has been said so far implies two other elements in the mercantilist view of society. First, mercantilists believed that the gain of one country was inevitably the loss of another. When the size of the pie was fixed, as they conceived, the slice your rival gained must be yours. Hence a favorable balance of trade for one country arithmetically entailed an unfavorable balance for another—an actual gain for the first nation and an actual loss of the other. We profess, at least, to believe that the gains of international trade benefit all trading nations. We believe also that wider and freer trade means larger total product and greater economic welfare for all. The narrowness and the hostility which the mercantilist doctrine promoted go far to explain mercantilism's fre-

[8] *Ibid.*, p. 162.

quent commercial wars. In contrast to laissez faire, mercantilism wears the unpleasant aspect of narrow nationalism.

The mercantilist tended to emphasize the disharmony of interests. Two disharmonies have been identified: disharmony among states and disharmony between the state and its own citizens. Laissez faire could advocate minimum interference by the state because it was confident that, in promoting their own self-interest, human beings enriched the community. In the absence of this confidence, the statesman had to intervene. His tasks were onerous: ordering the actions of individuals, reconciling rich to poor, regulating wages, supervising the conditions of employment, examining the quality of finished goods, and, in every respect, acting as the final arbiter of economic life.

REGULATION OF ECONOMIC LIFE

It is one thing to affirm the need for statesmanlike control of everyday life. It is another to enforce this control against a host of local interests. Steuart advised enlisting the self-interest of each man. But how was the statesman to do so, when his own zeal for the national interest hurt so many local interests? Like consistent laissez-faire policy, consistent mercantilist policy was an illusion. In practical fact, effective mercantilist policy compromised. In countries like Germany and Italy, its failure was complete. In France, its victory was incomplete. How did statesman get their way? What was their way?

Internal policies included a varied assortment of devices, including price control, quality control, regulation of labor, sumptuary acts, monopolies, and special privileges. Our discussion must be brief. One important inconsistency harassed policy persistently. Mercantilists favored protection: they feared foreign goods. But they failed to slough off entirely the medieval theory of provision, the policy which anxiously attempted to satisfy the basic needs of population by imports. Some goods mercantilists were so eager to possess in adequate quantity that they forbade export—an extension of the medieval policy of provision. Such a prohibition conflicted with the usually overriding desire to keep foreign goods out of the country and speed the departure of domestic goods. Because this conflict raged most intensely over food, the attempt to compromise between protection and provision is most striking in the English Corn Laws and the internal regulation of the price of grain which complemented them. Not repealed until 1846, the Corn Laws had a long and complicated history. Suffice it to say that they included regulations which encouraged corn imports above a given domestic price and allowed corn exports when domestic prices dropped beyond a certain level. The conflict of interests among landlords, corn merchants, consumers, and the state was recorded in the numerous alterations of prices and changes in regulations which marked the tumultuous history of the laws. It was recorded also in the sporadic efforts of English local authorities to control prices and eliminate monopolies. Despite such intervention, price regulations on the Continent were more complex, general, and severely enforced than they were in England.

Mercantilists were even more eager to control the quality of manufactures, since upon this quality successful export depended —the key to a favorable balance and all the other good things of the mercantilist world. In a triumph of logic over life, Colbert, the greatest of seventeenth-century French mercantilists, clamped enormously detailed controls upon manufactures. Colbert sought national uniformity of finished products, a formidable aim in any age, an almost impossible objective in the jungle of local interests which was France. His regulations or *règlements* were meticulous and minute. The decrees for the period 1666–1730 filled four quarto volumes and totaled 2200 pages. Three supplements, nearly as substantial, reinforced them.

The cloth *règlement* comprised 59 articles. The two dyeing *règlements* contained, respectively, 62 and 98 articles, and the largest of the general dyeing instruction achieved the magnificent total of 317 articles. Each had the force of law, behind each one was the King's authority. Supposedly, regulation followed the course of production, from raw material to finished product.

Specifications covered the appropriate handling of raw materials and each succeeding stage. Weaving and dyeing received special emphasis. Measurements were precisely prescribed. A sample rule required that the fabrics of Dijon be put in reeds 1¾ ells wide, that a warp must contain 1408 threads, 44 by 32 including the selvages, that when cloth came to the fulling mill it must measure in width precisely one ell. The *règlements* distinguished three categories of dyers: piece dyers of genuine colors, piece dyers of other colors, and the dyers of silk, wool, and yarn. This sort of thing went on indefinitely and interminably.

Enforcement was a constant worry. The intendant, the King's representative in each district, was responsible for the obedience of manufacturers and merchants. Therefore his agents made periodic, unheralded inspections. When they found cloth at any stage which fell below specification, their authority enabled them to slash it. This was the penalty for a first offense. Later transgressions brought fines or even imprisonment. But despite all efforts, violations were frequent.

Four institutional arrangements combined to control the free movement and payment of labor, sometimes in the pursuit of general mercantilist objectives, more frequently in those of guilds and other employers. Insofar as these measures kept wages low, they served mercantilist ends, but not always was this their aim or result. By prescribing artificially long periods of training and limiting the number of apprentices, the laws of apprenticeship added to the cost of labor and diminished its supply. In regulating the opening of new shops, the quality of merchandise, and the prices charged in towns, the guilds only partially served mercantilist objectives. When wages were set by law, the result was usually wages lower than those a free market might have set. Finally, especially in England, laws of settlement sharply curtailed the mobility of labor. These laws, which made each parish responsible for its own poor but also gave each the privilege of refusing relief to those not legally settled, put a premium upon the quick discovery and summary deportation of workers who had migrated from other parishes in search of employment. In *Tom Jones,* Henry Fielding devoted some of the best farcical pages in English literature to the problems of Squire Western as justice of the peace in enforcing the acts of settlement.

A spate of sumptuary laws attempted to control the consumption of various articles. In general, the principle restricted the use of imports and promoted the market for domestic rivals. Thus it was declared illegal for anyone to be buried in a shroud made of anything but wool. Dead or alive, the loyal Briton supported English industry. At various times laws discouraged the use of tobacco, tea, and sugar, on the familiar ground that they cost treasure to import.

Finally a tangle of monopolies and special privileges, granted by royal favor, protected numerous items from open competition and completed the armory of internal regulations. The best that could be said for the tremendous forest of regulation was that enforcement frequently failed to match the spirit of enactment. Because the discrepancy was widest in England, laissez faire had a chance to take root earlier and more firmly than anywhere else.

External economic policy rested upon five types of regulation: navigation acts, colonization, import duties, bounties, and drawbacks. Even the shortest examination demonstrates their remarkable consistency. The motives of the men who fostered the English Navigation Acts were perfectly plain, and, granted the national egotism of mercantilist policy, perfectly proper: they were designed to impede the carrying trade of Britain's rivals, expand the English carrying trade, foster a larger navy, and make of England an entrepôt for colonial goods. Even Smith, out of a preference of defense to opulence, exempted the Navigation Acts from his severer strictures against mercantilist interference with free trade. Viewed from the American angle, the Navigation Acts forced our ships to stop in England and transship their cargoes onto British vessels, wherever we had destined the cargoes and whatever the cost and inconvenience of the maneuver. Steps were taken to impede the construction of American ships. When they were built, other regulations hindered their trade in the ports of other British colonies.

To the English, all of this was quite fair, since the role assigned to the colony was the production of raw materials, not an independent merchant marine or its own finished goods. The raw materials exported by the colonies to the home country could be worked up into manufactures and then exported, to the inestimable benefit of the balance of trade. Some of the more ecstatic mercantilists found colonies a substitute for the gold and silver mines so enviably possessed by the Spanish. The home country gained treasure not only by selling manufactures but also by not sending coin to foreign lands for the raw materials of which they were composed. Therefore the obvious interest of the home country forbade or, at least, severely limited colonial processing. In return, the logic of the position demanded that the home country refrain from growing raw materials. So persuasive was this line of argument that England ruthlessly eliminated a thriving tobacco-growing industry within the British Isles to avoid competition with the colonial tobacco industry. Because many mercantilist restrictions were not enforced and most of the remainder were not aimed at the colonists' vital interests, it is possible that mercantilist restraints impeded colonial development very slightly. Such, however, was not the opinion of the colonists. The American Revolution was as much a war against mercantilism as a war for freedom.

Brief mention suffices for the three remaining devices. Import duties were an aspect of the mercantilist fear of goods and the mercantilist lust for a favorable balance of trade. Even more aggressive in their attack upon the foreigner's goods, bounties subsidized exports so that manufacturers, otherwise unable to compete with foreigners, could become competitive. As Adam Smith acidly commented, if foreigners could not be persuaded by competitive quality and price to buy English goods, the English government proposed to pay them to take the goods. Drawbacks were remissions of duties granted to merchants who imported goods only to reëxport them. So far as they went, they limited the effect of import taxes.

Comments on mercantilism have frequently condescended to the holders of such outmoded, fallacious notions. Fallacious they might be, outmoded they are not. With infinite ingenuity, the commercial policy of almost all contemporary nations attests the living strength of mercantilism.

ECONOMIC WRITERS IN THE AGE
OF MERCANTILISM

The awkward heading to this section is an attempt to suggest how much sense, by later criteria, can be found in the best writings of men who, if not mercantilists themselves, wrote when mercantilist policies dominated the scene. The first section of this chapter summarized typical mercantilist doctrine. What follows is less typical: it is the best available.

Of the dozens, if not hundreds, of mercantilist writers of some note, we will discuss only five: three seventeenth-century figures, Petty, North, and Locke; and two eighteenth-century political economists, Cantillon and Hume. They illustrate how diverse economic thought was during these centuries. They suggest, as well, something of the caliber of the economics available to Adam Smith when he began to write the *Wealth of Nations*. In profession, these writers were typical of their time: none was primarily an economist. Petty and North were men of affairs, Locke and Hume were philosophers, and Cantillon was a merchant. In every instance, economics was a by-product, not a specialty.

SIR WILLIAM PETTY (1623–1685)

The son of a poor clothier, Petty was a self-made man of almost appalling versatility. A partial list of his occupations includes inventor, linguist, doctor, friend and student of Thomas Hobbes, sailor, professor of music, vice-principal of Brasenose College, Oxford, army doctor, experimental shipbuilder, not to mention writer and political economist. The diarist Samuel Pepys called him "the most rational man that ever he heard speak with a tongue." In politics, Petty was a disciple of Hobbes and in Petty's writings can be found traces of Hobbes's belief that the power of the sovereign was limited only by his own will. In economics, however, Petty's method owed most to Francis Bacon. He was one of a group of experimenters in the spirit of Bacon's *Novum Organum*. True, the experiments were in modern eyes ludicrous. Against the background of centuries of medieval thought, they were intelligent and inevitable. One experiment placed a toad in the middle of a circle of powder made from unicorn's horn (source unspecified) to test the proposition that the powder's charm could confine the toad within the circle. The toad hopped out time after time. But the point was Petty's eagerness to subject the propositon to the test of experiment.

In economics Petty was the pioneer of political arithmetic, the term applied to early statistical methods. Although Adam Smith was to affirm his distrust of political arithmetic, Petty has good claim to the title of founder of modern quantitative methods. His description of his method indicated how well aware of his originality he was:

The Method I take is not yet very usual; for instead of using only comparative and superlative Words, and intellectual arguments, I have taken the course (as a specimen of the Political Arithmetick I have long aimed at) to express my self in terms of *Number, Weight,* or *Measure;* to use only Arguments of Sense, and to consider only such Causes, as have visible Foundations in Nature; leaving those that depend upon the mutable Mind, Opinion, Appetite, and Passion of particular men, to the Consideration of Others: Really professing myself as unable to speak satisfactorily upon those grounds (if they may be call'd grounds), as to fortel the case of a Dye; to play well at Tennis, Billiards or Bowles (without long practice) by virtue of the most elaborate Conceptions that ever have been written De Projectilibus et Missilibus or of the angle of Incidence and Reflection.[9]

Although Petty did not always follow his own precepts, and, when he did, many of his numbers were guesses or implausible estimates, he deserves the credit and the indulgence of the pioneer.

Petty wrote voluminously, particularly about the condition of

[9] Sir William Petty, *Economic Writings*, Cambridge, 1899, Vol. I, p. lxv.

Ireland, where he resided a good part of his life. His *Political Arithmetic* was a collection of statistical papers. Because it was most connected in style and most prescient in content, his most famous essay was the *Treatise of Taxes and Contributions* (1662). A summary of the contents will suggest the orientation of this early treatise on public finance. Throughout, the viewpoint was the ruler's, as befitted the admirer of Hobbes. He began by classifying public expenditure into six main branches. The first was defense. The second was the payment of officials "in such a degree of plenty and splendour, as private Endeavours and Callings seldom reach unto: To the end, that such Governours may have the natural as well as the artificial causes of Power to act with."[10] Petty had made two points: the importance of their work entitled public officials to high rewards, and power depended not only upon legal authority but also upon the financial strength of its wielders. Out of the same motives, Petty wished to maintain the clergy in a "proportionable splendour."

The care of army, government, and church was a familiar mercantilist objective. But the next three outlets for public expenditures imputed wider views to Petty. He proposed to support schools and universities, and to succor the unfortunate, somewhat in the manner of the modern welfare state. Among the unfortunate he included orphans, defectives, and unemployed workers. His argument seems unanswerable: ". . . it is unjust to let any starve, when we think it just to limit the wage of the poor, so as they can lay up nothing against the time of their impotence and want of work." [11] This position brought Petty fairly close to the laissez-faire judgment that if a man was free his freedom implied the right to starve. Its corollary stated that a man not allowed to make his own bargains could not be entirely responsible for life's contingencies. Finally, Petty charged the state with the proper maintenance of roads, rivers, aqueducts, and bridges.

What was a good tax system? Many passages in Petty's examination of this question anticipated Adam Smith's later discussion

[10] *Ibid.*, p. 18.
[11] *Ibid.*, p. 20.

and the celebrated canons of taxation themselves. Why, he asked, did taxes tend to increase? There were many reasons. Because people were unwilling to pay their taxes, collection was expensive and additional levies were necessary. Here, in embryo, was Smith's canon on economy in collection. Collection was impeded also by the need to pay in money, at stated times, rather than in goods at dates more convenient to taxpayers. Citizens were reluctant to pay because of "obscurities and doubts concerning the right of imposing."[12] Scarcity of coin and confusion of coinage added to the difficulties of payment, and the fewness of taxpayers made taxes the heavier on each person liable. Petty ground his own statistical axe when he noted, as a reason, "ignorance of the numbers, Wealth and Trade of the people, causing a needless repetition of the charges and trouble of new additional levies, in order to amend mistakes."[13]

Next, Petty indulged himself in a number of statistical explorations. He computed the savings to be made by reducing the number of parishes and, therefore, the number of clergymen employed at state expense. He argued, rather curiously, that since there were more men than women in England, the clergy might just as well return to celibacy and live on smaller incomes. He proposed to regulate the number of medical students according to statistical calculations of mortality and disease. He would also have reduced the number of merchants. His triumphant conclusion ran:

Now if the numerous Officers and Fees relating to the Government, Law, and Church; and if the number of Divines, Lawyers, Physicians, Merchants, and Retailers were also lessened, all which do receive great wages for little work done to the Public, with how much greater ease would common expense be defrayed? and with how much more equality would the same be assessed?[14]

Petty wished to spend these savings on the care of the poor. Resembling the public-works proposals of contemporary econom-

[12] *Ibid.*, p. 21.
[13] *Ibid.*, p. 21.
[14] *Ibid.*, pp. 28–29.

ics, his plans for the poor incorporated the usual mercantilist warning to economize on imports. The work of the poor should be ". . . without expence of Foreign Commodities, and then 'tis no matter if it be employed to build a useless Pyramid upon *Salisbury Plain*, bring the Stones at *Stonehenge* to *Tower-Hill*, or the like; for at worst this would keep their minds to discipline and obediance [sic], and their bodies to a patience of more profitable labours when need shall require it."[15] Which was no less picturesque than Keynes's remarks about the pyramids of Egypt or the digging up of old cans filled with money.

Petty advanced a program for the abatement of the difficulties of tax collection. People might think that the King asked too much, but surely they were mistaken, since the King injured his own power when he took from his subjects funds which they could profitably employ in trade. However, if taxes were proportional, people would grumble less, for the interesting reason that each person's relative position on the ladder of wealth would be preserved. Citizens' complaints about public expenditure on entertainments and displays were misguided: the money so spent, said Petty, passed into the hands of useful men, like brewers and bakers. Nor should taxpayers repine because the King enriched his favorites. Not only was this the King's right, but every man had his chance to be the King's favorite—a new view of equality of opportunity and the open society.

Petty concluded this portion of his analysis by observing that a certain amount of money was necessary to drive the trade of a nation. Emphasizing the significance of the velocity of circulation, he noted that banks economized upon the use of money. He consoled his readers with the reflection that taxes spent at home did little general harm. At worst, they altered the fortunes of individuals, "particularly by transferring the same from the Landed and Lazy to the Crafty and Industrious."[16]

An extremely interesting chapter examined the relative merits of particular taxes. The state should seek to have taxes "most

[15] *Ibid.*, p. 31.
[16] *Ibid.*, p. 36.

easily, speedily, and insensibly collected." More interesting than this general admonition was Petty's occasionally subtle analysis of shifting and incidence. A quitrent on land, to take one example, was a good tax only in a new state or in a state newly reformed. In an old state, landlords, saddled with long leases, suffered injustice bec..use they could not shift the quitrent to their tenants by charging higher rents. A tax on "the Rent of Housing" had its advantages, but difficulties of definition impeded enforcement. It was hard to tell whether a house was a dwelling or a place of business.

Almost incidentally, Petty advocated a labor-time theory of value, when he argued that rent should equal the surplus over necessities of the farmer, plus the replacement of seed. The price of corn in silver depended upon the amounts of labor required to produce each commodity. As Petty put it, "If a man can bring to *London*, an ounce of Silver out of the Earth in *Peru*, in the same time that he can produce a bushel of Corn, then one is the natural price of the other."[17]

Petty held interesting opinions on many other topics. He opposed the usury laws on common sense, commercial grounds: ". . . when a man giveth out his money upon condition that he may not demand it back until a certain time to come, whatsoever his own necessities shall be in the meantime, he certainly may take a compensation for this inconvenience which he admits against himself. And this allowance is what we commonly call usury."[18] What was a fair rate of interest? Petty's answer was: an amount at least as high as the rent that an equal sum, invested in land, brought. And, since money was portable and land fixed, a risk premium was appropriately added.

On foreign trade, Petty was brief and not entirely consistent. In standard mercantilist fashion, he argued that export taxes should not be so high as to make English prices higher than those of rivals. But no hint of the concept of elasticity of demand informed his comment. When it came to import duties, Petty

[17] *Ibid.*, p. 50.
[18] *Ibid.*, p. 47.

wished to make necessities imported from abroad more expensive than competitive home produce, to tax heavily goods "tending to Luxury and sin," and to burden only very lightly raw materials destined to be processed for later export. At the same time, his practical eye told him that heavy customs duties encouraged smuggling and increased the number of officials. In the end, other taxes had to supplement them. Petty played with the idea either of a tonnage charge on each ship or an insurance premium.

No trace of brotherly affection marred his comments about the Dutch. The best way to meet their ferocious competition was to entice away their skilled workers or, as an alternative, send English skilled workers to the Netherlands to learn Dutch secrets. These sage mercantilist reflections did not completely satisfy him. He commented that, in general, "as wiser Physicians tamper not excessively with their Patient, rather observing and complying with the motion of nature, than contradicting it with vehement Administrations of their own; so in Politicks and Oconomics the same must be used."[19] But he stopped far short of the unequivocal free-trade posture which his follower, Sir Dudley North, adopted.

His most famous, most-quoted remark proclaimed that "Labour is the Father and active principle of Wealth, as Lands are the Mother,"[20] an insight into the nature of the factors of production. An interesting anticipation of Jeremy Bentham's nineteenth-century theory of punishment can be inferred from his argument that when the state executed its citizens for crimes, it hurt itself. Much thriftier remedies were fines for the rich and slavery for the indigent.

In some ways, Petty was a representative man of his period. His belief in political absolutism, his unquestioning nationalism, even some aspects of his views on the poor, marked him as still a mercantilist. However, much in his work anticipated classical doctrine and stretched beyond it to modern techniques. Though

[19] *Ibid.*, p. 60.
[20] *Ibid.*, p. 68.

contemporary deficiencies tempted him into unscientific use of the few available data, he recognized the importance of the measurable. He identified the apparently permanent staples of public finance: shifting and incidence, tax administration, and expenditure policy. He employed the labor theory of value. He took a market view of the phenomenon of interest. More than a century later Adam Smith failed to see as clearly.

SIR DUDLEY NORTH (1641–1691)

Of Petty's two most important followers, North and Locke, the former was the more original. A leading student of the period, Jacob Viner, considered North one of the first free traders. Ricardo commented in a letter to McCulloch: "I had no idea that anyone entertained such correct opinions, as are expressed in this publication, at so early a period."[21] Ricardo might even have recognized a premonition of his own fondness for "strong cases" in North's description (in the third person) of his own method: ". . . he reduceth things to their Extreams, wherein all discriminations are most gross and sensible, and then shows them; and not in the state of ordinary concerns, whereof the terms are scarcely distinguishable."[22] North, like Ricardo, enjoyed clear and distinct problems, unmuddled by too many facts.

Professing himself an admirer of Descartes, North wrote anonymously. He explained that "the Publick is an acute as well as merciless Beast, which neither oversees a failing, nor forgives it."[23] Unafraid of heterodoxy, North was exceedingly sharp in analysis. So much was suggested by this merchant's criticism of mercantile activity: ". . . whenever Men consult for the Publick Good, as for the advancement of Trade, wherein all are concerned, they usually esteem the immediate Interest of their own to be the common Measure of Good and Evil. And there are many, who to gain a little in their own Trades, care not how much others suffer;

---

[21] Cited in the introduction to Sir Dudley North, *Discourses upon Trade*, Johns Hopkins, 1907, p. 3.
[22] *Ibid.*, p. 11.
[23] *Ibid.*, p. 7.

and each man strives that all others may be forc'd in their dealings, to act subserviently for his Profit, but under the cover of the Publick."[24]

As strongly as any other mercantilist, North believed in the strength of self-interest, but his conception of that motive's effects diverged far indeed from seventeenth-century opinion. Though it took no noble view of trading motives, the following passage did concede that unregulated trade benefited the community: "The main spur to Trade, or rather to Industry and Ingenuity, is the exorbitant Appetites of Men, which they will take pains to gratify, and so be disposed to work, when nothing else will incline them to it; for did Men content themselves with bare Necessaries, we should have a poor World."[25] Was there, here, across the centuries a premonition of the world of consumer durable goods? As strongly as any nineteenth-century classical economist, North affirmed the harmony of economic interests. The whole world was a trading area. No trade could be unprofitable or else men would leave it. "Wherever the Traders thrive, the Publick, of which they are a part, thrives also."[26] To force a man to trade in a line against his inclination could only damage the general welfare. No flatter contradiction of general mercantilist precept could be made.

North's other opinions were consistent with this standpoint. Laws should not regulate trade. The state should not interfere with the free flow of money. The supply of money conformed to the needs of trade and even the outward flow of money in the service of trade enriched the nation. "Money exported in Trade is an increase to the Wealth of the Nation; but spent in War, and Payments abroad, is so much Impoverishment."[27] This astounding man even preferred peace to war, for wars led to losses, not to gains. "If Peace be procured, easie Justice maintained . . . the Industrious encouraged . . . the Stock of the Nation will in-

[24] *Ibid.*, p. 12.
[25] *Ibid.*, p. 27.
[26] *Ibid.*, p. 13.
[27] *Ibid.*, p. 14.

crease, and Consequently Gold and Silver abound, Interest be easie, and Money cannot be wanting."[28]

No medieval taint adulterated North's opinions on interest. Should the government limit interest rates? In answering the question negatively, North erected a comparison between the landlord who rented land and the capitalist who rented stock for interest. Of the two, the capitalist deserved the higher return, because his risks were greater. Money responded to the same market pressures as did other commodities: ". . . so if there be more Lenders than Borrowers, Interest will also fall; wherefore it is not low interest makes Trade, but Trade increasing, the Stock of the Nation makes Interest low."[29] High interest rates attracted hoarded funds. Low interest rates kept money hidden. It was that simple. Moreover, since most loans supported the luxuries of the rich, rather than the fruitful activities of merchants, the usury laws aided luxury, not trade. Therefore, it was best to permit borrowers and lenders to make their own terms, in the manner of the "wise Hollanders." Rather contemptuously, North disposed of centuries of canonist subtlety in a sentence: "I will not say any thing to the Theological Arguments against Interest of Moneys; but their 3 *per Cent* is no more lawful than 4, or 12."[30]

Enough has been said to suggest how far in advance of his time North was. Even this sketchy account identified in his brief *Discourses* these central features of the *Wealth of Nations:* almost unqualified adherence to free trade, aversion to governmental tampering with the economy and belief in the natural harmony of interests, reliance upon self-interest to increase the general welfare, enlightened regard for other nations, preference for peace over war, and monetary views which stressed the natural flow of specie within countries and between countries. The rationalism of the eighteenth century, not the dogmatism of the mercantilist era, spoke through Dudley North. He was probably wise to write anonymously.

[28] *Ibid.,* p. 33.
[29] *Ibid.,* p. 18.
[30] *Ibid.,* p. 21.

JOHN LOCKE (1632–1704)

The name of John Locke is much greater in philosophy than it is in economics. His economics were neither so original as Petty's, nor so clear-sighted as North's. Appropriately, his major contribution to economics was a philosopher's: he provided the metaphysical justification for the labor theory of value in the famous essays *Of Civil Government*, published in 1690, but written before the Glorious Revolution, which they are sometimes mistakenly credited with justifying.

The sanction for labor as the source of value came in his chapter on property. His reasoning was this: God had given the earth in common to all men. How then did private property emerge? The answer was pragmatic. Property which belonged to everybody served the interests of none. Before property could benefit an individual, it had to be appropriated by that individual for his exclusive use. What was lawful appropriation? Here was the heart of Locke's answer:

> Though the earth and all inferior creatures be common to all men, yet every man has a "property" in his own "person." This nobody has any right to but himself. The "labour" of his body and the "work" of his hands, we may say, are properly his. Whatsoever, then, he removes out of the state that Nature hath provided and left it in, he hath mixed his labour with it, and joined to it something that is his own, and thereby makes it his property. It being by him removed from the common state Nature placed it in, it hath by this labour something annexed to it that excludes the common right of other men. For this "labour" being the unquestionable property of the labourer, no man but he can have a right to what that is once joined to, at least where there is enough, and as good left in common for others.[31]

Land mixed with labor created private property. But the statement seemed to imply limits, since each man commanded in himself only a finite amount of labor:

> As much as any one can make use of to any advantage of life before it spoils, so much he may by his labour fix a property in. What-

[31] John Locke, *Of Civil Government*, Everyman, 1943, p. 130.

ever is beyond this is more than his share, and belongs to others. Nothing was made by God for men to spoil or destroy. . . . As much land as a man tills, plants, improves, cultivates, and can use the product of, so much is his property.[32]

Thus far the theory was egalitarian. Most men's abilities were similar. If men were more nearly alike than different, then the property which the mixture of land and labor created would be of much the same size for different men. In two circumstances, Locke accepted this interpretation without reservation: in empty lands like the American colonies, where acres of fertile land waited for the industrious; and in earlier times before developed institutions complicated property tenure. What then of England, a long-settled land, destitute of acres held in common to be appropriated by him who would work them? Locke's answer amounted to a defense of inheritance and legal precedent: ". . . where the increase of people and stock, with the use of money, had made land scarce, and of some value, the several communities settled the bounds of their distinct territories, and, by laws, within themselves, regulated the properties of the private men of their society, and so, by compact and agreement, settled the property which labour and industry began."[33] In other words, although labor originally justified private property, once created, private property did not demand continued reaffirmation of title by repeated acts of labor. If the son were idle, his father's property nonetheless "by compact and agreement" became his.

Money added to the inequality of men's fortunes. Money derived its value, said Locke, from the general consent of mankind. If men were not willing to accept gold or silver for their produce or labor, gold or silver would cease to possess value, since they were of little use in themselves. Once men imputed value to money, they consented also "to a disproportionate and unequal possession of the earth."[34] For, because money was durable, "a man may, rightfully and without injury, possess more than he

[32] *Ibid.*, pp. 131–132.
[33] *Ibid.*, p. 138.
[34] *Ibid.*, p. 140.

himself can make use of by receiving gold and silver, which may continue long in a man's possession without decaying for the overplus."[35] The last statement seemed to remove all limits to appropriation which arose from the narrow capacity of any one man to enjoy the good things of the earth.

In sum, Locke's theory justified inherited property by past labor, and new property by contemporary labor. Past or present, labor, not land, was the mainspring of economic output. In the *Wealth of Nations*, Smith extended Locke's account of value when he advanced one theory for primitive society and another for his own time.

Locke's economics merit short comment. Sharing the mercantilist confusion between capital and money, he favored a large money supply as a thing good in itself, as well as a way of lowering interest rates. He did not favor legal control of these rates for fear that men would hoard rather than employ their funds. Locke may have been among the first to explain with fair clarity the self-adjusting mechanism of international trade, through changes in the flow of merchandise and precious metals. The following passage suggested equalization of commodity prices and money flows which achieved this end:

That in a country, that hath open commerce with the rest of the world, and uses money, made of the same materials with their neighbors, any quantity of that money will not serve to drive any quantity of trade; but there must be a certain proportion between their money and trade. The reason whereof is this, because to keep your trade going without loss, your commodities amongst you must keep an equal, or at least near the price of the same species of commodities in the neighboring countries; which they cannot do, if your money be far less than in other countries: for then either your commodities must be sold very cheap, or a great part of your trade must stand still, there not being money enough in the country to pay for them . . . at that high price, which the plenty, and consequently low value of money, makes them at in another country. . . .[36]

[35] *Ibid.*, p. 141.
[36] Cited by Jacob Viner, *Studies in the Theory of International Trade*, Harper, 1937, pp. 76–77.

However, the suggestion may exist more in the mind of the modern reader than in the thought of Locke, for he made no explicit mention of the usual correctives and appeared to consider it just as likely that trade would shrink as that prices would change. He seemed more aware that exchange rates depended upon the flow of merchandise and liquid funds. Unlike North, he shared the mercantilist preference for a favorable balance of trade. While his theory of the origins of private property made labor the source of value, he stopped short of making labor also the measure of value as Petty before him did. Like Petty, he thought that only land produced a surplus and wondered how money, barren by nature, could do the same.

RICHARD CANTILLON (c. 1685–1734)

Sometimes thought "the greatest economist before Adam Smith," Cantillon was apparently little read by his contemporaries, and completely mislaid until Jevons resurrected him in 1881. A transitional figure, there was much of the mercantilist about him: concentration upon the power of the state, fondness for gold and silver, emphasis on favorable trade balances, deprecation of luxury, assumption of mutual hostility among states, and willingness to regulate trade. Nevertheless, his systematic treatise anticipated a great deal of late-eighteenth- and nineteenth-century doctrine.

His three books dealt with value, money, and international trade. Even brief examination identifies the opposing elements held in suspension by Cantillon. Cantillon made a central distinction between intrinsic price and market price. Intrinsic price or value "is the measure of the quantity of Land and of Labour entering into its production, having regard to the fertility or produce of the Land and to the quality of its Labour."[37] Like Petty, Cantillon was content with two factors of production. Capital was the joint creation of land and labor, not an independent factor. More ephemeral in quality, market price was determined by

[37] Richard Cantillon, *Essai sur la Nature du Commerce en Général,* edited and translated by Henry Higgs, Macmillan (England), 1931, p. 29.

supply and demand. Cantillon approached very close to the modern concept of the schedule. His illustration of market price determination almost cried for a diagram on which supply and demand triumphantly intersected.

Cantillon's discussion of wages was followed very closely by Smith in the famous Chapter 10 of the *Wealth of Nations,* which dealt with the net advantages of different employments. Something of Cantillon's quality emerges from this passage: "The crafts which require the most Time in training or most Ingenuity and Industry must necessarily be the best paid. . . . The Arts and crafts which are accompanied by risks and dangers like those of Founders, Mariners, Silver miners, etc. ought to be paid in proportion to the risks. . . . When capacity and trustworthiness are needed, the labour is paid still more highly as in the case of Jewellers, Bookkeepers, Cashiers and Others."[38] Cantillon had identified three of Smith's influences upon monetary wages: cost of training, risk, and trustworthiness.

Cantillon's attitude toward wealth betrayed an odd mixture of emphasis on the virtues of land, which may have influenced the physiocrats a generation later, and attachment to the precious metals. He sketched something very like the physiocratic Tableau Économique in his picture of how the spending of the agricultural classes affected city dwellers and their spending in turn flowed back to the farmers. Everything depended on the land, and objects acquired value only because of the land. The landowner conferred benefits on all other classes and he alone was "naturally independent in a State . . . all other classes are dependent whether Undertakers or hired, and . . . all the exchange and circulation of the State is conducted by the medium of these Undertakers."[39] Cantillon's undertaker much resembled the modern entrepreneur, who takes risks in buying, in the hope of selling at a profit.

At the same time, Cantillon entirely failed to share the physiocratic contempt for foreign trade or their willingness to leave it

[38] *Ibid.,* p. 21.
[39] *Ibid.,* p. 57.

unregulated as not worth the attention of the state.[40] His attitude toward commodities and precious metals as wealth can be deduced from statements like this one: "The point which seems to determine the comparative greatness of States is their reserve Stock above the yearly consumption, like Magazines of Cloth, Linen, Corn, etc. to answer in bad years or war. And as Gold and Silver can always buy these things, even from the Enemies of the State, Gold and Silver are the true reserve Stock of a State, and the large or smaller actual quantity of this Stock necessarily determines the comparative greatness of Kingdoms and States."[41] And, like the mercantilists of his day, Cantillon was willing to discourage the import of foreign goods and to encourage home manufactures.

Book II, which centered on money, contained some of Cantillon's most original ideas. Three of the most striking were his discussions of the velocity of circulation, almost a cash balance theory; his improvements on earlier versions of the specie flow mechanism; and his explanation of how prices rose when the quantity of money was increased. He started his discussion of velocity with an old question: How much money is needed to carry on business, to drive trade? The answer depended partly on how rapidly the money changed hands—the velocity of circulation. Others had said this much. But Cantillon then proceeded to examine the behavior of each group toward the holding and spending of money. He broke his aggregate up into its important parts. At the same time, he recognized that banks and goldsmiths, their forerunners, increased the velocity of circulation. There was also a close discussion of internal differences of prices in the capital and in the provinces.

Cantillon's description of monetary flows between nations made it plain that he understood the effect upon prices of favorable and unfavorable merchandise balances, although he stopped a little short of making these adjustments automatic:

. . . if a State or Kingdom which supplies all Foreign countries with work of its own Manufacture does so much of this commerce that it

[40] See Chap. 4.
[41] *Ibid.*, pp. 89–90.

draws every year a constant balance of money from abroad, the circulation will become more considerable there than in foreign countries, money will be more plentiful there, and consequently Land and Labour will gradually become dearer there. It will follow that in all the branches of commerce the State in question will exchange a smaller amount of Land and Labour with the Foreigner for a larger amount, so long as these circumstances continue."[42]

Cantillon identified two other items in the international balance of payments, when he indicated that the tourist trade and foreign payments (investments) also affected the flow of funds.

His most ingenious bit of analysis was an explanation of Spanish price inflation. His account stressed the unfavorable effects upon the Spanish economy of the gold inflow from Spanish possessions. Mine workers were the first to enjoy an increase in their income. They bought goods from merchants, who, by increasing their own spending, added to employment, enlarged the demand for meat, wine, and wool, and, consequently, raised their prices. In time, prices rose so high that imports at lower prices expanded and, as a result, domestic mechanics and manufacturers were ruined. Money left the state to pay for imports; poverty and misery followed.

Cantillon's estimate of human history was somber: each nation passed through cycles of prosperity and decay. The sophistication of Cantillon's thought appeared to advantage in this description of the effects of increases in the money stock: "The proportion of the dearness which the increased quantity of money brings about in the State will depend on the turn which this money will impart to consumption and circulation. Through whatever hands the money which is introduced pays, it will naturally increase the consumption; but this consumption will be more or less great according to circumstances. It will be directed more or less to certain kinds of products or merchandise according to the idea of those who acquire the money."[43] A far cry indeed from the certainties of some of the earlier mercantilists.

Passing beyond most mercantilist conceptions, Cantillon saw

[42] *Ibid.*, pp. 157, 159.
[43] *Ibid.*, p. 179.

clearly that states which enjoyed favorable balances of trade, arising from merchandise exports, were soon emulated by other nations. In consequence, these favorable balances vanished. Cantillon's statement of the conclusion was dramatic: "When a State has arrived at the highest point of wealth (I assume always that the comparative wealth of States consists principally in the respective quantities of money which they possess) it will inevitably fall into poverty in the ordinary course of things."[44]

Because it is almost a short anthology of mercantilist foreign-trade prescriptions, we reproduce, in conclusion, Cantillon's summary of his own opinions: "I will conclude this by saying that the trade most essential to a State for the increase or decrease of its power is foreign trade, that the home trade is not of equally great importance politically, that foreign trade is only half supported when no care is taken to increase or maintain large merchants who are natives of the country, ships, sailors, workmen and manufacturers, and above all that care must always be taken to maintain the balance against the foreigner."[45]

DAVID HUME (1711–1776)

Hume, who saw most subjects more clearly than his contemporaries, made no exception of economics. Nevertheless, he wrote little about the subject, all of it in the form of brief essays. By the criteria of any age, Hume's enlightenment was exceptional. The welfare of individuals he considered parallel to that of the sovereign: ". . . according to the most natural course of things, industry and arts and trade encrease the power of the sovereign as well as the happiness of the subjects; and that policy is violent, which aggrandizes the public by the poverty of individual."[46] Adopting almost casually a labor theory of value ("Everything in the world is purchased by labour"), Hume included the poor in his concern for human happiness: "A too great disproportion among the citizens weakens any state. Every person, if possible, ought to enjoy

[44] *Ibid.*, p. 243.
[45] *Ibid.*, p. 243.
[46] David Hume, *Writings on Economics*, ed. by Eugene Rotwein, Nelson, 1955, p. 10.

the fruits of his labour, in a full possession of all the necessaries, and many of the conveniences of life. No one can doubt, but such an equality is most suitable to human nature and diminishes much less from the happiness of the rich than it adds to that of the poor."[47] Among other things, this was a declaration of the diminishing marginal utility of money, the basic premise of progressive taxation.

A complete cosmopolitan, Hume exalted the virtues of free trade: "Nature, by giving a diversity of geniuses, climates, and soils, to different nations, has secured their mutual intercourse and commerce, as long as they all remain industrious and civilized."[48] A fair statement of the principle of natural advantage. As for the effects of this intercourse, "I shall therefore venture to acknowledge, that, not only as a man, but as a British subject, I pray for the flourishing commerce of GERMANY, SPAIN, ITALY, and even FRANCE itself. I am at least certain that GREAT BRITAIN and all those nations, would flourish more, did their sovereigns and ministers adopt such enlarged and benevolent sentiments towards each other."[49] Even France! Could man say more?

Hume's favorite subjects were money and foreign trade. Although free of the mercantilist thirst for gold and silver, he did glimpse an interesting use for the gold and silver which flowed into a country, a use which foreshadowed the Keynesian concept of a profit inflation. If new money entered the realm, a temporary gap between prices and costs resulted. Since prices increased first, the immediate impact of monetary inflow was to raise profits. Higher profits stimulated industry and output. It followed that an appropriate monetary policy promoted progress by increasing the supply of money. But, in general, want of money never hurt a nation internally, "for men and commodities are the real strength of any community."[50] Hume made the explicit point that an unfavorable balance of trade turned exchange rates against importers, and encouraged exporters.

[47] *Ibid.*, p. 15.
[48] *Ibid.*, p. 79.
[49] *Ibid.*, p. 85.
[50] *Ibid.*, p. 45.

Less fortunately, Hume was responsible for a strong statement of the distinction between productive and unproductive labor which plagued economics through much of the nineteenth century: ". . . lawyers and physicians beget no industry; and it is even at the expense of others they acquire their riches; so that they are sure to diminish the possessions of some of their fellow-citizens, as fast as they encrease their own. Merchants, on the contrary, beget industry, by serving as canals to convey it through every corner of the state."[51] Nor did Hume avoid occasional mercantilist relapses: too much money was a nuisance because it increased prices, but a benefit because it gave the nation weight and power in wars and external affairs. However, Hume dwelled in the mercantilist world less than any other thinker of his time. If he had written a treatise instead of a few essays, it might well have resembled the *Wealth of Nations*.

---

[51] *Ibid.*, p. 53.

PART II

The Classical Tradition

Chapter 4

Adam Smith

The *Wealth of Nations* does not contain a single analytic idea, principle, or method that was entirely new in 1776.

J. A. Schumpeter

The most successful not only of all books on economics but, with the possible exception of Darwin's *Origin of Species*, of all scientific books that have appeared to this day.

J. A. Schumpeter

It is again a tribute to the greatness of Smith that all schools of thought may trace to him their origin or inspiration.

Sir Alexander Gray

These testimonials and demurrers to Smith's achievements are samples of many, early and late, which have punctuated a continuing flow of commentary on Smith himself, his book, and his ideas. Like Schumpeter, the same commentators both admired and detracted. One thing is clear, by now Smith's work is as much a fact of historical influence as it is a feat of economic analysis. It has been argued, even, that Smith's analytical ambiguities increased his ultimate influence on other economists, diverse in interest, and won him a wider public among the literate of his own time. Why was Smith the starting point of nineteenth-century English economics? How did his influence spread? How could the *Wealth of Nations* be so popular at the end of the eighteenth century and still so readable in the twentieth? The content and style of the book, the historical setting, and the personality of the author all contribute to the answers to such questions.

ENGLAND IN 1776

Frequently, economic historians date the beginning of the Industrial Revolution (when they admit the validity of the concept) in the last quarter of the eighteenth century. Business-cycle students often locate in the same period the more or less rhythmic alternation of expansion and contraction in economic activity which characterizes modern fluctuations. Valid though these generalizations seem to be, they demand hindsight. England in 1776 was not a modern economic community by any modern criterion. For one thing, agriculture was the principal industry. In most years England exported rather than imported grain. The illustrations used by Smith confirm the evidence of the few available statistics, that industry, such as it was, consisted largely of textile manufacturing. This activity centered in the home of the rural worker and in the small workshop of the modest enterpriser. As a central economic institution, the factory was a later development. So also was corporate organization as the typical legal form of the enterprise. Smith thought it self-evident that the individual businessman, who owned as well as operated his property, had every advantage over the hired agent of the corporation or joint stock company. The latter could never take the same interest as its owners in the prosperity of the enterprise.

Tools were simple. In Smith's famous illustration of division of labor, the pin manufactory, the advantages of division of labor derived from increased dexterity rather than from improved machinery. It was invention which flowed from division of labor, not division of labor which flowed from invention. The picture can be distorted. The large manufacturing enterprise was not entirely unknown in the eighteenth century. Coal and iron works gathered together hundreds of workers, and organized their production and payment after capitalist models. In

1776 such enterprises were rare and the extension of their techniques to textiles lay in the future.

For the great majority of English workers, life was hard, whether they struggled in the city or in the country. Samuel Johnson, who had himself fought to survive in the metropolis until fame came his way, once tried to compute the number of people in London who annually died of starvation. His estimate was less interesting than the hard reality of the endeavor. Rural life in the picturesque but unsanitary cottages of the farm laborer was no better. In 1750, probably two-thirds of the agricultural population owned no land. Necessarily, they worked for wages and supplemented their incomes with home industry. Much of the evidence suggests that their employers treated them meanly, docking their wages for poor workmanship, alleged or real, and cheating them on rates. In recompense, workers scamped workmanship and embezzled materials. Such were the unpromising roots out of which capitalism grew.

What does not emerge in this gloomy account is the ferment of the time.[1] England was an agricultural society indeed, but a society seething with change. Some of the more relevant changes were in agriculture itself. At the beginning of the eighteenth century, large tracts of land were uncultivated waste. As the century wore on, much of these lands was brought into use. On these lands and on properties already cultivated, landowners began to invest increasing amounts of capital. As that fact implies, techniques of cultivation were improved in several ways. More thorough cultivation and more systematic rotation patterns improved crop growing. Animal-breeding experiments improved livestock strains. Finally, the enclosure movement went hand in hand with an increase in the number of large estates run, on rational principles, for the profit of their owners.

Growing population was a symptom of increasing agricultural and industrial production. Since the first English census was not

---

[1] A wonderfully evocative account of this English background is to be found in W. C. Mitchell, *Lecture Notes*, Kelley & Millman, 1954. I have drawn upon it heavily.

taken until the start of the nineteenth century,[2] we can only guess at the change. That first census counted a population of something over ten millions. Undoubtedly the population was considerably smaller a century before. When people live as close to the margin of subsistence as the English of the eighteenth century, increase in numbers demands increase in the means of subsistence.

At home and abroad, English commerce was expanding, not spectacularly, but steadily and noticeably. During the years that Adam Smith taught at the University of Glasgow, he observed the founding of many enterprises, and the steady enlargement of the shipping industry. Glasgow was not unique. Larger and larger fleets of English merchantmen carried a mounting volume of English goods to other countries. Within the country, improvements in roads and public order widened the scale of domestic exchange. The evolution of financial institution facilitated the operations of both domestic and international traders.

The ferment was artistic and literary, as well as economic. The eighteenth century was the great century of English painting—Gainsborough and Reynolds; English philosophy—Hume, Berkeley, and Paley; English science; and English pottery and furniture. As every student of the English novel knows, the form was an eighteenth-century inspiration. *Tom Jones* appeared in 1749 and *Clarissa Harlowe* began her sufferings in 1747. The latter has proved sufficiently durable to evoke imitation as late as 1955 in Herman Wouk's *Marjorie Morningstar*.

Economics enjoyed a quickening of thought and an increase of publication. As early as 1749, Smith conducted with great éclat a public class in political economy, in Edinburgh. In 1750, Robert and Andrea Fontin began to reprint economic texts, among them works by Child, Petty, and Law. In 1752, Hume's *Political Discourses*, many of them devoted to economic topics, appeared and won unprecedented acclaim. Cantillon's *Essai sur le Commerce*, written a generation earlier, was made available in

---

[2] Indignant citizens had rebuffed earlier efforts as an infringement upon the liberty of the individual. What would they have thought about market research?

1755. Quesnay, the founder of the physiocratic school, published his first economic article in 1756.

There were signs and tokens enough that thoughtful men were analyzing changes of their own time. Yet, in 1776, England was a country still ostensibly devoted to mercantile principle. Perhaps the best, and surely the longest, defense of mercantilist theory and practice appeared in 1767, Sir James Steuart's two-volume quarto, *An Inquiry into the Principles of Political Economy*. The law of the land gave no comfort to novelty. In combination, the Navigation Acts, the Statute of Apprenticeship, and the Poor Laws impeded the free movement of workers from one parish to another, out of fear that they might become public charges; harassed the commerce of the American colonies; placed heavy burdens on imports via duties and treaties of commerce; and ineffectively meddled with the prices of necessities. "Ineffectively" was the key word, for one of the century's major achievements was the gradual breakdown of mercantilist enforcement. Nothing could stop men from moving illegally from farm to city, especially when they were pushed by enclosure on the land, and pulled by higher wages in the town. High duties meant simply greater profits for a flourishing tribe of smugglers, some of them recruited from the better classes of English society. The American colonies first grumbled, then evaded, and finally revolted.

The period called for a prophet. It got one: "a certain absent-minded Scotch professor" who "so greatly met" an "insistent opportunity"[3]—the chance to construct a theory closer to the facts Englishmen lived with and kinder to the sentiments which guided them.

SMITH'S LIFE

"Man," said Adam Smith, "is an anxious animal."[4] It is hard to understand how Smith grasped a truth so popular in our day,

---

[3] J. M. Clark, *et al.*, *Adam Smith, 1776–1926*, Chicago, 1928, pp. 51–52.

[4] Adam Smith, *Lectures on Justice, Police, Revenue, and Arms*, ed. by Edwin Cannan, Oxford, 1896, p. 179. This edition was based on notes taken by a student, probably in 1763.

especially since his own life was singularly pleasant and successful. An only child, he was born on June 5, 1723, in the small
town of Kirkaldy, Scotland. His father, a Writer to the Signet,
as lawyers were called, and a minor government official, died
several months before his son's birth. He left his widow ample
means to support herself and her child. A tender, affectionate
mother, she cared for the frail boy so effectively that he grew
into a healthy adult.

When he was 14, he enrolled in the University of Glasgow,
where he remained until 1740. There he came under the influence of Francis Hutcheson, in his words, "the never-to-be-for-
gotten Hutcheson." A teacher of rare force and persuasiveness,
Hutcheson should be remembered not because he lectured in
English rather than Latin, but because he numbered among
his students both Adam Smith and David Hume. Hutcheson was
the author of the phrase "the greatest happiness of the greatest
number," a catchword whose appeal has never been diminished
by its lack of logical meaning. His particular influence on Smith
was in the direction of greater religious and political liberty.
Hutcheson may have anticipated some of Smith's notions of
value.

Smith won a scholarship, a Snell Exhibition, to Oxford. He
spent the years 1740–1746 at Balliol College. It was not a happy
period. Smith, a man who made friends everywhere else he went,
made none at Oxford. A major explanation was the discrimination at the time against Scottish students. But, in addition, Oxford
during this period had fallen into a deep slumber, in which intellectual activity was a disturbance rather than a raison d'être.
Not that Smith wasted his time. If there were few lectures to
attend, because the lecturers evaded their duties, there was the
more time to read in the library. For six years, accordingly, he
browsed widely in belles-lettres, philosophy, and history. One
story of the period warrants repetition, though it is not quite
completely substantiated. He was punished for reading Hume's
Treatise of Human Nature. It is as certain as such a thing can be
that his bitter remarks on teachers and teaching in the *Wealth*

of Nations derived from memories of teachers who did not lecture and tutors who did not guide. His remedy recommended paying teachers according to the number of their students.

Not desiring to take holy orders, Smith returned in 1747 to Kirkcaldy and his mother, and began to cast about for a job. In 1748 he moved to Edinburgh. In that year and in 1749, he delivered a course of lectures on literature. These lectures were quite popular although, or probably because, their contents were quite conventional. Smith rated Shakespeare rather low and Racine very high. He thought little of Milton's shorter poems. Opinions of this sort led Wordsworth to remark that he was "the worst critic, David Hume excepted, that Scotland, a soil to which this sort of weed seems natural, has produced."[5] Sometime before 1752, he met David Hume and the two enjoyed a friendship terminated only by Hume's death in 1776.

Bad or good, the lectures accomplished their purpose: they won Smith a position as professor of logic at the University of Glasgow. A year later, in 1752, when the chair in moral philosophy became available, he shifted to it and held it until 1763. As a lecturer he was so popular that "even the small peculiarities in his pronunciation or manner of speaking, became frequently the objects of imitation."[6] His courses covered ample ground. Their first part was natural theology, a discussion of the proofs of being and the attributes of God. Next he came to ethics. A third division considered justice, and a final section analyzed expediency. The last he interpreted to be riches, power, and prosperity.

His lectures on ethics provided the basis for his first great literary success, the *Theory of Moral Sentiments*, which appeared in 1759. With a charm undiminished by time, Smith conducted his readers on an exploration of the springs of human behavior. Although the Hutcheson who made benevolence the principle of human action walked these pages, Smith was too skeptical a

[5] John Rae, *Life of Adam Smith*, MacMillan, 1895, p. 34.
[6] Dugald Stewart, *Account of the Life and Writings of Adam Smith*, read by Stewart before the Royal Society of Edinburgh in 1793, reprinted as an introduction to the *Wealth of Nations*, ed. by E. G. Wakefield, 1843, p. xxxi.

soul to rest a whole system on unalloyed kindness. Instead, he argued that we acted as we did out of a regard for the opinion of others. We shape our actions to please an impartial spectator, the possessor of enlightened reason. What we call conscience is the representative within our own breast of the enlightened observer. When we sympathize with a friend in trouble, our criteria are those we conceive will win the approval of this judicious soul. This enlightened observer, this impartial spectator of all our actions, did not teach universal benevolence. Though he felt the softer human emotions, he expected human beings to pursue their own interest, in ways which violated no ethical canons.

The immediate success of the *Theory of Moral Sentiments* was not astonishing. The style was easy and ample, the illustrations and the author's fund of curious knowledge entertained even those who disagreed with his notions. For the history of economics its vogue had a momentous consequence. The book fell into the hands of Charles Townshend, statesman, wit, and man of fashion. According to Hume, he was "so taken with the performance, that he said . . . he would put the Duke of Buccleuch under the author's care."[7] So it turned out that, in 1763, Smith resigned his professorship and became a traveling tutor to the young duke, a shift not nearly so strange then as it might appear now. By it, Smith gained £300 per annum, not only during the period of his responsibility, but for the rest of his life.

The tutor and his noble pupil went abroad early in 1764, first for a week or two in Paris, and then for 18 months in Toulouse, in the south. In Toulouse he began a book, as he said in a letter to Hume, "to pass away the time."[8] This book became the *Wealth of Nations*. It was an expansion of the fourth part of his Glasgow lectures, those devoted to expediency. Economics might have taken a different course if that "clever fellow," Charles Townshend, had not happened to read the *Theory of Moral Sentiments*.

[7] *Ibid.*, p. lxiii.
[8] Rae, *op. cit.*, p. 178.

In France, Smith met and talked with the physiocrats,[9] although the evidence of his *Lectures* seems to prove that much of what he appeared to borrow from this group, he had, earlier and independently, discovered for himself. At any rate, he met Turgot, an ally of the physiocrats; Quesnay, the founder of the system; and Necker, D'Alembert, Helvétius, and Marmontel. Hume's recommendation opened all doors to him. Even though the main contours of the *Wealth of Nations* were already clear in his mind, physiocratic influence was present in the details and organization of Book II. Prior to Quesnay's death, Smith had apparently intended to dedicate his book to him. In the event, he paid the physiocrats the compliment of generous praise, tempered by only mild criticism.

In 1766 he returned to London, content with his travels and determined to venture no more abroad. On both sides it had been a happy, productive period. His pupil testified that "we spent near three years together, without the slightest disagreement or coolness. . . . We continued to live in friendship till the hour of his death; and I shall always remain with the impression of having lost a friend whom I loved and respected, not only for his great talents, but for every private virtue."[10] And so he returned once more to Kirkcaldy, where he spent the decade ending in 1776, writing and rewriting the *Wealth of Nations*.

The book brought him fame and fortune, the one slowly as its influence spread, the second indirectly in the shape of an appointment in 1778 as Commissioner of Customs in Scotland. Its payment, plus his pension, gave him a very large income for the period. In 1787 his old school elected him to the honorary post of rector. On the occasion, he wrote: "No man can owe greater obligation to a society than I do to the University of Glasgow. They educated me; they sent me to Oxford . . . they elected me one of their own members. . . . The period of thirteen years, which I spent as a member of that society, I remember as by far the most useful, and as by far the happiest and most

[9] See pp. 80–86.
[10] Stewart, *op. cit.*, p. lxxv.

honourable of my life."[11] His last years were shadowed by the death of his mother in 1784. Since he lived in a pre-Freudian era, it is possible that Smith, a bachelor by choice, was bound to his mother by no more than sincere affection, for he came and went as he chose, not seeing her for long intervals, content always to return to her and the village he loved. In 1790 he died of a chronic intestinal obstruction. He bore his pain with exemplary fortitude and expressed anxiety only that his friends destroy his unpublished manuscripts.

PHYSIOCRACY

Justice demands that a sketch of the physiocrats precede any account of the *Wealth of Nations*. Perhaps the brevity of the summary suggests the bias of English-speaking economists. Perhaps it suggests as well the simplicity of physiocratic notions (always excepting the Tableau Économique), despite the prolixity of their presentation.

The physiocrats were the first "school" in the history of economic thought. In the same sense, Benthamites, Marxists, and Keynesians constituted schools. Unlike the mercantilists, the physiocrats were in close touch with each other, acknowledged a common leader, established organs of propaganda, and presented a united front to the world. Above all, they taught a common doctrine. Although their vogue was brief—their publications bear dates between 1756 and 1778, and their influence had begun to wane well before 1780—in their time, they converted the great and left a permanent mark on economics.

Something should be said about physiocracy as a social phenomenon before we consider its major teachings on wealth, the natural order, the role of the state, and freedom of trade. To begin with, their single leader, often praised by them in the most extravagant terms,[12] was François Quesnay, a physician who

---

[11] *Ibid.*, p. cv.

[12] The elder Mirabeau ranked Quesnay's invention of the Tableau Économique with the invention of writing and money as the three greatest contributions to human civilization.

came to economics as an amateur in his sixties. Quesnay was the court doctor who had won his position by his successful treatment of the Dauphin for smallpox. If his position did not completely account for his influence, Mme. de Pompadour had also made him a favorite. It has been conjectured[13] that many who professed themselves disciples of the doctor hoped that he would drop a word to their advantages into the ear of that powerful lady. The major disciples attracted by Quesnay included the Marquis de Mirabeau, Mercier de la Rivière, and Dupont de Nemours.[14] Turgot has been frequently numbered among this group. Actually, he differed from it at important points and refused to confine the meaning of productive labor to agricultural pursuits. Although the physiocrats' economic ideas were original, their social standing was impeccable and their devotion to the maintenance of property and to the preservation of absolute monarchy was intense.

Physiocracy became the fashion in other countries also. Carl Friedrich, the Margrave of Baden, became a disciple and corresponded with Mirabeau. Voltaire was both a critic and an admirer. Catherine of Russia was sufficiently taken by the doctrine to engage in a dialogue with Mercier de la Rivière. Little came of it. The following excerpt from a report of one of the conversations may explain why:

"Sir," said the Czarina, "could you tell me the best way to govern a State well?"—"There is only one, Madame," answered the pupil of Quesnay; "it is to be just, i.e. maintain order, and enforce the laws." —"But on what basis should the laws of an empire repose?"—"On one alone, Madame, the nature of things and of men."—"Exactly, but when one wishes to give laws to a people, what rules indicate most surely the laws which suit it best?"—"To give or make laws, Madame, is a task which God has left to no one. Ah! what is man, to think himself capable of dictating laws to beings whom he knows not, or knows so imperfectly? And by what right would he impose laws upon beings whom God has not placed in his hands?"—"To

[13] By Joseph Schumpeter in his *History of Economic Analysis*, Oxford, 1954.
[14] Thomas Jefferson carried on animated correspondence with Dupont de Nemours. Physiocracy in a new country must have seemed attractive.

what, then, do you reduce the science of government?"—"To study well, to recognize and manifest, the laws which God has so evidently engraven in the very organisation of man, when He gave him existence. To seek to go beyond this would be a great misfortune and a destructive undertaking."—"Monsieur, I am very pleased to have heard you. I wish you good-day." She sent him home richly rewarded, and wrote to Voltaire: "He supposed that We walked on all fours, and very politely took the trouble to come to set us up on our hind legs."[15]

What did the physiocrats preach so vehemently? One of the major achievements of modern quantitative economics is the concept and the measurement of national income. Never before could the analyst understand the physiology of economic society so clearly. The physiocrats anticipated, however crudely, this analysis. The Tableau Économique endeavored to trace the flow of income through society. It thus embraced the purposes if it could not match the triumphs of national income measurement. More important than their faulty analysis was their grasp of the notion of economic science as a unified whole. They had a sense of system unrivaled up to their arrival. They tried to see how things hung together. No one can say they did badly for a first attempt.

Two French scholars located "the essence of the Physiocratic system . . . in their conception of the 'natural order.' "[16] Now, "natural" is a treacherous word. Cultivated gentlemen of means like the physiocrats had no affection for Rousseau's state of nature, one famous meaning of the word "natural." Life in the woods would have struck them as chilly, monotonous, and risky. They sought regularity, not adventure. They hunted for and felt sure that they had found repetitive patterns in human behavior which could be called laws, analogous to the physical relationships which control the material universe. These regularities were the work of God, who intended us to conform to them. As Mercier de la Rivière had said to Catherine of Russia, God

[15] Henry Higgs, *The Physiocrats* (1897), Langland Press, 1952, pp. 88-89.
[16] Gide and Rist, *A History of Economic Doctrines*, Heath, 1949, p. 25.

had planted these laws deep in human nature. The proper study of man was the quest for what was already there, the divine principles of human organization.

Perhaps there was a problem. Who was to say that he had discovered these laws? The physiocrats had a ready answer. Surely, cultivated gentlemen like themselves were the likeliest candidates. Once the laws were disclosed, appropriate human behavior reduced itself to the propriety of obeying them. All that government needed to do was to allow each man to follow his own "natural" tendency, implanted by God. Here was the rational and, still more, the theological sanction for laissez faire. This was not the first time, nor the last, that "natural" has been taken to mean "good" and the "good" opposed to existing arrangements.

Many economists remember the physiocrats primarily for their odd views about the role of the land. So long as a follower of Henry George and the single-tax movement is left, these views still convince someone. What did they believe? First, that land was different from any other agent of production. Nature or God, working through the soil, produced more wealth than was consumed in its creation. This special gift of God applied only to land. The net product, a famous concept, was the difference between wealth consumed and wealth produced.

Commerce, transportation, and manufacturing were incapable of producing new wealth. They might shift the location of old wealth. They might alter its shape in the process of fabrication, but they added nothing to the land's produce. The distinction between productive labor and unproductive labor was even more extreme than Hume's. As late as John Stuart Mill, it led to the most fruitless controversies over the precise qualities which make one kind of labor productive and another the reverse. Insofar as other classes earned profits, these profits were transferred from the agriculturists, their only source, to other groups. On various grounds, the physiocrats frequently approved such transfers.

No one can seriously claim that the Tableau Économique

was free of obscurity. Its purpose was at any rate clear: it traced the circulation of income among the great classes of society. There were only three: a productive class of agriculturists; a proprietory class which included the King and the landowners; and the sterile class which consisted of merchants, manufacturers, domestic servants and members of the liberal professions. All wealth originated with the first class. Imagine the total product of that class to be worth five million francs. Suppose that two of the five million were needed to maintain the productive class, that is to feed and clothe it. These two millions, remaining where they were, did not circulate. The remaining produce, worth three million, was distributed to the other classes. Since the productive class needed some manufactures, it bought these for one million from the sterile class. The remaining two millions passed into the hands of landowners and other propertied groups, including the government. This propertied group lived on its two millions, which it acquired through taxes and rents. It spent one million for food and the other for manufactures. Although, by definition, the sterile class produced nothing, it received two million francs from the productive and propertied classes for manufactures. These it used to buy necessities and raw materials. These two millions had now returned to their starting point, the agriculturists. Since the landed proprietors had also spent one million on food, the whole of the original five million francs was replaced. The cycle began once more.

Something was surely peculiar. Landowners appeared to do nothing: artisans worked desperately hard. Yet the latter were termed sterile and the former, though not honored with the title "productive," were revered. The justification sounded in parts like Locke. After all, landowners were the descendants of the men who had cleared the fields and made today's cultivation possible. Somebody, sometime, had mingled his labor with the land.

There was an even more important warrant for the landowners' position. Private property, thought the physiocrats, was the strongest of social cements, the institutional arrangement which enabled a society to manage its affairs in peace and prosperity.

The corollaries of this claim were numerous obligations which fell upon the shoulders of the property owner. Landowners were responsible for bringing into cultivation new lands. Ideally, they set an example by their personal conduct, and they spent their money in ways which benefited the community. Their obligations to their tenants should restrain them from ever taking away from the tenants more than their net product. Worst of all, the landlords should pay all the taxes. This last followed logically from the theory of the net product. If land alone produced a surplus and this surplus was drained off by landlords, the other classes received no more than a subsistence minimum. Only one group, the landowners, should pay taxes. Moreover, only this group could pay them, because wherever the tax was laid, in the end it was shifted to the landowners. Here was the basis of the single tax, as preached by Henry George, and as later adopted by the English Labor Party.

Since exchange was barren and unproductive of wealth, what difference did it make whether trade were free or controlled? With some departure from logical consistency, the physiocrats argued strenuously for free trade, conceivably because they expected trade to decay all the more speedily as an effect, conceivably because free trade between nations was linked, as a goal of their propaganda, with the removal of internal restrictions.

Their conception of the state was strange. Although they wished to relieve it of the need to enforce the burdensome restrictions of mercantilism, the physiocrats were strong supporters of absolute state power. Their argument was ingenious. The role of the monarch was to identify himself with the natural order. This done, he should make sure that everyone else acted according to the demands of the natural order. He was a despot who had read the physiocrats. In practical fact, such a despot had a great deal of work to do before the natural order could hold sway. Before the state could restrict its action, it had first to eliminate the tangle of restrictions, local and external, which hampered freedom.

As a school the physiocrats enjoyed only brief glory. But their insights, and their obfuscations, became a part of nineteenth-century economics through the writings of Adam Smith and his followers.

THE *WEALTH OF NATIONS*

"Adam Smith is a teller of stories about political economy. His book entertains those even whom it does not instruct, and instructs others by means of entertaining them."[17] Although not every economist would rejoice in this description of his own work, Wakefield's judgment was both apt and complimentary. The reader, new to the *Wealth of Nations*, perhaps new to economics, found to his pleasure that this famous economist led him gently by the hand, never quite descending to triviality, never leaping over knotty points, always willing to pause to tell a curious story or point an apt illustration. The style was easy and graceful, yet capable of genuine indignation. The always reasonable analysis advanced by stages which neither insulted nor overtaxed the normal reader's intelligence. Digressions were numerous, some of them were very long: that the book was not tidily organized only added to its charm.

Attractive even to readers of the eighteenth century was the spirit of generosity which the book so frequently displayed. The obiter dicta breathed a sympathy for the poor and the oppressed quite alien to his mercantilist predecessors and antagonists. Although the ignorant and the tendentious have used Smith as an apologist for a rising industrial capitalist class, his own heart beat with the laborer and the rural worker. Numerous well-turned expressions of these sympathies can be cited: "Masters are always and every where in a sort of tacit, but constant and uniform combination, not to raise the wages of labour above their actual rate."[18] Or, "Our merchants and master-manufacturers complain

---

[17] Adam Smith, *Wealth of Nations*, ed. by E. G. Wakefield, 1843, Introduction, p. vii.

[18] Adam Smith, *Wealth of Nations*, ed. by Edwin Cannan, Modern Library, 1937, pp. 66–67.

much of the bad effects of high wages in raising the price, and thereby lessening the sale of their goods at home and abroad. They say nothing concerning the bad effects of high profits. They are silent with regard to the pernicious effects of their own gains. They complain only of those of other people."[19] On trade gatherings he commented: "People of the same trade seldom meet together, even for merriment and diversion, but the conversation ends in a conspiracy against the public, or in some contrivance to raise prices."[20] His preference for the rural life was strong, as in this passage: "Country gentlemen and farmers are, to their great honor, of all people, the least subject to the wretched spirit of monopoly."[21] For the consumer he had one of the first good words in the record of economic thought: "Consumption is the sole end and purpose of all production; and the interest of the producer ought to be attended to, only so far as it may be necessary for promoting that of the consumer. The maxim is so perfectly self-evident, that it would be absurd to attempt to prove it. But in the mercantile system, the interest of the consumer is almost constantly sacrificed to that of the producer."[22]

The optimistic temper of the book also pleased, particularly in contrast with the mercantilists who came before and the Malthusians who came afterwards. Smith's analytical conclusions produced his optimism, but it was also something with which he began, a part of the "vision," as Schumpeter put it, with which every important economist begins. What were the contents of this vision? Smith believed that in human affairs progress was the ruling tendency. This was no woolly Utopian wish. On the contrary, Smith founded his confidence on the innate selfishness of man and the natural harmony of interests. He stated and restated these affirmations. "Every individual is continually exerting himself to find out the most advantageous employment for whatever capital he can command. It is his own advantage, in-

---

[19] *Ibid.*, p. 98.
[20] *Ibid.*, p. 128.
[21] *Ibid.*, p. 428.
[22] *Ibid.*, p. 625.

deed, and not that of the society, which he has in view. But the study of his own advantage naturally, or rather necessarily leads him to prefer that employment which is most advantageous to the society."[23] Or again, "The uniform, constant, and uninterrupted effort of every man to better his own condition, the principle from which public and national, as well as private opulence is originally derived, is frequently powerful enough to maintain the natural progress of things toward improvement, in spite both of the extravagance of government, and of the greatest errors of administration."[24]

Join to these remarks two more and the vision is complete. "This division of labour, from which so many advantages are derived, is not originally the effect of any human wisdom, which foresees and intends that general opulence to which it gives occasion. It is the necessary, though very slow and gradual, consequence of a certain propensity in human nature which has in view no such extensive utility; the propensity to truck, barter, and exchange one thing for another."[25] Completing this view of human nature was this egalitarian passage: "The difference between the most dissimilar characters, between a philosopher and a common street porter, for example, seems to arise not so much from nature, as from habit, custom, and education, When they come into the world, and for the first six or eight years of their existence, they were, perhaps, very much alike, and neither their parents nor playfellows could perceive any remarkable difference."[26]

What Smith said was that man was a rather feckless creature, born into this world with few if any special capacities. Fortunately, God or nature implanted in him certain instincts, among them a drive to "truck" and "barter." These instincts, combined with his "uniform" and "uninterrupted" attempt to make more money and rise in the world, led him to work harder, save more

[23] *Ibid.*, p. 421.
[24] *Ibid.*, p. 326.
[25] *Ibid.*, p. 13.
[26] *Ibid.*, p. 15.

money, produce the goods society needed, and enrich the community. Men were "naturally" like this.

If government kept its hands out of economic affairs, the "natural order" could speedily flower. Like his physiocratic friends, Smith did not mean that the natural order was quite spontaneous. Men had to behave wisely. At many points, Smith despaired of that much wisdom. Nevertheless, the natural order was something to strive for, since God and nature intended it for man. More frequently, Smith believed that men's natural drives were so strong that not even a meddling government could stop, though it could impede, inevitable progress. "Progress" always implied rising per capita real income, a better deal for the poor. Because human beings resembled each other so closely by nature, agricultural laborer, factory employee, small artisan, and rich merchant alike shared the benefits of natural liberty. Natural liberty implied free competition, free movement of workers, free shifts of capital, and freedom from government intervention.

As an analytical performance, the *Wealth of Nations*, despite its rambles and digressions, fulfilled the title's promise. It was truly a quest for the "nature" and the "causes" of the "wealth of nations." To digress after the example of Smith, one notes that for many years economics emphasized not wealth but prices, income distribution, and income determination. (Only recently, in connection with the problems of underdeveloped countries, has economics turned again to the causes of economic growth.) A good deal of Smith's analysis reads as though written with today's underdeveloped countries in mind. To him, all European countries, except Holland, and the entire remainder of the world, except China, were underdeveloped. In a very important respect, then, this book was a theory of economic development.

Therefore, Book I started sensibly with a discussion of the division of labor, because the "greatest improvement" in productivity was the effect of this principle. The division of labor led to increased dexterity, saving of the time usually lost in moving from one occupation to another, and invention of machinery by workmen. Although these advantages of the division of labor were considerable, even tremendous, Smith perceived drawbacks as well, which he mentioned in a widely separated passage:

The man whose whole life is spent in performing a few simple operations, of which the effects too are perhaps, always the same, or very nearly the same, has no occasion to exert his understanding, or to exercise his invention in finding out expedients to removing difficulties which never occur. He naturally, therefore, loses the habit of such exertion, and generally becomes as stupid and ignorant as it is possible for a human creature to become. . . . His dexterity at his own particular trade seems, in this manner, to be acquired at the expence of his intellectual, social, and martial virtues. But in every improved and civilized society this is the state into which the labouring poor, that is, the great body of the people, must necessarily fall, unless government takes some pains to prevent it.[27]

However, Book I displayed no reservation about the beneficence of the division of labor. Division of labor was limited by the extent of the market. Some trades could be carried on only in towns. Any improvement in transportation promoted the widening of the market and the division of labor. At some stage, as markets widened and division of labor increased, barter became a nuisance and money an enormous convenience. After experiments with nonmetals (Smith offered a list of the curious objects which had been used as money) and then with other metals, men settled on gold and silver.

Pleasantly led on by his subject, Smith came at the end of Chapter 4 to value. Value could be either in use or in exchange. Lingering briefly over the paradox of water and diamonds, the first precious in use and valueless in exchange, and the second valueless in use and precious in exchange, he then promised to concentrate on value in exchange, how it was measured, what were its component parts, and why market price sometimes ex-

---

[27] *Ibid.*, pp. 734–735.

ceeded or fell below the natural price or true exchangeable value.

The remaining chapters in Book I contained the heart of Smith's theory of value. As later commentators observed, they were full of confusions, but, as the commentators occasionally failed to observe, they were full of better things also. Stripped of the obscurities, these chapters told this story. "In that early and rude state of society which precedes both the accumulation of stock and the appropriation of land,"[28] the amount of labor needed to produce the commodity for which it exchanged, determined the value of a commodity. When capital was accumulated and land appropriated, two additional claimants to society's income appeared, the "undertaker" or capitalist, and the landlord. Thus the laborer no longer enjoyed full title to the entire product. Nevertheless, the real value of all kinds of income, wages, profits, and rent, was measured "by the quantity of labour which they can, each of them purchase or command."[29] Although the market made rough adjustments for different kinds of skill, by and large, an hour's labor was an hour's labor, whenever and by whomever applied. Smith's reason was again egalitarian. The real measure of labor was psychic—the toil and trouble, the actual pain involved in working rather than resting. Since men resemble each other more than they differ from each other, these pains tended toward equality.

The actual prices at which commodities sold were market prices, but the prices toward which they moved were natural prices. Natural prices resembled equilibrium prices. Although they differed from time to time, according to the advancing, declining, or stationary condition of the economy, at any one moment there was "an ordinary or average rate both of wages and profit in every different employment of labour and stock."[30]

The natural price compensated laborers, employers, and landlords at their natural rates. Smith described the relation between

[28] This was a beginning much satirized by Thomas Love Peacock in his admirable nineteenth-century comic novels. See, for example, *Crotchet Castle*.
[29] *Wealth of Nations*, Modern Library ed., p. 50.
[30] *Ibid.*, p. 55.

natural and market rates in the following way: If "the quantity of any commodity which is brought to market falls short of the effectual demand, all those who are willing to pay the whole value of the rent, wages, and profit, which must be paid in order to bring it thither, cannot be supplied with the quantity which they want. Rather than want it altogether, some of them will be willing to give more. A competition will immediately begin among them, and the market price will rise more or less above the natural price, according as either the greatness of the deficiency, or the wealth and wanton luxury of the competitors, happen to animate more or less the eagerness of the competition."[31] If the reverse possibility occurred and too much was brought to market, the competition of sellers sank market price below natural price.

Observe what followed: an automatic mechanism brought natural and market price into equality. If market price exceeded natural price, then landowners and employers shifted their land and capital into the more profitable employment where their resources could earn the higher returns. If natural price exceeded market price, then either land, labor, or capital had to be receiving less than the natural rate. Accordingly, its owners withdrew it from less, and shifted it to more, remunerative employments. In the first case, resources flowed into a profitable industry, in the second they left a depressed one. State intervention was unnecessary, because self-interest directed resources where they could best and most profitably be used.

How were the natural rates of wages, profits, and rent determined? In primitive times, Smith remarked somewhat wistfully, no problem existed because only one claimant presented himself. Now wages were the result of a contract between worker and master, in which the latter always had the advantages of superior organization, power, and wealth. Despite the inequality of the contest, masters could not reduce wages below a subsistence rate and enough more to support a family to replace the worker and his wife. Death was the ultimate retort of

[31] *Ibid.*, p. 56.

the underpaid worker. Although subsistence was, thus, the **natural** level of wages, the market level might be higher, when a society was progressing and the funds for the employment of labor were expanding more rapidly than the number of laborers. Here Smith suggested simultaneously a part of Malthusian population doctrine and Ricardian wages fund theory. "The liberal reward of labour, therefore, as it is the necessary effect, so it is the natural symptom of increasing wealth."[32] Therefore saving was critically important. Saving increased the fund of capital which spelled economic progress and higher wages.

In comparison with his wage doctrine, Smith's theory of profits received scrappy treatment. It amounted to little more than the statement that "the rise and fall in the profits of stock depend upon the same causes with the rise and fall in the wages of labour, the increasing or declining state of the wealth of the country, but those causes affect the one and the other very differently."[33] By the last clause, Smith meant that progress caused the rate of profit to fall, because larger numbers of capitalists competed for a limited number of profitable opportunities. On the other hand, progress made wages rise.

Chapter 10, "Of Wages and Profit in the Different Employments of Labour and Stock," has been justly famous.[34] In it, Smith skillfully analyzed wage and profit equilibrium in different employments, according to nonpecuniary as well as pecuniary advantages. He approached the old puzzle of why some worked for lower monetary wages than others of similar abilities, by considering five factors which, even in a condition of perfect liberty, would result in differences of money wages or profits. These included the agreeableness of the employment, the cost of learning the skill, the constancy of employment, the trust reposed in the workman, and, strangely, the probability of success. Teachers and clergymen like their work. Doctors take many years to learn their trade. Building employees depend upon

[32] *Ibid.*, p. 73.
[33] *Ibid.*, p. 87.
[34] Yet Cantillon anticipated at least three of Smith's five causes of monetary inequalities in wages. Fame does not always reward the original.

the vagaries of the weather. Accordingly, the first two earn little and the last two earn a good deal. Twentieth-century illustrations of the role of trust are harder to find. Rather than pay them high salaries, banks bond their tellers. The lottery implied in the last factor might apply to lawyers, some of whom hit jackpots and others of whom barely scrape a living.

The long second part of the chapter inveighed against the "inequalities occasioned by the Policy of Europe."[35] Most eloquently, Smith attacked guilds (corporations was his term), apprenticeship rules which are a "manifest encroachment upon the just liberty both of the workman, and of those who might be disposed to employ him,"[36] monopolies, high tariffs, Acts of Settlement, and subsidized employments. It was ridiculous, for example, to subsidize curates. The only result was an oversupply of underemployed clergymen.

Smith was of several minds about the final distributive share, rent. At one point, he regarded rent as simply a constituent element of price, a deduction from gross revenue. On other occasions he termed it a monopoly price. Still elsewhere, he implied that rent was a result of high prices rather than their cause, much in the later Ricardian manner. But of one thing he was confident, the interest of the community and the landlord coincided. Only when society was progressing did rents rise. Though landlords loved "to reap where they have not sown," their prosperity symbolized the general good.

In one respect, Smith's rent theory was superior to the more consistent, analytically superior Ricardian construction. Even though his classification failed to carry conviction, Smith did endeavor to distinguish different land-tenure arrangements and the contrasting market situations of land in different uses. Perhaps carried away by vague physiocratic notions, he alleged, for example, that land which produced food always paid rent and that other land might or might not pay rent. He recognized, as Ricardo did not, that, although conceptually rent was a payment

---

[35] *Wealth of Nations*, Modern Library ed., p. 118.
[36] *Ibid.*, p. 122.

for land only, in practice capital improvements inextricably entangled themselves in the natural fertility of the soil. Inevitably, therefore, actual rent was a composite payment of pure rent and profits on investment.

Flaws are easy enough to find in the value and distribution theory of the first book. Later economists always find errors in the work of earlier. Somehow, they commit errors of their own. Perhaps economics is a difficult subject. The first book contained three theories of value: a pure labor-quantity theory which applied largely to primitive societies, but which appeared also incongruously at other points; a cost-of-production theory in which actual prices were explained as the sum of wages, profits, and rents at their natural rates; and a market-price theory which rested upon the forces of supply and demand. Not only did Smith waver among these theories; he also tried, sometimes in the same passage, to use his theory of value for two different purposes, to explain the central tendencies of prices, and to measure changes in prices. Even after he abandoned the pure labor quantity explanation, he clung to the hope that labor might measure the value of profit and rent, in a manner not very easy to grasp. No clear justification of profit ever emerged. Finally, there was a confusion in the labor-quantity version itself about whether Smith meant that the amount of labor needed to produce a product determined its value, or the amount of labor needed to produce the product for which it exchanged. The modern student, nurtured on a theory of price, often impatiently dismisses Smith's anxiety about value as an underlying substance, as a piece of metaphysics rather than a part of economics.

The capital theory of Book II, like almost everything else written on this intricate subject then or later, does not enchant by virtue of its clarity. At the outset Smith declared capital accumulation vital, because it and division of labor marched together. He never paused to demonstrate the relationship. A long list of distinctions followed. Stock was either means of subsistence, conceived as a heap of food and clothing advanced by un-

dertakers to laborers, or the materials and tools which the laborers used. It soon turned out that stock and capital were not
identical. Stock might be either capital, which afforded its owner
a revenue, or the source of immediate consumption by its owner.
The frugal Smith much preferred those who possessed stock to
turn it into capital. Capital itself was subdivided into circulating
or fixed components. Circulating capital was the food and clothing advanced to laborers while they fabricated finished goods.
But money (its inclusion was a real analytical lapse on Smith's
part) and completed work in the hands of merchants or manufacturers, were also circulating capital. Fixed capital—land improvements or useful machines—remained in the hands of owners. The principle of classification followed use, not the nature of
product. The food the capitalist ate was no part of capital. The
food eaten by an employed laborer was an item of circulating
capital. Occasionally Smith confused the issue by referring to
capital as a sum of money, rather than a heap of goods.

Many traces of physiocratic doctrine marred this book. One
example was the distinction between productive and unproductive labor. To the physiocrats only agricultural labor was productive. Less extreme but no more logical, Smith drew the line
between the two according to the outcome of the labor. Productive labor "fixes and realizes itself in some particular object."[37] Unproductive labor "generally perishes in the very
instant of their performance."[38] Teachers, statesmen, doctors,
lawyers, poets, and writers labor unproductively, though, added
Smith, often usefully. Bricklayers, opium fabricators, painters,
printers, and cigar makers labor productively. The finished
product is the proof. The lecture is unproductive. Printed in a
book it becomes miraculously a productive product.

Although Smith had modified extreme physiocratic notions,
he continued to believe that, in some way, land was a resource
superior to its complements. "In agriculture too nature labours

[37] *Ibid.*, p. 314.
[38] *Ibid.*, p. 314.

along with man."[39] Smith ignored the certainty that if nature did not do as much in manufacturing, no process could be completed. He labored to establish a hierarchy of capital uses. Agriculture, naturally, headed the list.

Even in this generally unsatisfactory book, good things abounded. One of them was Smith's constant emphasis on the virtues of thrift, which recalls Bagehot's acute observation that Smith thought there was a Scotsman inside each of us. Smith wisely remarked that the American colonies had advanced so rapidly because they concentrated on agriculture, in which their natural advantage was greatest. Underdeveloped countries in a tearing rush to industrialize might still profitably ponder this bit of wisdom. In a careful discussion of money, Smith indicated the advantage of paper currency as a replacement of gold and silver. Finally, in the middle of his confusions, Smith held fast to his belief in the indispensability of capital accumulation to progress.

The high point of the treatise when it appeared was Book IV, a ringing attack upon mercantilism and a conditional defense of physiocracy. Smith was a polemicist as well as a scholar. Mercantilist restrictions were evil on general grounds and, frequently, even on mercantilist grounds. Again and again, he sounded the clarion call of natural liberty.[40]

He demolished the mercantilist arguments one after another.[41] "Fleets and armies are maintained not with gold and silver, but with consumable goods."[42] If we need anything, free trade will get it for us: "We trust with perfect security that the freedom of trade, without any attention of government, will always sup-

---

[39] *Ibid.*, p. 344.

[40] North had anticipated the heart of Smith's arguments. His presentation lacked Smith's literary effectiveness. His greatest mistake, however, was being born at the wrong time.

[41] Smith naturally attacked the worst examples of mercantilist thought he could find. The preceding chapter suggested how diversified so-called mercantilist thought actually was. To some degree, Smith's "mercantilism" was a straw man.

[42] *Wealth of Nations*, Modern Library ed., p. 409.

ply us with the wine which we have occasion for: and we may trust with equal security that it will always supply us with all the gold and silver which we can afford to employ, either in circulating our commodities, or in other uses."[43] This was Smith's way of saying that even if economic policy recommended larger gold stocks, the free way was the best way to increase them. There is no reason to linger over the details of Smith's attack: he unmistakably disliked bounties, drawbacks, exclusive trade treaties, internal restrictions. In each case the touchstone was the superior economic results which flowed from a system of liberty. When they were free, individuals, keen in their own interest, directed their labor and their capital into channels which enriched them and the community.

Interesting reservations dotted this verbal onslaught. Smith was no unqualified free trader. Because "defence . . . is of much more importance than opulence,"[44] Smith advised the retention of the Navigation Acts. In peace they made the nation weaker, but in war they enlarged the reservoir of trained seamen. He was willing to levy a tariff which counterbalanced taxes levied on home produce. On practical rather than theoretical grounds, Smith considered and rejected the germ of the infant-industry argument for protective tariffs. Retaliatory action was a poor device, because it added a second injury to the one inflicted by foreigners. Out of humanity, he proposed to approach free trade by slow gradations. But what did humanity demand? Smith was confident that individuals thrown out of work by the repeal of tariffs would quickly find new, better-paid employment, if they were free to move about without restraint from guilds and apprenticeship rules. Nowhere was Smith a Utopian: "To expect, indeed, that the freedom of trade should ever be entirely restored to Great Britain, is as absurd as to expect that an Oceania or Utopia should ever be established in it."[45]

[43] *Ibid.*, p. 404.
[44] *Ibid.*, p. 429.
[45] *Ibid.*, p. 437.

Smith ended this book with a short, sympathetic account of the physiocrats. A trace of condescension flawed the sympathy: "it would not, surely, be worth while to examine at great length the errors of a system which never has done and probably never will do any harm in any part of the world."[46] Smith praised the physiocrats' belief that "the most advantageous method in which a landed nation can raise up artificers, manufacturers and merchants of its own, is to grant the most perfect freedom of trade to the artificers, manufacturers and merchants of all other nations."[47] However, the physiocrats made the important mistake of "representing the class of artificers, manufacturers and merchants, as altogether barren and unproductive."[48] So much for the physiocrats, whose system was "the nearest approximation to the truth that has yet been published upon the subject of political economy."[49] Smith's peroration was triumphant: "All systems of preference or of restraint, therefore, being thus completely taken away, the obvious and simple system of natural liberty establishes itself of its own accord."[50]

On public finance, Book V, Smith's views became famous, though once more they had their anticipators, first among them, Petty. Two major questions engaged his attention: What should the state do? How should the state raise the funds to implement its aims? His answer to both questions is still quoted. In a system of natural liberty, the sovereign has three legitimate functions: defense of the realm, "exact administration of justice," and public works individuals would not undertake because they were unprofitable. The first two categories explained themselves. By the third, Smith apparently meant aids to commerce like roads and harbors, and schools. The teachers in the schools, however, should be paid by the fees of the students. Schools enlightened the poor and counteracted the dulling effects of ex-

[46] *Ibid.*, p. 627.
[47] *Ibid.*, p. 636.
[48] *Ibid.*, pp. 638–639.
[49] *Ibid.*, p. 642.
[50] *Ibid.*, p. 651.

cessive division of labor. Otherwise, individuals conducted the economic life of the country. "An invisible hand" guided them to the general welfare.

On taxation, Smith proposed four rules or canons. A tax should be equal. Equality implied two characteristics: proportionality and impact on all categories of income. Much depends on standpoint. When Smith wrote, regressive taxation was the rule. Proportional taxation represented an advance. Today, proportional taxes strike most people as a retreat from a more equitable progressivity. At that, Smith hinted at a lurking fondness for progressive taxation when he said that "it is not very unreasonable that the rich should contribute to the public expence, not only in proportion to their revenue, but something more than in that proportion."[51] Taxes, Smith thought in a way that persists, should not damage incentives. A tax on rent discouraged no activity because there was none to discourage. It was an excellent tax. Although in general Smith opposed sumptuary legislation, he favored taxes designed "to give some discouragement to the multiplication of little ale-houses."[52]

The other canons were refinements of common sense, one of Smith's specialties. Certainty implied that the taxpayer knew when he had to pay, the manner of the payment. and the amount to be paid. Astonishingly at the time, convenience was the taxpayer's rather than the government's. Other things equal, the taxpayer should be allowed to pay when it hurt him least. Other things equal, the best tax cost the least to collect. If import duties were widely evaded by smugglers, and the cost of policing the coasts exceeded the receipts from the customs, tariffs were bad taxes on this ground alone.

SMITH'S INFLUENCE

The quality of Smith's achievement was not, his critics have been right to say, its originality. He found his belief in natural

[51] *Ibid.*, p. 794.
[52] *Ibid.*, p. 804.

liberty in the mainstream of eighteenth-century thought. On many major points in trade and exchange, Hume had anticipated him and had dealt more truly with the analytical difficulties. The physiocrats had produced a complete system. The much maligned mercantilists had contributed to his knowledge. Even the cynical Mandeville, in his *Fable of the Bees*, must have suggested Smith's guiding principle of self-interest, however little he relished Mandeville's form. Smith was not always clear or consistent. Often he failed to stick to his subject.

If all this is true, what is left? For one thing, a treatise. In economics, with few exceptions, durable contributions are bulky, though the proposition is not reversible. Hume's short essays frequently tossed off his keenest insights. Smith knew better. The book was so long, not because the analytical principles were so numerous or subtle, but because Smith knew how to make one principle illuminate a great many problems. The most obvious example is the weight the division of labor is made to bear. It is a complete theory of production. Upon it the progress of nations depends.

Length has other advantages. In this long book, Smith avoided few of the major economic problems of his era. Here they were: taxes, foreign trade, Poor Laws, Corn Laws, Acts of Settlement, agricultural improvement, colonies, education, banking, usury, highways, and harbors. There was system in their appearance, for principles illuminated problems. Hume's paradoxes became old friends, after Smith's copious illustration and unhurried discussion. Smith brought his own connotations with him. Even the case-hardened reader must have felt that here was no theorist, here was a sensible, hard-headed Scot, with more time at his disposal than busy men of affairs to reach conclusions that any man of sense might have worked out for himself.

The originality in Smith was arrangement and exposition. He arranged what he borrowed, selected illustrations so telling that few have palled, combined historical and analytical materials in an unusually effective way, and furnished a model to his successors.

In England, the nineteenth century was a long postscript to Smith's *Wealth of Nations*. Other economists quoted him, disputed his facts, and corrected his principles. In form, Ricardo's *Principles of Political Economy* was a commentary on the *Wealth of Nations*. That book had interested Ricardo in economics to begin with. Smith was the great starting point for all.

Smith's influence upon the politics of his day is more difficult to trace. 1783 was the first time that the *Wealth of Nations* was quoted by title in the House of Commons. The circumstances did not flatter. Fox, who cited the book, opposed its principles and declared that he had not read it. It was mentioned once more in support of a commercial treaty with France, four years later. A most distinguished admirer was William Pitt. In a speech made in 1792, emphasizing the importance of capital accumulation, Pitt said:

> Simple and obvious as this principle is, and felt and observed as it must have been in a greater or less degree even from the earliest periods, I doubt whether it has ever been fully developed and sufficiently explained, but in the writings of an author of our own time, now unfortunately no more (I mean the author of the celebrated treatise on the *Wealth of Nations*), whose extensive knowledge of detail and depth of philosophical research will, I believe, furnish the best solution of every question connected with the history of commerce and with the system of political economy.[53]

As panegyric, this may be the best a politician ever offered an economist.

In 1779, members of the British cabinet consulted Smith on their plans to concede free trade to Ireland. Smith wrote to Lord Carlisle: "Should the industry of Ireland, in consequence of freedom and good government, ever equal that of England, so much the better would it be not only for the whole British Empire, but for the peculiar province of England."[54]

Some of Smith's tax reforms were quickly introduced. But these are the sum of Smith's immediate, identifiable impact upon

[53] John Rae, *Life of Adam Smith*, 1895, pp. 290–291.
[54] *Ibid.*, p. 355.

legislation or public policy. For more than a generation, the conservative reflex to the French Revolution stifled liberal ideas. In this frozen period, educated opinion relished Malthus more happily than Smith.[55]

---

[55] A list of Further Readings for Part II appears on pp. 405–409.

Chapter 5

Jeremy Bentham

I have travelled the world and that old man's fame
Wherever I went shone brightly
To his country alone belongs the shame
To think of his labours lightly.

John Bowring

A teapot he named Dick
And Dapple was his stick
He cherished pigs and mice
A fact which will suffice
To hint, from all we hear
He was a little queer.

They say he cherished men,
Their happiness, and then
Calmly assumed one could
Devise cures for their good,
Believing all men the same,
And happiness their aim.

He reckoned right and wrong
By felicity—lifelong—
And by such artless measure
As the quantity of pleasure.
For pain he had a plan,
Absurd old gentleman.

Helen Bevington

By his own generous admission, Jeremy Bentham "owed everything," as a technical economist, to Adam Smith. His single contribution to economic discussion still remembered, was the *Defence of Usury* (1787), and this was less a novelty than the correction of a bad piece of reasoning by Adam Smith. Bentham argued that Smith was wrong to support the general principle of natural liberty while simultaneously defending public regulation of interest rates. Bentham's arguments in essential points resembled Smith's: "[there is] no more reason for fixing the price of the use of money than the price of goods."[1] Moreover, "no legislator can judge, so well as each individual for himself, whether money is worth to him anything, and how much, beyond the ordinary interest."[2] Although scarcely more was needed to establish his point, Bentham, never one to stint, generously added five defects of the laws: many could not borrow at all; some were forced to secure funds in disadvantageous ways; others had to borrow "upon disadvantageous terms in the very way forbidden"; a useful class of men—projectors or promoters—were exposed to unmerited suffering and disgrace; and, finally, the laws encouraged treachery and ingratitude.

Of these points, Bentham, an inventor and projector himself, attached most importance to the fourth. He pleaded quite eloquently for the innovations which such activities created. Although Bentham did not so much as imply a theory of interest, he did conclude that the effect of usury laws was to raise interest rates higher to compensate lenders for the risk of apprehension—one reason why loan sharks' rates are always high.

Even though Bentham's economic writings filled three substantial volumes and included two efforts to write manuals designed to express Adam Smith's analysis more concisely, kindness suggests that no more be said of them. But if Bentham was a minor economist, he was a major influence upon major economists, and the key figure of an important group of practical

[1] Jeremy Bentham, *Economic Writings*, ed. by W. Stark, Burt Franklin, 1952, Vol. I, p. 124.
[2] *Ibid.*, p. 125.

reformers, the Philosophical Radicals. In these roles, Bentham continues to deserve respect and merit analysis.

BENTHAM'S LIFE

Born in 1748, Bentham died in 1832, just three days before the passage of the great Reform Act which met some of the criticisms which he had made of English representative institutions. The son of an ambitious attorney, Bentham was something of an infant prodigy, able to read without instruction and adept at the violin. He was so assiduous as a scholar that he managed to avoid flogging at school, an impressively rare feat for the time. He attended Queen's College, Oxford, between 1760 and 1763. He later recalled with horror that he had been compelled to signify his consent to the notorious Thirty-Nine Articles. Young and undersized even for his age, he was unhappy at Oxford, as he had been earlier at school. With little trouble, a long list of eminent Englishmen who hated their schools could be compiled.

At 16, he took his degree and, in comformity with his father's wish, began to study law first at Lincoln's Inn and then, as a student of Blackstone, at Oxford. Dutiful son though he was, he could not confine his interests to law. Set up in rooms of his own, he began to read widely in only moderately respectable authors, among them Montesquieu, Hume, Priestley, Hartley, Beccaria, and Helvétius. With this reading he combined numerous experiments in chemistry and physics. Although he was admitted to the bar in 1769, he thought less and less of practicing, and more and more of benefiting the world.

This wish to become the Newton of the moral universe, joined to the eccentricities which grew upon him with age and continued bachelorhood, explained the faint air of ridicule in many contemporary estimates, which, in turn, set the tone for modern students. However, there is fair evidence that as a young man Bentham had the ordinary tastes of a cultivated gentleman. He loved music and admired the theater. His celibacy was neither principled nor constitutional. He seems to have fallen deeply in love with a Miss Polly Dunkly. When the match was disapproved by his father, who supported him, he hesitated in agony between a life's work and his love. If he chose the former, it cannot have been the first such choice made. Moreover, he later made a half-hearted attempt to conclude a marriage with an heiress, spurred by his father's emphatic approval.

More and more he turned to his writing. In it he aimed at little less than the complete reformation of English institutions and, especially, English law. His first published work appeared anonymously in 1776. Entitled *A Fragment on Government*, it was a most vigorous assault upon Blackstone's *Commentaries*. The book caused considerable stir, largely, it turned out, because readers attributed authorship to various famous people, among them Lord Mansfield, an opponent of Blackstone. When Bentham's proud father disclosed the secret of the authorship, the flurry of interest died down, little to Bentham's surprise. In 1789 he published his *Introduction to the Principles of Morals and Legislation*, a work written in 1780 and released only at the insistence of his friends. Through life, it was always Bentham's habit to write, accumulate, never revise and never publish. If publication came, it was because faithful disciples pieced together books from the thousands of pages which Bentham industriously deposited into boxes. Although this book was much superior to the slightly different effort of William Paley in 1785, it aroused no comment. At home, Bentham was a prophet without honor. Abroad, his fortune was greater. The faithful Dumont, declaring himself a disciple, had prepared translation after translation of Bentham into French.

The turning point in his English reputation came in 1808, when he met James Mill, the father of the more famous John Stuart Mill. This was a historic meeting. When it occurred, Bentham was a man of 60, known in England, if at all, as the inventor of a new model prison, the Panopticon, constructed on circular principles so that a single warder could observe each cell. James Mill was a man of 35, a Scot, come to London, like so many others, to make his way. At the time he was supporting himself by hack journalism, superintending the education of children destined to reach the noble number of nine, and trying to make his reputation by writing a *History of British India*. The disappointed, reputedly eccentric philosopher and the rising young man had much to offer each other. What Bentham gave Mill was a doctrine. What Mill gave Bentham was a school. It has been said that Mill was a born intellectual entrepreneur, a vigorous and convincing conversationalist, a forceful and logical writer. As writer and talker, he was energetic beyond the limits of ordinary men. Since the remainder of Bentham's life was entwined with the group James Mill did so much to organize, we will examine next the doctrine Bentham gave them and, afterwards, the use they made of it.

BENTHAM'S SYSTEM

Bentham's conception of human nature, a major influence upon Ricardo and John Stuart Mill, was clearest in his *Introduction to the Principles of Morals and Legislation*. "Nature," said Bentham, "has placed mankind under the governance of two sovereign masters, *pain and pleasure*."[3] All men are alike in loving pleasure and hating pain. Granted this axiom, Bentham judged public as well as private actions according to their effects upon happiness. Happiness was always simply a matter of pleasures and pains. Hence the famous principle of utility, as interpreted by Bentham, was a handy way of summarizing our observations on human happiness: "The principle of utility is the foundation of the present work. . . . By the principle of utility is meant that principle which approves or disapproves of every action whatsoever, according to the tendency which it appears to have to augment or diminish the happiness of the party whose interest is in question."[4] The word "interest" was important. Men, thought Bentham, were essentially egoistic creatures, each acting to bene-

[3] Jeremy Bentham, *Introduction to the Principles of Morals and Legislation*, Haffner, 1948, p. 1.
[4] *Ibid.*, p. 2.

fit himself. Although private interest might coincide with public interest, Bentham was convinced that, in the event of conflict, it was private interest which won. A characteristic passage from his later writings made the point this way:

Taking the whole of life together, there exists not, nor ever can exist, that human being in whose instance any public interest he can have had, will not, in so far as it depends upon himself, have been sacrificed to his own personal interest. Toward the advancement of the public interest, all that the most public-spirited, which is as much as to say the most virtuous of men, can do, is to do what depends upon himself towards bringing the public interest to a state as nearly approaching to coincidence, and on as few occasions amounting to a state of repugnance, as possible with his private interest.[5]

But did not this most benevolent of men, who sacrificed his own love in order to benefit humanity, take account of the same quality in others? Only very cautiously: "Yes. I admit the existence of *disinterestedness*. . . . I admit the existence of *philanthropy*. . . . But my children! it is on what has been seen most commonly to happen . . . it is upon *this*, that all practice, if it has any pretension to the praise of prudence, must be built."[6]

Man was hedonistic and selfish. For Bentham, it followed that "the community is a fictitious body" and its interests "the sum of the several members who compose it."[7] Society was individualistic. Government, properly conceived, was no more than a mechanism for increasing the happiness and diminishing the pain of individuals.

Thus far any eighteenth-century reader would have found himself on familiar ground: everybody was a utilitarian in the closing portion of that century. Hume was utilitarian on deistic grounds, Paley on Christian premises. In fact, the latter had informally calculated the pleasures and pains of the afterlife when he defined virtue as "the doing good to mankind, in obedience [sic] to the will of God, and for the sake of everlasting happi-

[5] Bentham, *Economic Writings*, Vol. III, p. 430.
[6] *Ibid.*, p. 435.
[7] Bentham, *Introduction to the Principles of Morals and Legislation*, p. 3.

ness."[8] As Paley saw human motivation, we behaved like Christians because the pleasures of heaven awaited us. We did not behave otherwise because we feared the pains of hell.

What distinguished Bentham from all the rest? At least three qualities. Above all, he was a demon classifier. Anxious to describe minutely his subject matter, he listed 14 simple pleasures, among them wealth, skill, amity, good name, power, piety, benevolence, malevolence, memory, imagination, expectation, association, and relief; and twelve simple pains, among others desire, disappointment, and regret. Aware here at least that men differed, he categorized no fewer than 32 circumstances which influenced sensibility to pleasure and pain: health, firmness of mind, pecuniary circumstances, sex, age, rank, and education were seven of them. Sixteen subheadings further illuminated the subject of rank. And each of the other circumstances received similar treatment. Where other utilitarians had been vague, Bentham was excessively concrete.

His applications of utilitarian doctrine were also original. A major illustration was punishment for crime. What penal code promoted best the happiness of the community? Bentham's reasoning was straightforward. If every man sought pleasure, the criminal was essentially a bad calculator who traded, on bad terms, the pleasures of his crime for the pain of his punishment. On sound utilitarian principles, a government should help the criminal to become a better calculator. Imagine, Bentham asked, a criminal hesitating between the commission of two crimes. At least two rules applied. "The value of the punishment must not be less in any case than what is sufficient to outweigh that of the profit of the offence."[9] The second rule read: ". . . when two offences come in competition, the punishment for the greater offence must be sufficient to induce a man to prefer the lesser."[10] Since punishment was always a source of pain, "the punishment ought in no case to be more than what is necessary to bring it into

---

[8] William Paley, *Works*, 1838, Vol. III, p. 20.
[9] Bentham, *Introduction to the Principles of Morals and Legislation*, p. 179.
[10] *Ibid.*, p. 181.

conformity with the rules here given."[11] In passing sentence, the Benthamite judge considered all 32 conditions affecting the criminal's sensibility. At a time when the death sentence was the usual penalty even for trivial offenses, the sheer enlightenment of Bentham's analysis must have startled his readers. At the time, they were few.

Bentham's boldest and most bizarre effort was his attempt to calculate the actual quantity of pleasures and pains. How can we assign numerical values to psychic magnitudes? In the following manner, said Bentham. If we take a single pleasure or pain in isolation, we can identify four characteristics which affect its size: intensity, duration, certainty or uncertainty, and propinquity or remoteness. If we hold any three of these qualities constant we prefer the pleasure which offers more of the fourth. Longer novels are to be preferred to shorter ones of equal merit, a certain holiday to an uncertain, a treat today to a treat tomorrow. This was far from the end of the matter. Some pleasures led to others, some carried in their train sobering pains. Thus, the pleasure of intoxication was marred by the pain of hang-over. On the other hand, the joy of a good night's sleep increases the pleasure of tennis. "Fecund" pleasures evoke other pleasures and "fecund" pains evoke other pains. "Purity" or "impurity," a sixth characteristic, deals with the tendency of pleasures or pains to induce their opposites. Finally, when we deal with a group of people, "extent" becomes a seventh consideration: we count the number of individuals affected.

Bentham's own description of a mode of evaluating the impact of an act upon the community cannot be duplicated by paraphrase:

Begin with any one person . . . take an account,
1. Of the value of each distinguishable *pleasure* which appears to be produced by it in the *first* instance.
2. Of the value of each *pain* which appears to be produced by it in the *first* instance.

[11] *Ibid.*, p. 182.

3. Of the value of each pleasure which appears to be produced by it *after* the first. This constitutes the *fecundity* of the first *pleasure* and the *impurity* of the first *pain*.

4. Of the value of each *pain* which appears to be produced by it after the first. This constitutes the *fecundity* of the first *pain* and the *impurity* of the first pleasure.

5. Sum up all the values of all the *pleasures* on the one side, and those of all the pains on the other. The balance, if it be on the side of pleasure, will give the *good* tendency of the act . . . with respect to the interests of that *individual* person; if on the side of pain, the *bad* tendency. . . .

6. Take an account of the *number* of persons whose interests appeared to be concerned; and repeat the above process with respect to each. *Sum up* the numbers expressive of the degrees of good tendency. . . . do this again with respect to each individual, in regard to whom the tendency of it is *bad*. . . .[12]

There remained the critical question of assigning numerical weights to these dimensions of pleasure and pain. Although Bentham made many stabs at an answer, he never carried a sample calculation all the way through. He suggested that the proper intensity unit was the "faintest sensation that can be distinguished to be pleasure or pain," that "a moment of time" made an appropriate unit of duration, that "degrees of intensity and duration are to be counted in whole numbers, as multiples of these units," and that "certainty and propinquity are reckoned as fractions whose limit is immediate actual sensation; from this limit fractions fall away."[13] Increasingly, he doubted whether it were really possible to measure intensity. He wondered also how qualitatively different pleasures—say, eating and friendship—could be quantitatively compared. In *Utilitarianism*, John Stuart Mill extended these doubts considerably further.

Momentarily, Bentham rescued himself by using money as a guide to the measurement of pleasure and pain, an insight which

---

[12] *Ibid.*, pp. 30–31.

[13] Wesley C. Mitchell, *The Backward Art of Spending Money*, Augustus Kelley, 1950, pp. 181–182.

made him one of the anticipators of the marginalist schools of the 1870's. In one passage, he said: "If of two pleasures a man . . . would as lief enjoy the one as the other, they must be reputed equal. . . . If between two pleasures the one produced by the possession of money, the other not, a man had as lief enjoy the one as the other, such pleasures are to be reputed equal. . . . Money is the instrument for measuring the quantity of pain or pleasure."[14] But a second analytical anticipation of Bentham's canceled the usefulness of the first. Money meant different things to different people, according to the various amounts they possessed. To a rich man, ten pounds might mean nothing, to a poor man the difference between penury and modest comfort. Bentham had grasped the popular later concept of the diminishing marginal utility of money: each unit of currency yielded less pleasure than its predecessor. Here Bentham was forced to give the problem up, at a loss to assign values to pleasures purchased by pounds which measured different satisfactions.

Bentham's man—passive, hedonistic, individualistic, and egoistic—was not the man of modern psychology, and still less of modern psychiatry. A modern reader often finds it hard not to laugh at the thought of solemnly measuring pleasure or assigning dimensions to pain. Undoubtedly, Benthamite psychology is outmoded. A modern admirer of Bentham has noted, however, that we pretend to measure qualities as strange as pleasure, among them intelligence and personality traits.

Bentham carried to a logical conclusion the utilitarian strain of reasoning in England. Since logic is a horrid virtue, he undoubtedly revealed most cruelly some of utilitarianism's flaws. His achievements extended beyond his doctrine. A legal reformer of enormous originality, he eventually caused great changes in legislative and judicial procedures. He offered the natural democrats who followed him a central core of democratic doctrine: one man, for most purposes, was as good as another.

[14] *Ibid.*, pp. 186–187.

THE PHILOSOPHICAL RADICALS

Who were the Philosophical Radicals whom James Mill rallied around the Benthamite standard? What did they believe? What did they accomplish? East India official and journalist, James Mill himself was also an historian, logician, free thinker, and economist. James Mill recruited David Ricardo. He and Bentham (at Mill's instigation) encouraged Ricardo to write his *Principles*, and had a little to do with what went into it. Other utilitarians included Black, the editor of the *Morning Chronicle;*[15] George Grote, the historian of Greece; and Francis Place, the celebrated radical tailor of Westminster, who actively promoted the group's many parliamentary projects.[16] In Parliament, the sect could count on Joseph Hume, Roebuck, and, less dependably, Burdett. After 1824, a remarkable group of younger men, led by John Stuart Mill, assumed leadership.

In the earlier group were writers and thinkers, practical politicians like Place, journalists like Black, and organizers like James Mill. After they founded their own organ, the *Westminster Review*, in 1824, the fame of the group spread still more rapidly. They were all avid controversalists. Much later, John Stuart Mill commented on "the air of strong conviction with which they wrote, when scarcely any one else seemed to have an equally strong faith in as definite a creed; the boldness with which they tilted against the very front of both existing political parties; their uncompromising profession of opposition to many of the generally received opinions and the suspicion they lay under of holding others still more heterodox than they professed."[17] They were unreconstructed intellectuals.

Their beliefs were no less definite than their personalities. Although probably no single Philosophical Radical agreed without qualification to all of the positions which follow, they approxi-

---

[15] Friends knew when Black had seen Mill by the tone of the next day's editorials. Mill's forensic skill was not small.

[16] See Graham Wallas' charming and informative *Life of Francis Place*, Burt Franklin, 1951.

[17] John Stuart Mill, *Autobiography*, Oxford, 1924, p. 84.

mate the sense of the group. Though they were discreet on the subject, they regarded religion in terms scarcely less extreme than Marx's. James Mill's own position was agnostic, a word invented later in the century. His famous son thought him obsessed on the subject: "I have a hundred times heard him say, that all ages and nations have represented their gods as wicked, in a constantly increasing progression, that mankind have gone on adding trait after trait until they reached the most perfect conception of wickedness which the human mind can devise, and have called this God, and prostrated themselves before it. This *ne plus ultra* of wickedness he considered to be embodied in what is commonly presented to mankind as the creed of Christianity."[18] Religion had no utility. More likely, it caused large quantities of pain.

In psychology, the Philosophical Radicals were admirers of Hartley, the associationist. His and their belief was an extension of Locke. Hartley believed that men possessed no innate ideas. As children, we received sense impressions from the people and the objects around us. By the process of association,[19] these impressions combined to produce complex ideas. But environment only produced these ideas. Change the environment and changed with it are the old ideas. Any schoolmaster could teach any child the arts and graces of the gentleman, or the more useful habits of the scholar. It was a matter only of catching the child young, exposing him to proper associations, and accepting the congratulations of envious spectators. Universal education on proper principles could create an enlightened electorate of intelligent people. In the minds of both, the famous education James Mill subjected John Stuart Mill to was a practical demonstration of Hartleian and Benthamite psychology. It was simple: John was protected from bad associations, the company of ill-taught children and the ministrations of scarcely better-taught schoolmasters, and abundantly exposed to good associations, the company and tuition of a father who knew what and when to teach. In John Stuart Mill's

[18] *Ibid.*, p. 34.
[19] As one student translated this dignified phrase, ideas stick together.

opinion, the program gave him a head start of a quarter century over less fortunate contemporaries and converted an ordinary child into a useful citizen.

No ambiguity surrounded the group's politics. The members believed in representative government and complete freedom of discussion. They had not the slightest notion that a fairer system of representation could produce anything except public benefit. In a fair discussion, truth always triumphed. This last belief was the confidence of a tremendously verbal group, who outargued, outfought, and, above all, outthought their opponents. Thus they proved that the truth won. The practical implications of their position induced opposition to the notorious Six Acts, which severely limited freedom of assembly and publication; the Stamp Act, which placed heavy taxes on all periodicals and afflicted, in particular, radical organs; and the Combination Acts, which made trade-union organization almost impossible. Differing over the details, they united in favor of electoral reform. Although James Mill had little taste for feminine suffrage, his famous son was a sturdy exponent of women's rights. None of them contemplated immediate universal manhood suffrage, because suffrage demanded education and the educated man's capacity for rational decision. It was no fault of the Benthamites that not every citizen had the chance to acquire these qualifications.

In economics they were devout Malthusians and Ricardians.[20] They gave Malthus a cheerful twist. Mill described how they did it in this passage:

Malthus's population principle was quite as much a banner and a point of union among us, as any opinion specifically belonging to Bentham. This great doctrine, originally brought forward as an argument against the indefinite improvability of human affairs, we took up with ardent zeal in the contrary sense, as indicating the sole means of realizing that improvability by securing full employment at high wages to the whole labouring population through a voluntary restriction of the increase of their number.[21]

[20] Chap. 6 considers Malthus and Chap. 7 Ricardo.
[21] Mill, *op. cit.*, pp. 89–90.

Of the group, Francis Place openly advocated birth control. James Mill wrote tentative passages which might yield to similar interpretation. A not entirely verified legend had it that John Stuart, as a boy, was arrested for distributing birth-control literature. They welcomed the Ricardian theory of rent. James Mill's own textbook in economics was based upon Ricardo.

In ethics, they waved before them the flag of the greatest happiness of the greatest number, eager, however grimly, to increase the quantum of human joy. It is one of the sadder paradoxes of intellectual history that this exceedingly worthy group, full of public spirit and general benevolence, took so little joy in life themselves. They had little humor, and Bentham exhausted the corporate stock of playfulness. As was said of them, they were a collection of vegetarians raising beef cattle.

Their economics and ethics led them to other public positions. On sound Malthusian grounds, they favored Poor Law reform. The contemporary Poor Laws, it seemed to them, were capriciously administered, interfered with labor mobility, and fostered imprudent marriage in the blithe expectation of public charity. The infamous system of public grants as supplements to wages, begun in 1795, threatened to pauperize much of the working class.

Convinced on Ricardian grounds of the iniquity of rent and the virtues of profits, the Philosophical Radicals strenuously supported Corn Law repeal. The repeal promised to accomplish two ends: remove the umbrella of protection under which landlords collected high rents and charged high prices, and allow a generation's breathing space to inculcate prudential habits.

The Combination Acts caused rather more difficulty, because two cherished principles conflicted. Economics taught them that the sum available at a given time to pay wages was fixed. Trade-union agitation could not increase it. Trade unions could share the total among a smaller number of men, causing the unemployment of the remainder. Alternatively, unions could raise the wages of their members and depress those of nonmembers. So far unions seemed pernicious. The Radicals were still more attached, however, to freedom of speech and agitation. As a result, though only Place was whole-hearted on the issue, the group did support his successful fight for repeal. They hoped that unions would soon learn the imprudence of excessive wage demands.

For the rest, they supported numerous libertarian measures: repeal of taxes on knowledge, removal of dissenters' and Catholics' disabilities, abolition of ecclesiastical pluralities, and legal reform on Benthamite prescription.

In appearance, their degree of success in so many causes appears astounding. The Reform Act of 1832 did much to abolish the inequities of the old system of representation: rotten boroughs were eliminated, the franchise was cautiously extended, and the new industrial capitalists secured direct in place of virtual representation. In 1834 the new Poor Law Act abolished outdoor relief completely and established a system of workhouses, which segregated the sexes and made life as hard as possible. It was in one of the new Poor Law workhouses that Oliver Twist raised his piteous, unprecedented plea for "more." Although outdoor relief never vanished completely in practice, and the English penchant for administrative illogic softened the law's full impact, an important principle had been established. In 1846 the Corn Laws were repealed, and, soon afterwards, the remaining vestiges of commercial protection. Adam Smith's dream was realized: free trade came, briefly, to England. As the century wore on, universal free education slowly became established. Most of Bentham's legal reforms became law or practice. Parliament repealed stamp taxes. Place's determined activity earned its reward in the displacement of the Combination Acts. Dissenters, Catholics, and even Jews won full civil rights.

But the credit was far from the Philosophical Radicals', entirely. In most of their fights they had allies: they would have enlisted the devil himself in a good cause. Richard Cobden and his Anti-Corn Law League, not the Benthamites, repealed the Corn Laws. In many other instances, the Philosophical Radicals simply rode a wave of liberalism and humanitarian feeling. Probably this prickly group, who savaged both major parties, did accelerate events, provide coherent programs, and push some ideas further than their phlegmatic countryman, at the time, wanted.

CONCLUSION

What did all of this mean to economics? First of all, it was the atmosphere in which two great economists flourished, Ricardo and John Stuart Mill. The latter was the creed's finest product and its best advertisement. Since Ricardo imparted a lasting shape to economic analysis, a major influence upon him was a major influence upon economics. Second, the agitations and the successes of the Philosophical Radicals and their shifting allies, transformed England. English economists found new materials and new problems in a new England. Thus the creed not only imparted a lasting analytical bent and a pervasive psychological tone to English economics, but it also helped create the conditions upon which this analytical mechanism operated.

These are large claims, as much sociological as economic. They amount to the proposition that intellectual association, group sympathy, and mutual support count much in the development of technical economics. Perhaps this is not a bad Benthamite conclusion.

Chapter 6

Thomas Robert Malthus

Parson! I have, during my life, detested many men; but never any one so much as you. . . . No assemblage of words can give an appropriate designation of you; and, therefore, as being the single word which best suits the character of such a man, I call you *Parson*, which amongst other meanings, includes that of Borough-monger Tool.

William Cobbett

Philosopher Malthus came here last week. I got an agreeable party for him of unmarried people. There was only one lady who had had a child; but he is a good-natured man, and if there are no appearances of approaching fertility, is civil to every lady.

Sydney Smith

Bachelors and spinsters I decidedly venerate. The world is overstocked with featherless bipeds. More men than corn, is a fearful pre-eminence, the sole and fruitful cause of penury, disease, and war, plague, pestilence, and famine.

Thomas Love Peacock in *Melincourt*

A benefactor to mankind, on a level with Adam Smith.

Nassau Senior

Seldom has a theory so simple and unoriginal, fathered by so mild a scholar, caused so violent and protracted a commotion as Malthus' theory of population. This theory thoroughly conquered the minds of the leaders of society. Driven into the intellectual underground, the book's opponents desperately expended as much energy attacking the man as his ideas. Few ideas accord so well with their time and influence social action so quickly.

MALTHUS' LIFE

Malthus himself was a cheerful, even-tempered man in the classic manner of those who preach pessimism. As a collegian he enjoyed practical jokes, as an adult he laughed appreciatively at his friends' jokes. His life was uneventful. He was born in 1766 at the Rookery, the country seat of his father, Daniel Malthus. The father, an eccentric country squire in the best English tradition, entertained himself in reading and argument. An ardent believer in the perfectibility of mankind, he was probably the only one of Rousseau's friends who never aroused the angry philosopher's displeasure. Daniel Malthus took a major share in the early education of his son, and surrendered him to Oxford in 1785. There Malthus did well enough to graduate as ninth wrangler in mathematics, even though he read widely in philosophical subjects as well. He later received a fellowship at his old college, took holy orders, and briefly held a curacy near Albury.

In 1798 the first edition of the *Essay on Population* appeared anonymously. A rousing success, the *Essay* determined his future. In search of supporting evidence for its propositions, Malthus traveled as widely as possible on the Continent, consulted masses of printed materials, and published a much enlarged second edition in 1803. In 1805 he became professor of history and political economy at Haileybury College, a training school for the young men who were destined to govern India in the name of the East India Company, which at that time administered British India as its private preserve. True to his principles, he did not marry until 1804, when he was 38. The remainder of his life passed smoothly. Edition of the *Essay* followed edition. Each contained new evidence and additional refutations of his critics. He became the friend and amicable antagonist of David Ricardo. The length, even tone, and topical range of their letters have not been rivaled. In 1821, he was among the original members of the Political Economy Club. His own *Principles of Political Economy*, in which Keynes found so many anticipations of his own preoccupations, was written as an attack on Ricardo. He was elected a member of the Royal Society. Increasingly regarded as an oracle, he gave evidence before parliamentary committees on colonization, Poor Laws, Corn Laws, and population. He died in 1834.

THE *ESSAY ON POPULATION*

Possibly the *Essay* would never have been written, and probably it would not have appeared in 1798, if William Godwin had not published, in 1793, his *Enquiry Concerning the Principles of Political Justice, and Its Influence on General Virtue and Happiness*. At once sublime and ridiculous, this book was the sensation of the moment. Even at this remove in time, its argument has a nostalgic charm. Although by the time of its third edition in 1798 *Political Justice* had swollen to two huge volumes, its central argument was extremely simple: "Man is perfectible, or in other words susceptible of perpetual improvement";[1] "truth is omnipotent";[2] and "what is born into the world is an unfinished sketch, without character or decisive features impressed upon it."[3]

None of this was original. The optimism had good eighteenth-century antecedents. The view that children were born into the world receptive to all outside influences could be traced to John Locke's *Essay on Human Understanding*. Early and late, rationalists have cherished and exaggerated the power of truth. Godwin achieved his impact by literary charm and the extravagant lengths

[1] William Godwin, *Political Justice*, ed. by F. E. L. Priestly, University of Toronto, 1946, p. 86.
[2] *Ibid.*, p. 91.
[3] *Ibid.*, p. 37.

to which he pushed his principles. The sources of *all* human troubles were bad government and poor institutions. Education could remedy *all* difficulties. The human reason could easily triumph over sexual instincts and it could even indefinitely expand the length of human life, so that men could become immortal. The charms of intellectual interchange far exceeded the transitory sensual pleasures to which men clung, out of ignorance of better. Godwin never preached violent revolution: he appealed only to men's understandings. When men understood, they would perceive that simplicity of life, equal distribution of income, anarchism rather than government, assured a future full of unprecedented happiness. "Truth is omnipotent."

When Daniel Malthus read this essay, so completely attuned to his generous, quixotic soul, immediate conviction followed. But his son was not so readily persuaded. Thomas Robert all his life belonged to the race of cheerful pessimists who take heart as they observe the world's insoluble problems. So the two walked and argued. Although neither convinced the other (when does anyone convince an antagonist?), Daniel Malthus considered his son's arguments so strong that he suggested publication. Nothing loath, his son, the author of one unpublished pamphlet already, dashed off his famous book.

The *Essay*, when it appeared in 1798, soon swept poor Godwin into disrepute. Polemical in form, it tried to answer Godwin, Condorcet, and other proponents of the proposition that the human race could be indefinitely improved. With the exception of the American population increase, no statistical evidence buttressed the argument. In tone the *Essay* was aprioristic, theological, and sweeping. The theme was simple. Human progress was forever limited, because population always tended to increase more rapidly than the food supply. After giving due credit for their anticipations to David Hume, Adam Smith, and Robert Wallace, Malthus clinched his case with illustrative ratios. Waiving or ignoring the point that there were many geometric ratios, Malthus considered himself conservative in concluding that population, if unchecked, would double every 25 years. Why could not the food of the people increase as rapidly? Here the small extent of arable land, and the limited possibilities of improvements in cultivation combined to make doubling improbable. At best, we might expect increase in arithmetic ratio. So, cried Malthus triumphantly, population increased in this manner, 2–4–8–16–32–64–128–256–512–1024; and food, in the same time, only increased 2–4–6–8–10–12–14–16–18. This enormous disparity flowed from two simple, "basic postulata": food was necessary for life, and the passion between the sexes was an enduring, unchanging sentiment.

Of course population was checked. A thousand and twelve cannot live on food adequate for 18. Long before we reached the ninth or even the third term of these progressions, two kinds of checks operated, the preventive and the positive. The first implied delay in marriage out of fear of poverty or descent in the social scale. Unfortunately, those most susceptible to this reasoning were the upper and middle classes. Most in need of postponement, the poor were least likely to delay. Worse even than premature marriage was the vice which so often accompanied delayed marriage: "vices that are continually involving both sexes in inextricable unhappiness."[4] Hot passion led to overpopulation. Cold reason led to sin.

While the preventive check influenced the upper classes, the positive check operated upon their inferiors. The positive check included every cause of premature death. In this edition, infant mortality and famine occupied favored places. In later editions Malthus listed 11 aspects of the positive check: unwholesome occupations, severe labor and exposure, bad and insufficient food and clothing, bad nursing of children, excesses of all kinds, great towns and manufactures, common diseases and epidemics, wars, infanticide, plague, and famine—a dreary catalogue. The eloquence which these prospects inspired appeared to excellent advantage in this passage:

Famine seems to be the last, the most dreadful resource of nature. The power of population is so superior to the power of the earth to

4 Thomas Robert Malthus, *Essay on Population*, 1798, pp. 69–70.

produce subsistence for man, that premature death must in some shape or other visit the human race. The vices of mankind are active and able ministers of depopulation. They are the precursors in the great army of destruction; and they often finish the dreadful work themselves. But should they fail in this war of extermination, sickly seasons, epidemics, pestilence and plague, advance in terrific array, and sweep off their thousands and ten thousands. Should success be still incomplete; gigantic, inevitable famine stalks in the rear, and with one mighty blow, levels the population with the food of the world.[5]

After he read this passage, Thomas Carlyle, no optimist himself, called political economy a "dismal science." The name has stuck. "To prevent the recurrence of misery, is, alas! beyond the power of man."[6]

Therefore, all Godwin's schemes of human equality fell to the ground. Implacable instinct, not human institutions, was the trouble. Equality would simply increase population faster and render more inevitable the positive check. Did no hope exist for diminishing poverty? Not very much. "Were I to propose a palliative; and palliatives are all that the nature of the case will admit; it should be, in the first place, the total abolition of all the present parish-laws."[7] Malthus, in other words, proposed to deprive the unemployed of automatic relief. Since 1795, parishes, following the example of the Justices of Speenhamland, had been granting aid to the unemployed and also to those of the employed whose wages fell below subsistence levels. Malthus thought that so long as the right to public assistance persisted the poor would marry and have children, regardless of their prospects in life. If they were deprived of this support, they might hesitate, postpone marriage, and diminish the number of mouths brought into the world. "These are the unhappy persons who, in the great lottery of life, have drawn a blank."[8]

The only other "palliatives" Malthus thought useful were premiums for the cultivation of new land and public encouragement

[5] *Ibid.*, pp. 139–140.
[6] *Ibid.*, p. 98.
[7] *Ibid.*, p. 95.
[8] *Ibid.*, p. 204.

of farmers to turn from grazing to cultivation, where their efforts would feed a larger population. As an ultimate measure, "for cases of extreme distress, county workhouses might be established. . . . the Fare should be hard and those that were able obliged to work."[9] But these stern measures afforded Malthus little hope. Man's emotions were too strong for his reason: "The cravings of hunger, the love of liquor, the desire of possessing a beautiful woman, will urge men to actions, of the fatal consequences of which, to the general interest of society, they are perfectly well convinced, even at the very time they commit them."[10] It was the godless Godwin who thought that sexual passion would abate as men became more reasonable.

What could the Deity mean by these unpleasant prospects? As his enemies never let him forget, Malthus was a clergyman. Accordingly, he offered a theological interpretation. In order "to urge man to further the gracious designs of Providence, by the full cultivation of the earth, it has been ordained that the population should increase much faster than food."[11] Besides, "the sorrows and distresses of life . . . seem . . . necessary . . . to soften and humanize the heart, to awaken social sympathy, to generate all the Christian virtues, and to afford scope for the ample exertion of benevolence."[12] The poor could console themselves that they improved the characters of the rich. On the same point, Malthus added: "It seems highly probable, that moral evil is absolutely necessary to the production of moral excellence."[13] There was a last justification of God's ways to men: "Evil exists in the world, not to create despair, but activity."[14]

Thus ran the first essay. Its authority induced a prime minister, William Pitt, to withdraw, in 1800, a new bill for poor relief, out of deference to the objections of "those whose opinions he was bound to respect."[15] A new disciple of Malthus, Pitt had come a

---

[9] *Ibid.*, p. 97.
[10] *Ibid.*, pp. 254–255.
[11] *Ibid.*, p. 361.
[12] *Ibid.*, p. 372.
[13] *Ibid.*, p. 375.
[14] *Ibid.*, p. 395.
[15] James Bonar, *Malthus and His Work*, Macmillan, 1885, p. 43.

long way from the remarks he made in 1796: "Let us make relief a matter of right and honour, instead of a ground for opprobrium and contempt. This will make a large family a blessing and not a curse; and this will draw a proper line of distinction between those who are to provide for themselves by their labour, and those who, after enriching their country with a number of children, have a claim upon its assistance for their support."[16]

Malthus was in accord with his time. The excesses of the French Revolution were alarming the English upper classes. The heavy and increasing burden of the poor rate hurt them financially. Malthus' admirable theory explained that poverty was the fault of the poor. They should neither marry nor propagate. The troubles these activities caused were properly their own. Nature and human frailty caused poverty. If improvement came, better individual behavior, not government intervention, would cause it.

The first essay was a young man's book. After its enormous initial success, Malthus reflected and grew uncomfortable with two of the essay's aspects: its paucity of empirical evidence, and its pessimistic tone. To remedy the first defect, he traveled about Europe and read practically everything written about population. The second edition, dated 1803, was a very different volume from the original. For one thing, it was enormously enlarged. The enlargement destroyed much of the literary appeal of the 1798 essay. Malthus omitted entirely the philosophical discussion of evil and gave much less attention to the Utopian speculations of Wallace, Godwin, and Condorcet. He very much expanded his discussion of the Poor Laws, and added a long new section on the Corn Laws. Above all, he incorporated tremendous quantities of historical illustrations of the operations of the principle of population. The illustrations ranged from the American Indians, the Hottentots, and the Patagonians, to Western Europe and England. Only loosely tied to Malthus' theme, these illustrations became rapidly wearisome. Despite all the historical additions, the principal piece of empirical evidence continued to be the experience of the United States.

[16] *Ibid.*, p. 30.

Malthus believed that he remedied the pessimistic tone of the first essay by his description of a new population check, moral restraint. If, said Malthus, men could be persuaded to postpone marriage and remain continent, avoiding vice, then population could be restrained and famine averted. With the addition of moral restraint, Malthus' classification became confused. Bonar suggested that objectively there were still only two checks, the preventive (including moral restraint) and the positive. Extra mouths either did not appear or one of Malthus' catalogue of disasters killed them. But, subjectively, there were now three checks: vice, the preventive check accompanied by incontinence; misery, the product of the positive check; and moral restraint, the preventive check unaccompanied by immorality.

Malthus did not really alter his conclusions between editions, despite the addition of a third check and the changes in the book's form. Malthus had few hopes of immediate improvement in men's conduct. It was mildly encouraging to him that, on the Continent, the preventive check appeared to influence the actions of all classes and the positive check was called little into action. But as for the Christian duty of moral restraint, "few of my readers can be less sanguine than I am in their expectation of any sudden and great change in the general conduct of men on this subject."[17] In all of Europe, commented Malthus plaintively, only the Swiss seemed completely to understand the principle of population.

On the Poor Laws, Malthus was more judicious than he had been in 1803. Their administration was, in his opinion, capricious, cruel, and wasteful. Nevertheless, he now favored nothing more extreme than "their *gradual* and *very gradual* abolition."[18] He recommended, as a transitional device, "a regulation . . . declaring that no child born from any marriage, taking place after the expiration of a year from the date of the law, and no illegitimate child born two years from the same date, should ever be entitled to parish assistance."[19] The frivolous might have com-

[17] Thomas Robert Malthus, *Essay on Population*, Everyman, 1914, Vol. II, p. 168.
[18] *Ibid.*, p. 64.
[19] *Ibid.*

mented that it took twice as long to convince the licentious as to persuade the virtuous.

After weighing the matter carefully, Malthus supported a bounty on corn export. This action would promote English agriculture and encourage the cultivation of new lands. Although in general he favored free trade, here he made an exception, for he was not one, he declared, to push general principles too far.

THE MALTHUSIAN CONTROVERSY

Respectable opinion quickly became Malthusian. The *Edinburgh Review*, one of the two leading quarterlies, under McCulloch's influence, immediately vociferated Malthusian doctrine. Although the *Quarterly Review* took a little longer, by 1817 it too had succumbed. As for the *Westminster Review*, the not entirely respectable Radical organ, it supported Malthus strenuously, although with birth-control overtones, which, however guarded, could not fail to disturb him. Malthus was taught even to children. Mrs. Marcet's *Conversations on Political Economy*, addressed to proper pupils and proper governesses, must have nauseated hundreds of defenseless children. On a somewhat higher level, Harriet Martineau produced her *Illustrations of Political Economy*, which Malthus himself endorsed as the best simple exposition of his doctrine. In 1807 the *Edinburgh Review* declared that Malthus had "enlarged the boundaries of science and entitled himself to the rare commendation of having added to that class of important truths which have only to be explained to command our immediate assent."[20] James Mill, Ricardo, John Stuart Mill, and Francis Place swallowed Malthus whole.

Respectable opinion was less than the whole of opinion. By no means everybody admired Malthus. The tone of the attacks ranged from the reproachful to the scurrilous. The merits of the criticism are the harder to assess because sometimes the most violent critics had the best arguments. Some critics attacked Malthus' originality. Others concentrated on his theology. A third

[20] *Edinburgh Review*, October, 1807, p. 102.

group analyzed his principal piece of factual evidence, the American experience of population growth. Still another tack was demolition of the ratios. Some laid their fire on the checks. One group attacked Malthus as a hard-hearted oppressor of the poor. The allegations were various and critics did not limit themselves to single points.

ORIGINALITY

Every important idea has its predecessors. Here they were quite numerous. Sir Walter Raleigh had labeled war and pestilence as checks to population. In 1677 Sir Matthew Hale enumerated the checks to population as plague, famines, wars, floods, and fire. In 1753 Robert Wallace noted that "it is not owing to the want of prolific virtue, but to the distressed circumstances of mankind that every generation does not more than double themselves."[21] And, as he tossed off so many other important notions, David Hume described a theory of population in one concise paragraph:

For as there is in all men, both male and female, a desire and power of generation more active than is ever universally exerted, the restraints, which they lie under, must proceed from some difficulties in their situation, which it belongs to a wise legislature carefully to observe and remove. Almost every man who thinks he can maintain a family will have one; and the human species, at this rate of propagation, would more than double every generation. How fast do mankind multiply in every colony or settlement; when it is an easy matter to provide for a family; and when men are nowise straitened or confined, as in long established governments . . . if every else be equal, it seems natural to expect, that, wherever there are most happiness and virtue, and the wisest institutions, there will also be most people.[22]

Much of Malthus reposed in this passage: the passion between the sexes; the checks, implied rather than described; the Ameri-

---

[21] Kenneth Smith, *The Malthusian Controversy*, Routledge and Kegan Paul, 1951, p. 19.
[22] Quoted in *ibid.*, p. 18.

can experience, a fair inference from the remarks on colonies; and even the geometric ratio, in the reference to doubling.

Obviously, Malthus was no innovator. People listened to him, not to his anticipators, partly because the time was ripe, but also because the first edition of the essay displayed rare sweep, passion, and intensity. Where ideas are as scarce as they have been in economics, form and emphasis must substitute for inventiveness.

THEOLOGY

Probably, moral restraint's addition to the other checks resulted from Malthus' sensitivity to the judgment that he had made of the world an evil, dismal place and that such a world was a poor testimonial to the good intentions of the Creator. By arguing that God had enjoined moral restraint upon human beings as their duty, Malthus hoped to silence the critics. He did not succeed. As late as 1831, the criticism was repeated in the popular form of execrable doggerel:

Squire Thimble

Pray, young folks, of procreation
  Of breeding children, shun the woes;
Check the surplus population;
  Restraint that's moral interpose.

Dick

Of children full that I my quiver
  Might have, you heard the parson pray;
Can you, then, where God's the giver,
  Behold the gift and turn away?

Betsy

Didn't he pray for God to bless me,
  And make me fruitful on the vine;
And charge my Richard to caress me,
  And sick or well, not to repine?

All the Young Men and Girls

Hang that Thimble, what can he know?
The Bible bids us to increase:
Back to London, then, may he go;
And let us live and love in peace.[23]

The heart of the theological count against Malthus was that his recommendation of late marriage contravened scriptural teaching.

AMERICAN INCREASE

In every edition Malthus averred that population's growth in the new American state definitely proved geometrical doubling, in the absence of checks. Critics attacked this evidence in several ways. Godwin pointed out an obvious weakness of Malthus' demonstration. The latter assumed that the entire increase of population in the United States was the result of procreation by the original settlers and their descendants. Substantial immigration into the country was an important modification, of which Malthus took no account.

Ravenstone, in a much more sophisticated way, analyzed population growth according to age classes. The demographic explosion in the United States was the result of an abnormal concentration in the country of young people. Since the circumstance was accidental and temporary, the demographic situation was bound to alter. Ravenstone and others made the general point that the experience of one country was an inadequate basis of generalization.

THE RATIOS

There was a good deal of nonsense in these geometric and arithmetic formulations. Occasionally, supporters of Malthus, and even Malthus himself, expounded the doctrine of population as though the ratios were entirely incidental to it. Yet, if the ratios were dismissed, what had Malthus added to the theory of population? It was the common gossip of the learned that popu-

[23] William Cobbett, *Tracts*, 1831, Vol. I, No. XII, p. 292.

lation tended to increase more rapidly than the food supply, and well known that various checks kept the two in balance. The ratios caught the fancy of Malthus' first audience and he was never willing to give them up entirely.

Criticisms of them were many. On the score of language, Malthus was asked whether he meant that population actually did increase in geometric ratio, that it tended to increase at this rate, or only that it had the power to do so. Save possibly for the United States, the first interpretation plainly controverted the facts. In language never distinguished for its precision, Malthus wavered between the second and the third interpretations. But a world of difference separated them. If population tends to double, then the danger of famine was never far away. If only a remote power existed, then we could move on to more pressing problems. Malthus' opponents naturally preferred the last version. They argued powerfully that the earth was still relatively unpeopled, vacant lands were numerous in many parts of the world, and the present danger of population did not exist, whatever might be its potentialities.

Moreover, Malthus had not said what stage in the mathematical progressions we had reached. If we were between the first and the second term, then we had a whole generation of grace, for by Malthus' own demonstration, here food and population kept pace. In 25 years, much could happen. Perhaps, moral restraint could catch the imagination of the general population.

CRITIC OF THE POOR

Hazlitt and Cobbett especially accused Malthus of hardhearted attacks upon the poor. His efforts to repeal the Poor Laws struck them as entirely reprehensible. His proposal to suspend their operation for the newly married aroused their derision. How could a poor man know that he could support a family? How could he estimate the spells of unemployment or the wages which awaited him? In fact, how could Malthus expect the ordinary man to penetrate the veil of the future, when his betters did so badly in the effort? Although there was every reason to believe that Malthus was a benevolent man, there was unquestionably an air of the theoretical about his remarks where they concerned ordinary men, and a certain unpleasant relish in the description of misfortune, which gave ammunition to modern and contemporary critics. Malthus' embittered critics pointed to the luxuries of the rich and the weight of the taxes on the poor, as sufficient explanations of the wretched state of the English masses.

THE CHECKS

When examined narrowly, the logic of Malthus' checks became dubious. War was not the same as flood or famine. Men controlled the first, but not the other two. As men improved, they might hope to diminish the number and ferocity of wars. Malthus' gloomy view of moral restraint neglected the better side of human nature, his opponents emphasized. If women were notoriously pure, why could not men act as well? Some did so voluntarily: priests and monks. During a portion of their lives, why could not other men remain continent?

Malthus had lumped contraception with vice? But, his critics argued, he had little theological sanction. Place and Mill saw no sound argument against contraception. It is a historical joke upon Malthus that the neo-Malthusians were advocates of birth control.

CONCLUSION

Malthus' importance was twofold. He supplied an essential theoretical pillar of the analytical structure which David Ricardo and John Stuart Mill erected. Through them, he passed into the mainstream of the history of economic doctrine. Also, he powerfully influenced the public policy of his age. Malthusian doctrine was the strongest ideological cause of the new Poor Law of 1834. He was a potent conservative force, as believers in nature rather than men usually are. On the general issues of the day his voice was frequently raised, and always listened to.

Some things Malthus did not accomplish. He did not construct a useful science of demography. Experience has shattered the principle of population. Neither the ratios nor the checks now convince, except when they are altered out of recognition. His simple book had a great influence: the influence did not make it a better book. So little did his population doctrine have to say that when Keynes came to discuss Malthus he ignored the population theory and talked only about his analysis of oversaving and underemployment.

Chapter 7

David Ricardo

In the *Wealth of Nations*, Adam Smith enunciated the major themes of political economy: value and its origins, the production and the distribution of wealth, and the meaning of economic progress. Simultaneously, Adam Smith disposed of the ancient errors of mercantilism, at the relatively slight cost of some new confusions of his own. He presented England with a set of principles and, more important, a program. The program was designed to liberate England from governmental restraint and establish that system of natural liberty best calculated to enrich the citizens of the community. For upon their prosperity the nation's depended.

THE BACKGROUND

Between the publication of the *Wealth of Nations* in 1776 and the appearance of David Ricardo's *Principles of Political Economy and Taxation* in 1817, 41 years elapsed and England fought and won its greatest war. In those four decades a radically transformed England evoked from economists altered responses to new problems. Theoretical controversy had resolved some disputed points and sharpened disagreement upon others. Economics was ready for another stage in its development, a new synthesis. Ricardo, like Smith, attracted legions of disciples because this badly written, highly abstract, frantically disorganized tract registered England's evolving fortunes and responded to England's needs. That it also sharpened the analytical tools of the professional economist may strike us as more important than it did Ricardo's contemporaries.

What had changed in the British economy? What ideas dominated the intellectual scene? How did Ricardo's own experience and character combine in the issue of economics' most influential theory?

CURRENCY

Despite his hearty attacks upon mercantilism, Smith's attitude toward the future was cheerful. Hampered though it was, individual initiative was producing marvelous results all around him. As England grew richer, Smith was confident that capital increase could outrun population growth. So long as the relationship of the rates held, wages could rise and the lot of the workingman could improve. Even in 1776, Smith demonstrated ingeniously, English wages exceeded bare subsistence minima. Rising rents signalized prosperity. Under God, free enterprise promised to reconcile classes and enrich their members. This picture's warm colors did not reflect Smith's accurate prevision of English industrial hegemony. Division of labor and economic freedom, not machines and factories, were the sufficient agents of material prosperity.

The colors in Ricardo's palette were all somber shades of gray and black, even though industry had advanced so far in England that keen observation rather than the prophetic gift should have indicated where the future lay. Ricardo saw problems, not promises; and uncertainty, not progress. This was not strange. In the first two decades of the nineteenth century, England was a land of troubles. In economic affairs these troubles centered around two obsessive words, "currency" and "corn," almost sign and countersign in the fraternity of economists.

Take currency first. In 1776 the organization of the English monetary system was comparatively simple. "Money" meant coin, and coin could be exchanged for paper currency at the Bank of England, which stood ready to redeem all notes issued by itself. A relatively small number of country banks, outside of

London, also issued paper notes, and these too could be exchanged for gold, through the intermediate stage of conversion into Bank of England notes. Although Smith favored the use of paper money, his chief argument emphasized its superior economy in circulation, not its connection with credit expansion. Paper currency substituted for gold coin, it had no independent life of its own.

In 1802, the year of Henry Thornton's *Enquiry into the Nature and Effects of the Paper Credit of Great Britain*, the position was drastically different. The number of country banks had increased rapidly. Since no agency regulated them, some rested on shaky foundations. Worse still, their collapse threatened to carry down with them their more reputable country brethren, involve the major London banks, and embarrass the Bank of England itself. This chain of connections signalized the growing complexity of finance. The growing use of checks led to the establishment of the London Clearing House, which minimized the cash transfers required among banks, on the usual principle of offsetting balances.

The prime change in the banking scene was greater recognition of the role of the Bank of England. Toward the end of the eighteenth century, this bank became recognized as a bank of last resort. Like all other central banks, it furnished credit when no one else would or could. Thornton's strikingly prescient analysis treated the Bank much less as the private institution which was its legal form, and much more as a government bank, whose responsibility to the business community at large transcended its narrower obligation to pay appropriate dividends to its own stockholders.

This shift in apprehension of the Bank of England's place in the scene occurred just when the pressures of the Napoleonic wars forced the bank to suspend cash payments in 1797. It no longer furnished gold in exchange for its own notes. This suspension of cash payments created a situation in which English currency lost its direct tie with gold. Henceforth its value had to be judged by other criteria. About this question of valuation, much debate raged during the first 15 years of the nineteenth century. One side took the position that the rise in English prices reflected an increase in the value of gold. The other, to which Ricardo allied himself, argued much more simply that English prices had risen because the Bank of England had printed too many banknotes, unchecked by any need to redeem them with gold. Ricardo concurred heartily in the report of the Parliamentary Bullion Committee, written largely by Francis Horner in 1810, which concluded "that the paper currency is now excessive, and depreciated in comparison to gold, and that the high price of Bullion and low rates of exchange are the consequences as well as the sign of such depreciation."[1] As the last half of the quotation suggested, Ricardo and others of his persuasion used as evidence the discount at which the paper pound sold in foreign markets and the high price which had to be paid in English paper currency to acquire gold from other countries. What concerned Ricardo was monetary management. His solution was less rather than more management. If the suspension of gold payments by the Bank of England were speedily ended, then free market forces would rapidly determine the correct value of English currency in England and the rest of the world.

What had the Bank of England in mind when it printed such extravagant numbers of bank notes? War finance was again the explanation. At an early point in the Napoleonic wars, the English government concluded that it could not finance English armies and navies by taxation alone. Therefore the government borrowed. It borrowed directly from the Bank of England or from individuals. Both devices created deposits, increased the money supply, and enlarged the demand for money. To men of the time, including Ricardo, the debt which the protracted struggle created seemed a crushing burden, a grim problem to which solution was not apparent.

[1] David Ricardo, *The Works and Correspondence*, ed. by Piero Sraffa, Cambridge, 1951–1955, Vol. III, p. 161.

CORN

Corn and population were a second set of difficulties at the beginning of the nineteenth century. In 1801 the population of Great Britain exceeded ten million only very slightly. By 1821, it had increased 34 percent and it continued to increase, despite substantial emigration, throughout the nineteenth century. Even in the first decades of the century, Englishmen were alarmed at the proliferation of mouths. The emotion was the response of a nation which still considered itself agricultural. As recently as 1750 England had been an agricultural exporter and an importer of manufactures. Although by the last quarter of the eighteenth century she had begun to import grain, England, in many years, fed herself, and in exceptionally good years, two as late as 1812 and 1813, actually exported grain. At worst, the amounts imported were small.

English farmers had a vital stake in the image of a rural nation. All during the Napoleonic wars, protection had awarded them almost a monopoly. By 1811 more Englishmen earned their livings in commerce, navigation, and manufacturing than agriculture, but the latter was still the largest single occupation. During the wars, English farmers and landlords had completed the process of enclosure, experimented with new techniques of soil and animal care, and sunk larger and larger amounts of capital in the land. Great interests were at stake, therefore, in the battle which raged over the issues of continued agricultural protection.

One of these interests was that of the poor. Even before England's industrialization gathered momentum, poor relief had been a venerable problem. Its cost was traditionally borne by local governmental units, the parishes, and financed out of local assessments, the rates. In form, this relief was mostly "outdoor," granted to the recipient in his own home, not in a workhouse. As we have seen, the Settlement Acts protected each parish from the poor of its neighbors.

The immediate condition of the poor was closely related to the price of bread, their principal diet. This price rose steadily between 1775 and 1825, to the point at which many employed workers could not support themselves on their wages. The various supplementary grants in aid of wages, begun in 1795, tied the amounts awarded to the price of bread. Undoubtedly, humanitarian motives spurred local justices of the peace to adopt this system. Nevertheless, its effects were little short of disastrous. What was conceived as a minimum wage rapidly became a maximum. The grants themselves turned out to be mostly benefits for farmers who hired laborers at substandard wages, in the full knowledge that poor relief would be forthcoming. Was there a more effective way to dull the normal incentives of labor, diminish working efficiency, and demoralize the morale of the labor force?

Worst of all, the arrangement intensified the dread danger of overpopulation. If workers were sure of subsistence, employed or unemployed, assiduous or idle, drunk or sober; if rewards failed to distinguish between the efficient and the inefficient, then how could the prudential check operate? Men married as their passions directed them, especially since their lot before marriage was little better than after marriage. As Malthus warned, population would bear ever more heavily upon the land. Unused acres would disappear and more intensive cultivation would yield diminishing fruits. The horrors of the positive check—disease, pestilence, death in infancy, and above all, famine—would disperse the redundant population. The replacement of agriculture by manufacturing was no solution, despite the fuller operation of division of labor in the latter. Manufacturing processes used raw materials which, as products of the soil, were subject to the same inexorable laws as food.

Machinery stimulated more immediate problems than solutions. In Ricardo's phrase, industry was subject to sudden interruptions in the channels of trade. While many agricultural workers were probably underemployed, few faced the complete unemployment which was sometimes the industrial worker's lot. These new industrial workers were probably somewhat better off than agricultural laborers, although the statistical evidence is exceedingly scanty. Nevertheless, there was something frightening about the spectacle of massed urban poverty, not matched by the concealment and dispersion of the rural poor. What could be expected of the inhabitants of the lowering mills which dominated their grimy cities? No one knew. Machines might ultimately set men free, but not many observers at the time were willing to say so. Many more saw greater benefits to the poor in the repeal of the Corn Laws.

Agricultural protection touched the interests of a third major economic group, the rising capitalists. To them the issue was simple: if corn could be freely imported, its price would fall, bread made from it would be cheaper, and wages could be cut. Lower production costs would enable English manufacturers to compete more effectively in foreign markets and expand their profits. Their adoption of this position was gradual. At the end of the eighteenth century, a majority probably preferred protected markets for their own products and granted the same boon to their fellow property holders in land.

To Ricardo, Corn Law repeal was a necessity. Repeal of these laws could temporarily raise the standard of life for a period as long as a generation. If workingmen grew used to this higher standard and came to recognize that its perpetuation depended upon their own acts, they might adopt moral restraint, the effective protection of their new position.

Such was Ricardo's economic universe, a world of disordered currency, towering debt, menacing increase in population, market disruption, and expensive Poor Laws. And perhaps here was sufficient explanation of the tone of the *Principles of Political Economy and Taxation*. But there was something more. Before the French Revolution, English leaders seemed relatively receptive to change and reform. In the reaction which followed the French Revolution, sentiment hardened, the mood of the country changed, and its leaders shifted abruptly to the most implacable conservatism, in whose eyes all change appeared equally repugnant. This attitude included mounting distrust of popular sentiment and popular action and induced Parliament to increase the restraints on free speech, free assembly, and free combination of workers in trade unions. We may look back upon the beginning of the century full of knowledge that it was destined to be one of England's greatest. No Englishman concluded as much then. To any liberal Englishman his country's salient characteristics must have appeared to be rigidity, repression, and control.

RICARDO'S LIFE

When a Bank proprietor, he argued strenuously and warmly against the inordinate gains of that body; he defended the cause of the fund-holders when he had ceased to be one; he was accused of an attempt to ruin the landed interest after he became a large landed proprietor; and while a member of parliament, he advocated the cause of reform, which, if adopted, would have deprived him of his seat.

Moses Ricardo

We had delightful conversation, both on deep and shallow subjects. Mr. Ricardo, with a very composed manner, has a continual life of mind, and starts perpetually new game in conversation. I never argued or discussed a question with any person who argues more fairly or less for victory and more for truth.

Maria Edgeworth

Though short by modern standards, the life of David Ricardo was a testimonial to the enlightened use of leisure by a man of great wealth, which he made for himself. Ricardo was born in 1772, in London, the third child among the numerous progeny of a devout father, Abraham Ricardo. An active and successful stockbroker, his father brought up his son in the same profession. In consequence, Ricardo's formal education ended at 14, when he went to work full time for his father. From the beginning, he won recognition as extremely able, preternaturally quick in the firm's intricate financial negotiations, and outstanding in the most intellectual and abstract branch of stock-exchange operation, currency arbitrage. In 1793, a breach between himself and his father developed over his marriage to Priscilla Ann Wilkinson, a

Quaker. The scanty evidence suggests that the marriage signalized rather than caused Ricardo's growing estrangement from the Judaism of his youth. However, he advanced no further along the path to conversion than Unitarianism, the most latitudinarian of dissenting sects.

Twenty years old, married, and penniless, Ricardo had to shift for himself. So fine was his reputation that he readily borrowed funds enough from associates to set up his own business. According to his brother's memoir, he rapidly amassed a large fortune. At the time of his death in 1823, his assets, including his magnificent county seat, Gatcomb Park, amounted to something between £675,000 and £775,000, and his annual income from investments was approximately £28,000. These were tremendous sums in nineteenth-century prices and by no means disgraceful totals even now.

Ricardo was a great deal more than a superb moneymaking machine. Perhaps because his mind was so sharp that making money inadequately challenged it, he turned to intellectual pursuits as soon as his fortune was solidly established. When he was 25, he fitted up a laboratory and started a mineral collection. In 1808 he became one of the first members of the Geological Society. One student has alleged that these scientific pursuits did more to form his economics than the notions of Jeremy Bentham and James Mill.[2]

He discovered political economy almost by accident. The story went that, in 1799, when he was boring himself at Bath, the period's most famous resort, he picked up a copy of the *Wealth of Nations*, which, it may be remembered, Adam Smith had begun to pass the time in the south of France. What might have been the history of economic doctrines, if Smith and Ricardo had not been subject to boredom? The *Wealth of Nations* caught Ricardo's attention at once, and he read it with mounting fascination. But he did not rush into print himself. He made his literary debut in 1809, in three letters to the *Morning Chronicle*. After that date, several pamphlets, a copious correspondence, and the

[2] *Ibid.*, Vol. X, p. 35.

Principles attested the central importance of political economy in his life.

If he had not been persuaded, he might have written nothing at all, for he said of himself, in a letter to Mill, "I have all the disadvantages too of a neglected education, which it is in vain to seek to repair."[3] The same James Mill was the firm instrument of persuasion. Few escaped Mill's presence without agreeing to carry out his plans. Over Ricardo, Mill took special pains. His son testified that Mill respected Ricardo's intellectual powers, and felt deep affection for him. The second was a rare sentiment in that austere soul. Presumably, Ricardo would not have written the *Principles* if Mill had not freely extended much advice in this vein:

Why do you cry, "Oh that I were able to write a book!" when there is no obstacle to your writing, but this want of confidence in your own powers. You want some practice in the art of laying down your thoughts in the way most easy of comprehension to those who have little knowledge, and little attention; and this is to be got infallibly by a little practice. As I am accustomed to wield the authority of a schoolmaster, I, therefore, in the genuine exercise of this honourable capacity, lay upon you my commands, to begin to the first of the three heads of your proposed work, rent, profit, wages—viz. *rent* without an hour's delay. If you entrust the inspection of it to me, depend upon it I shall compel you to make it all right, before you have done with it.[4]

However, it passes probability that Ricardo would have written nothing, save for the fortunate chance of an Egyptian captivity, enforced by a stern master. The strongest independent evidence of Ricardo's own drive was his correspondence with Malthus, which endured from 1811 until Ricardo's death. The letters examined currency and foreign exchange, rent, profits, the price of corn, and measures of value. In them many of Ricardo's ideas first achieved mention. From them he might well have constructed his more formal works.

[3] *Ibid.*, Vol. VII, p. 190.
[4] *Ibid.*, Vol. VI, p. 321.

Quite probably Mill did induce Ricardo to enter Parliament. In 1819 Ricardo became the representative of Portarlington, a pocket borough, which he purchased according to the practice of the period. In Parliament he displayed the same qualities of honesty, devotion to truth, and good manners which had distinguished him in controversies with Malthus and Bosanquet. He was no more effective as a speaker than as a writer. People listened to him, as they read him, with the attention evoked by the supremely well-informed and the completely public-spirited. In Parliament he naturally aligned himself with the Benthamite wing of the Whig opposition. According to one observer, he was a reformer who "spoke of Parliamentary reform and vote by Ballot as a man who would bring such things about and destroy the existing system tomorrow."[5] As always, Ricardo had pushed his principles hard.

Ricardo always tended to brush aside details of existing institutional arrangements and practices, in the interests of clear principle. It was this habit of mind that Brougham, himself sympathetic on occasion to reform, identified in the stately language of Parliamentary courtesy:

His hon. friend, the member from Portarlington, had argued as if he had dropped from another planet; as if this were a land of the most perfect liberty of trade—as if there were no taxes—no drawbacks—no bounties—no searchers—on any other branch of trade but agriculture; as if, in this Utopian world, of his hon. friend's creation the first measure of restriction ever thought of was that on the importation of corn; as if all classes of the community were alike—as if all trades were on an equal footing; and that, in this new state, we were called upon to decide the abstract question whether or not there should be a protecting price for corn. But we were not in this condition.[6]

Ricardo's own position on existing representation elicited the acid comment of an Irish member: "That honourable gentleman had talked gravely against the influence of the aristocracy, yet not-

[5] *Ibid.*, Vol. VIII, p. 152.
[6] *Ibid.*, Vol. V, p. 56.

withstanding, he did not believe he could himself mention one of his own constituents, although they did not amount to more than twelve in all; and it was equally certain, that the honourable gentleman was either returned by that very aristocracy, whose influence he so loudly deprecated, or by an interest quite equivalent, and not less cogent."[7] The last clause of this palpable hit was circumlocution for cash purchase.

In 1823, at the age of 51, Ricardo died quite suddenly of an ear inflammation. Since eulogies are an untrustworthy literary form, only one, from a Parliamentary colleague, need be cited. Huskisson's tribute pointed to qualities which Ricardo's friends had praised during his life: "There was no man who esteemed more highly the acuteness and ability of Mr. Ricardo than he [Huskisson] did, and no man who more sincerely lamented his loss. In all his public conduct there was an evident anxiety to do what he thought right, to seek the good of the country, and to pursue no other object; and his speeches were always distinguished by a spirit of firmness and conciliation that did equal honour to himself and to his country."[8]

Ricardo was a gentle, even long-suffering husband, as his *Journal of a Tour on the Continent* demonstrated; a most generous father; and a kindly friend. The young John Stuart Mill commented on his benevolence and the attraction he exerted upon the young. But the judicious cheerfulness of his outward manner disguised some melancholy of spirit. It appeared in a letter to Mill, written when Ricardo was only 48 and tolerably healthy:

I am led to set a light value on life when I consider the many accidents and privations to which we are liable. In my own case, I have already lost the use of one ear, completely—and am daily losing my teeth, that I have scarcely one that is useful to me. No one bears these serious deprivations with a better temper than myself, yet I cannot help anticipating from certain notices which I sometimes think I have, that many more await me. I have not, I assure you, seriously quarreled with life,—I am on very good terms with it, and

[7] *Ibid.*, Vol. V, p. 289.
[8] *Ibid.*, Vol. V, p. 332.

mean while I have it to make the best use of it, but my observation on the loss of esteem and interest which old people generally sustain from their young relations, often indeed from their own imperfections and misbehavior, but sometimes from the want of indulgence and consideration on the part of the young, convinces me that generally happiness would be best promoted if death visited us on an average at an earlier period than he does now.[9]

INFLUENCES ON RICARDO

Although his intellectual curiosity was strong, Ricardo was not a systematic reader. Perhaps he was the founder of that school of English economists which still prefers to make things up rather than look them up. Yet, a number of intellectual influences played upon his mind. First among them must be put Adam Smith. Ricardo's *Principles* followed the example of Smith's organization. More than that, they commented on and criticized point after point in the *Wealth of Nations*. Ricardo's procedure pointed to Adam Smith's continuing force and influence. Partly as a consequence of Smith's position, no systematic treatise on political economy had emerged between 1776 and 1817 from the flood of economic discussion in pamphlets and periodicals.

The influence of James Mill and Jeremy Bentham is harder to assess. It was, at all events, totally different in character. Ricardo, who greatly admired Mill, evidently borrowed from him, with little dissent, the system of philosophical ideas which has been discussed under the heading of Philosophical Radicalism. Ricardo accepted Bentham's hedonistic calculus, the measurement of pains and pleasures; the sect's intense belief in education and representative government; and its practical program, addressed to the widening of civil liberties and the repeal of Corn and Poor Laws. But it is a treacherous step to infer that Ricardo's economics directly reflected these ideological commitments. Few signs in the *Principles* indicate that the technical economics owed anything to Mill and Bentham, both much inferior to him in their understand-

[9] *Ibid.*, Vol. VIII, p. 253.

ing of the subject. Ricardo worked easily with the rough and ready hypothesis that most men sought their own gain, a notion no doubt as old as human thought. Making no effort to refine this notion with Benthamite tools, he wrote comfortably in a long English tradition which he breathed as he breathed air. Mill cannot be dismissed so readily. At the least, he had stimulated Ricardo to writing, if not to thought. Moreover, Mill assimilated Ricardo to the school he was so superbly fitted by nature to head. In the sociology of English economics, the Ricardian school owed as much to the organized propaganda of James Mill as to the original constructions of David Ricardo.

Whom else did Ricardo read and heed? On population and rent (despite his good independent title to the latter), Ricardo acknowledged indebtedness to Malthus. His enthusiastic devotion to Malthus' *Essay* deeply colored the tone of his own *Principles.* His endorsement was unconditional: "Of Mr. Malthus' Essay on Population, I am happy in the opportunity here afforded me of expressing my admiration. The assaults of the opponents of this great work have only served to prove its strength; and I am persuaded that its just reputation will spread with the cultivation of the science, of which it is so eminent an ornament. Mr. Malthus, too, has satisfactorily explained the principles of rent."[10] Ricardo's *Principles* supplied the economics to surround Malthus' demography.

Ricardo adopted and restated J. B. Say's proposition that supply created its own demand and, therefore, general glut must be impossible. In a time of economic maladjustment, Ricardo's statement had an Olympian ring:

M. Say has, however, most satisfactorily shown, that there is no amount of capital which may not be employed in a country, because demand is only limited by production. No man produces, but with a view to consume or sell, and he never sells, but with an intention to purchase some other commodity, which may be immediately useful to him, or which may contribute to future production. By producing, then, he necessarily becomes either the consumer of his own

[10] *Ibid.,* Vol. I, p. 398.

goods, or the purchaser and consumer of the goods of some other person. . . . There cannot, then, be accumulated in a country any amount of capital which cannot be employed productively, until wages rise so high in consequence of the rise of necessaries, and so little consequently remains for the profits of stock, that the motive for accumulation ceases.[11]

Though their minds never met in the same way as Ricardo's and Mill's, Say was one of Ricardo's more frequent correspondents. Through him, French economics and its emphasis upon laws had its chance to influence English political economy.

In one way or another, Smith, Malthus, Bentham, Mill, and Say did most to shape Ricardo's thought or publication. Ricardo read and approved a few other sources. He justly admired Thornton's brilliant work on paper credit: his own views suffered by comparison with Thornton's rare blend of institutional materials and analytical understanding. He knew Edward West's *Essay on the Application of Capital to Land*, which advanced a theory of rent similar to Ricardo's first effort in his *Essay on the High Price of Corn*, and to Malthus' *Essay on Rent*. He followed the controversy between Spence, a belated disciple of the physiocrats, and James Mill, on the usefulness of foreign trade.

But where someone like Alfred Marshall at the end of the century conscientiously reinterpreted his predecessors' doctrines, combined them into a new theory, and demonstrated the continuity of economics, Ricardo, in the manner of the self-educated, thought everything through for himself, even when he found what he wanted well expressed elsewhere. Whatever he embodied of changes in economic ideas since Adam Smith was more likely to derive from his own cast of mind than from his graduation from James Mill's school for economists and politicians.

RICARDO'S ECONOMICS

By the time Ricardo published his *Principles*, he had, in less than a decade, established his reputation as an authority on cur-

[11] *Ibid.*, Vol. I, p. 290.

rency and other economic problems. Although many of these earlier economic writings were extraordinarily interesting, the *Principles* incorporated Ricardo's mature convictions on economic theory and economic policy.

What was the book like? It was terribly abstract. It contained almost no facts, in any ordinary meaning of the word. Ricardo sought laws of economic behavior, regularities in the behavior of large masses of men. Two passages from his letters to Malthus indicated how he understood his goal: "Our differences may in some respect, I think, be ascribed to your considering my book as more practical than I intended it to be. My object was to elucidate principles, and to do this I imagined strong cases that I might shew the operation of those principles."[12] It was not the last time "strong cases" fascinated Ricardo. In the next passage he identified his own preference for investigation of the long run:

It appears to me that one great cause of our differences in opinion, on the subjects which we have so often discussed, is that you have always in your mind the immediate and temporary effects of particular changes—whereas I put these immediate and temporary effects quite aside, and fix my whole attention on the permanent state of things which will result from them. Perhaps you estimate these temporary effects too highly, whilst, I am too much disposed to undervalue them. To manage the subject quite right they should be carefully distinguished and mentioned, and the due effects ascribed to each.[13]

It still entertains that, in this dialogue, the practical man was Malthus, the professor of political economy, and the theorist, devoted to abstract principle, was Ricardo, the acute businessman who had made his fortune in the stock market. The way to solve England's problems, Ricardo was convinced, demanded understanding of the principles which underlay everyday actions. These principles he sought to elucidate.

The *Principles* were not only abstract, they were disorganized. More than one economist has tried to arrange the chapters in a

12 *Ibid.*, Vol. VIII, p. 184.
13 *Ibid.*, Vol. VII, p. 120.

sequence more coherent than Ricardo's. The results were inevitably disappointing, for the book was not a single piece of exposition, it was a collection of essays on value, rent, profits, wages, and other topics. Even the smaller units, the chapters, displayed grave flaws of composition. Ricardo was elliptical, undisposed to define terms, and prone to skip logical steps. Critics commented that the clearest part of the book was the index. This, it turned out, was prepared by James Mill, who misinterpreted Ricardo's meaning in several places.

The peculiar power of the *Principles* lay in the spectacle of great intelligence, however narrow and concentrated, forcing new truth out of old problems. It is possible to exaggerate the difficulties of reading Ricardo. Close attention, sympathy with his aims, and readiness to reread produce eventual understanding. The understanding is worth the trouble, because Ricardo poured some new wine into some new bottles. He shifted economics' emphasis from value, Smith's major analytical problem, to distribution. While Smith's principal practical problem, economic progress, concerned him also, here also his techniques and his conclusions differed from Smith's.

VALUE

Many of Ricardo's letters centered on value. His pamphlets approached the subject, and the first, longest, and most obscure chapter in the *Principles* represented a full-scale assault on its difficulties. But the search did not end there. In the very year of his death, still seeking an invariable measure of value, he summarized his position in a letter to Malthus: "We agree, I believe, that nothing can be a measure of value which does not itself possess value. We agree too I believe that a measure of value to be a good one should itself be invariable, and further that in selecting one thing as a measure of value rather than another we are bound to shew some good reason for such selection, for if a good reason be not given the choice is altogether arbitrary."[14] Although Ricardo retained doubts about the adequacy of his theory, John Stuart Mill

[14] *Ibid.*, Vol. IX, p. 320.

accepted it without reservation. Marx and the Ricardian Socialists used it as a starting point, and the English marginalists of the 1870's reacted sharply against it.

The theory's later importance demands extensive discussion of it here. Nevertheless, Ricardo's own preoccupation was the distribution of income among the three great classes of English society, landowners, capitalists, and workers. Where Smith rejoiced in an expanding economy, Ricardo feared an unchanging national product—a pie to be divided among the classes. In such circumstances, the principle of division became overwhelmingly important.

If value was a sideshow, it fascinated Ricardo's contemporaries. As he understood value, a good theory performed two functions: it identified the underlying causes of the multitudinous price fluctuations of actual experience; and it provided a measure of comparison for the various commodities whose prices changed. The twentieth-century student ignores the first objective and contents himself with theories of price in the short, middle, and long run. He handles the second objective as a technical index number problem and often ignores the philosophical questions which the construction of any composite measure provokes.

How well did Ricardo's theory meet his tests? By running together a number of sentences from the *Principles*, we can derive an outline of the theory: "Possessing utility, commodities derive their exchangeable value from two sources: from their scarcity, and from the quantity of labour required to obtain them. . . . There are some commodities, the value of which is determined by their very scarcity alone. . . . These commodities, however, form a very small part of the mass of commodities daily exchanged in the market. By far the greatest part of those goods which are the objects of desire, are procured by labour; and they may be multiplied . . . almost without any assignable limit. . . . In speaking then of commodities, of their exchangeable value, and of the laws which regulate their relative prices, we mean always such commodities only as can be increased in quantity by the exertion of human industry, and on the production of which competition operates without restraint."[15] The qualifications came later. What Ricardo said here directly might be paraphrased in this way. First of all, commodities had to possess utility, someone had to want them. But utility was a precondition of value, not its explanation. Ricardo's later comment on Say made that point plain: "He [Say] certainly has not a correct notion of what is meant by value, when he contends that a commodity is valuable in proportion to its utility. This would be true if buyers only regulated the value of commodities; then indeed we might expect that all men would be willing to give a price for things in proportion to the estimation in which they hold them, but the fact appears to me to be that the buyers have the least in the world to do in regulating price—it is all done by the competition of the sellers."[16]

Statues, pictures, old coins, and rare wines were among the commodities whose value was regulated by scarcity. Since supply was fixed, intensity of demand determined price. Because there were so few of these commodities, Ricardo dismissed them from further consideration. What was left were those commodities which could be "multiplied" almost without limit by human labor. Not quite all. Ricardo excluded goods produced by monopolies. In the end, the theory of value, applied to those objects (never services) which human labor, under competitive conditions, produced. This category, in Ricardo's judgment, covered most of the items which passed through markets.

At its simplest, the theory stated that commodities exchanged against each other in competitive markets according to the relative amounts of labor needed to produce them. In equilibrium, a clock priced at $100 required ten times as many man-hours to produce as a pair of shoes priced at $10. Ten times as much labor produced the shoes as a hammer priced at $1. Dispelling Smith's confusion, Ricardo stated that only labor embodied, never labor commanded, counted in this calculation. Labor time, while not perfect in its role, was a good measure of value: "In making la-

[15] *Ibid.*, Vol. I, p. 12.
[16] *Ibid.*, Vol. VIII, pp. 276–277.

bour the foundation of the value of commodities and the comparative quantity of labour which is necessary to their production, the rule which determines the respective quantities of goods which shall be given in exchange for each other, we must not be supposed to deny the accidental and temporary deviations of the actual or market price of commodities from this, their primary and natural price."[17] He made himself even more explicit in writing to Malthus: "You say that my proposition 'that with few exceptions the quantity of labour employed on commodities determines the rate at which they will exchange for each other,' is not well founded. I acknowledge that it is not rigidly true, but I say that it is the nearest approximation to truth, as a rule for measuring relative value, of any I have heard."[18]

What validated labor as a measure was a combination of practicality and psychological soundness. Most of the time, commodities did really exchange in rough proportion to the labor expended in their fabrication. On the second score, labor had approximately the same meaning for each person: it was a pain. In an age when people work at their leisure and play at their work, the distinctions may be blurred. But, as Ricardo saw it, "it requires an exertion of some magnitude to apply one's body and mind to productive labour for ten or twelve hours of the day, but no exertion at all to consume what one has before been at the pains of producing. The one gives pain, the other pleasure."[19] But even though the pains of labor were equal for all who worked, the market distinguished between the pains of different people. Ricardo's dismissal of the problem fell short of its solution: "The estimation in which different qualities of labour are held, comes soon to be adjusted in the market with sufficient precision for all practical purposes, and depends much on the comparative skill of the labourer, and intensity of the labour performed. The scale, when once formed, is liable to little variation. If a day's labour of a working jeweller be more valuable than a

---

[17] *Ibid.*, Vol. I, p. 88.
[18] *Ibid.*, Vol. I, p. xl.
[19] *Ibid.*, Vol. II, p. 364.

day's labour of a common labourer, it has long ago been adjusted, and placed in its proper position in the scale of value."[20]

Intensity accorded well with pain measures. Presumably, more intense labor gave more pain to the worker. But what had "comparative skill" to do with pain? Moreover, in the last sentence Ricardo committed the sin of circular reasoning. Labor quantity should have explained the market phenomena. The latter were improperly employed in explanation, since they were the things to be explained.

The theory's qualifications did not end here. There was the troublesome case of capital. In the real world, goods were produced with different proportions of fixed capital (machines and structures), and circulating capital (wages). Even when these proportions were identical, the machines frequently differed in durability. When the first two conditions were identical, some goods might take longer to produce than others. As Ricardo came to see, all of these difficulties were associated with time.

He dealt with these issues rather awkwardly, in arithmetic illustrations. One of his examples went like this: Imagine a farmer who employs 100 men at £50 per man, per year. At the end of 12 months, assuming profits are 10 percent, he could sell the produce of the labor at £5500. Suppose that a manufacturer employed 100 men in the construction of machines, paying them the same wages as the farmer. At the end of the year the machines will be worth £5500. Imagine that in the second year the manufacturer employs 100 men *and* these machines. The 100 men must produce goods worth more than £5500, in order to pay the manufacturer a return on the capital locked up in his machines. The return he expects is £550. Therefore his goods must sell for £6050. Thus, although the employees of the farmer and of the manufacturer expended equal amounts of labor in the second year, the latter's goods fetched a higher total price, solely because the proportions of durable and circulating capital differed.

How important were these qualifications of the labor theory of

[20] *Ibid.*, Vol. I, pp. 20–21.

value? Ricardo's first chapter was sufficiently ambiguous to pro-
voke several interpretations. There was good warrant for the
opinion that Ricardo's theory amounted to a cost-of-production
explanation. Since rent (as will be indicated) formed no part of
price, labor and waiting, both painful, required compensation,
and formed the constituent elements of price. Shortly after the
publication of the *Principles*, Ricardo shocked his faithful follower McCulloch by saying, "after the best consideration that I
can give to the subject, I think that there are two causes which
occasion variation in the relative value of commodities—1 the relative quantity of labour required to produce them, 2dly the relative times that must elapse before the results of such labour can
be brought to market. All the questions of fixed capital come under the second rule."[21] Yet, at about the same time, he stoutly defended the proposition that quantity of labor was still the best
single measure of value. Our conclusion, necessarily tentative,
supports the second version. Although Ricardo was uneasy about
value, he clung to the labor-quantity explanation and deprecated
the importance of his own modifications.

DISTRIBUTION

In Ricardo's theory of distribution, rent held central place.
This position resulted from what has been termed Ricardo's double dichotomy. Taking the pie which was the national product, he
deducted the share removed as rent by landlords. He subtracted
from the remainder wages, explained by a separate theory, and
left, as a second residual, profits. The beginning of the skein of
explanation was rent.

"Rent," said Ricardo, "is that portion of the produce of the
earth, which is paid to the landlord for the use of the original and
indestructible powers of the soil."[23] Here was one of economics'
durable definitions. Implicit in it were the peculiar institutional
features of English agriculture. It was this unique system of land
tenure which made foreign economists reluctant to accept Ri-

---

[21] *Ibid.*, Vol. VIII, p. 180.
[23] *Ibid.*, Vol. I, p. 67.

cardian dicta. On the land there were three classes: the landlord who did no farming, but simply rented his land to a farmer, a member of the second class; the farmer, in turn, hired agricultural laborers, the third group. In Ricardo's drastic simplification of economic processes, the farmer was simply a capitalist who happened to employ his capital on the land instead of in a factory. In much the same way, the agricultural laborer was simply a member of the wage-earning poor who chose the employ of an agricultural rather than an industrial capitalist.

Invariably Ricardo spoke in these terms. And, although some landlords dabbled in farming, and many farmers labored in their rented fields, the land-tenure arrangements were close to Ricardo's assumptions. Less plausible was Ricardo's notion that agricultural capital like industrial capital was mobile: the rural capitalist like his industrial brother alertly shifted his resources to the most profitable places. Yet the proposition appeared self-evident to Ricardo:

Whilst every man is free to employ his capital where he pleases, he will naturally seek for it that employment which is most advantageous; he will naturally be dissatisfied with a profit of 10 per cent., if by removing his capital he can obtain a profit of 15 per cent. This restless desire on the part of the employers of stock, to quit a less profitable for a more advantageous business, has a strong tendency to equalize the rate of profits of all, or to fix them in such proportions, as may in the estimation of the parties, compensate for any advantage which one may have, or appear to have over the other.[24]

"This restless desire" was the central motive force of equilibrium adjustment.

How did rent arise? Rent was never part of price, yet landlords received sums of money which had to be called rent. Ricardo offered an explanation of the paradox: "It is only, then, because land is not unlimited in quantity and uniform in quality, and because in the progress of population, land of an inferior quality or less advantageously situated is called into cultivation, that rent is ever paid for the use of it."

[24] *Ibid.*, Vol. I, pp. 88–89.

Here was the mechanism:

When in the progress of society, land of the second degree of fertility is taken into cultivation, rent immediately commences on that of the first quality, and the amount of that rent will depend on the difference in the quality of these two portions of land.

When land of the third quality is taken into cultivation, rent immediately rises on the second, and is regulated as before, by the difference in their productive powers. At the same time, the rent of the first quality will rise. . . .[25]

Ricardo's conception was both simple and ingenious. Profits per dollar of investment and wages per hour of employment on the land, must be equal. The mobility of capital and the tendency of wages toward conventional subsistence minima insured such a result. Since land differed in natural fertility, equal quantities of capital and labor applied to more fertile land had to yield more produce than equivalent quantities applied to poorer land. The difference between the two yields was rent.

Rent evolved historically. When population was scant, not all even of the best land could be cultivated. Rent did not exist. As population increased, the remaining first-quality land will be cultivated, and land of the second quality will be tilled. The price of the crop will be determined by the cost of wages and profits on the second-grade land. Now, land of the first quality can and must pay rent, since capital and labor can earn their normal rewards and there will still be something left over. If population grows still more, third-quality land will be taken into employment. At that stage, land of the second quality begins to pay rent, and land of the first quality pays a higher rent.

It was unnecessary to assume that landlords allowed their land to be used free of charge. Farmers were always free to cultivate poor land within their boundaries, or to push cultivation more intensively on land already worked, until diminishing returns just enabled them to pay the usual rates of wages and profits for the additional cultivation. Or, as Ricardo put it, "I am myself fully

[25] *Ibid.*, Vol. I, p. 70.

persuaded that a large quantity of corn is raised in every country, for the privilege of raising which, no rent whatever is paid. Every farmer is at liberty to employ an additional portion of capital on his land after all that which is necessary for affording his rent, has already been employed. The corn raised with this capital, can only afford the usual profits if no rent is paid out of it."[26]

We can now summarize Ricardo's theory. The expenses of cultivation on the worst land used set the price of corn. The quality of the land employed was determined by the size of the population. Granted Malthusian premises, population was likely to increase, the quality of land taken into cultivation decline, and the share of rent in the national product increase. Agriculture was an industry in which diminishing returns were the rule in every civilized country. Such were the consequences of the Ricardian theory of rent.[27]

WAGES

The judgment has frequently been made that the Ricardian theory of wages was a subsistence theory which condemned the laborer to perpetual existence on the thin margin of destitution. If it can be allowed at all, this view requires substantial qualification. Occasionally, it is true, Ricardo seemed to say that wages tended to find their level at the minimum needs of the laborers: "Labour, like all other things which are purchased and sold, and which may be increased or diminished in quantity, has its natural and its market price. The natural price of labour is that price

---

[26] *Ibid.*, Vol. IV, p. 240.

[27] Questions of originality are difficult to settle. Ricardo himself generously granted priority to this differential theory of rent to Malthus and Edward West. As far as publication went, the year 1815 witnessed the birth of no fewer than four related versions of differential rent theory: Malthus' *Inquiry into Rent,* West's *Essay on the Application of Capital to Land,* Torrens' *Essay on the External Corn Trade,* and Ricardo's own *Essay on Profits.* Malthus' formulation of the law of diminishing returns was vague, West's was more precise but stated in monetary terms, Ricardo discussed yet a third variant, in physical terms. All stated the law in proportional rather than marginal language. Ricardo's letters to Malthus and Trower in 1813 and 1814 suggested that the theory was clear in his mind that early. Even dates of publication make his claim to originality the equal of his rivals'.

which is necessary to enable the labourers, one with another, to subsist and to perpetuate their race, without either increase or diminution."[28] But Ricardo's qualifications removed the theory's sting. Subsistence needs were interpreted as conventional rather than physiological:

. . . it is not to be understood that the natural price of labour, estimated even in food and necessaries, is absolutely fixed and constant. It varies at different times in the same country, and very materially differs in different countries. It essentially depends on the habits and customs of the people. An English labourer would consider his wages under their natural rate, and too scanty to support a family, if they enabled him to purchase no other food than potatoes, and to live in no better habitation than a mud cabin; yet these moderate demands of nature are often deemed sufficient in countries where "man's life is cheap," and his wants easily satisfied.[29]

This made all the difference. Moreover, Ricardo emphasized, deliberate action was capable of altering "habits and customs." Laborers' tastes can rise: "The friends of humanity cannot but wish that in all countries the labouring classes should have a taste for comforts and enjoyments, and that they should be stimulated by all legal means in their exertions to produce them. There cannot be a better security against a superabundant population."[30]

In the last sentence the Malthusian devil brandished his cloven hoof. A second major qualification of pure subsistence doctrine might hold him in check. Ricardo only occasionally believed in the possibility of rapid capital increase, but when he did so, he believed its effects to be those that Smith had identified: "Notwithstanding the tendency of wages to conform to their natural rate, their market rate may, in an improving society, for an indefinite period, be constantly above it; for no sooner may the impulse, which an increased capital gives to a new demand for labour be obeyed, than another increase of capital may produce the same effect; and thus, if the increase of capital be gradual and con-

[28] Ricardo, *op. cit.*, Vol. I, p. 93.
[29] *Ibid.*, Vol. I, p. 97.
[30] *Ibid.*, Vol. I, p. 100.

stant, the demand for labour may give a continued stimulus to an increase of people."[31] What mattered the natural rate, if the market rate remained persistently above it?

Analytically, Ricardo's theory was a simple set of propositions. Labor was a commodity, like other commodities. Its price reflected the forces of supply and demand. The demand for labor was capital, the wages fund. On Malthusian principles, the supply of labor was regulated by the number of people born who survived to working age. This number, in turn, depended upon the available subsistence. After a time lag, an increase in the second caused an increase in the first. Major qualifications reduced the theory's starkness.

How important did Ricardo consider these qualifications? There were times when Ricardo hoped that freedom would teach prudence: "Like all other contracts, wages should be left to the fair and free competition of the market, and should never be controlled by the interference of the legislature."[32] If freedom reigned, if the Poor Laws, which hampered liberty, were removed, we might hope for a good deal: "The clear and direct tendency of the poor laws . . . is not, as the legislature benevolently intended, to amend the condition of the poor, but to deteriorate the condition of both poor and rich." There was a remedy: ". . . the nature of the evil points out the remedy. By gradually contracting the sphere of the poor laws; by impressing on the poor the value of independence, by teaching them that they must look not to systematic or casual charity, but to their own exertions for support, that prudence and forethought are neither unnecessary nor unprofitable virtues, we shall by degrees approach a sounder and more healthful state."[33]

How effective could education, that sovereign remedy, be? Here there was deep pessimism in Ricardo's mind. The mass of the population, he feared, were swayed considerably more by emotion than by reason. The single substantial hope was for a

[31] *Ibid.*, Vol. I, pp. 94–95.
[32] *Ibid.*, Vol. I, p. 105.
[33] *Ibid.*, Vol. I, p. 107.

generation of high wages, produced by a fortunate relationship between capital and population. Twenty-five years of prosperity might so accustom workers to the comforts of life that they might behave prudently in order to preserve them. Not a strong hope in the end.

Quite possibly the future was much dimmer: ". . . both rent and wages will have a tendency to rise with the progress of wealth and population."[34] When population rose, worse land was cultivated and better land was cultivated more intensively. Each recourse yielded diminishing returns. Each raised the rent on land which already paid rent, and added new classes of rent-paying land. When corn prices rose, wages rose. Since Ricardo assumed a fixed money supply, a smaller share remained to be paid to the last and most useful class of all, the capitalists.

PROFITS

Profits must fall. As Ricardo unhappily put it: "The natural tendency of profits then is to fall; for, in the progress of society and wealth, the additional quantity of food required is obtained by the sacrifice of more and more labour." Was there any escape? Perhaps: "This tendency, this gravitation as it were of profits, is happily checked at repeated intervals by the improvements in machinery, connected with the production of necessaries, as well as by the discoveries in the science of agriculture which enable us to relinquish a portion of labour before required, and, therefore, to lower the price of the prime necessity of the labourer."[35]

At best, these were possibilities. The opposition between laborer and capitalist was a fact. The landlord's share passed inexorably to him. It increased with population. The other two classes fought over what was left. The conditions of conflict were stringent: the national product was invariant, and the money which facilitated its distribution was stable in quantity and velocity. Since the landlord's share rose, Ricardo's next proposition had the force of inevitability: "There can be no rise in the value of

[34] *Ibid.*, Vol. I, p. 102.
[35] *Ibid.*, Vol. I, p. 120.

labour without a fall of profits. If the corn is to be divided between the farmer and the labourer, the larger the proportion that is given to the latter, the less will remain for the former. So if cloth or cotton goods be divided between the workman and his employer, the larger the proportion given to the former, the less remains for the latter."[36] In this grim system, "in every case, agricultural, as well as manufacturing profits are lowered by a rise in the price of raw produce, if it be accompanied by a rise of wages."[37] Even though farmers ultimately pay no rent, the incidence falling on consumers, they have the same interest as other capitalists in preventing the rise of rents. For, when rents rise, wages rise for agricultural as for industrial laborers, and profits fall.

The fall of profits diminished the incentive to accumulation. When accumulation slowed, the wages fund shrank and the lot of the worker deteriorated. Nothing was further from Ricardo's mind than expropriation of the land. Nevertheless, it is easy to see how both Ricardian and Marxist socialists found this line of analysis an exceedingly useful starting point.

EVALUATION

What judgment can be rendered on these theories of value and distribution? One of Ricardo's severest critics conceded the explanatory force of his economics. The accents were grudging, but the concession was unmistakable: "If we could view Ricardo's system in a purely historical light, as an explanation of contemporary events, it would, in a general way, fit the facts as to the outstanding change in England during the half-century prior to the date of the book." The striking phenomenon that demanded interpretation, "was an increase of several fold in the prices of agricultural relative to manufactured products. And it would be correct to explain this, in the main, and speaking superficially, by the increase of 'labour' in manufactures through inventions, and its decrease in agriculture, in consequence of the pushing outward

---

[36] *Ibid.*, Vol. I, p. 35.
[37] *Ibid.*, Vol. I, p. 115.

of the margin of cultivation."[38] Despite Ricardo's infuriating abstractions, his world was the real world and the abstractions explained it, at least "superficially." In this respect, he resembled other great English economists. His economics superseded Smith's because they better explained the world of 1817. John Maynard Keynes's economics superseded his predecessors' because they better explained a world as confused as Ricardo's.

Ricardo's popularity and influence depended, then, mainly on his immediate applicability. There was another side to his achievement. Ricardo left a permanent mark on economics, a fact which has been deplored by Keynes and Schumpeter, and welcomed by Marshall. It was not that his economics were faultless. A most important flaw was the absence of integration between his value and distribution theories. Probably the principal technical achievement of economics up to Keynes was the demonstration that the prices of commodities and the prices of services—land, labor, and capital—were so closely interrelated that a single explanation sufficed. After the 1870's, economics became an increasingly refined mode of valuation, in which the marginal principle constituted a complete exposition of how economic resources were allocated and how individual wants set the process in motion.

Little of this appeared in Ricardo. The marginal principle was not his. His discussion of the law of diminishing returns confused proportional and marginal returns. There was no theory of consumer demand. Recognizing no alliance between value and distribution, he handled distribution as three separate problems, not as a single issue susceptible to a single resolution. What, then, was the "permanent mark," which he left on economics? It was the characteristic method of economic theory. This economic method examines one cause at a time and analyzes its effects upon a situation otherwise invariant. His strong cases still suggest the regular tactics of the economic theorist.

Keynes deplored the victory which Ricardo won over Malthus

[38] Frank Knight, "The Ricardian Theory of Production and Distribution," *Canadian Journal of Economics and Political Science*, May, 1935, p. 17.

on the existence of general gluts. In Malthus he descried a neglected forerunner. Although he was unable to clothe his insight with the weapons of analysis, Malthus did perceive that general unemployment was a possibility, and did guess its cause, a deficiency of spending. Keynes's complaint contained the irony that his own Ricardian methods produced Malthusian conclusions. Like Ricardo, he traced the impact of a single cause, sought to understand the economy as a mechanism, and identified movements to equilibrium. Theoretical brilliance, not empirical solidity, was as much Keynes's as Ricardo's, major strength. The forte of modern price theory is also logical power, accompanied by factual inadequacy.

FOREIGN TRADE

Ricardo's major contribution to the theory of foreign trade was the principle of comparative advantage, still a staple in modern theoretical discussion. Like Smith, Ricardo began his account with a generalized statement of absolute advantage (in later terminology): "It is quite as important to the happiness of mankind, that our enjoyments should be increased by the better distribution of labour, by each country producing those commodities for which by its situation, its climate, and its other natural or artificial advantages, it is adapted, and by their exchanging them for the commodities of other countries, as that they should be augmented by a rise in the rate of profits."[39] It is silly to grow bananas in Scotland, or rye in South America. As Ricardo put the matter here, foreign trade raised living standards in much the same way as an increase in the wages fund.

Ricardo's next step was epochal. Trade, he claimed, might take place to the advantage of *both* trading partners, even when one of the pair was more efficient in the production of *both* the commodities exchanged. Ricardo's demonstration is one of the enduring illustrations of the subject. It merits full quotation:

> The quantity of wine which she [Portugal] shall give in exchange for the cloth of England, is not determined by the respective quanti-

[39] Ricardo, *op. cit.*, Vol. I, p. 132.

ties of labour devoted to the production of each, as it would be, if both commodities were manufactured in England, or both in Portugal.

England may be so circumstanced, that to produce the cloth may require the labour of 100 men for one year; and if she attempted to make the wine, it might require the labour of 120 men for the same time. England therefore would find it to her interest to import wine and to purchase it by the exportation of cloth.

To produce the wine in Portugal, might require only the labour of 80 men for one year, and to produce the cloth in the same country, might require the labour of 90 men for the same time. It would therefore be advantageous for her to export wine in exchange for cloth. This exchange might even take place, notwithstanding that the commodity imported by Portugal could be produced there with less labour than in England. Though she could make the cloth with the labour of 90 men, she would import it from a country where it required the labour of 100 men to produce it, because it would be advantageous to her rather to employ her capital in the production of wine, for which she would obtain more cloth from England, than she could produce by diverting a portion of her capital from the cultivation of vines to the manufacture of cloth.

The exchange was advantageous for England also:

> Thus England would give the produce of the labour of 100 men for the produce of the labour of 80. Such an exchange could not take place between the individuals of the same country. The labour of 100 Englishmen cannot be given for that of 80 Englishmen, but the produce of the labour of 100 Englishmen may be given for the produce of the labour of 80 Portuguese, 60 Russians, or 120 East Indians. The difference in this respect, between a single country and many, is easily accounted for, by considering the difficulty with which capital moves from one country to another, to seek a more profitable employment. . . .[40]

With his typical indifference to factual plausibility, Ricardo assumed in the illustration that Portuguese efficiency exceeded English efficiency in both wine and cloth. The point was that the interests of both countries were best served by Portuguese spe-

[40] *Ibid.*, Vol. I, pp. 134–136.

cialization in wine and English concentration on cloth. The proof boiled down to the proposition that the total quantity of cloth and of wine enjoyed by the citizens of *each* country was larger in trade's presence than in its absence. When England exported to Portugal the cloth produced by the labor of 100 men, in exchange for the wine processed by 80 Portuguese, she imported what would have required the labor of 120 Englishmen to produce. As for Portugal, she gained by her 80 men's labor, cloth that it would have taken 90 of her laborers to complete. Both countries were better off.

The example and the principle convinced as far as they went. Several questions remained unanswered: how were the gains of foreign trade divided among the partners? How could the theory be expanded to cover several nations and several products? What was the role of money? Ricardo supplied an answer only to the last question: money was not very important: "The exportation of the specie may at all times be safely left to the discretion of individuals; it will not be exported more than any other commodity, unless its exportation should be advantageous to the country. If it be advantageous to export it, no laws can effectually prevent its exportation. Happily in this case, as well as in most others in commerce where there is free competition, the interests of the individual and that of the community are never at variance."[41] The "never" in the last sentence of the quotation said something, in its firm way, about the doctrinaire strength of Ricardo's convictions.

Two implicit assumptions dominated this theory. The first declared that the pure labor-quantity theory explained domestic value. The qualifications of the chapter on value did not reappear. The second alleged that commodities, produced by unequal quantities of labor, exchanged against each other in international trade solely because capital was immobile. The reasons for the immobility were irrational. Even at some cost to themselves, businessmen preferred to keep their capital at home. Thus even the most rational of Ricardo's social groups feared foreigners and valued the familiar.

[41] *Ibid.*, Vol. III, p. 56.

Ricardo drew large inferences from his theory. In a Parliamentary speech, in 1820, he declared that "this would be the happiest country in the world, and its progress in prosperity would be beyond the powers of imagination to conceive, if we got rid of two great evils—the national debt and the corn laws."[42] Although even Ricardo was willing to temper his extreme free-trade position in specific instances, these were few and temporary. On the subject of Corn Laws, he granted that "after the quantity of capital employed under the faith of legislative enactments in agriculture, it would be a great injustice to proceed to an immediate repeal of those laws."[43] After appropriate notice, Parliament was to do its duty. There was a rare endorsement of Smith's preference for defense over opulence: "It is, then the dangers of dependence on foreign supply for any considerable quantity of our food which can alone be opposed to the many advantages which, circumstanced as we are, would attend the importation of corn."[44] For the rest, tariffs were permissible only "whenever any peculiar tax falls on the produce of any one commodity, from the effects of which all other producers are exempted."[45] Ricardo's free-trade position was a great deal firmer than Smith's. Ricardo's confidence in the self-adjusting specie flow mechanism reinforced his faith in free trade.

TAXES

Although many pages of the *Principles* analyzed taxes and their incidence, Ricardo's position permits easy summary. Taxation was unequivocally a burden. Not a hint of compensating benefits from government expenditure mitigated the judgment. Therefore taxes should be so levied as "to press on all equally, so as to interfere as little as possible with the natural equilibrium that would have prevailed if no disturbance whatever had been given."[46] At all costs, taxes should avoid penalizing capital. When

[42] *Ibid.*, Vol. V, p. 55.
[43] *Ibid.*, Vol. V, p. 34.
[44] *Ibid.*, Vol. IV, p. 27.
[45] *Ibid.*, Vol. IV, p. 243.
[46] *Ibid.*, Vol. VIII, p. 101.

wages were at subsistence or near that level, direct taxes either on wages or on the products laborers bought had to be shifted. There was only one place to which they could be shifted: profits. But when profits shrank, the motive for accumulation weakened and the size of the wages fund diminished. As Ricardo put it, "it is only because taxation interferes with the accumulation of capital, and diminishes the demand for labour, that it is injurious to the working classes. Sometimes it only retards the rate of accumulation, at other times it arrests it altogether, and on some occasions the taxes by being supplied at the expence of capital itself actually diminish the means of the country to employ the same quantity of labour as before."[47]

MACHINERY

Ricardo's evaluation of the effects of machinery are interesting in themselves and also as an example of their author's persistent honesty of intellectual opinion. Ricardo's original view of machinery's impact was unequivocally favorable. By promoting the division of labor, machines increased per capita output and moderated the effects of diminishing returns from the land. Moreover, machines increased profits, the size of the wages fund, and the wages of labor. Machinery was an almost unqualified boon. The "almost" had to be added because, even in his first edition of the *Principles*, Ricardo admitted that an industrial nation was liable to more severe *temporary* fluctuations than an agricultural nation. His reasoning identified the possible frictional dislocations: "A great manufacturing country is peculiarly exposed to temporary reverses and contingencies, produced by the removal of capital from one employment to another." Why? "The demand for any particular manufactured commodity is subject not only to the want, but to the tastes and caprices of the purchasers." Always, too, there were wars and taxes: "A new tax . . . may destroy the comparative advantage which a country before possessed in the manufacture of a particular commodity; or the effects of war may so raise the freight and insurance on its con-

[47] *Ibid.*, Vol. VIII, pp. 168–169.

veyance, that it can no longer enter into competition with the home manufacture of the country to which it was before exported." The effects might be serious: "In all such cases, considerable distress and no doubt some loss, will be experienced by those who are engaged in the manufacture of such commodities; and it will be felt not only at the time of the change, but through the whole interval during which they are removing their capitals, and the labour which they command, from one employment to another."[48]

In the same year as Ricardo's first edition of the *Principles*, John Barton wrote a pamphlet called the *Condition of the Labouring Classes of Society*, in which he questioned, even in normal times, the favorable effect of new machinery. The nub of his argument was an arithmetic demonstration that the capitalist's profit depended only in some cases on the number of laborers he employed. In many instances the capitalist might do better to employ fewer laborers and more machines. Ricardo read and believed. With the appalling logic which dumfounded his supporters, he reversed his position. As Ricardo came to see the problem in his third edition, the key distinction was between the net revenue which comprised the profit of the employer and the gross revenue which provided the funds to employ labor. He concluded that "an increase of the net produce of a country is compatible with a diminution of the gross produce, and that the motives for employing machinery are always sufficient to insure its employment, if it will increase the net produce, although it may, and frequently must, diminish both the quantity of the gross produce, and its value." Workers were right, after all, to distrust machinery, for "the opinion entertained by the labouring class, that the employment of machinery is frequently detrimental to their interests, is not founded on prejudice and error, but is conformable to the correct principles of political economy." However, there was this consolation: ". . . if the improved means of production, in consequence of the use of machinery, should increase the net produce of a country in a degree so great as not to

[48] *Ibid.*, Vol. I, p. 263.

diminish the gross produce . . . then the situation of all classes will be improved."[49] One of his letters to McCulloch, the most shocked of his followers, even contemplated a fall in total output: "The whole change of my opinion is simply this, I formerly thought that machinery enabled a country to add annually to the gross produce of its commodities, and I now think the use of it rather tends to the diminution of the gross produce."[50]

Ricardo was a dangerous man: he followed his own logic wherever it led. This relentless logic led him, in a Parliamentary speech, made in 1819, to propose, great capitalist that he was, a capital levy. The report of his speech revealed his usual decorous utterance:

He would, however, be satisfied to make a sacrifice, the sacrifice would be a temporary one, and with that view he would be willing to give up as large a share of his property as any other individual. By such means ought the evil of the national debt to be met. It was an evil which almost any sacrifice would not be too great to get rid of. It destroyed the equilibrium of prices, occasioned many persons to emigrate to other countries, in order to avoid the burthen of taxation which it entailed, and hung like a millstone round the exertion and industry of the country."[51]

None of his fellow capitalists rushed to the banner of the capital levy.

RICARDIAN SOCIALISTS

Great ideas lead to unexpected consequences. Mill and the Ricardians, the subject of the next chapter, were expected results, but the Ricardian Socialists and, still more, the Marxists, were surely not dreamed of by Ricardo. As a postscript to this chapter, we shall glance at the first group. It is hard to distinguish the Ricardian Socialists—William Thompson, John Gray, Thomas Hodgskin, John Francis Bray, and Charles Hall—from the Owenite school of Utopians. Like them, these Ricardian Social-

---

[49] *Ibid.*, Vol. I, pp. 391–392.
[50] *Ibid.*, Vol. VIII, p. 387.
[51] *Ibid.*, Vol. V, p. 21.

ists built model communities on coöperative principles. Like them also, they exaggerated human goodness and human rationality. However, to this Utopian element they added a faith in scientific economics and scientific psychology which set them off from the Utopians. The economic faith was Ricardian and their psychological trust was in Bentham's felicific calculus. Thus their efforts at reform were founded squarely on the best moral science of the time.

The school's leading representative was William Thompson, who was probably born in 1783 and died in 1833. Little is known of Thompson. He was an Irishman who derived an adequate income from rent. His health seems to have been poor and, whether as cause or effect, he was a vegetarian for two decades. His two major works, *An Inquiry into the Principles of the Distribution of Wealth* (1824), and *Labour Rewarded* (1827), attracted little attention. However, he was known to Bentham, who entertained him for some months, and John Stuart Mill, who recorded a three months' debate with Thompson, then associated with the Owenites.

Although it cannot be accurately said that his two important books were free of contradictions, his argument is worth repetition. He started by distinguishing himself from other economists. These economists were interested in the production of wealth. He, on the contrary, cared only about distribution, because of its impact upon human happiness. Coming to the first of his major claims, he attacked the concept of economic man. Man was far too complex to be categorized as a simple seeker of gain. Self-interest, at least in its narrow economic version, left too much out. Almost in the same breath, however, he tried to use Bentham's calculus to estimate individual susceptibility to pleasure and pain. He concluded that "all members of society (cases of malformation aside) being similarly constituted in their physical organization, are capable by similar treatment, of enjoying equal portions of happiness."[52] Then he demonstrated that it was really impossible to measure differing degrees of susceptibility, a point

[52] Quoted by Esther Lowenthal, *The Ricardian Socialists*, Columbia, 1911, p 21.

at which his conclusion paralleled Bentham's. However, he then affirmed that, *since* degrees of human susceptibility could not be measured, human beings must possess equal degrees of sensitivity, a conclusion which conspicuously did not follow from the premises.

Consistency suggested that Thompson should then have embraced a system of complete equality. That he did not do so immediately was the consequence of his concern for productivity. In his words, "the important problem to be solved is how to reconcile equality with security; how to reconcile just distribution with continued production."[53] This question was so important that Thompson devoted most of the book's remainder to examining the relationship of these objectives in different systems. The major systems included were the present method of "constraint by mingled force and fraud"; the system of "security," in which "each is to have his own through the recognition to the whole produce of labor"; and the system of equality, in whose favor Thompson enlisted Bentham.

The leading feature of the present system was inequality. As one member of the school put it, "All wealth is the product of labor. All men are equal or nearly so, and therefore capable of producing equal quantities of wealth. Wealth is unequally divided, therefore the few possessors must abstract it from the many producers."[54]

There were four other major counts against the present system. First, the "forced abstraction of the product of labour from any individual will cause more loss of happiness to him than any increase of happiness to the person acquiring."[55] Like Bentham, Thompson recognized the diminishing marginal utility of money. Second, since the worker was allowed to keep so little of the product of his labor, he had little motive to work. The system was extremely unproductive. Third, current arrangements promoted undue concentration of economic power. Finally, the

[53] *Ibid.*, p. 23.
[54] *Ibid.*, pp. 23–24.
[55] *Ibid.*, p. 24.

maldistribution of wealth gave rise to hosts of unproductive laborers, the menial servants of the rich.

The system of equality was a considerable improvement on existing arrangements. Three principles guided it. The first declared, "all labor ought to be free and *voluntary*, as to its direction and continuance." The laborer should get what he produces: "All products of labor ought to be secured to the producers of them." There was a final principle: "All exchanges of these products ought to be free and *voluntary*."[56] The system strongly promoted production. Did it do as well by equality? Here Thompson wavered. On the one side, he claimed, "so far from being irreconcilable with each other, it is only by an undeviating adherence to real security that any approach can be made to equality."[57] On the other, he admitted that "as far as concerns labour by individual competition . . . security is not reconcilable with equality of distribution."[58]

Two other major flaws vitiated the system of equality. First, it was impossible accurately to measure the individual contribution of the worker. So much Thompson admitted. Second, he had grave reservations about the value of competition. Competition had four major disadvantages, at least: its emphasis on selfishness, its misdirection of effort because of individual ignorance, its failure to provide for sickness and old age; and the despotism of property ownership.

Therefore, in the end, Thompson plumped for Owen's system of equality, if it were voluntarily introduced: "Though labor might be secured in the *right* to the whole product of its exertions, it does not follow that labor might not, in order to insure a vast increase of production and enjoyment to everyone, as well as mutual insurance against all casualties, *voluntarily agree before production* to equality of remuneration."[59] In this community, "supply and demand, population and other contested

[56] *Ibid.*, p. 26.
[57] *Ibid.*, p. 97.
[58] *Ibid.*, p. 150.
[59] *Ibid.*, p. 37.

questions of morals, legislation and political economy will be reduced to fixed data."[60]

Thompson's faith in Ricardo was direct. If labor truly was the source of all value, then laborers deserved their full product. At points Thompson argued that interest, profits, and rent were all deductions from labor's reward. Sometimes, he recognized labor's need for capital. He did not, like Hodgskin, suggest a way of reducing capital to labor. When, in *Labour Rewarded*, he came actually to consider wages in more detail, he concluded that "a variety of accidents and chances comprised in the phrases 'proportion of supply to demand' "[61] explained wages. Of these accidents, knowledge, political power, and the habits of the workers were most important.

For Thompson, the way of reform was not Ricardian. He saw little gain in population limitation and displayed little enthusiasm for Corn Law repeal. He regarded the latter as a capitalist agitation designed to reduce wages. So long as membership was voluntary, he approved of trade unions as efforts to restrict the evils of competition, but he considered their scope limited. Capital could shift out of unionized industries and new labor could shift into them. He advocated popular education, the emancipation of women, and a variety of other liberal measures, all within the frame of his wish for more radical social change.

---

[60] *Ibid.*, p. 28.
[61] *Ibid.*, p. 33.

Chapter 8

John Stuart Mill

It appears to the present writer that a work similar in its object and general conception to that of Adam Smith, but adapted to the more extended knowledge and improved ideas of the present age, is the kind of contribution which Political Economy at present requires.

John Stuart Mill

INTRODUCTION

Logician, reformer, journalist, and Ricardian economist, Mill was liberalism's greatest nineteenth-century figure, in Gladstone's phrase, the "saint of rationalism." He was open to the major intellects of his day: inevitably, his father, Bentham, and Ricardo, but also Coleridge, Saint-Simon, Comte, and Carlyle. Although his nineteenth-century reputation depended only slightly upon his fame as an economist, his *Principles of Political Economy*, published in 1848, was one of the most influential texts of any time. As late as 1919 it was still being used at Oxford.[1]

The book, as analytical economics, was not original. Anyone familiar with Mill's predecessors could read Mill with familiar feelings. Mill started by reiterating competition's central importance, in these words:

. . . only through the principle of competition has political economy any pretension to the character of a science. So far as rents,

[1] Mainly, no doubt, because the superior alternative, Marshall's *Principles*, had been written by a Cambridge man.

profits, wages, prices, are determined by competition, laws may be assigned for them. Assume competition to be their exclusive regulator, and principles of broad generality and scientific precision may be laid down. The political economist justly deems this his proper business: and as an abstract or hypothetical science, political economy cannot be required to do, and indeed cannot do anything more.[2]

This was Ricardo rendered articulate. It also came perilously close to saying that economic life had better be competitive for the sweet sake of economic theory, which otherwise would be destitute of ruling principle.

A second legacy which Mill cherished was the law of diminishing returns. He could scarcely have emphasized it more strongly: "After a certain, and not very advanced, stage in the progress of agriculture, it is the law of production from the land, that in any given state of agricultural skill and knowledge, by increasing the labour, the produce is not increased in an equal degree; doubling the labour does not double the produce; or, to express the same thing in other words, every increase of produce is obtained by a more than proportional increase in the application of labour to the land." Nothing economic was more important: "This general law of agricultural industry is the most important proposition in political economy. Were the law different, nearly all the phenomena of the production and distribution of wealth would be other than they are."[3] This presentation, incidentally, confused the short run, in which techniques and resources were fixed, with a long run in which all elements of the productive process varied.

What rule applied to manufacturing? Here, the law of diminishing returns battled "mechanical improvements" and "contrivances for saving labour." The outcome was cheerful: ". . . in manufactures, accordingly, the causes tending to increase the productiveness of industry preponderate greatly over the one

[2] John Stuart Mill, *Principles of Political Economy*, ed. by W. J. Ashley, Longmans, Green, 1909, p. 242.
[3] *Ibid.*, p. 177.

cause which tends to diminish it."[4] Even in agriculture, technology modified, though it could not reverse, the law. In both cases, Mill was more optimistic than Ricardo had been.

He could not escape from another classical doctrine. Cheerful about technological advances as, in one sense, he was, he remained a Malthusian. The truth was too plain to waste much time discussing it: "On this subject, the discussions excited by the *Essay* of Mr. Malthus have made the truth, though by no means universally admitted, yet so fully known, that a briefer examination of the question than would otherwise have been necessary will probably on the present occasion suffice."[5] He handled one of the frequent anti-Malthusian arguments sharply: "It is in vain to say, that all mouths which the increase of mankind calls into existence, bring with them hands. The new mouths require as much food as the old ones, and the hands do not produce as much."[6]

However, he could interpret Malthus more cheerfully than Malthus had chosen to interpret himself. In his *Autobiography*, he described how he and his group converted Malthusianism into progressive doctrine: "Malthus's population principle was quite as much a banner, and a point of union among us, as any opinion specially belonging to Bentham. This great doctrine originally brought forward as an argument against the indefinite improvability of human affairs, we took up with ardent zeal in the contrary sense as indicating the sole means of realizing that improvability by securing full employment at high wages to the whole labouring population through a voluntary restriction of their numbers."[7]

For the long run at least, Mill also accepted Say's law. Say, it will be recalled, had argued that no possibility of general glut could exist because supply created its own demand. He granted that a single commodity might temporarily be in oversupply. Mill came to add the possibility of short-run fluctuations, akin to

---

[4] *Ibid.*, pp. 185–186.
[5] *Ibid.*, p. 156.
[6] *Ibid.*, p. 191.
[7] John Stuart Mill, *Autobiography*, Oxford, 1924, pp. 88–89.

business cycles. But, he agreed, there was no chance of general overproduction. If people did not spend all of their incomes upon themselves, what could they do with them, except "invest them productively; that is, expend them on employing labour."[8]

As will be seen later, these general principles led to a conventional analysis of value, rent, wages, and profits. Mill's single point of originality was his distinction between the laws of production and the laws of distribution. This distinction, designed to give economic policy more leeway, Mill put in this way:

The laws and conditions of the Production of Wealth partake of the character of physical truths. There is nothing optional or arbitrary in them. . . . Whether they like it or not, their production will be limited by the amount of their previous accumulation. . . . Whether they like it or not, a double quantity of labour, will not raise, on the same land, a double quantity of food. . . . Whether they like it or not, the unproductive expenditure of individuals will *pro tanto* tend to impoverish the community, and only their productive expenditures will enrich it.

With distribution it was otherwise: "It is not so with the Distribution of Wealth. That is a matter of human institution solely. The things once there, mankind, individually or collectively, can do with them as they like."[9]

Mill fulfilled his desire to take account of the "more extended knowledge and improved ideas of the present age," by drawing heavily upon contemporary economic literature. In contrast to Ricardo, Mill had read widely. In his long and rather tiresome discussion of Russian, Prussian, English, and Austrian systems of land tenure, he cited Richard Jones, then an economist of comparatively minor reputation, who has come to be regarded as a precursor of historical economics. On peasant proprietorship in Switzerland, North America, and elsewhere, his authority was Sismondi, a pioneer student of industrial fluctuations. He quoted, approvingly, Tooke on the perils of inflation. He refuted Attwood, a leading member of the inflationist Birmingham cur-

---

[8] Mill, *Principles*, p. 560.
[9] *Ibid.*, pp. 199–200.

rency school. Mill relied upon Babbage on division of labor, and Wakefield on colonization and the relative advantages of large and small landholdings. On capital accumulation, he employed John Rae's *New Principles of Political Economy*. Although the major influences remained Malthus, Smith, and Ricardo, the book gave abundant evidence of Mill's endeavor to keep up with the times. The effort extended to a sympathetic, though ultimately disapproving, association with socialism.

MILL'S LIFE

In these enlightened days, experts advise parents either to leave their children's personalities alone or, at most, to guide them with tactful discretion. When his son was born in 1806, James Mill took a decidedly different attitude. He decided to treat him to a Benthamite education. Its principles were charmingly simple: one exposed the child to good associations and protected him from bad associations. Since no association was better than James Mill's, the father took his gifted child's training into his own hands.

What hands they were. The tot began Greek at 3, and Latin at 8. When he was 12, his father started him on logic, philosophy, and political economy. During this period, no holiday interrupted the rhythm of his work; no children, except his brothers and sisters whose tuition was largely in his hands, diminished his concentration, and no light reading was permitted.[10] In view of his father's opinions upon religion, neither the blessings nor the rigors of spiritual consolation varied the boy's life.

Brought up in the company of adults, the child was naturally solemn, prematurely old, and disposed to express his opinions like the responsible intellectual he had become. However, he had no notion of his intellectual superiority until he was 14. Just before he left for a French visit, his father and he had a heart-to-

[10] Michael St. John Packe's excellent *Life of Stuart Mill*, Macmillan, 1954, spent some space arguing that John Stuart Mill overstated the case against his father. Even modified by Packe, the regimen was severe enough to evoke retrospective shudders.

heart talk. In a scene at once touching and comic, James Mill warned him that he might find that he knew things his contemporaries did not know. But, continued the unfond parent, he had no reason for pride. It was all the result of having a father who was capable of teaching according to Benthamite principles. Any other child, raised in the same way, could do as well. This opinion John Stuart Mill held through life. He believed that his father had given him a generation's head start over his contemporaries.

It is sad to mention what excited the boy when he was 16. He had been reading Bentham's *Treatise on Legislation* in Dumont's French translation. Here was how it impressed him:

When I laid down the last volume of the *Traité*, I had become a different being. The "principle of utility" understood as Bentham understood it, and applied in the manner in which he applied it through these three volumes, fell exactly into its place as the keystone which held together the detached and fragmentary component parts of my knowledge and beliefs. It gave unity to my conceptions of things. I now had opinions; a creed, a doctrine, a philosophy; in one among the best senses of the word, a religion; the inculcation and diffusion of which could be made the principal outward purpose of a life. And I had a grand conception laid before me of changes to be effected in the condition of mankind through that doctrine.[11]

His father had done his work well. Boys of 16 are still prone to enthusiasm, but not very often, one guesses, over three-volume expositions of the principle of utility.

What could this precocious but complete Benthamite do as he approached manhood, except spread the gospel according to his masters, his father and Jeremy Bentham. His financial needs were met by a position in the East India Company, where his father had preceded him after publication of the successful *History of British India*. In the winter of 1822–1823, he founded the Utilitarian Society. Its members, choice spirits all, were young men dedicated to Benthamism. They read papers to each other, debated with other groups, and studied worthy books intensively.

[11] Mill, *Autobiography*, p. 56.

Less than a year afterwards, the Philosophical Radicals founded the *Westminster Review*. Its leading spirit was James Mill, and his son soon began to contribute articles and reviews. Between 1825 and 1830, Mill and his friends debated vigorously with Owenites, Coleridgians, and Thompsonites. Thus he extended his acquaintance to Utopian Socialists, Romantics, and Ricardian Socialists.

In the middle of all this activity occurred what Mill called a crisis in his mental history: the machine rebelled and broke down. His description of his condition is still poignant: "I was in a dull state of nerves, such as everybody is occasionally liable to; unsusceptible to enjoyment or pleasurable excitement; one of those moods when what is pleasure at other times, becomes insipid or indifferent; the state, I should think, in which converts to Methodism usually are, when smitten by their first 'conviction of sin.'" In this mood, he thought of a horrifying possibility: ". . . it occurred to me to put the question directly to myself: 'Suppose that all your objects in life were realized; that all the changes in institutions and opinions which you are looking forward to, could be completely effected at this very instant: would this be a great joy and happiness to you?'" Imagine the effect of a negative answer: ". . . an irrepressible self-consciousness distinctly answered 'No!' At this my heart sank within me: the whole foundation on which my life was constructed fell down. All my happiness was to have been found in the continued pursuit of this end. The end had ceased to charm, and how could there ever again be any interest in the means? I seemed to have nothing to live for."[12]

Ultimately he recovered, assisted by his discovery of Wordsworth, whom he thought ideally suited to unpoetic natures. The experience taught him two lessons: the best way to achieve happiness was not to aim at it directly; and, he must belatedly remedy a major deficiency of his education, he must cultivate his feelings. Obviously, they were capable of disturbing him.

From this crisis dated his wistful flirtation with modes of

[12] *Ibid.,* p. 113.

thought and feeling, alien to everything that he had been taught. He borrowed from, as well as argued with, Coleridge and his followers, Maurice and Sterling. He met Carlyle, listened to him sympathetically, and deluded that dour prophet into the belief that Mill was one of his disciples. For several summers, Carlyle, persuaded that Mill was really a mystic, endeavored to persuade Mill to visit him in his remote Scottish fastness, Craigenputtock. Mill always refused, and Carlyle finally decided that he was poor human material. Mill found much to admire in the Saint-Simonians, whose tone was more rational and whose questioning of the justice of hereditary property he approved. For a time, Saint-Simon's great pupil Auguste Comte impressed him. In Comte's philosophy of history as a series of stages, theological, metaphysical, and positive, he found a key to social understanding. It did not fit very long. Somehow, Mill became nobody's disciple. Struggle as he might, his father was too strong. A Benthamite he remained.

The great emotional event of his life was his long friendship and eventual marriage to Harriet Taylor. When Mill met her in 1830, she was the wife of a prosperous businessman and the mother of several small children. Nevertheless, love rapidly ripened and during the next two decades the two occasionally traveled together on the Continent and spent holidays in the English countryside. It was one of the unconventional relationships of which the highly conventional Victorians were capable. When Mr. Taylor died in 1851, his widow and Mill became man and wife.

Reputed a beauty, Harriet Taylor was surely a formidable bluestocking. Mill credited her with enormous influence upon him. He claimed that the *Essay on Liberty*, his most eloquent piece of writing, was as much hers as his. Her inspiration and persuasion led him to soften his attitude toward socialism in the successive editions of the *Principles*. The extravagant epitaph which Mill composed after Harriet's death in 1858, testified to the warmth of his adoration:

As Earnest for the Public Good
As She Was Generous and Devoted
To All Who Surrounded Her
Her Influence Has Been Felt
In Many of the Greatest
Improvements of the Age
And Will Be in Those Still to Come
Were There but a Few Hearts and Intellects
Like Hers
The Earth Would Already Become
The Hoped-For Heaven[13]

Friends considered Mill's feelings excessive. They found her neither so beautiful nor so intelligent as her husband did.

The rest of Mill's life was devoted to the liberal causes of his time. During the Civil War, his was a powerful voice for the North, against the prevailing pro-Southern sympathies of the respectable. In Parliament, where he served two terms during the 1860's, his record was consistent. He favored extension of male suffrage and the vote for women. He attacked the government's repressive Irish policy. He led the public agitation against Governor Eyre of Jamaica, who repressed disorder in his colony by shooting and flogging, with abandon, guilty and innocent alike. One incident in his electoral campaign suggested the man's quality. Here was a proof of his claim that honesty helped his campaign.

In the pamphlet "Thoughts on Parliamentary Reform," I had said, rather bluntly that the working classes, though differing from those of some other countries, in being ashamed of lying, are yet generally liars. This passage some opponent got printed in a placard, which was handed to me at a meeting, chiefly composed of the working classes, and I was asked whether I had written and published it. I at once answered "I did." Scarcely were these two words out of my mouth, when vehement applause resounded through the whole meeting.[14]

[13] Packe, *op. cit.*, p. 408.
[14] Mill, *Autobiography*, pp. 240–241.

It is possible, barely, to imagine the like at a modern political meeting.

THE *PRINCIPLES*

VALUE

Mill's discussion of value started with one of the most-quoted statements of the nineteenth-century: "Happily, there is nothing in the laws of value which remains (1848) for the present or any future writer to clear up; the theory of the subject is complete."[15] In the light of the work of the 1870's, Mill could scarcely have been more wrong. Starting with this opinion, Mill thought his task was restatement of Ricardian value theory in simpler, clearer, and ampler terms. Like Ricardo, he distinguished between value in use and value in exchange, discarding the first and concentrating upon the second. Like Ricardo, once more, Mill stated that "the value of commodities . . . depends principally (we shall presently see whether it depends solely) on the quantity of labour required for their production."[16] But where Ricardo had been logical, though abstruse, Mill, in his efforts to clarify the theory, actually substituted something different for it. He added: ". . . wages do enter into value."[17] Moreover, "profits . . . as well as wages enter into the cost of production which determines the value of the produce."[18] Mill left his readers with a cost-of-production theory, parallel to the labor-quantity theory and quite different from it. Wages and profits were monetary measures, the quantity of labor was a physical amount. Even if he had not lumped disparates together, he, in common with Ricardo, had given quite different explanations of wages and profits.

Otherwise the theory was safely Ricardian. Items fixed in quantity—rare wines and old masters—depended on supply and demand, not cost of production. He maintained that "the intro-

[15] Mill, *Principles*, p. 436.
[16] *Ibid.*, pp. 457–458.
[17] *Ibid.*, p. 461.
[18] *Ibid.*, p. 461.

duction of money does not interfere with the operation of any of the Laws of Value."[19] Money itself had a value, determined like that of other commodities, by its cost of production.

DISTRIBUTION

Mill faithfully reproduced the disjointed treatment of rent, profits, and wages, so noticeable in Smith and Ricardo. There were still three separate explanations of the major elements of income, these were still imperfectly coördinated, and their relation to value was tangential.

On rent, Mill was a pure Ricardian. Rent was differential: "Rent . . . is the difference between the unequal returns of different parts of the capital employed on the soil."[20] Rent had no effect on price: "Rent . . . forms no part of the cost of production which determines the value of agricultural produce."[21] Finally, rent was less important than the other income shares: "Wages and profits represent the universal elements in production, while rent may be taken to represent the differential and peculiar."[22]

Mill explained wages by extending the wages-fund doctrine. "Wages depend, then, on the proportion between the number of the labouring population, and the capital or other funds devoted to the purchase of labour; we will say for shortness, the capital."[23] Given this generalization, it followed that "it is impossible that population should increase at its utmost rate without lowering wages."[24] Plainly, if workers wanted high wages, they had to behave prudently. Prudence demanded of them limitation of their numbers. Mill devoted many pages to proving that no other remedy for low wages could be effective. Education was essential to enable workers to understand their situation: "An effective national education of the children of the labour-

[19] *Ibid.*, p. 488.
[20] *Ibid.*, p. 472.
[21] *Ibid.*, p. 472.
[22] *Ibid.*, p. 477.
[23] *Ibid.*, p. 349.
[24] *Ibid.*, p. 251.

ing class, is the first thing needful."[25] Coincident with education, relief of poverty for a generation would give society a breathing spell. Colonization and aid to a new class of small proprietors might diminish poverty.

The size of the capital available was the second determinant of the general wage level. Simple arithmetic proved that the larger the wages fund, granted a stable number of workers, the higher the wage level. Thrift was the key. The less that potential savers spent on luxuries and servants, the more would be available for the employment of productive labor. Probably because he wished to emphasize the importance of the wages fund, Mill retained the untidy distinction between productive consumption and unproductive consumption, and between productive labor and unproductive labor, which had deceived Smith into some odd statements. Mill's view was narrow: "By unproductive labour, will be understood labour which does not terminate in the creation of material wealth."[26]

Although Mill later recanted of the wages-fund doctrine which encountered mounting criticism, all editions of the *Principles* during his lifetime explained wages primarily by recourse to the wages-fund doctrine. In Mill's opinion, the doctrine implied no reason for pessimism. He apparently considered that adherence to it, after he was convinced of its inaccuracy, did no damage to his analysis.

When it came to profits, Mill borrowed an explanation from Nassau Senior. Senior had maintained that the justification for profit was analytically the same as the justification for wages. In both cases pains suffered justified incomes received. The pain suffered by the saver was abstinence, postponement of the pleasures of consumption. The sufferings of workers *and* capitalists determined the value of a commodity. To call profits the rewards for the abstinence even of the wealthy, might have seemed a little strong. However, even more than Ricardo, Mill was haunted by the fear that profits tended to fall as civilization ad-

25 *Ibid.*, p. 380.
26 *Ibid.*, p. 49.

vanced. In fact, profits would be at their minimum now, were it not for a series of new outlets for capital. Mill's fears explained passages of this kind: "When a country has long possessed a large production, and a large net income to make savings from, and when, therefore, the means have long existed of making a great annual addition to capital . . . the rate of profit is habitually . . . within a hand's breadth of the minimum, and the country therefore on the very verge of the stationary state. . . . The expansion of capital would soon reach its ultimate boundary, if the boundary itself did not continually open and leave more space."[27] In the short run, profits and wages varied inversely.

TECHNICAL NOVELTIES: BUSINESS CYCLES, FOREIGN TRADE

The portion of Mill's economics so far described did not rise above the level of his predecessors. In two fields, Mill did make technical advances: international trade and business cycles. Among respectable economists, business cycles were not a fashionable subject. Ricardo had spoken briefly of "sudden interruptions in the channels of trade" and had said little more about the subject. Mill was able to reconcile adherence to Say's Law with an interest in fluctuations by regarding the latter as the basic explanation of long-run full employment, while admitting fluctuations in employment and income in the short-run.

As a business-cycle analyst, Mill was astonishingly modern in his approach. For one thing, he applied labels to the phases of the cycle. He identified only three: the speculative state, commercial revulsion, and the quiescent state. The first was the period of expansion, the second approximated the upper turning point, and the third the period of contraction. Although he neglected a crucial part of cycle theory, the lower turning point, his analysis of what happened in a business cycle was remarkably close to some current theories. Somewhat in the manner of Hawtrey,[28] Mill emphasized the importance of inventory specu-

[27] *Ibid.*, p. 731.
[28] See pp. 358–360.

lation in the expansion phase. In addition, he discussed errors of optimism and pessimism in a way which anticipated some aspects of A. C. Pigou and J. M. Keynes. Almost alone in this period, Mill centered attention upon the role of fixed capital.

In his attitude toward business-cycle policy, Mill was less modern. He reposed no trust in monetary measures and his interest in preventing inflation exceeded his concern over unemployment. On general grounds, he opposed government intervention into economic affairs.[29]

Mill's contribution to the theory of international trade was a major extension of Ricardian theory. Ricardo had left unanswered an important question: how were the benefits of international trade divided among the trading nations? What was the mechanism which distributed the gains? Mill's answer ran in two-country terms and depended upon drastically simplified assumptions, a state of affairs not very different today. If Germany and England were the two countries in question, and they traded in only two commodities, cloth and linen; if, in addition, output in each country proceeded at constant real cost; and if, finally, in England, 10 yards of cloth cost as much to produce as 15 yards of linen and, in Germany, 10 yards of cloth cost as much to produce as 20 yards of linen, then the principle of comparative advantage made it certain that England would import linen and export cloth.

However, the real prices at which the transactions took place determined the distribution of benefit. Mill began by setting out the limits of these prices. Exchange would take place, if, at one limit, 10 yards of cloth exchanged for 15 yards of linen, and, if, at the other limit, 10 yards of cloth exchanged for 20 yards of linen. Suppose, said Mill, that actual exchange was 10 yards of cloth for 17 yards of linen. What might produce such a result was the relative strength of the demand for cloth and linen in the two countries.

A change in any of the conditions of the problem altered its

---

[29] This discussion has depended quite heavily on R. G. Link, *English Theories of Economic Fluctuations*, Columbia, 1959.

conclusion. Imagine, Mill asked, that a technical improvement in German linen manufacture reduced its price one-third. The German demand for linen would increase and its price, in terms of cloth, decrease. What would happen to the English demand for linen after the German offering price were lowered? Mill's answer employed the comparatively modern notion of elasticity of demand. If English demand for linen increased by the same percentage as its price decreased—an elasticity of unity—then at the new equilibrium 10 yards of English cloth would exchange for $25\frac{1}{2}$ yards of German linen. If elasticity were less than unity, equilibrium occurred when 10 yards of cloth exchanged for more than $25\frac{1}{2}$ but less than 30 yards of linen. Finally, if demand elasticity were more than unity, the equilibrium solution demanded that 10 yards of cloth exchange for less than $25\frac{1}{2}$ but more than $22\frac{1}{2}$ yards of linen.

Mill's cumbersome arithmetic example determined trade equilibrium under the highly simplified conditions it assumed. From this analysis, Mill concluded that trade equilibrium between two countries found each one exporting just enough to cover its imports. This was the "equation of international demand" or the "law of international values." It was a model for Alfred Marshall's elegant geometry and a jumping-off place for twentieth-century theorists. Of Mill's work, a leading authority commented: "Mill's discussion of the relationship between reciprocal demand and the commodity terms of trade was in the main a pioneer achievement, and probably constitutes his chief claim to originality in the field of economics."[30]

SOCIAL POLICY

If, on the whole, Mill restricted himself to his predecessors' economics, he amply fulfilled his promise of novelty in the domain of economic applications, that area of human affairs where the mutable laws of distribution, rather than the fixed rules of

[30] Jacob Viner, *Studies in the Theory of International Trade*, Harper, 1937, p. 535.

production, applied. Nowhere was the point plainer than in Mill's treatment of the English working classes and their proper, as well as probable, future. Mill, as has been noted, was a realistic judge of the English workingman, capable of saying that "as soon as any idea of equality enters the mind of an uneducated English working man, his head is turned by it. When he ceases to be servile, he becomes insolent."[31] But the English worker's imperfections increased the need to improve his position and, even more essential, his character.

What could be done to achieve aims so laudable? Mill's answer mingled realistic analysis and idealistic aspiration. His starting point was a heresy: he alleged that the progressive state in which population and output rose was not conducive to improvement in the quality of life. On the contrary, the stationary state, characterized by stability of capital and population, offered the most hope of human development and a higher kind of life. Mill's conviction was strong:

I cannot, therefore, regard the stationary state of capital and wealth with the unaffected aversion so generally manifested by political economists of the old school. I am inclined to believe that it would be, on the whole, a very considerable improvement in our present condition. I confess that I am not charmed with the ideal of life held out by those who think that the normal state of human beings is that of struggling to get on; that the trampling, crushing, elbowing, and treading on each other's heels, which form the existing type of social life, are the most desirable lot of human beings.[32]

To this harsh judgment he added bitterly: ". . . hitherto it is questionable if all the mechanical inventions yet made have lightened the day's toil of any human beings."[33] Could an essay on the perils of the subway and the charms of the rural life say more? In his time, Mill was rare among economists in his distrust of material progress as a sufficient goal.

He sharply questioned the adequacy of his society's treatment

[31] Mill, *Principles,* p. 110.
[32] *Ibid.,* p. 748.
[33] *Ibid.,* p. 751.

of the poor. In his central chapter on this subject, "On the Probable Futurity of the Working Class," Mill concluded, after an analysis of how the rich and the powerful acted, that the poor could not trust either the wisdom or the benevolence of their superiors. All the dreams of aristocratic magnanimity which had endured even in Bentham's early writings were just that— dreams, nothing more. Upon their own exertions depended the fate of the poor: "The poor have come out of leading-strings and cannot any longer be governed or treated like children. To their own qualities must now be commended the care of their destiny."[34]

As things stood, there was an overwhelming reason why the poor could not raise the quality of their life. At the center of their daily routine was a cancer. This cancer was the very nature of the relationship between worker and employer. As Mill described this nexus, it was an association of mutual suspicion. Employers coldly insisted upon the last possible ounce of effort from their employees. The latter retorted with conscientious malingering. The experience demeaned both groups. In the mouth of Mill, heir to the economists who had cherished this central market relationship, this was a radical statement.

Although Mill's diagnosis was bold, his remedies with few exceptions were comparatively timid. Mill's flirtation with Utopian socialism (there is no evidence that Mill ever read Marx) was long, tentative, and inconclusive. A reader might trace through the *Principles'* successive editions an increasing sympathy with the aims of socialism, the personalities of leading socialists, and even socialism's diagnosis of capitalist ailments. It all went for nothing, for Mill boggled at a critical point: central direction of economic activity. His faith in competition remained too strong to allow him to become a socialist: "I agree . . . with the Socialist writers in their conception of the form which industrial operations tend to assume in the advance of improvement. . . . I utterly dissent from the most conspicuous and vehement part of their teaching, their declamations against competition. . . .

[34] *Ibid.*, p. 757.

They forget that wherever competition is not, monopoly is; and that monopoly in all its forms is the taxation of the industrious for the support of indolence, if not of plunder."[35] Mill reminded his readers that two changes might render even capitalism tolerable: "One of these conditions is universal education; the other a due limitation of the number of the community."[36]

If socialism was not the remedy and private enterprise had not been given an adequate trial, what was the answer? In Mill, it came in two parts: the first, the province of private action, the second that of the state. Something had to be done to dignify life's central economic relationship by changing industrial relations. The interests of workers should run parallel to those of masters, not oppose them. Mill laid considerable stress upon profit sharing as a hopeful technique. In many illustrations from the industrial experience of the middle of the century, Mill argued that laborers worked harder, improved their habits, increased their incomes, and even raised the profits of capital. Because workers maintained their own internal discipline and punished severely malingerers who reduced everyone's income, the quality of the finished product soared.

Thus profit sharing substantially improved normal arrangements. Nevertheless, Mill considered the form transitional. Ideally, workers acquired factories and ran them for themselves. Mill's ideas about how these factories could be managed were vague, though no vaguer than most syndicalist theories. If the details were obscure, the vision was noble: ". . . the relation of masters and workpeople will be gradually superseded by partnership, in one of two forms: in some cases, associations of the labourers with the capitalists; in others, and perhaps finally in all, associations of labourers among themselves."[37] What was the path to the noble prospect? How could the ill-paid workers in English factories acquire the resources to buy factories? How

[35] *Ibid.*, p. 792.
[36] *Ibid.*, p. 209.
[37] *Ibid.*, p. 764.

many employers were sufficiently enlightened to adopt voluntary profit-sharing arrangements? Alas, Mill never answered these uncomfortable questions.

On the role of the state in improving the life of the masses, Mill was not always consistent. In the spirit of his predecessors, he stated this general rule: *"Laisser-faire* . . . should be the general practice: every departure from it, unless required by some great good, is a certain evil."[38] While not especially original, his case against government intervention was powerful. According to the principle of the division of labor, government was inefficient, tyrannically disposed, and ineffective in realizing the wishes of the governed. Moreover, individual action was superior not alone because of government's defects, but also because individual action developed individual character.

A good case, but it left Mill uncomfortable. His discomfort took the shape of a long list of exceptions to the general rule that government should not intervene. The state could legitimately compel school attendance against parental opposition. The children were too young to judge for themselves. As for the parents, the community must judge when the individual (lacking education himself) has no basis of judgment. By extension, lunatics and idiots occupied the same category. There was another, more dubious set of cases which justified intervention: instances in which community sentiment, united in support of some proposition, required governmental action to implement their preference. In Mill's own example, a Factory Act, the agreement of most employers to shorten hours was ineffective so long as a small minority refused to join in the action. The exception might seem broad enough to encompass almost all of the legislation of the modern welfare state. The state could intervene when people acted for others, like the trustees of charities. Again, there was gound for action when the effects of some decision would be long felt, as in colonization.

Mill was a reluctant interventionist. There was a tension be-

[38] *Ibid.,* p. 950.

tween his urge to ameliorate the condition of the poor and his distrust of state action. Part of his program was radical in 1848: some of it is radical in 1958. He was perfectly willing, for example, to limit inheritance. Here was a means of promoting equality without damaging incentives. Quite consistently, he opposed a measure which in the current spectrum seems less radical, progressive taxation: "To tax the larger incomes at a higher percentage than the smaller is to lay a tax on industry and economy; to impose a penalty on people for having worked harder and saved more than their neighbors. It is not the fortunes which are earned, but those which are unearned, that it is for the public good to place under limitation."[39]

There were other instances of this blend of the conservative and the liberal. The notion of eminent domain pleased Mill: he approved taking away land from large private owners for the public convenience. All that the Benthamite principle of security of property seemed to demand was proper compensation. Could a New Dealer say more than this: "The claim of the landowners to the land is altogether subordinate to the general policy of the state. The principle of property gives them no right to the land, but only a right to compensation for whatever portion of their interest in the land it may be the policy of the state to deprive them of. To that, their claim is indefeasible."[40] Mill favored special taxes on rent increases.

On the other hand, his position on poor relief and factory legislation was conservative, according to later lights. Granted the structure of incentives which activated economic life, we could not efficiently extend unconditional poor relief. The means test and restrictions on the liberty of the unemployed, alike obnoxious to modern tastes, were both endorsed by Mill: ". . . the guarantee of support could be freed from its injurious effects upon the minds and habits of the people, if the relief, though ample in respect to necessaries, was accompanied with conditions which they disliked, consisting of some restraints on their

---

[39] *Ibid.*, p. 808.
[40] *Ibid.*, p. 233.

freedom, and the privation of some indulgence."[41] If work was painful, men worked only when necessity spurred them.

On factory legislation, Mill discriminated by age and sex. While it was desirable to protect children, it was wrong to restrict men's freedom. Probably, Mill argued, it was also mistaken to apply such measures to women, or it would be wrong "if women had as absolute a control as men over their own persons and their own patrimony or acquisitions."[42]

Mill's position could scarcely strike any one in the 1950's as consistent. Its humanitarianism was crippled by a view of the market directly opposed to it. The drive toward equality foundered on the rock of competition. Mill's concrete solutions were Utopian. However, if to be modern is to be torn between alternative goods and to be aware of some of life's complexities, Mill was a modern.

[41] *Ibid.*, pp. 365–366.
[42] *Ibid.*, p. 959.

Chapter 9

Karl Marx

The English Established Church . . . will more readily pardon an attack on 38 of its 39 articles than on $\frac{1}{39}$ of its income.

Karl Marx

I hope the bourgeoisie will remember my carbuncles all the rest of their lives.

Karl Marx

The conditions under which men produce and exchange vary from country to country, and within each country again from generation to generation. Political economy, therefore, cannot be the same for all countries and for all historical epochs.

Friedrich Engels

INTRODUCTION

Marxism is at once philosophy, sociology, history, and economics. Its great leaders, Karl Marx, and his scarcely less original collaborator, Friedrich Engels, were scholars, propagandists, journalists, refugees, and revolutionists. If the world has ever since been somewhat confused about Marxism's intellectual meaning, and if economists, especially, have tended to dismiss Marxist economics as special pleading rather than dispassionate investigation, these were the reasons. On one occasion, Marx complained that in Germany Proudhon was admired as an eminent French economist, though it was conceded that his philosophy was weak;

and in France he was admired for his command of German philosophy, though it was readily admitted that his economics was faulty. In somewhat the same way, Marx's economics has frequently been criticized as poor metaphysics and his theory of history, as poor economics—attacks made the easier by the example of Marx's own slashing, polemical style.

MARX'S LIFE

Karl Marx's life was the career of a dedicated fanatic. He was the son of a prosperous Rhineland jurist. Marx, Jewish by birth, was baptized a Christian, and attended German universities. There he soon identified himself with the radical Hegelians. In consequence, when he graduated, he could not secure a university appointment. Instead, he dabbled in radical journalism. His efforts sufficiently impressed the authorities to cause his expulsion from Germany. In turn, Belgium and France forced him to leave. Finally, he came to rest in London, where he spent the last 30 years of his life as one of the most celebrated and assiduous users of that great library, the British Museum. The reasons why the English, in their turn, did not expel him probably included English tolerance, Marx's apparent harmlessness, and the notorious British aversion to abstract systems constructed by foreigners.

These were years of grinding poverty for Marx, his devoted wife, and suffering children. He lived partly on the proceeds of hack journalism—for a period he was English correspondent of the New York *Tribune*—and mostly on the bounty of his friend, disciple, and collaborator, Engels. Engels was fortunate in the possession of a rich father and considerable business talent of his own. Among the many easy paradoxes which surround Marxism was the circumstance that unless a well-to-do bourgeois had supported an impoverished bourgeois in the citadel of capitalism, the revolutionary theory designed to overthrow that citadel could not have been constructed.

During these years, Marx and Engels produced an impressive series of books, separately or collaboratively. In 1845, as a youth of 24, Engels wrote his *Condition of the Working Class in England*, a descriptive account of the appalling poverty in English industrial districts. In 1848 the two produced jointly one of the famous pamphlets of history, the *Communist Manifesto*. In a style closer to the concise Engels than to the professorial Marx, this pamphlet contained three inflammatory elements. It was an exultant call to arms in a year when, all over Europe, revolution promised to triumph. It was a program of reform for the successful revolutionary parties. Finally, it was a concise theory of history. More succinctly and more forcefully than ever again, the two portrayed human events as the product of class struggle, determined by changing economic circumstances.

The year before, Marx wrote a bitter attack on Proudhon, which he called *The Poverty of Philosophy*, a play upon Proudhon's original title, *The Philosophy of Poverty*. Even this early there was apparent the tone of personal vilification which marks Marxist controversy. It is a manner strangely at variance with the Marxist conception of ideology as independent of personal attributes.

These formal productions, only a few of them described above, much understate the amount of writing the two produced. They attacked many individuals, commented upon many specific situations, and scribbled endless letters to each other and to third parties. Marx and Engels were ever hopeful of revolutionary success. Their steady interest in revolutionary tactics led to close associations and frequent communications with radical groups everywhere. Naturally, none of these groups pleased them. Either their leaders sold out to the enemy, in the manner of Lassalle to Bismarck; or they were doctrinally untrustworthy like Proudhon, the anarchist Bakunin, the later revisionist Bernstein, or many others; or they were personally inadequate, like Hyndman, the leading English Marxist. In only one country, Germany, did Marx and Engels during their lifetimes witness the growth of a party based avowedly on Marxism. Their hopes and fears shifted with the political tides. England had been their earliest hope, but they came to despair of the English, especially during the prosperity which succeeded the crisis of the middle of the century. The Paris of the Commune won their admiration. Toward the end of his life, Marx began, cautiously, to hope for revolution in Russia. Engels complemented this effort by speculating that the Russians, by drawing upon their primitive forms of agricultural association, might skip capitalist revolution and move directly to socialism.

Marx's major work, the container of all his doctrines, was *Capital*. This is a strange book, with an even stranger publication history. Its first volume appeared in 1867; but the second and third, only after Marx's death; and the fourth, itself divided into three substantial parts, not until this century. The first three volumes, in English translation, fall little short of 3000 pages, inordinately long for a revolutionary tract, not brief for anything else. Nor did the manner ingratiate. *Capital* opened with 150 pages of subtle, philosophical discussion of the concept of value. In these pages, hairsplitting distinctions jostled rude attacks upon other economists and capitalists in general. (Everything was bathed in a wash of footnotes of the most erudite variety, drawing upon works in Greek, Latin, German, English, French, and Italian.) Suddenly the manner changed and the remainder of the first volume illustrated several simple theoretical points. The exploitation of worker by capitalist, a theoretical necessity of capitalism, was described in impressive detail. Marx drew his facts from the reports of the English factory inspectors, the heroes of his grim tale. These pages burned with indignation at workers' wrongs, anger at their oppressors, and thirst for revolt. Strange materials for an economic treatise!

Edited for publication by Engels from Marx's sketchy notes, Volume II dealt entirely with capital theory. Full of tedious arithmetic schemes of capital production and reproduction, it must be one of an eminent economist's least-read works. Volume III meticulously described distribution. As will be seen later, it was also a descent to a lower plane of abstraction, on which actual market prices received their explanation. Volume IV, edited by Karl Kautsky after Engels' death, was a scholarly history of theories of surplus value.

INFLUENCES ON MARX

Marx's economics bore the imprint of Ricardo, to whom he made generous acknowledgment. Marx extended Ricardo's labor theory of value (in a form considerably more absolute than Ricardo had ultimately considered satisfactory). Although he reduced the major economic classes to two by eliminating the landlords, Marx borrowed a good deal from Ricardo's handling of distribution. Starting with Ricardo's growing doubts about the favorable impact of machinery upon the working class, Marx developed a tremendous indictment of technology in a capitalist society.

Capital owed other debts. Marx had read the Ricardian Socialists, particularly William Thompson. From them he may have derived the concept of surplus value and a hint of the critical importance of class struggle. These were, of course, inferences he might equally well have drawn directly from Ricardo. Even though Marx excoriated Bentham almost as violently as his favorite targets, Malthus and Senior, he owed him something. In the end, revolution came because workers, acting upon rational calculation, rebelled against the pains of capitalism, and exchanged them for the pleasures of socialism. Marx's workers were hedonists. Revolution did not come more quickly because these workers were imperfect pleasure machines. One of capitalism's historical missions was to educate them the better to appreciate their position. The factory was like the school. Both made students more proficient seekers of pleasure and more adroit dodgers of pain.

The influence upon Marx which English-speaking readers found most difficult to bear was German. English students are not happy when metaphysics is mingled too openly with their economics. Marx's Hegelian metaphysics, an especially abstruse philosophy, inserted itself at the foundation of his theory of history, and manifested themselves insistently in other Marxist theories.

What were the theories which such disparate influences helped to create? The rest of this chapter is an attempt to answer the question. One last introductory comment, however, addresses itself to Marx's originality. All of his ideas can be traced to others. But the same comment applies to all other economists. What counts is form, emphasis, and inference. Marx's age was the age of the machine. His emphasis upon capital was, therefore, well chosen. His inferences from the labor theory of value helped him to a theory of capitalist change. No doubt, like other theories of history, this one was inadequate. But its conception was grand and its details were impressive. What is even more important, Marx, using so many classical materials, broke out of that world. The view was exhilarating, even though the direction was wrong. Undoubtedly it was the imagination and sweep of Marxist theory, as much as its actual contents, which attracted so many intellectuals. It seemed to explain so much.

MARXIST THEORIES

Marxists frequently maintain that individual analysis of the various Marxist theories destroys the unity of the doctrine. Nevertheless, separate examination is inevitable. There is no other way to handle a complex problem except to divide it into parts. Moreover, there is less than Marxists claim to this idea of doctrinal unity. Finally, separation might save something from the Marxist wreck which, if the Marxist claim of "organic unity" were taken seriously, could only be total. Here are the reasons for discussing separately Marxist philosophy, history, ideology, and economics.

PHILOSOPHY

Official Marxist philosophy was dialectical materialism. It was essentially a description of how change in human affairs, and even in the physical universe, occurred. Change was development and development took place by stages, each stage "higher" than its predecessor. An initial situation was a "thesis," its successor an "antithesis," and the third stage a "synthesis." All phenomena followed the rule of three here suggested, but the process did not end here, for change itself was continuous. The synthesis itself became the first stage in a new development. No situation, idea, or activity was fixed; each contained within itself the seeds of change. Thus capitalism succeeded feudalism, and socialism is destined to replace capitalism. The flat statement conceals the essence of the dialectical phenomenon, the seeds of change in each form of organization. Narrowly examined, feudalism demonstrated the signs of emerging capitalism. Subjected to the scrutiny of a Marx, capitalism yielded its portents of socialism.

Three rules applied to this dialectical process. The first, the unity of opposites, explained the coexistence of uneasy, hostile elements. In capitalist society, bourgeosie and proletarians temporarily exist and coöperate, as well as struggle. In mathematics, the expression $-a^2$ is the product of a and $-a$, a unity of opposites. Development is possible and inevitable because social and economic forms of the utmost apparent stability and uniformity are actually coalitions of disparate elements.

The second rule, the negation of negation, summarized the mechanism of change. All historical victories have been temporary and incomplete. Capitalism negated a feudalism which, in its glory, appeared indestructible. Capitalism, too, seems eternal, but its span is actually brief. Unfortunately, Marxist terminology was vague. Phenomena are negated by their "opposites." But what was an opposite? Dialectical philosophers still argue the question. In what respect did change imply negation? How did one distinguish between "opposites" and mere differences? Did these dialectical triads apply to all aspects of life, as Marx and Engels sometimes insisted?

The final rule referred to the change of quantity into quality. If heat were applied to water in a kettle, to use Engels' example, at first the only result would be hotter water. Eventually, when the temperature of the water reached 212 degrees at sea level, a qualitative change would occur: water would be transformed into steam. Similarly, when capitalists increased their oppression of proletarians, the early effect was only increased misery. However, the ultimate effect was revolt, a qualitative shift in human reaction. Some of the definitional difficulties were obvious. Was not a higher water temperature a different quality of that water? And in what sense was temperature quantity and steam and water quality?

In Hegel, Marx's master, the dialectical process was idealist. The important sphere of its activity was the human mind; the outside world was subsidiary to mental activity. Marx reversed the priority. Important change, for him, occurred in the world of material objects; its basis was economic. Therefore the sphere of spirit and thought could only reflect the *real* changes in the material universe. Change remained dialectical, even though it did its work in non-Hegelian locations. For Marxists, then, dialectical materialism postulated triads of development centered in the material universe. Marx's definition of the material universe, his isolation of social and economic tendencies, both belong to the theory of history.

HISTORY

In the *Communist Manifesto*, Marx and Engels summarized the past as the history of class struggles. These class struggles reflected themselves in literature, religion, science, art, politics, and all other human affairs. There was a terminology to accompany the theory. Change took place in the "base." This "base" included the technical state of production and the legal conditions of property ownership. In the full flush of capitalist development, appropriate legal arrangements paralleled capitalism's characteristic technology, complex machines systematically deployed in large factories. Factory owners, the capitalists, faced free workers. These workers were free to sell their labor, move from employment to employment, and act as commodities. They were free, in another sense, of the implements of production—one illustration of the sour Marxist sense of humor. Because they no longer owned their tools, they had to sell their ability to work—labor-power was the Marxist term—to capitalist employers.

In capitalism's growth, technological advance marched hand in hand with alterations in proletarian legal position. Before modern capitalism could evolve, "the expropriation of the agricultural producer, of the peasant, from the soil . . . ,"[1] had to occur. Only in this way could capitalists be sure of a supply of labor to use and to exploit. From Marx's standpoint, steps in the process included the enclosure movement which began at the end of the fifteenth century, the expropriation of Church lands coincident with the Reformation, and the land transfers which followed the Glorious Revolution. Masquerading as political and religious events, these were actually approaches to the free labor market of modern capitalism.

As such transformations succeeded each other, the triumph of the modern factory system became feasible. Technology and property relationships moved together. The struggle within this base was the dynamic of capitalist change. As capitalism matured, the implacable hostility between owners and proletarians, notable in capitalism's earliest dawn, became more and more marked—the tensions between opposites compressed in unity became ever more severe.

Capitalism itself was a changing phenomenon. More and more peasants were forced off the land. As the few remaining peasants were compelled to work as agricultural laborers, the distinction between the rural and the urban working class disappeared. Big capitalists gobbled little capitalists and the middle class vanished. Complete explanation of these promising events must await analysis of Marxist economics. Marx's tacit assumption suggested that fate or nature demanded the progressive increase of industrial output. Capitalists were driven to increase their output. Ultimate progress from capitalism to socialism was the result of incompatibility between the techniques of production (an ability to create ever more goods), and society's legal arrangements. When the latter became a "fetter" upon production, revolution fol-

[1] Karl Marx, *Capital* (Vol. I), Modern Library, 1906, p. 787.

lowed. In his own way, Marx was as addicted to notions of progress as any cheerful Englishman of the nineteenth century. But only Marx's own language did justice to the apocalyptic character of that progress:

Along with the constantly diminishing number of the magnates of capital, who usurp and monopolise all advantages of this process of transformation, grows the mass of misery, oppression, slavery, degradation, exploitation; but with this too grows the revolt of the working-class, a class always increasing in number, and disciplined, united, organised by the very mechanism of the process of capitalist production itself. The monopoly of capital becomes a fetter upon the mode of production, which has sprung up and flourished along with it and under it. Centralisation of the means of production and socialisation of labour at last reach a point where they become incompatible with their capitalist integument. This integument is burst asunder. The knell of capitalist private property sounds. The expropriators are expropriated.[2]

A glorious passage. The changing organization of capitalism was the historical irony which insured the ultimate revolt of a "disciplined" working class. Trained to coöperate with his fellows in the factory, the worker found in his desperation the motive to turn coöperation to new ends.

So much for the changes which occurred in the base. The "superstructure" included all derivative human activities. Political democracy accompanied maturing capitalism because democracy was a convenient device of domination for capitalists. In religion, Christianity altered its form in accord with economic necessity. In the Middle Ages, the Church condemned usury: the age was pre-capitalist. On the other hand, the Calvinism of early capitalism sanctioned not only interest, but also the complete apparatus of the capitalist search for gain.[3] Thought itself corresponded to economic circumstances. Smith's economics signalized capitalism's emerging triumph and Marx's theories the imminent victory of

[2] *Ibid.*, pp. 836–837.
[3] Later scholars, among them Tawney, found this view of Calvinism much too simple.

socialism. It was no accident (a famous Marxist phrase) that Marx appeared when he did. In Engels' words, ". . . while Marx discovered the materialistic conception of history, Thierry, Mignet, Guizot, and all the English historians up to 1850 are the proof that it was being striven for."[4] Later Marxists have applied this insight to art, music, and literature. From the Marxist standpoint, the Soviet control of the arts proceeded from an effort to identify the music, painting, and literature which were the appropriate reflection of the productive forces, released and organized in Russia.

Although all of this was drawn faithfully from Marxist sources, Marx and Engels, in writing so much over so long a span of time, inevitably altered some of their opinions. The foregoing depended heavily upon the *Communist Manifesto* and, moderately, upon *Capital*. Certain problems obtruded themselves. The first was that old philosophical problem, determinism. The problem for Marxism was this: if immanent in society was the unfolding force of production, if, at some stage, private property hindered rather than promoted this unfolding, if this "contradiction" changed worker attitudes and promoted more militant class action, then it was hard to see what needed to be done except to wait patiently for deliverance from oppression. At the close of the century, Eduard Bernstein and his German followers drew such a conclusion. Bernstein argued that orderly parliamentary tactics, trade-union activity, and democratic pressures were appropriate, dignified, and effective—since revolution was, in any case, inevitable. Here was something of a dilemma for revolutionary leaders. The banner of inevitability was an attractive device to follow, for it always comforts to know that one's own side will win. But if inevitability led to inaction, would not revolutionary hopes be dimmed?

Engels rather than Marx wrestled with this dilemma, mostly in letters composed in the 1880's and early 1890's. By then the question was more than academic: it was a problem of practical politics in Germany and some other countries. Engels' resolution

---

[4] *Selected Correspondence of Karl Marx and Frederick Engels,* International Publishers, 1942, p. 518.

or attempted resolution of the difficulty can be conveniently discussed in the company of a second major difficulty, the rigid one-to-one relation of events in superstructure to events in base. This relation, at its most extreme, denied importance to the historical uniqueness of countries, independent developments in the arts and sciences, and mutual influence among the various spheres of base and superstructure. Engels' key statement is unfortunately long:

According to the materialist conception of history the determining element in history is *ultimately* the production and reproduction in real life. More than this neither Marx nor I have ever asserted. If therefore somebody twists this into the statement that the economic element is the *only* determining one, he transforms it into a meaningless, abstract, and absurd phrase. The economic situation is the basis, but the various elements of the superstructure—political forms of the class struggle and its consequences, constitutions established by the victorious class after a successful battle, etc.—forms of law—and then even the reflexes of all these actual struggles in the brains of the combatants: political, legal, philosophical theories, religious ideas and their further development into systems of dogma—also exercise their influence upon the course of the historical struggle and in many cases preponderate in determining their *form*. There is an interaction of all these elements, in which, amid all the endless *host* of accidents . . . the economic movement finally asserts itself as necessary.[5]

The statement appeared to leave Engels uncomfortably poised on both horns of his dilemma: between inevitability and uncertainty, and monism and pluralism, for the statement answered less than it appeared to answer. What did "ultimately" mean? How could the economic movement be in the end "necessary" if it were not the "only determining one"? Could the "course" of events be the same if their "form" were different? Upon questions of this kind Engels' exposition was suspended. To them he gave no good answers. To impute a large role to human will was to admit that history presented choices. To assign inevitability to

[5] *Ibid.*, pp. 475–476.

the course of events diminished the incentive to human action.

Perhaps there was more faith than logic in Marxist predictions, even a note of despised Utopianism. Here is an illustration of this wistful note: "The struggle for human existence comes to an end. . . . Man cuts himself off from the animal world, leaves the conditions of animal existence behind him and enters conditions which are really human. The conditions of existence forming men's environment, which up to now have dominated man, at this point pass under the dominion and control of man, who now for the first time becomes the real conscious master of Nature, because and in so far as he has become master of his own social organization."[6] Utopianism dominated the Marxist conception of the state. Contained briefly in his *Critique of the Gotha Program* (1871), Marx's analysis was excessively simple. The state was an instrument of class domination and class oppression. Under capitalism it represented the interests of capitalists, the ruling class. When socialist revolution came, capitalists would be dispossessed and proletarians would succeed them. The successor state would represent only the workers. Since it was ruled by a dictatorship of the proletariat, the state's sole task should be elimination of the remaining class enemies, the capitalists. When this work was completed, the need for the state—by definition—vanished. When all belonged to the single class of workers, the state withered away. In the economic world, the dialectic process had reached its conclusion.

IDEOLOGY

In Marx, ideology was the set of beliefs appropriate to the class position of the believer. Thus the capitalist naturally adopted the economic, political, religious, social, and artistic tenets of his role. His religion, like his politics, made him a better capitalist, at least in the days of capitalist power. In the same way, as the contradictions of capitalism manifested themselves, workers began to adopt the economics and politics of Marxism. As the worker became

[6] Friedrich Engels, *Herr Eugen Dühring's Revolution in Science* (Anti-Dühring), International Publishers, 1939, p. 309.

conscious of his position in society, he realized that he could improve that position only by belief in capitalist exploitation and the reality of the class struggle.

This corollary to the usual relation between base and super-structure had interesting implications. Truth became relative. Because of his class position, a personally honest man might believe in false ideas. A personally dishonest man, who in his day-to-day dealings cheerfully perjured himself, might believe in correct ideas, because his class position directed him to them. In 1776 Marxism would have been less "correct" than the laissez-faire economics of Adam Smith, because the objective conditions of capitalism had not developed to the stage which demanded Marxism. Of course, it is un-Marxist to put the matter in this way. Marxism was impossible in 1776. It was inevitable in 1867.

All of this conformed to Marx's view that history was on the side of the unfolding, productive forces of technology. The *Wealth of Nations* aided capitalism when capitalism still had an historical mission to fulfill. *Then* it was true doctrine. *Capital* aided the next occupant of history's leading part, the proletariat. *Now* it was true doctrine. What men think and feel, according to Marx, is much less the effect of their individual capacities than it is the result of their class position and its necessities.

The doctrine conveyed another meaning. The brightest man cannot see the truth, if he is a capitalist in capitalism's waning. Nor can the stupidest man evade the truth, if he is a proletarian on the eve of the revolution. Hence the ridicule which Marx poured on bourgeois morality. Revolutionary morality recognized as good and true whatever promoted the revolution and castigated as bad and false only what retarded the revolution. What the capitalist called a "lie" might be revolutionary truth.

MARXIST ECONOMICS

Capital contained several theories. Inevitably, there was a theory of value. There were also explanations of capitalist development, economic crisis, and economic breakdown, closely related to each other and to the theory of value. The theory of value doubled as an explanation of relative prices, the problem of most of the first volume, and as a clue to economic change. Its second aim rendered incomplete a good deal of the criticisms of such keen analysts as Eugen von Böhm-Bawerk, who centered their attention upon the theory only as an explanation of actual prices in real markets.[7]

VALUE

Like Ricardo, Marx began with value. He identified the central problem of exchange value as the explanation of why goods exchanged for each other in given ratios, through the intermediary of money. Why did a quarter of wheat exchange for x blacking, y silk, or z gold? If exchange were rational, said Marx, there was some common valuable element in each of these objects. The language in which Marx couched these observations was formidable: ". . . the valid exchange values of a given commodity express something equal; secondly, exchange value, generally, is only the mode of expression, the phenomenal form, of something contained in it, yet distinguishable from it."[8]

What could this common element be? Not any natural or technical attribute, for "such properties claim our attention only in so far as they affect the utility of those commodities . . . [and] . . . the exchange of commodities is evidently an act characterized by a total abstraction from use-values. Then one use-value is just as good as another, provided only it be present in sufficient quantities."[9] What was left? Only a single common property: all commodities were the products of labor. This was a highly abstract labor. The residue of each product became "a mere congelation of homogeneous human labor, of labor-power expended without regard to the mode of its expenditure."[10] This residue was Value. Two comments are in order. Much of Marx's labo-

[7] See his *Karl Marx and the Close of His System*, Augustus Kelley, 1949.
[8] Marx, *Capital*, Modern Library ed., p. 42.
[9] *Ibid.*, p. 44.
[10] *Ibid.*, p. 45.

rious demonstration was play-acting. The Value with which he concluded was the value with which he started. There was no serious attempt to prove that the common element could not be utility, bulk, or extent. For this, Marx had a reason. He knew that labor was the source of value, because labor was at the heart of human relations, as he dealt with them. His was the theory of social relations, not of price. Second, unlike Ricardo, Marx did not emphasize pain as the justification of payment.

In Marx, a useful article was valuable only because it embodied human labor. Use value was mentioned, only to be dismissed, its usual fate. Marx quickly introduced a qualification. Labor created value only when it was socially necessary labor, defined as "the labor time . . . required to produce an article under the normal conditions of production, and with the average degree of skill and intensity prevalent at the time."[11] The definition was oddly evocative of Marshall's much later Representative Firm. The point of Marx's qualification was to deal with the ridiculous possibility that the less efficiently workers performed, the more valuable their product became, because more hours of labor went into its creation.

Above all, value was a social relation, characteristic of a market economy, Marx's period of commodity production. Relationships were between people, not between commodities. Exchange occurred when goods which were not use values to one owner were traded for goods held in the same low esteem by another owner. By definition, a commodity produced for sale was a non-use value to its producer. It had to be exchanged. As commodity production widened in scope, the need for a universal equivalent to facilitate exchange also increased. Here was the origin of money as a measure of value and a standard of price.

Despite its terminological oddities, Marx's discussion, up to this point, differed little from Ricardo. Then Marx made the key logical distinction upon which the major burden of the subsequent analysis came to rest. This was the distinction between labor

[11] *Ibid.*, p. 46.

and labor power. Value, Marx had said, was found in "homogeneous congelations of undifferentiated labor,"[12] Ricardo's ordinary common labor. This undifferentiated labor consisted of labor hours, but when the employer hired a laborer, he bought labor power, the worker's capacity to labor during a standard factory day. Human labor power "in motion creates value, but is not itself value. It becomes value only in its congealed state, when embodied in the form of some object."[13]

Marx used this distinction to explain how profit, or surplus value, emerged from a market in which only equivalents were exchanged. The riddle was, if everything sold at its value, how did surplus value arise? The answer began in early economies, where sales occurred only to facilitate later purchases. The cycle was Commodity-Money-Commodity and the nature of the transaction was barter. Capitalism introduced a variant, M-C-M, a cycle in which money was advanced by the capitalist, with the object of recovering it, not with the purpose of purchasing a good. Since the capitalist aimed at profit, accurate notation rewrote the cycle M-C-M' $(M + m)$, when M equaled the capitalist's original monetary outlay and m equaled the transaction's profit. This profit Marx labeled surplus value.

It remained to identify surplus value's source. Exchange could not be the origin, because commodities, Marx assumed in Volume I of *Capital*, exchanged at the prices determined by the amounts of labor needed to produce them. Even if it were momentarily granted that these laws of exchange were violated and all goods sold above their values, each seller as he became a buyer would necessarily discover that his increased income was dissipated in paying the higher prices of the commodities he bought rather than sold. Marx's solution has been implied: he assumed the existence of a unique commodity, alone capable of creating value. That commodity was labor power.

Since labor power was a commodity, produced and sold in a market like other commodities, its value was determined, like

[12] *Ibid.*, p. 52.
[13] *Ibid.*, p. 59.

theirs, by the labor time socially necessary for its reproduction. That span of time was the amount essential to produce the means of subsistence, which, in Marx as in Ricardo, differed in amount and quality in different societies. To be added were the means of subsistence of wife and children and the education necessary for the worker's trade. For Marx as for Ricardo, skilled labor was simple labor multiplied. The higher wages of skilled labor measured the increased outlay on the means of subsistence caused by longer education.

Because only labor created value, the workman was entitled to the whole product of his labor. Actually he received only that portion of his labor necessary for his subsistence and reproduction—the value of his labor power. The remainder, surplus value, comprised profits, interest, and rent. The machines and factories which the capitalists had amassed enabled them to exploit the propertyless worker. In Marx, machines could no more create value than could money in Duns Scotus. Marx, as Tawney said, was the last of the Schoolmen. The secret of primitive accumulation, the first collection of capital, was nothing more than the force and the fraud which wrested from the peasants their fields, and from the artisans their tools.

Much of Volume I of *Capital* then examined surplus value and the exploitation of the proletariat. The degree of exploitation of labor power Marx measured solely by reference to variable capital, his term for wages. Constant capital—machines and raw materials—did not affect the measurement. The simple formula for the computation was s/v where s was surplus value and v was variable capital. S/v could be translated as surplus labor time/necessary labor time, if necessary labor time were defined as the period required to produce the workman's means of subsistence, and surplus labor time as the extra portion of the day worked only for the benefit of the capitalist.

Necessary labor time and surplus labor time together constituted the working day. The longer that day, the greater the surplus value produced. Therefore it was in the employer's interest to increase the working day as much as possible and in the workman's interest to shorten it. Lengthening the working day increased absolute surplus value. But there were limits to such extension, arising partly from the physical limits of the worker's strength. Factory legislation, which, over time, shortened the working day, reinforced this restriction. As Marx interpreted this legislation, it was a belated defense of capitalism by capitalists who became fearful that the very source of surplus value, labor power, was being destroyed. Marx cherished the factory inspectors who enforced these acts against the opposition of the more benighted capitalists.

When the capitalist was thwarted in his efforts to increase the working day, he shifted his attention to the creation of relative surplus value, derived by decreasing the amount of socially necessary labor time devoted to producing the worker's means of subsistence. Such was the explanation of greater mechanization, improved technology, and persistent efforts to cheapen food. From the Marxist standpoint, the prolonged agitation to repeal the Corn Laws was simply an attempt to diminish the length of time the worker labored to support himself and to increase, correspondingly, the portion of the day which benefited the capitalist.

It was obvious to Ricardo that the owners of machinery deserved a reward for employing it. Senior had called the abstinence which preceded the creation of machinery a pain like labor. Quite differently, Marx held that the machine could do no more than transfer the value in it, the hours of socially necessary labor time consumed by its creation, to the finished product. True, the more labor a machine contained, the more it could transfer, but of that value it created not an iota. Then why did capitalists persist in buying machines? Marx's answer was this: The first capitalist to introduce a machine will be able, temporarily, to produce a given quantity of goods with less total labor and to receive the same market price. He will be able to sell his goods above their value. Granting an urge to accumulate and competitive markets (both assumed by Marx), his incentive was strong. However, his advantage must prove temporary. Competition soon induces other capitalists to introduce the same improvement. Then prices fall and capitalists are worse off than they were, because they have less labor to exploit.

Some of Marx's most eloquent pages described the impact of machinery upon the English working classes. The effects were almost wholly bad. Because many mechanical operations required dexterity rather than strength, capitalists employed women and children. These unfortunates worked horribly long hours, in wretched surroundings, under stern discipline. Of the male laborer, owners made a free slave dealer. Frequently without employment himself, he trafficked in the blood of his family. The mortality rate was high for adults and murderous among children. Because men and women were mingled in heat and grime, because little hope remained for them, and because only violent entertainments could arouse their dulled senses, they wallowed in moral degradation. The intellectual desolation of the new mill towns complemented this degradation. Adults had no time to read. Children had no opportunity to learn to read. When compelled by the Factory Acts to attend some sort of school, the children, exhausted by their hard labor, slept rather than learned. Frequently, their schoolmasters were themselves barely literate. Marx tellingly quoted the results of examinations of pit boys. Some could not identify Jesus Christ. Others did not know who the Queen of England was. Stunted physically, they were in no better condition intellectually.

Machinery had one favorable effect. Machinery demanded a disciplined work force and central factory control. One day, workers could employ their training to overthrow their employers. For this day of deliverance, strikes were a preparation and their bloody repression a lesson in class consciousness.

As for the capitalist, capitalism causes increasing tension. In the passage which follows, Marx emphasized the capitalist's acquisitive nature, and something else as well:

At the historical dawn of capitalist production—and every capitalist upstart has personally to go through this historical stage—avarice, and desire to get rich, are the ruling passions. But the progress of capitalist production not only creates a world of delights; it lays open, in speculation and the credit system, a thousand sources of sudden enrichment. When a certain stage of development has been reached, a conventional degree of prodigality, which is also an exhibition of wealth, and consequently a source of credit, becomes a business necessity to the "unfortunate" capitalist. . . . there is at the same time developed in his breast, a Faustian conflict between the passion for accumulation, and the desire for enjoyment.[14]

But the whole of Volume I ignored one of the problems which had afflicted Ricardo, the effects of different proportions of constant and variable capital upon the determination of value. According to the labor theory of value's explanation of market prices, surplus value and, hence, profit, should have been higher in occupations which used relatively large amounts of variable capital (labor) and relatively small amounts of constant capital (machinery). If such were the case, there would be a number of different rates of profit. But, said Marx, "a difference in the average rate of profit of the various lines of industry does not exist in reality, and could not exist without abolishing the entire system of capitalist production."[15] This reaffirmed Ricardo's and Smith's assumption that in competitive markets, profits in different lines approached equality. They could differ only when the mobility of resources was impeded, contrary to the logic of capitalism.

How could this market fact be reconciled with Marxist assumptions? Marx's solution entailed descent to a lower level of abstraction. The first volume did not really explain market prices, save on the unreal assumption of identical organic compositions of capital—equal percentages of machinery and labor. Its purpose, ran the Marxist apology, was to examine capitalism's inner secrets, concealed beneath the market ephemera which contented most economists. The third volume propounded a new theory, designed to explain relative prices. It offered a new concept, prices of production; and a simple aggregative technique.

Marx's explanation depended substantially upon arithmetic ex-

[14] *Ibid.*, pp. 650–651.
[15] Karl Marx, *Capital*, Kerr and Co., 1909, Vol. III, p. 181.

ample, a bad habit he may have borrowed from Ricardo. Suppose, he asked, that we examined five different enterprises in five different occupations and discovered that average technique resulted in the following picture of capital structures:

TABLE 1. Sample Capital Structures

Capitals		Rate of Surplus Value	Amount of Surplus Value	Value of Product	Rate of Profit
I	80c 20v	100%	20	120	20%
II	70c 30v	100	30	130	30
III	60c 40v	100	40	140	40
IV	85c 15v	100	15	115	15
V	95c 5v	100	5	105	5

The table represented an impossible situation. While minimal conditions of capitalist production were fulfilled, there could not be five different rates of profit in the same market.

What was a more realistic picture? Actually, the competitive market redistributed surplus value and the actual prices at which goods were sold (Marx's term was prices of production) were either above or below the values of the commodities sold. This was the story which the next table tells.

TABLE 2. Capital Structures and Prices of Production

Capitals		Amount of SV	Value of Product	Price of Production	Deviation from Value	Rate of Profit
I	80c 20v	20	120	122	2	22%
II	70c 30v	30	130	122	−8	22
III	60c 40v	40	140	122	−18	22
IV	85c 15v	15	115	122	7	22
V	95c 5v	5	105	122	17	22
Average	78c 22v	22			0	

Using Smith's and Ricardo's familiar competitive mechanism, Marx simply assumed that competition would attract capital to industries where profits were high and away from industries where profits were low. When the movement was complete the first set of rates would fall, and the second rise. One ruling rate, then, emerged. If he had been able to realize the full value of his product, the third capitalist would have earned a profit of 40 percent. Unfortunately for him, competition forced him to settle for the average rate of profit. The average was simple to derive. The total profit produced by these five enterprises was 110. If that profit were so divided that each capitalist earned the same rate of return on his outlay of 100, each price had 22 added to it and the average rate of profit was 22 percent. These prices of production or selling prices departed from the true values of the goods by amounts indicated in the next-to-last column of Table 2.

How much was lost by this transition from the values of the first volume to the prices of production of the third? According to Marx, not very much: "The average rate of profit which determines the price of production must, however, always be approximately equal to the amount of surplus-value which falls to a given capital as an aliquot part of the total social capital. . . . Now, as the total value of the commodities governs the total surplus-value, and this again determines the amount of the average profit and consequently the general rate of profit, as a general law or a law governing fluctuations, the law of value regulates the prices of production."[16]

How valid was the Marxist theory of value? To a non-Marxist, the "proof" that labor alone was the source of value was metaphysical assumption, not logical demonstration. How sound was the price-of-production hypothesis erected upon it? Marx's most damaging critic, Eugen von Böhm-Bawerk, emphasized the circularity of the reasoning. Marx's prices of production included wages as well as profits. These wages were set according to the prices of the means of subsistence. But these prices, as actual market prices, were also prices of production. Hence Marx explained prices of production by prices of production. As a piece of sheer economic reasoning, Marx's rescue of his theory failed to impress.

The weaknesses impressed his critics, not Marx. On this precarious foundation, Marx erected a remarkable series of prophe-

[16] *Ibid.*, p. 189.

cies, hypotheses, and speculations. Since keen observation and acute historical analysis accompanied Marx's exposition, the defects of the theory did not necessarily destroy these predictions.

ECONOMIC DEVELOPMENT, CRISIS, AND BREAKDOWN

Marx's predictions were an extraordinary mixture of prevision and inaccurate diagnosis. They included concentration and centralization of capitals, a falling rate of profit, an ever larger reserve army of labor, increasing misery, polarization of classes, and revolution. Crises, wars, and imperialism paralleled these changes.

Here was the story. Two tendencies in capitalism were concentration and centralization of capitals. By concentration, Marx meant the increasing average size of the manufacturing enterprise. In contrast to Ricardo who assumed constant returns to scale in manufacturing, Marx believed that increasing returns resulted from finer subdivision of process and more intricate machinery, which the larger enterprise could afford and the smaller one could not. Improving technology added its weight to the scale. The capitalist's obsessive acquisitiveness and the competition of his fellows drove him to introduce improvement and enlarge the scale of his operations.

The other half of the process was centralization. Because the market for finished goods was limited, increasing size implied a smaller number of enterprises. Even if the market grew larger, technology advanced still more rapidly and, with it, the optimum size of the average plant. Which of the capitalists disappeared? What was the mode of their disappearance? The answer to the first question was obvious. The small capitalist was forced to the wall and the large capitalist became still larger, a conclusion rendered inevitable by Marx's assumption of falling cost curves.

The mechanism of their disappearance was closely connected with the hastening circumstance of crisis. There are at least three strands in Marx's explanation of capitalist crisis. Nowhere did he weave them together into a coherent explanation of business cycles. Marx made two factual assumptions about the character of contemporary fluctuations. Their period, he thought, was ten

years. Their phases he described as "moderate activity, prosperity, over-production, crisis, and stagnation."[17] His explanations included the conception of a disproportion between the production of capital goods and consumer goods, a hint of the emphasis upon the structure of production of which the Austrians made so much. But he appeared to rely more frequently upon an under-consumptionist explanation which emphasized the disparity between capitalism's powers to produce and the capacity of its consumers to purchase, when incomes were so unevenly distributed. These were insights, not theories. Here was a sample: "The enormous power, inherent in the factory system, of expanding by jumps, and the dependence of that system on the markets of the world, necessarily begets feverish production, followed by over-filling of the markets, whereupon contraction of the markets brings on crippling of production."[18] In Marx's Hegelian language, this was a contradiction between the forces of production and the forces of consumption. Even if ideology allowed him to glimpse the truth, the most enlightened capitalist could not escape the consequences of the contradiction, for inexorable competition compelled him to pay the lowest wages he could. These low wages narrowed his market and rendered crisis inevitable.

Marx devoted most attention to the falling tendency of the rate of profit. As he put this generalization, ". . . the same rate of surplus-value, with the same degree of labor exploitation, would express itself in a falling rate of profit, because the material growth of the constant capital, and consequently of the total capital, implies their growth in value, although not in the same proportion."[19] As industry grew larger, constant capital expanded more rapidly than variable capital. Since surplus value was the product of labor power, the rate of profit necessarily declined. Marx's analysis usually assumed a constant rate of surplus value or exploitation. This was a difficult assumption to share, in the face of labor's increasing productivity. The increase in

---

[17] Marx, *Capital*, Modern Library ed., p. 495.
[18] *Ibid.*, p. 495.
[19] Marx, *Capital*, Kerr and Co., 1909, Vol. III, p. 248.

productivity appeared to insure either larger profits for capitalists or a higher standard of life for the workers. Presumably, Marx regarded the answer to the difficulty to be the fact of periodic unemployment. The filling and refilling of the industrial reserve army served the same function in Marx as Malthusian theory played in Ricardo. Both implied a depressing effect on worker welfare.

Marx identified counteracting forces which might delay, though never avert, the operations of the law of the falling rate of profit. Temporarily, the rate of exploitation might be increased. If the worker labored harder and devoted a smaller proportion of each day to his own support, this would delay declining profits. Again temporarily, wages might be forced below the value of labor power—subsistence, a phenomenon which occurred also in the population cycles which have been inferred from Malthus' theory. The elements of constant capital could be cheapened. If machinery cost less, total invested capital declined or, at least, increased more slowly. And, since profit was figured on total capital, the decline in its rate was once more arrested. Finally, foreign trade was capable of cheapening raw materials. Insofar as these materials entered into the means of subsistence, the degree of exploitation could be raised. At best (or worst) these forces delayed the operation of falling profits. Raising the degree of exploitation or cheapening the means of subsistence appeared to offer hope, but exploiting workers more intensively curtailed employment and narrowed the opportunities to exploit. No ultimate escape existed from capitalism's contradictions.

Why should a drop in the rate of profit be so disastrous to capitalism? Apparently, when the rate of profit fell capitalists were so alarmed that they sought desperately to restore it. Their efforts, in a typical contradiction, only intensified the danger they feared. Their reduction of wages, more vicious competition for existing markets, and search for new markets abroad destroyed small capitalists, lowered the cost of constant capital, and made it more profitable for the remaining large capitalists to continue. Recovery found a larger reserve army of unemployed, fewer capitalists, and larger enterprises. Each cycle repeated the process.

Crises were accompanied by polarization of classes. By something of a sociological tour de force, Marx conceived of classes as conforming to economic categories. The distinction between classes, then, was a matter of ownership only. Capitalists owned the machines and tools of production. Proletarians owned only their labor power. Different classes meant different interests, an easy step, in the classical tradition. Capitalism entailed a two-class division, just as socialism implied a one-class society. Full class consciousness meant full realization by the proletariat of just how different their interests were from those of their capitalist oppressors.

Capitalism tended to disguise these facts of life. Workers frequently suffered from a false class consciousness which led them to identify themselves with capitalists. Farmers misunderstood their position. Small proprietors, professional workers, and the white-collar class might all think that they were allied to capitalism. The role of the business cycle was to clarify the real class opposition. During crises the small proprietors who were bankrupted sank into the proletarian mass. Small farmers lost their land to bigger farmers, and the latter, it became clear, were only a branch of capitalism in general. The dispossessed small farmer, too, was either forced into the rural proletariat or compelled to swell the reserve army of unemployed in the cities. Even skilled workers suffered unemployment. Their efforts to improve their economic position were bloodily repressed. Thus did crisis sharpen the class struggle.

Over time, the lot of the working class must become progressively more wretched. In each crisis unemployment rises to new heights and, even in prosperity, the reserve army of the unemployed never disappears. This increasing misery is the harder to bear, because their masters live in increasing luxury. When true class consciousness has been achieved, and the misery of the workers is intolerable, the proletariat revolts and "the expropriators will be expropriated."

Everything was inevitable. The story's irony was capitalism's preparation of its own end. Its historic mission to develop productive forces is ultimately finished. Then it must yield to a new, "higher" mode of organization. As Marx put the role of capital, ". . . it is one of the civilizing sides of capital that it enforces this surplus labor in a manner and under conditions which promote the development of the productive forces of social conditions, and the creation of the elements for a new and higher formation better than did the preceding forms of slavery, serfdom. . . . it creates the material requirements and the germ of conditions, which make it possible to combine this surplus labor in a higher form of society, with a greater reduction of the time devoted to material labor."[20]

CONCLUSION

What have been the reasons for Marxism's enduring appeal? Surely not its economics. Marx's economics were the Ricardian school's last gasp, in their relentless extension of the labor theory of value, adherence to the classical scheme of distribution, reliance on Benthamite psychology, and exclusive interest in supply. Only a few scant years after the first volume of *Capital*, Jevons, Menger, and Walras attacked classical theory and substituted new economic doctrines. Marxist economics were outdated before the second and third volumes of *Capital* were published.

Events certainly have not completely verified the theory of history. In Western Europe and the United States the misery of the masses has increased neither relatively nor absolutely. Although the evidence on the other predictions is subject to diverse interpretations, no conclusive proof is available that crises are more severe, the average amount of unemployment greater, and the relative number of capitalists smaller than Marx's own day. Classes refuse to polarize. False class consciousness is an international scandal. Monistic historical explanations are out of intellectual fashion.

[20] *Ibid.*, pp. 953–954.

The reasons for Marx's enduring influence transcend his intellectual achievement. Much of his work was a superb appeal to the emotions. His account of the woes of the working classes can still arouse a retrospective fury that men had to live so long like beasts. Marx appealed, as well, to the hopes of everybody who sought a heaven on earth. Marx's heaven was within our reach. Although Marx wrote little about the future socialist society, that little made it evident that men will be better, governments will wither, and human beings, at last, will lead fully human lives.

None of this should deny Marx's intellectual achievement. Though his view of classes was oversimple, he at least recognized the crucial importance of the concept and made a beginning at systematic analysis of class structure. No doubt his view of history was incomplete and contradictory. Nevertheless, it combined history and analysis in a fashion which had eluded his predecessors. (Marx's world was larger than Ricardo's and Mill's.) His generalizations appeared to apply to every country, not to England alone. Marx's history and economics were dubious. It remains true that, with the honorable exception of Joseph Schumpeter, no succeeding economist has really tried to handle the application of theory to history, and history to theory. It is hard to deny the Marxist claim to magnificent failure.

PART III

Marginalists and Opponents

Chapter 10

The New Economics: 1870

Economic science is, and must be, one of slow and continuous growth. Some of the best work of the present generation has indeed appeared at first sight to be antagonistic to that of earlier writers; but when it has had time to settle into its proper place, and its rough edges have been worn away, it has been found to involve no real breach of continuity in the development of the science.

The present treatise is an attempt to present a modern version of the old doctrines with the aid of the new work, and with reference to the new problems, of our own age.

Alfred Marshall

In the last few months I have fortunately struck out what I have no doubt is *the true Theory of Economy*, so thorough-going and consistent, that I cannot now read the other books on the subject without indignation.

W. S. Jevons

INTRODUCTION

The literature of economic theory written in the last 30 years of the nineteenth century, especially in England and the United States, but also in France, Austria, and Italy, would not strike as strange a reader familiar only with contemporary economic analysis. Economists like W. S. Jevons in England, Léon Walras in France, and Carl Menger in Austria dealt in the now conventional problems of individual price determination. Their explanation of market price centered on the equally familiar notion of utility. Followers of the path-breaking trio—John Bates Clark in the United States, Wieser and Böhm-Bawerk in Austria, and Alfred Marshall in England—extended the theory of market price from commodities to factor services. Emerging from these efforts was the marginal productivity theory of wages, interest, and rent, a theory which dominates explanation even now. By 1900 the pattern of price and distribution theory was complete.

Not only did these economists set the precedent for the problems and the solutions of much modern economics, they also invented, improved, or rediscovered techniques of continuing relevance. The key to their technique was the marginal principle, the generalization which explains market price by concentrating on the satisfaction or utility received by a consumer from the purchase and use of the last unit of any commodity. The consumer, they taught, was in personal equilibrium when the price that he paid for each of the commodities he acquired was proportional to the satisfactions yielded by each commodity's last unit. In this position, no shift in his pattern of spending could increase his gratifications. The path to this conclusion was varied, as the discussion below will suggest, but within four years of each other, Walras, Menger, and Jevons reached similar conclusions independently.

A mathematical principle, marginal utility appeared to demand the application of differential and integral calculus. Not astonishingly, therefore, Jevons' and Walras' demonstrations (though not Menger's) relied on mathematical notation and reasoning. Even elementary demonstrations, in the modern world, of market equilibria now employ the simpler concepts of calculus. The plane geometry of the economic diagram was also a product of this period. Although Walras' and Jevons' diagrams seem oddly labeled, they contain the essential determination of market equilibrium by the intersection of supply and demand at a single price.

How great a break with the past did these innovations represent? In one sense, the break was only moderate, because numerous unknown and unsung writers of the first half of the century had anticipated large parts of marginalist doctrine. The Frenchmen Dupuit and Cournot, the Germans von Thünen and Gossen, the Englishmen Jenkins and Senior, and even the Australian Hearn, were among these anticipators. Jevons, Menger, and Walras were subjectively original—they had read none of these men, but their title to objective priority was clouded. But these pioneers wrote almost for themselves alone. The dominant Ricardo-Mill school in England and the historical school in Germany controlled the teaching and writing of economics. A break with the past meant a break with Ricardo and Mill.

On the existence or seriousness of this departure, different opinions were possible, as the quotations at the head of this chapter hint. The case for the novelty of the marginalists was very strong, though possibly less strong than the enthusiastic Jevons thought. Did not Ricardo and Mill, in the footsteps of Adam Smith, take utility for granted and seriously analyze only supply? Because their vision was limited to supply, the bulk of their theoretical analysis produced the labor theory of value. While Jevons derived the value of goods from the intensities of satisfactions they evoked, Ricardo and Mill (with qualifications) inferred value from the amount of labor needed to produce finished products. Could any two emphases be more opposed?

Not only did the two groups concentrate upon different explanations of price; they appeared to live in different worlds as well. Malthusian speculation on population dominated the world of Ricardo and Mill. To them, the danger of overpopulation seemed greater than the hope of rapidly expanding output. As a practical issue, the repeal of the Corn Laws bulked large: the first edition of Mill's *Principles* was published only two years after their repeal. Joined to this issue were questions of popular suffrage, freedom to publish, and impediments to labor organization. In the 1870's these disputes were anachronisms. Because the future was dark and uncertain, the great economists of the century's first half looked anxiously at the long run. The emotional coloration of the 1870's was much lighter.[1] To think of the Victorian as uniformly optimistic is an inaccurate cliché. The more cautious claim that economists became more cheerful is defensible. Malthusian gloom yielded to happier assumptions of continued economic progress, rising labor productivity, and higher rewards for all classes. The English attitudes of the last third of the nineteenth century anticipated the current American conviction that standards of life can be infinitely improved. In such a world, concern with the short run was legitimate and strategic. This temporal difference was one of the sharpest contrasts between the English marginalists and their illustrious predecessors.[2] Thus, in their best work, men like Jevons and, a generation later, Edgeworth and Wicksteed, took their society for granted and happily turned to technical questions.

The techniques themselves were very different. Marginalism's increments, mathematics, and diagrams were undreamed of by Mill, Ricardo, and Smith. Different theories, techniques, and problems appeared to validate the proposition that something really new had happened in the 1870's.

It was Alfred Marshall, one of marginalism's most original minds, who challenged this conclusion most strongly. Decorum and propriety demanded, in the opinion of this very proper Englishman, continuity and progress in any science. His firm belief that nature made no leaps supported the judgment that marginalism was simply an improvement on old techniques, possibly a shift in old emphases, but no revolution. His argument ingeniously interpreted the work of the English economists. In his view, Ricardo and Mill, even Smith, had been aware of all price determination's problems, and of the significance of utility. Not ignorance but strategy induced them to neglect value in use and explain market prices as derived from value in exchange. In their

---

[1] Old ideas do linger. Jevons' analysis of English coal reserves simply translated corn into coal, and inferred Malthusian conclusions from coal shortage instead of from corn shortage.

[2] Even Alfred Marshall, an apparent exception to this generalization, had least to say about the longest of his time periods, the secular period.

time this emphasis was entirely appropriate. Properly and charitably interpreted, the emphasis was not as lopsided as many assumed. Even Ricardo's theory depended on more than labor. If we note his qualifications, we must conclude that he favored a cost-of-production explanation of price. In it, labor and capital were both costs. Cost of production, said Marshall, was at least as good a theory (with utility held constant) as utility was (with cost of production held constant). As for the mathematics, Marshall, himself an excellent mathematician, argued that this was only a way of expressing more clearly, and more briefly, ordinary ideas. While Ricardo was no mathematician, he reasoned like one. Therefore marginalism deserved no acclaim because of its superior mathematical credentials.

Marshall's critique implied that Ricardo and Mill and the marginalists had been guilty of excessive emphasis on a part of price theory. Ricardo and Mill underplayed utility. The marginalists, even worse, paid little attention to cost of production.[3] The truth was to be found in Marshall's own combination of cost, as explanation of supply, and utility, as explanation of demand.

As in most controversies, there was something to be said on each side. The novelties of the marginalists were sufficiently numerous, the shift in their problems sufficiently sharp, and their conclusions sufficiently different, to change the face of economics. But some of the change was in appearance, not in substance. Ricardo and Mill had also wanted to know how prices were determined. Adam Smith had lucidly described the mechanism of price equilibrium. No doubt the marginalists argued a much more cogent case for the welfare-maximizing effects of perfect competition, but their predecessors had handled the problem.

The marginalists borrowed from earlier English economists some of the subject's organizing principles: human rationality, equilibrium technique, and the high valuation of competition.

---

[3] Marshall was never completely fair to the marginalists of the 1870's, especially Jevons. The group's theories did discuss cost of production. They explained it with the same marginal principle which they applied to demand.

They added an emphasis on demand, and a refined technique. Technique was the heart of the issue. To some economists, the real story of economics is the improvement of its techniques. For them, the marginalist revolt was a genuine liberation, a shift from fuzzy literary generalities to precise logical formulations. Economists who are also interested in economics' assumptions, conclusions, and practical applications will find more development and less revolution in marginalism.

A postscript is necessary. English marginalism was most successful in a version which emphasized continuity. Marshall, not Jevons, won the battle for English minds. And it was Marshall, not Jevons, who made the smallest claims for himself, who spoke of his own great book simply as "an attempt to present a modern version of the old doctrines with the aid of the new work."[4] Marshall's triumph may intimate that the English value the proprieties, among them respect for one's elders, more than they value exact accuracy in the evaluation of doctrinal novelties.

ANTICIPATORS: COURNOT, THÜNEN, GOSSEN

Justice demands that some attention be paid to the unlucky who, in the history of any subject, make their discoveries too early to win the approval of their contemporaries. There are many anticipators of marginal analysis. Three major names were Augustin Cournot (1801–1877), J. H. von Thünen (1783–1850), and H. H. Gossen (1810–1858).

Cournot's originality and analytical ingenuity can hardly be exaggerated. In 200 small pages,[5] he described and defined the downward-sloping demand curve, completely analyzed the maximization of profit under conditions of monopoly, advanced an ingenious explanation of duopoly pricing, proved that equilibrium price occurred when aggregate supply equaled aggregate demand, and exactly defined the market form which we call

---

[4] Alfred Marshall, *Principles of Economics*, Macmillan, 1920, p. v.
[5] See his *Researches into the Mathematical Principle of Wealth*, 1838. Translated by N. T. Bacon, 1927.

perfect competition and he called "unlimited competition."[6] And the book went unread.

Thünen, like Cournot, was one of the gifted amateurs who have enriched economics. A scientific farmer, he spared no efforts to associate results with causes, in his experiments on his land. From his incredibly detailed records, stretching over many years, Thünen furnished proof of the law of diminishing returns, extended his speculations to location theory, and consistently applied the marginal principle. He reached, if he did not solve, the basic problem of imputation theory: how to distribute the proceeds from the sale of finished products among the factors of production which combined to complete the goods.

Gossen completely described utility as the basis of value, although he did not extend his conclusions to the explanation of exchange. His book advanced two original laws, both familiar parts of demand theory today. The first generalization stated that the satisfaction from successive units of the same commodity, in a limited time period, diminished as the amount in the hands of the consumer increased. His second conclusion defined, as a condition of personal equilibrium, satisfactions from the last units of commodities, proportional to the prices of the commodities. When Jevons identified Gossen as his predecessor, he accorded him no more than justice. Walras, while pointing out how much further he (Walras) had advanced, still spoke of Gossen in extravagant terms: "Gossen claimed the glory of Copernicus, which is due to him because of his concept of the mathematical equilibrium of the economic world. In my opinion, he combines the glory of Copernicus with that of Newton because of his solution of the social question."[7]

[6] The following definition says something about the precision and severity of Cournot's thought: "The effects of competition have reached their limit, when each of the partial productions D_k is *inappreciable*, not only with reference to the total production D equals $F(p)$ but also with respect to the derivative $F'(p)$ so that the partial production D_k could be subtracted from D without any appreciable variation in the price of the commodity." (*Ibid.*, p. 90.) Or, in perfect competition, no seller is important enough to alter market price by varying the amount that he supplies.

[7] Henry W. Spiegel, *The Development of Economic Thought*, Wiley, 1952, p. 485.

A word can be spared for W. E. Hearn, whose book *Plutology; or, the Theory of the Efforts to Satisfy Human Wants* was cited respectfully by Jevons. This diffuse, rambling work did contain the germs of marginal-utility and marginal-productivity doctrine. In a rare concise passage, Hearn stated the law of satiable wants: "There are [objects] of which the pleasure depends in a great degree, upon their scarcity. But in hardly any case does the increase of the object bring with it a proportional increase of enjoyment. The sameness soon falls upon the taste; and if, as is usually the case, an extraordinary quantity of one object involves a corresponding diminution in the supply of others, one faculty or class of faculties is gratified to the full extent that its nature will bear, while the other faculties are left unsupplied."[8] Save for Jevons' endorsement, it would be hard to rate Hearn very high. Senior spoke as clearly a generation earlier: "Not only are there limits to the pleasure which commodities of any class can give, but the pleasure diminishes in a rapidly increasing ratio long before those limits are reached. Two articles of the same kind will seldom afford twice the pleasure of one, and still less will ten give five times the pleasure of two."[9]

W. S. JEVONS (1835–1882)

Jevons was almost a model Mid-Victorian. His *Letters and Journals*, the major source of biographical information, portrayed a man of strong family affections, extended first to his father and siblings, and then to his wife and children. At the age of 19, when an opportunity came his way to go to Australia as an assayer in the Sydney mint, he initially refused, out of reluctance to leave his family, and eventually accepted the lucrative post only when his father urged him to do so. During his six years in Australia, he groaned constantly in his letters to his family about his homesick eagerness to return to England. Yet these were productive

[8] Hearn, *Plutology*, 1864, pp. 17–18.
[9] Nassau Senior, *An Outline of the Science of Political Economy*, 1836, pp. 11–12.

years financially. They enabled Jevons to accumulate the modest capital which allowed him to choose his later career freely. Intellectually, the Australian years gave birth to Jevons' interest in meteorology and economics. When he left Australia and took up life as a London student, he carried with him the germ of his future theories.

Equally strong in Jevons were the sense of duty and the aspiration to achieve some great end. In him, the noncomformist conscience—in this instance Unitarian, came to full flower. His remark, "I began to think I could and ought to do more than others,"[10] was characteristic. Later in his life, he exhausted himself rushing up to London to give testimony or act as an external examiner, and then hastening back to Manchester to meet his classes on time. He was so dull a lecturer that his students might have excused an occasional absence. He found it almost impossible to abstain from work. Again and again, he complained of the fatigue which his intense labors had caused him.

His individualism was intensely held. He suspected the merits of free medical services and trade unions, at a time when both were gaining general public acceptance. But he feared that they would undermine the incentives to labor and self-improvements upon which so much rested. The plight of the poor aroused in him a mixture of anxiety, trepidation, and sympathy. All three feelings appeared in this typical passage: "I wish with all my heart to aid in securing all that is good for the masses, yet to give them all they wish and are striving for is to endanger much that is good beyond their comprehension. I cannot pretend to underestimate the good that the English monarchy and aristocracy, with all the liberal policy actuating it, does for the human race, and yet I cannot but fear the pretensions of democracy against it are strong, and in some respects properly strong."[11] He concluded weakly: ". . . compromise, perhaps, is the only resource."[12]

---

[10] *Letters and Journals of W. S. Jevons*, 1886, Macmillan, p. 12.
[11] *Ibid.*, p. 231.
[12] *Ibid.*, p. 232.

Reform puzzled and worried him: "It is very difficult to know what view to take of the Reform agitation. I am not a democrat . . . and don't much care to adopt popular views to please the mob. However, I don't think any Reform Bill that is likely to pass will really upset our system here, while it may lead to many improvements."[13] He extended to women the condescension of these passages. When his sister Lucy was depressed about her progress in painting, he consoled her with these manly words: "I think that women are often quite sufficiently admirable in themselves and their characters without accomplishments and works."[14] Lucy's reaction has been lost to history.

About his own work and ideas, Jevons was justifiably confident. He was disposed to find error among those who failed to appreciate his performances, not in his performances. When he was 25, he anticipated "every success from my theory of political economy, which seems to develop itself with that facility which is a proof of its soundness."[15]

At first, his hopes were disappointed. When he sent a sketch of the theory to the Royal Society, it passed unnoticed, although a second paper he submitted received favorable attention. His reaction was in character: "The year of which only five minutes have now to run seems to have been a long one. It has seen many of my hopes fulfilled, many frustrated. It has made me an M.A. It has seen my theory of economy offered to a learned society (?) and received without a word of interest and belief. It has convinced me that success in my line of endeavor is even a slower achievement than I thought. This year has taken much youthfulness out of me."[16] He was 27.

He was less pleased with his social qualities and his capacity to arouse the love of others. "May I not hope to become passably social? May I not hope by making myself better known to those around me, to use my acquirements with better advantage, and gain position, which I desire more as a means than an end? And

---

[13] *Ibid.,* p. 232.
[14] *Ibid.,* p. 223.
[15] *Ibid.,* p. 155.
[16] *Ibid.,* p. 175.

may I not even find the society of ladies and friends generally a relaxation from my own devouring thoughts, much needed if I am to avoid all chance of a breakdown?"[17] Equally affecting was this cry from the heart: "My ideals seem to involve contradictories. I would be loved and loving. But the very studies I have to cultivate absorb my thoughts so that I hardly feel able to be what I would in other ways."[18]

This complex man was also generous, though not to the mighty. He abhorred Mill. At some damage to his own reputation, he constantly attacked Mill's economics and, even more strenuously, his logic. Jevons, like Mill before him and Keynes after him, was a powerful logician, who produced his own systematic treatise. He hated Mill's authority because it perpetuated error and suppressed truth. Conceivably, he hated him on the more personal ground that Mill's followers criticized his work most harshly. His letters to Foxwell on the subject of Marshall's originality were acerbic. They indicated something about what it was like to be outside the centers of influence: "I have been very much interested in your letter concerning my paper. It has told me much, which I had no previous means of knowing, concerning ideas current in philosophical subjects in Cambridge. I was not aware that Marshall had so long entertained notions of a quantitative theory of political economy, and think it a pity that he has so long delayed publishing something on the subject."[19]

His stately correspondence with Léon Walras, like himself at first unappreciated, revealed the generosity of both writers. The major events were these. A copy of the first part of Walras' book fell into Jevons' hands. At once he wrote to Walras. The letter first complimented Walras on his paper's contents, and then pointed out that he, Jevons, had reached the same conclusions in 1871, if not in 1862. Was Walras, he asked, familiar with his book? Would he like a copy? Walras reacted promptly and honorably: he offered to publish an acknowledgment of Jevons'

[17] *Ibid.*, p. 199.
[18] *Ibid.*, p. 214.
[19] *Ibid.*, p. 331.

priority in the *Journal des Économistes*. Rather ruefully, Jevons accepted the offer:

> After receiving your very friendly letter . . . and after seeing a full statement of your mode of arriving at the equation of exhange, I cannot for a moment entertain the least doubt of the entire independence of your own researches as regards my own. As to the question of priority of publication, it is of course of less importance than that of the truth of the theory itself. But I confess that I have always in my own mind attached much importance to this mathematical theory of economy. . . . I cannot, therefore, help accepting your very kind offer to make known in the *Journal des Économistes* or otherwise the fact that I had already gone over part of the same ground as yourself, although in a different manner. . . .[20]

Jevons closed with the hope that "the theory of exchange will . . . become the origin of the exchange between us of many friendly letters." The two continued a friendship until Jevons' death.

The drama had another act. After he published his *Theory of Political Economy*, Jevons began to look about for other mathematical economists. His hunt uncovered Gossen. He gave him generous credit: ". . . it is quite apparent that Gossen has completely anticipated me as regards the general principles and method of the theory of Economics. So far as I can gather, his treatment of the fundamental theory is even more general and thorough than what I was able to scheme out."[21] In the same preface he praised Dupuit's measurement of utility in 1849 and Cournot's work on supply and demand in 1838.

The other major events in Jevons' life can be rapidly told. After the failure of his paper for the Royal Society, Jevons in 1863 produced his essay "On a Serious Fall in the Value of Gold." Although its reception was not encouraging, the paper displayed an important talent: Jevons' remarkable command of inductive techniques. In this paper he considered problems of measurement

---

[20] *Ibid.*, pp. 305–306.
[21] W. S. Jevons, *The Theory of Political Economy*, 4th ed., Macmillan, 1911, p. xxxv.

and developed an index number. Keynes considered his achievement the equal of all previous work on index numbers put together.

Full recognition came to him in 1865, after the publication of the *Coal Question*. Bold and ingenious, the book's Malthusianism persuaded its author to neglect many of the more optimistic arguments for continued English industrial growth. The errors in the book proved of less importance to Jevons than the circumstance of Gladstone's reading it and citing it in a debate on the national debt. John Stuart Mill spoke of it approvingly in the House of Commons. The reputation of the still youthful author was made.

Meanwhile, his academic career continued. He taught first at Owens College, Manchester. He moved in 1876 to University College, London, as professor of political economy. Though he worked hard at his job, he was never happy as a lecturer. Partly the cause was shyness. But another source of his discomfort was the necessity to teach Mill's doctrines to students whose careers depended partly on imbibing "correct" political economy.

He was a prolific writer on logic, philosophy of science, and the sciences themselves. His major economic work, *The Theory of Political Economy*, appeared in 1871. Of its reception, Jevons noted that the only leading economist who reviewed it was Cairnes, who, without fully understanding the theory, was all the more hostile to it. In an anonymous review, Marshall was, in Keynes's words, "tepid and grudging."[22] The best Marshall could say was this: "We may read far into the present book, without finding any important proposition which is new in substance. . . . The main value of book does not lie in the more prominent theories, but in its original treatment of a number of minor points, its suggestive remarks and careful analogies."[23]

Jevons led a quiet domestic life with a devoted wife. Increasingly bad health forced him to resign his professorship and seek frequent rest in Norway. In 1883 he died of a drowning accident.

[22] Spiegel, *op. cit.*, p. 510.
[23] *Ibid.*, p. 510.

An important economic document, *The Theory of Political Economy* resembled a hasty sketch, not a finished portrait in oils. Although it was full of bright ideas, the ideas frequently were not worked out. It had none of Marshall's majesty. These defects had their virtues. The book was lively where Marshall was grave, rash where Marshall was cautious, and original at points where the equally original Marshall pleased himself with cautious platitudes. No wonder Jevons irritated Marshall: their mental habits were quite different.

Jevons' preface took an uncompromising stand. He was a mathematician and a Benthamite: ". . . I have attempted to treat Economy as a calculus of pleasure and pain, and have sketched out, almost irrespective of previous opinions, the form which the science as it seems to me, must ultimately take. I have long thought that as it deals throughout with quantities, it must be mathematical in matter if not in language."[24] Ricardo and Mill were bad guides:

When at length a true system of economics comes to be established, it will be seen that that able but wrong-headed man, David Ricardo, shunted the car of Economic science on to a wrong line—a line, however, on which it was further urged towards confusion by his equally able and wrong-headed admirer, John Stuart Mill. There were economists, such as Malthus and Senior, who had a far better comprehension of the true doctrine (though not free from the Ricardian errors), but they were driven out of the field by the unity and influence of the Ricardo-Mill school."[25]

When he attacked the theory of value, his position was unmistakable. On the first page, he stated that "value depends entirely upon utility," and on the next he paid his respects to labor by limiting its effect upon value. Labor, by altering supply, was capable of changing the final degree of utility (his term for marginal utility) of the last unit marketed. Although we could never measure feelings directly, we could estimate their force by their effects on prices. In this emphasis upon money as the measure of

---

[24] Jevons, *The Theory of Political Economy*, p. xxx.
[25] *Ibid.*, pp. li–liii.

psychic states, Jevons followed Bentham and anticipated Marshall.

Jevons insisted upon the marginal nature of his theory. It centered upon those "critical points where pleasures are nearly, if not quite equal."[26] Total utility never concerned Jevons. What counted instead was final degree of utility—Marshall's marginal utility and Walras' rareté. And, Jevons carefully noted, "there is never, in any single instance, an attempt made to compare the amount of feeling in one mind with that in another. I see no means by which such comparison can be accomplished."[27]

Jevons considered economics a deductive science, because we had to begin with ready-made generalizations and draw inferences from them. Examples of such generalizations included men's inevitable choice of the "greater apparent good," the satiability of human wants, and the increasing pain of prolonged labor. At the same time, he stressed the need to "verify" and make "useful" this deductive science by the "purely empirical science of statistics." In a sophisticated way, he was aware of the enormous difficulties of adorning theory with the "reality and life of fact."

Chapter 3 contained the heart of his utility theory. He defined utility as "the abstract quality whereby an object serves our own purpose, and becomes entitled to rank as a commodity. Whatever can produce pleasure or prevent pain *may* possess utility."[28] This utility was not proportional to the quantity of the commodity, but quantity did influence its amount. Jevons' diagram illustrated his proposition that utility had two dimensions, the quantity of the commodity and the intensity of the effect upon the consumer. In Figure 1, each rectangle equaled the utility of an increment of food. Because Jevons assumed that the first two increments were vital to continued life, he left them undefined. They had no limit. If we assumed that the increments of food were infinitely small, we could draw a continuous curve, as in Figure 2. As Jevons amplified this diagram, total

[26] *Ibid.*, p. 13.
[27] *Ibid.*, p. 14.
[28] *Ibid.*, p. 38.

utility was an area, and degree of utility was a line, such as *ab*.
If *u* equaled the whole utility of consuming *x*, then *u* was a
function of *x*. On the diagram, *aa'* was an increment of *x*,
abb'a was an increment of *u*, and *ab* equaled increment of
u/increment of *x* or the degree of utility. Finally, since the
limit of increment of *u*/increment of *x* was du/dx, then
"... *the degree of utility is* ... *the differential coefficient
of u considered as a function of x*."[29] Final degree of utility
was "the last addition or the next possible addition of a very

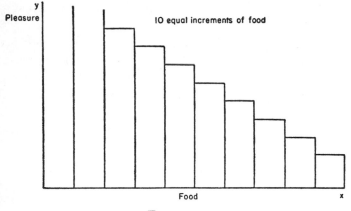

Food   x

FIGURE 1

small, or infinitely small, quantity to the existing stocks."[30] Said
Jevons triumphantly, "The final degree of utility is that function
upon which the Theory of Economics will be found to turn."[31]
The resolution of the water-diamonds paradox was now child's
play. In temperate climates, men set little or no value upon water,
"simply because we usually have so much of it that its final degree
of utility is reduced nearly to zero."[32] Jevons' concluding observation pointed out that, in equilibrium, the final degree of utility

[29] *Ibid.*, p. 51.
[30] *Ibid.*, p. 51.
[31] *Ibid.*, p. 52.
[32] *Ibid.*, p. 52.

of a commodity serving two or more purposes was equal in each employment.

From the theory of value Jevons advanced to the theory of exchange, the set of propositions which elucidated prices in actual markets. Jevons' market contained at least two persons trading in two or more commodities. Each trader was aware of the size of other traders' stocks and the nature of their intentions to sell at various prices. The behavior of the traders conformed to utilitarian assumption: each sought his own interest, "so that any one

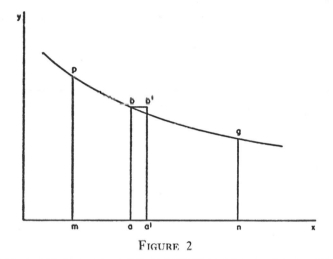

FIGURE 2

will exchange with anyone else for the slightest apparent advantage."[33] Complete knowledge was so essential to the smoothly functioning competitive market that Jevons, the individualist, recommended compulsory collection of statistics.

So much for individual demand and supply. In handling market demand and supply, Jevons introduced a dubious concept, the trading body. Vague in definition,[34] the trading body was de-

[33] *Ibid.*, p. 86.
[34] "The trading body may be a single individual in one case; it may be the whole inhabitants of a continent in another; it may be the individuals of a trade diffused through a country in a third." *Ibid.*, p. 88.

signed to solve the problems of competitive price determination. Since the trading body appeared to behave no differently from the individual, Jevons obscured the characteristics of competitive markets and failed to explain how market prices were formed.

Although his demonstration of exchange equilibrium was incomplete and defective, Jevons' account of the conditions of equilibrium has survived without substantial change. Consumers acted to maximize their satisfactions. Such maximization implied equality of satisfaction derived from the expenditure of equal sums in every direction, or, what is an extension of this proposition, quantities of utility proportional to the last amounts expended in all directions.

Jevons' examination of the difficulties and complexities of exchange was remarkably prescient. Indivisibility was one complicating case. Suppose, said Jevons, that someone wanted to buy a house, an indivisible object, for money, a divisible object. Suppose also that the owner of the house were willing to sell at £1900 and the buyer to purchase at £2100. Then the price was indeterminate, the ratios of exchange failed, and the solution depended upon the bargaining capacities of the two negotiators. Substitutes also engaged his attention. He defined a close substitute as a commodity of a "different strength" from its rival. While he did not solve the difficulty adequately, he recognized the distorting possibilities of the differing marginal utility of money to rich and poor. He concluded that exchange produced equality of final degrees of utility for each individual, but not for different individuals. His welfare inferences from this conclusion were necessarily guarded. Exchange maximized utility only for a given income distribution. Other income distributions, presumably nearer to equality, might increase total benefit.

At the end of the chapter on exchange, Jevons summarized his theory in these words:

. . . though labour is never the cause of value, it is in a large proportion of cases the determining circumstance, and in the following way:—*Value depends solely on the final degree of utility. How can we vary this degree of utility?—By having more or less of the*

commodity to consume. And how shall we get more or less of it?—
By spending more or less labour in obtaining a supply. . . .
  Cost of production determines supply;
  Supply determines final degree of utility;
  Final degree of utility determines value.[35]

Even this role of labor was circumscribed by the fact that labor
itself was variable. The value of produce determined it. It did
not determine the value of produce.

Jevons' theory of distribution was a much sketchier affair. Al-

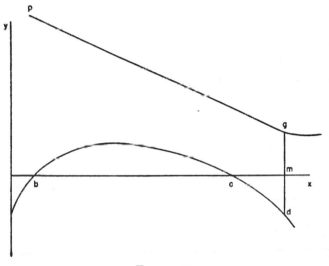

FIGURE 3

though it contained many good things, including an anticipation
of Austrian capital theory and an account of the backward-
bending supply curve of labor, it was full of Ricardian residues.
The theory of rent was pure Ricardo, and the capital theory was
weakened by Ricardian formulation. However, great virtuosity
marked Jevons' discussion of the balance of pleasure and pain in
the theory of wages. Figure 3 ingeniously pictures the situation.
Hours were the unit on the *x*-axis and utility was the unit on the
y-axis. The top curve, which measured the utility of the wage to

[35] *Ibid.*, p. 165.

the worker, declined according to the law of diminishing satisfaction. The bottom curve measured the disutility or pain of labor to the worker. On the assumption that it was hard to begin work, there was a negative portion of the curve to the left of *b*. Moderate amounts of labor give pleasure and generate the curve segment between *b* and *c*. Larger amounts of work cause pain once more, and explain the negative segment to the right of *c*. The point at which *qm* equals *md* identifies the amount of labor at which the pain of the extra work just matched the utility of the extra wage. Here the laborer stopped.

CARL MENGER (1840–1921)

At some small cost to accuracy, it was possible to argue until the 1870's that political economy was an English subject. Only in England had a dominant school won so many adherents. Only in England could its members point to such glowing triumphs as free trade and unhampered industrialization. The line of descent from Smith to Ricardo to Mill bespoke a continuity of English economics missing from less happy lands.

This strong English conviction of splendid uniqueness was an optical illusion. English economics never won complete acceptance in other countries. A French school, which harked back to Condillac and Say, preserved its influence not only in France but also in Germany. In Germany pure theory was in disrepute and historical economics dominated the intellectual scene. Worse still, the primacy of the English theoretical school depended partly on the underestimation or ignorance of important innovations made by Dupuit and Cournot, and von Thünen and Gossen. English primacy, by the 1870's, was partly insularity. With Menger the fiction became transparent. Menger founded an effective, widely read school of economists, the Austrians.

Before examining Menger's *Principles of Economics*, we should say something about the German situation in 1871. When Menger wrote, he found not only that English classical economics were in disrepute in Germany (although he cited Smith, he failed to mention Ricardo and Mill), but also that economic theory, as such, was a discredited approach. This intellectual bias had important consequences for Menger's later career and the propagation of his doctrine. Two years after the publication of his *Principles*, he won appointment to the chair of economics in the University of Vienna, a speedy recognition denied to Jevons and Walras. But because of the unpopularity of economic theory and the popularity of the historical method, Menger felt compelled to devote his efforts less to extending his own theory and more to defending his own method and attacking his opponents' techniques. Thus his next major work, his *Studies in the Methods of the Social Sciences and of Political Economy in Particular*, was a harsh and acute polemic against his adversaries. The historical school will receive separate treatment.[36] Here it will suffice to say that the attack evoked reprisal. Schmoller answered the book in a biting review. Menger rejoined in a heated pamphlet. The *Methodenstreit*, the conflict over method, thus well begun, lasted a generation. In retrospect, the controversy appeared singularly fruitless. What could be more platitudinous than the statement that history and theory both have their importance, and that some problems yield to one technique and other problems to its alternative. The argument was anything but trivial to its participants. Schmoller, who said that no partisan of pure theory should get a teaching post, had a powerful enough position in German academic life to lend force to his pronouncement. Less given to passion about abstract method, English economists never duplicated this scholarly imbroglio.

Menger's claim to the invention of the marginal principle was as good as Jevons'. His book, too, appeared in 1871. These simple truths aside, the contrast between the two volumes was greater than the similarity. Jevons clothed his argument in mathematics. Menger was utterly nonmathematical. His illustrations were simple and numerical, and he used not a diagram. For these reasons, and because his exposition was careful, polished, and beautifully proportioned, Menger was the easiest of the pioneer-

[36] See Chap. 12.

ing trio to approach. Unlike Jevons, no haste or incompleteness marred Menger's work. In the German manner, its definitions were a trifle excessive in length and subtlety, but it was no more earnest than Mill and no less lucid than David Hume.

In summarizing this book, we shall examine value, exchange, and distribution. Menger began by defining the qualities which defined an economic good. There were four: a human need, satisfaction of this need by the good, human knowledge of the object's capacity to satisfy the need, and the technical ability to direct the object to the satisfaction of the need. As civilization progressed, Menger noted cheerfully, the number of imaginary needs (for goods which really failed to satisfy) diminished.

Menger classified goods according to the directness with which they satisfied human wants. Goods of the first order satisfied human desires immediately, goods of the second and higher orders satisfied these needs only indirectly. Although bread was a good of the first order, flour was in the second order, and wheat in the third. The concept had its difficulties. Presumably, an expense-account lunch would be a good of the second order. But the same lunch, eaten at the expense of the eater, was a good of the first order. To the home baker, flour might be a good of the first order.

An object did not assume the character of an economic good (Menger's "goods character") at a higher stage, unless complementary goods were available. Menger instanced the shortage of cotton in England during the American Civil War. The labor and plant of the industry were idle, because their complement, cotton, was missing. Complementarity grew more complex, as the order of goods examined became higher. Third-order goods required complements, and so did second-order goods, in order to produce the first-order goods which were economic production's ultimate objective. In fact, the goods character of higher-order objects could be derived only from the possession of this attribute by goods of lower order. In the transformation of higher-order goods into lower-order goods, time was essential. The more complex was the structure of production, the longer was the time period which had to elapse from the beginning to the end of the productive process. In Menger, economic progress sprang from the increasing use of goods of higher order. Presumably, division of labor was a corollary of this tendency.

Men's needs arose from drives deeply imbedded in their natures. The more civilized a nation was, the more complex was the process by which these drives were gratified, and the more essential it was to arrange in advance for their satisfaction. The record of the past, said Menger, demonstrated that men grew ever more capable of estimating precisely the quantity of goods their needs demanded and the times when these needs were most insistent. Economic rationality implied choice. For Menger, choice was balancing at the margin, though he was innocent of this terminology. Man's efforts to select those needs which they wished most to satisfy out of scarce available means, defined the phenomenon of economizing. The economic character of goods was the consequence of this single cause—scarcity. If anything, Menger was more vehement than Jevons in his deprecation of labor as an explanation of value: "The value of goods arises from their relationship to our needs, and is not inherent in the goods themselves. With *changes in this relationship*, value arises and disappears."[37]

Satisfactions differed in their importance. The continuance of life depends on the gratification of some wants. Other satisfactions serve less important purposes. Menger implied that men agreed on their priorities: ". . . there can . . . be no doubt that, when men have a choice between doing without a comfortable bed or doing without a chessboard, they will forego the latter more readily than the former."[38] However, different quantities of an item, whatever its significance to continued life, possessed different meanings. Although food was essential to life, a person could skip a meal and live. Time was the important point. He shortly came to a clear statement of the marginal principle:

[37] Carl Menger, *Principles of Economics*, translated by James Dingwall and Bert F. Hoselitz, Free Press, 1950, p. 120.
[38] *Ibid.*, p. 123.

". . . further attempts to satisfy the same need will bring at first a greater and then a smaller enjoyment, until eventually a point can be conceived, for each person, at which the further *employment* of available accommodations would become a matter of complete indifference to him, and finally even burdensome."[39]

To this definition Menger appended a notable illustration. Table 3, though cumbersome in form, on the whole clarified Menger's procedure.

TABLE 3.

Food				Tobacco					
I	II	III	IV	V	VI	VII	VIII	IX	X
10	9	8	7	6	5	4	3	2	1
9	8	7	6	5	4	3	2	1	0
8	7	6	5	4	3	2	1	0	
7	6	5	4	3	2	1	0		
6	5	4	3	2	1	0			
5	4	3	2	1	0				
4	3	2	1	0					
3	2	1	0						
2	1	0							
1	0								

Menger assumed that the consumer chose, in this table, among ten commodities, of which food, the most important, was first, and the fifth in importance was tobacco. If expenditure of the same amount of money could purchase a unit of any of these commodities, and if the satisfactions derived from consuming one are unrelated to the satisfactions of consuming others, the consumer chose according to the satisfactions yielded by each commodity. The numbers in the table represented the satisfactions resulting from consuming successive units of the commodities. If the consumer had only $1 and the price of the commodity units was $1, he bought food. If he had $2, he was indifferent between more food and a unit of the second commodity. If he had $10, he purchased four units of *I*, three of *II*, two of *III*, and one of *IV*. His total satisfaction was 80. No other distribution of his

$10 yielded as high a total. Tobacco was not a rational choice until he had available at least $11. Thus, "the end result of this procedure is that the most important of the satisfactions that cannot be achieved have the same importance for every kind of need, and hence that all needs are being satisfied up to an equal degree of importance of the separate acts of satisfaction."[40] Therefore a good's value to an individual equaled the least important of the satisfactions yielded by any unit of the good. Since the last unit was least important, the consumer, in estimating value, concentrated on last units.

The values of higher-order goods depended upon "the expected value of goods of lower order they serve to produce."[41] The possibility of lengthening the time structure of production by increasing the amount of capital was limited by time preference for the present, a phenomenon "deeply embedded in human nature." This was one of the universals of human behavior which Menger persistently sought. Interest was a payment for the use of a productive resource, capital. Another higher-order good was entrepreneurial activity. The entrepreneur collected information, calculated rationally, and performed an "act of will" in assigning goods of higher order to particular productive processes and supervising the execution of production plans.

This was Menger's transition to the theory of distribution. His explanation of imputation pointed directly to the more complex theories of the 1890's: "The aggregate present value of all the complementary quantities of goods of higher order (that is all the raw materials, labor services, services of land, machines, tools, etc.) necessary for the production of a good of lower or first order is equal to the prospective value of the product. But it is necessary to include in the sum not only the goods of higher order technically required for its production but also the services of capital and the activity of the entrepreneur."[42] He made the point probably plainer in this statement: ". . . the value of a

[40] *Ibid.*, p. 131.
[41] *Ibid.*, p. 50.
[42] *Ibid.*, p. 161.

concrete quantity of a good of higher order is equal to the difference in importance between the satisfactions that can be attained when we have command of the given quantity of the good of higher order whose value we wish to determine and the satisfaction that would be attained if we did not have this quantity at our command."[43] This was one way of describing the marginal product. There was a significant difference between Menger's definition and the definitions of his followers: his marginal product was satisfaction, not either physical or monetary units.

An outstanding merit of Menger's distribution theory was the single analytic treatment applied to all the productive services. "Land occupies no exceptional place among goods."[44] Wages were like other prices: ". . . the *prices* of actual labor services are governed, like the prices of all other goods, by their *values*. But their values are governed . . . by the magnitude of importance of the satisfactions that would have to remain unsatisfied if we were unable to command the labor services."[45] In modern translation, this might read: the demand for labor services was derived from the demand for finished products, and depended upon the valuation put upon these finished products.

Like his theory of imputation, Menger's explanation of exchange extended his analysis of value. Classifying methodically, Menger discussed barter between two individuals in isolation, monopoly, and bilateral competition. There is no need to linger over his very awkward numerical examples. What these horse- and cow-trading illustrations demonstrated was the mutual gains from trade, resulting from the offer of goods of less utility to one person and more to another, to a second market trader whose estimates reversed those of the first. Both parties gained when a man rich in horses and poor in cows dealt with another man rich in cows and poor in horses. In such negotiations, equilibrium was attained when *"one of the two bargainers has no further quantity of goods which is of less value to him than a quantity of*

[43] *Ibid.*, p. 165.
[44] *Ibid.*, p. 165.
[45] *Ibid.*, p. 171.

another good at the disposal of the second bargainer, who, at the same time, evaluates the two quantities of goods inversely."[46] Menger's conclusion does not astonish: competition was much the more efficient form of organization because the incentive to cut cost in the hope of making profit was greatest. Competition increased satisfaction for everybody.

This theory of price was less satisfactory than Menger's theory of value. It neglected the role of diminishing returns in explaining supply, and the absence of diagrammatic devices made the verbal analysis exceedingly labored. Such comments cannot dim the luster of Menger's masterly explanation of utility and the limited but sound theory of income distribution derived from it.

LÉON WALRAS (1834–1910)

Like Mill and Keynes, Walras was the son of an economist. In all three cases, the fame of the son exceeded that of the father. In Walras' lifetime, it was far from certain that fame would be his ultimate lot. His *Éléments d'Économie Politique Pure*, to some the towering achievement of all economics, fell as flat before a French audience as Jevons' *Political Economy* did before an equally inattentive English public.

In part, this was Walras' own fault. Of the three great marginalists, he was the least accessible. Not only were his mathematics difficult and unrelenting, but the prose style, in the words of his patient American translator, William Jaffé, was "crabbed." His level of abstraction, which diminished as he proceeded, ended much higher than that upon which most theorists began. Cairnes, who was stopped by Jevons' calculus, could only have been horrified by the Frenchman.

There was another reason, even less creditable to his readers, why Walras won only belated acceptance. In the 1870's, French economics was in a bad way. Although the roster of distinguished French theorists included Condillac, Cournot, Dupuit, and Say, only Say received attention. More politicians than economists,

[46] *Ibid.*, p. 187.

French practitioners, in the spirit of Bastiat, devoted themselves to the unrelenting advocacy of the extremer versions of laissez faire. More than a mathematician, Walras was a land reformer, even something of a socialist, though opposed on theoretical grounds to the Marxist theory of value. His opponents lacked the discrimination to see that this "radical" reached theoretical conclusions which established the efficacy of competition on a scientific basis. In fact—much to his credit—his conclusions did not differ from those of the individualistic Jevons. He was willing to contemplate, on other grounds, more state intervention than Jevons allowed on any ground.

In France, Walras' career was a failure. Twice flunking the examination for the École Polytechnique, he ultimately entered the École des Mines. Here he soon turned to literature. All his novels were failures. Next, he passed 12 years in varied ways, as journalist, clerk, editor, and public lecturer. He turned to economics at his father's suggestion. In 1870 he obtained the position which he retained until retirement in 1892, the new chair of economics in the faculty of law at Lausanne, Switzerland. His masterpiece was published in 1874 and 1879.

Up to a point, it is accurate to link the names of Walras, Menger, and Jevons. Like the German and the Englishman, the Frenchman independently discovered marginal utility, *rareté* in his terminology. He used the principle to explain value and exchange, and production. But, as Walras himself pointed out,[47] there he and his contemporaries parted company. Walras went much further. He completed the mathematical theory of exchange by extending it to markets where there were many commodities and many participants. From the theory he derived the doctrine of maximum satisfactions. He developed a mathematical theory of production. His greatest triumph was his conception of the economy as a whole. His mathematical constructions were nothing less than a model of the economy's interrelationships. Especially for the nonmathematical, the importance of this achieve-

[47] See "Walras on Gossen" in Spiegel, *op. cit.*, pp. 471–488.

ment demands emphasis. Adam Smith had had a vision of the economy as a system in 1776. His "invisible hand" was a vague literary statement of the beneficent effects of free markets. In no sense was it a proof. Walras offered a proof. His markets for consumer goods, productive services, and capital produced determinate solutions for the prices of products, land services, personal services, and capital services.

Inevitably, the solutions were abstract. Like Jevons and Menger, Walras was confident, nevertheless, that information could be secured to solve the numerous equations of exchange. He suggested interviewing individuals about their tastes, an interesting anticipation of contemporary market research and consumer attitude studies. In the mind of this formidable theorist, pure economics was only a prelude to applied economics. Undoubtedly Walras was too optimistic. Conceptual as well as statistical problems made the solution of the equations hard to imagine. This by no means invalidated them. They continue to offer an unrivaled picture of markets as a whole.

What was this picture like? Walras offered his own summary. He asked first: under the assumption of perfectly free competition (never defined), how were prices determined? The theory of exchange supplied the answer for consumers' goods and services. The theory of production answered the query for the prices of raw materials and productive services. The theory of capitalization yielded prices for fixed capital goods. Finally, the theory of circulation gave prices for circulating capital goods.

Suppose we started with consumers' goods and services. Select one of these goods as a measure of the others, a unit of account. Call this good the *numéraire*, or money. Ratios of exchange, prices, will be "cried at random." At such prices, each individual offers goods or services, of which his supply is too great. He seeks to acquire those of which he has too little. Save by accident, it is unlikely that the amounts offered and the amounts demanded of each commodity, at these prices, will be equal. Assuming that they are not, offering price rises when demand exceeds supply. When supply exceeds demand, offering price falls. Now a new set of prices are cried. Again prices rise or fall according to the relation of demand and offer. After a series of gropings or approximations (*tâtonnements*), equilibrium prices are reached and exchange takes place. Walras' exposition contained an ambiguity. It was not plain whether any exchange actually took place at nonequilibrium prices. If exchange did occur, that fact affected the location of the equilibrium point. If exchange did not occur, then the institutional features of the actual market were exceedingly vague.[48] Walras constructed this theory upon the foundation of value premises similar to Jevons' and Menger's. In equilibrium, each consumer derived equal satisfaction from his last equal outlays in every direction.

In the case of multicommodity exchanges of three or more goods, with m commodities there were $m(m-1)$ prices (of each good in terms of all the others), and $m(m-1)/2$ "partial markets," in which goods exchanged for each other. The equation system was determinate, even though it was hard to imagine finding and using the data required to derive numerical solutions.

Walras extended this line of analysis to production, Menger's goods of higher order. The key figure was the entrepreneur, the coördinator and director of production. Production implied two markets. In one, landowners, workers, and capitalists sold productive services and bought consumers' goods and services. Entrepreneurs bought the first and sold the second. In the other market, for commodities instead of services, products were offered only by entrepreneurs, and bought by other entrepreneurs. Once more, prices were cried at random. As consumers, the three economic groups offered their services and demanded consumers' goods, in ways designed to maximize their utility. Simultaneously, entrepreneurs offered finished goods and demanded the services of land, labor, and capital, according to the technical requirements of production. On the last score, Walras assumed that there was just one way of producing a given product, only one set of proportions among various materials, types of labor, and varieties

---

[48] Edgeworth handled this difficult problem by the device of recontract. See pp. 292–293.

of machines, capable of completing the product. This assumption of fixed coefficients of production made it impossible for him to develop a full marginal productivity theory. Such a theory depends upon recombining productive services according to changes in their relative prices.

The movement toward equilibrium was familiar. Entrepreneurs expanded output when selling prices exceeded their costs of production, the prices paid to the owners of productive services. They contracted output when selling price fell short of the prices paid for productive services. The double conditions of equilibrium demanded equality of demand and supply for every product and service, and equality of selling price and cost of production. In equilibrium, profit, appropriately defined, was zero. Although Walras suffered much criticism of this concept, it followed logically from the system he had constructed. As the owner of a productive service, the entrepreneur had already received his reward. Profit was a surplus designed to move the system toward equilibrium.

Capital goods were exchanged in a separate market. On one of its sides, there were individuals who saved. Savers demanded part of their incomes in new capital goods, rather than consumers' goods and services. On the market's other side were entrepreneurs who manufactured capital goods instead of consumers' goods. The ratio of exchange between savings and capital goods depended directly upon the values of the services yielded by the machines, and ultimately upon the theories of production and exchange which indicated how those values were determined. Like other manufacturers, those who made capital goods expanded or contracted their output in response to changes in the selling prices of their machines. Interest was the price paid to the saver for his funds. A similar demonstration for circulating capital completed Walras' theory of equilibrium.

This summary could not begin to do justice to the intricacies of Walras' conception and the rigor of its execution. Nevertheless, one major conclusion was correct only with severe qualifications. Walras concluded from the theory of exchange that a competitive market maximized total utility. This conclusion was tenable only on the assumption that money had equal utility for rich and poor. Otherwise, the only possible conclusion was Jevons', a free competitive market maximizes the utility derived from a given distribution of income. Other income distributions, other total utilities.

For Walras, the oversight was unexpected. As a practical reformer, he contemplated a good deal of state intervention. He wished compulsory education, so that consumers could increase the utility of their purchases. He favored restrictions of working hours and curbs upon monopoly. At times he sounded like Henry George. He advocated state control of incomes earned because of general social improvement, rather than by individual effort. Why, he asked, should landowners benefit from increases in the value of their holdings which they had done nothing to cause? This was a perennial question, asked in the nineteenth century by Henry George, and in the twentieth by the British Labour Party. As a reformer, Walras conceived that the state should intervene to improve the effectiveness of resource allocation. When the mechanism worked well, there was no reason for the state to act.

In time, Walras attracted many followers. He numbered among his admirers such eminent economists as the American Irving Fisher, the Swedish Knut Wicksell, and the Austrian Joseph Schumpeter. Of contemporary economists, J. R. Hicks is the leading exponent of Walrasian economics. Thus, Walras founded a school. Of the three marginalist giants, only Jevons remained a lone figure. The English marginalist school was Marshallian.[49]

---

[49] A list of Further Readings for Part III appears on pp. 409–410.

Chapter 11

The New Economics: the 1880's and After

A man can be neither a saint, nor a lover, nor a poet, unless he has comparatively recently had something to eat.
P. H. Wicksteed

Marginalism started its life as an international phenomenon—anticipated by a German, a Frenchman, and an Englishman—and triumphantly formulated by an Austrian, a second Frenchman, and a second Englishman. In its later development, the subject of this chapter, Italy, Sweden, and the United States added themselves to the international set in the persons of Vilfredo Pareto, Knut Wicksell, John Bates Clark, and Irving Fisher. Alfred Marshall and Philip Wicksteed in England, and Böhm-Bawerk and von Wieser in Austria complete the list of great names in marginalism's second generation.

MARGINALIST AIMS

The marginalists addressed themselves to four tasks. The first was the completion of the main theoretical structure. Jevons, Walras, and Menger had furnished an adequate explanation of consumer choice in the theory of marginal utility. They had not succeeded in extending that theory consistently or completely to problems of resource allocation. Although all three had recognized that producers' goods derived their value from finished goods, none adequately explained how the amounts paid for finished goods were divided among the owners of the resources used in their manufacture. The later marginalists' single major achievement was the creation of the marginal-productivity theory, as the twin of marginal-utility theory. When they were finished, the marginal principle could claim to explain the decisions of entrepreneurs, the size and division of incomes, and the spending of these incomes. Some of the marginalists were persuaded that the marginal principle ran through the whole life of men.

The second job was improvement of the analytical apparatus. Since a great many ingenious minds engaged in this activity, many of their efforts inevitably resulted in technical refinements, rather than major new doctrines. Cumulatively, these refinements altered the form of later exposition and infused it with greater precision. Attributions will be made later. Here we note a few of the major novelties introduced by this group. They greatly improved their use of fictions. Although economists had always imagined simple states, primitive societies, or mariners stranded on lonely islands, never before had they described their parables so precisely and depended on them so heavily. Three of these powerful simplifications were the stationary state, partial equilibrium, and natural value. The stationary state implied stable population, resources, and methods. Partial equilibrium enabled the economist to examine a small industry, isolated from disturbances arising in the remainder of the economy. Natural value enabled its originator to demonstrate the inevitability of rent and interest in any social order, even a communist one. An enduring piece of apparatus was the indifference curve. Marginalists used it to analyze substitution and complementarity, equilibrium in barter, and consumer equilibrium.

As marginalism gained confidence, it increased in technicality. The diagrams became more complex. In some instances they sprang boldly from the footnotes and appendices to the text itself. Marshall operated extensively with an armory of elasticities. He developed the notion of consumers' surplus. Wieser advanced the notion of opportunity cost. Böhm-Bawerk started interminable controversy with his period of production. These illustrations were evidences of how much harder the path of the student was becoming. The plight of the businessman or the ordinary intelligent citizen was becoming hopeless.

Nevertheless, the marginalists tried to communicate their discoveries. This third task was handled in the systematic treatise. Marshall's *Principles of Economics*, Wicksteed's *Common Sense of Political Economy*, Clark's *Distribution of Wealth*, and Wicksell's *Lectures on Political Economy* were four major contributions to the correction of other economists and to the instruction of a wider public. In economics the systematic treatise was no novelty. But the approach and manner of the new treatises was new. The historical and sociological material which bulked so large in Smith and Mill shrank to negligibility in the books of these latter-day system builders. The number of principles of explanation diminished and the refinement of exposition increased. Consistency was the jewel won.

The final job of the marginalists was the isolation of scientific conclusion from personal preference. The point is exceedingly significant. Marxists, Veblenites, and others have often accused the marginalists of producing a theory designed deliberately to justify existing social and economic arrangements. Their intention, it was alleged, was to prevent or delay much-needed social reforms. Much in the marginalist canon made this accusation plausible. There were hymns of joy to the beauties of competition, the natural laws of distribution, and social equities of those laws.[1] However, any intelligent reader could separate these obiter dicta from the scientific content. At its best, the new economics justified Marshall's description: it was "not a body of concrete truths, but an engine for the discovery of concrete truths."[2] Even the moderately attentive could see that, whatever the opinions of individual marginalists about society and life, the tools of their trade were ethically neutral. Implacably hostile to socialism, both Pareto and Barone proved that a socialist market could

---

[1] The criticism did not fairly apply to Fisher, Pareto, or Wicksell, and only with severe modifications to Wieser and Marshall. The guiltiest party was Clark.

[2] A. C. Pigou (ed.), *Memorials of Alfred Marshall*, Cambridge, 1925, p. 86.

operate efficiently. With the best motive in the world, Marxist economists were not able to do as much. Although Wicksell was a reformer, he was able to write a finished exposition of marginal productivity. The radical Walras concluded that free competition generally maximized satisfaction. So it has always gone. The theory of welfare economics owes a good deal to Marshall. The theory of monopolistic competition is an extension of hints contained in Marshall and Wicksell. A good socialist can be a marginalist; a conservative can be an institutionalist. Neither need be a hedonist.

Leaders cannot control their disciples. Followers of this responsible group frequently used marginalist arguments ignorantly and malevolently as crude justifications of the status quo. Ricardo shocked his follower McCulloch by his open-mindedness about his own theories. Marx claimed that he wasn't a Marxist. Before his death, Keynes seemed uncertain whether he was a Keynesian. The marginalists could be criticized only for occasionally so mingling the ethical and the technical as to encourage misinterpretation.

Three marginalist schools were one of the fruits of these intellectual activities. The prophets of the Lausanne school were Walras and Pareto. The leaders of the Austrian school were Menger, Böhm-Bawerk, and Wieser. Marshall and Pigou headed the English school. Vested academic or national interest (a school combines the two) always makes it harder for the original outsider to obtain a hearing. Some of the differences in exposition among the marginalists were related more closely to membership in different schools than to differences in concept. Fortunately, some of the greatest marginalists, Marshall, Wicksell, and Wicksteed, were eclectic, not doctrinaire.

ALFRED MARSHALL (1842–1924)

. . . in my vacations I visited the poorest quarters of several cities and walked through one street after another, looking at the faces of the poorest people. Next, I resolved to make as thorough a study as I could of Political Economy.

Alfred Marshall

He wanted to enter the vast laboratory of the world, to hear its roar and distinguish the several notes, to speak with the tongues of business men, and yet to observe all with the eyes of a highly intelligent angel.

J. M. Keynes

Marshall has been called the great father figure of English economics.[3] Much in his life and character supported the judgment. His emphasis upon continuity in economic thought took the shape of veneration for his great predecessors, especially Ricardo and Smith, and of reprimand to scornful youths like Jevons who danced upon the intellectual graves of their elders. In his own case, veneration fostered extreme caution, even intellectual timidity. He avoided controversy, and wished above all to be right.

Marshall's father was cashier in the Bank of England. A masterful man, of the sternest religious principles, he destined his son for the ministry. Something of a domestic tyrant,[4] he early recognized Alfred's abilities. In the manner of James Mill, he directed his son to the classics, worked him hard in Hebrew, and prohibited the mathematics which Alfred loved. Nevertheless, when his father endeavored to send him to Oxford on a scholarship which would have led to the church, the son rebelled. With the aid of a loan from an uncle and another scholarship, he went to Cambridge.

There his career was entirely successful. In 1865, he was second wrangler in mathematics and was elected to a fellowship. Sometime during his Cambridge years, he lost his religious faith and became an agnostic. But he continued to admire the religious spirit and never wrote or spoke against religion. In 1867, while he was teaching mathematics at Cambridge, he grew interested in metaphysics, then psychology, and finally economics. He reinforced this last taste with a year in Germany which enabled him to meet, among other economists, Wilhelm Roscher.

The reason for his shift, a little unusual for a man who had expected to make his career in molecular physics, was the not uncommon Victorian wish to do good. Marshall wished to end

---

[3] T. W. Hutchison, *A Review of Economic Doctrines*, Oxford, 1953, p. 62.
[4] He wrote a tract called *Man's Rights and Women's Duties*.

poverty; much more, he hoped to lead the poor to live noble lives. The study of political economy, he hoped, would improve the quality of human existence. Therefore, from 1867 on, while he lectured on economics in Cambridge, he slowly developed his own system. In 1875 he visited the United States to study the problem of protection in a new country. In 1876 he married Mary Paley, an early bluestocking, a student of Marshall's, and a lecturer in economics in Newnham College. Forced to give up his fellowship because of his marriage, he became, in turn, principal of University College, Bristol, and lecturer in political economy at Oxford. In 1885 Cambridge called him back as professor of political economy. He held the chair until his retirement in 1908. His intensive work on the *Principles of Economics* began in 1885.

When that great book finally appeared in 1890, English economists hailed it with instant acclaim. Nevertheless, its originality failed of full appreciation. The fault was Marshall's. He made few claims to originality, and the smooth, almost soporific style, the air of platitude, and the relentless consignment to footnotes of many novelties, aided him to convince inattentive readers of his own estimate. What Marshall wanted most was agreement. Thin-skinned man that he was, he hated controversy and criticism. These emotional attitudes had their use. English economics avoided the fruitless German battle of methods partly because Marshall, himself a good economic historian, carefully made only limited claims for analytic methods, and offered measured tribute to the historian's craft.

One instructive exception marred the harmony of Marshall's life. William Cunningham, a leader of the historical school in England, criticized Marshall quite sharply for perverting economic history.[5] Marshall, he charged, assumed the universality of economic laws, neglected the relativity of economic conclusions, and perpetrated many misinterpretations in the historical sketch which began the *Principles*. For the first and only time, Marshall answered a criticism. The answer was firm, but con-

[5] *Economic Journal,* Vol. II, 1892, pp. 1–16, 492–506, 507–519.

ciliatory. Cunningham had misunderstood him: "Speaking broadly, his criticisms proceed on assumptions that I hold opinions which in fact I do not hold."[6] The difference between them, said Marshall, was emphasis alone.

Marshall's reputation for originality suffered for a second reason. He had waited too long. There was evidence by the early 1870's that the main outlines of his theory and, certainly, the graphic apparatus were complete. The testimony of the students to whom he taught his new doctrines was convincing. Foxwell's correspondence with Jevons stressed Marshall's achievements. Jevons' answer was the only one: Why doesn't he publish? Thus, Marshall's claim was good to subjective originality in the discovery of both marginal utility and marginal productivity, the twin triumphs of marginalism. But he refined, rewrote, and sought the single masterful production rather than the collection of bright ideas of which Jevons' work consisted.

For this decision there was a penalty. On the Continent it took the shape of wonder at the reception England gave ideas which for the most part seemed 20 years old. This reaction possibly explained Marshall's petulance toward his marginalist predecessors. He insisted that Menger, Walras, and especially Jevons had not taught him. No, it was von Thünen and Cournot, who preceded the trio of the 1870's as well as Marshall.

In the *Principles*, Marshall's concern with ethics, wish to improve business practice, and enlighten the poor shined forth on most pages. This was more than mere obiter dicta. These concerns influenced the book's organization and even the form of some of its technical contributions. The book was organized around supply and demand. But of the two, Marshall said much more about the first. His reason was characteristic: ". . . while wants are the rulers of life among the lower animals, it is to changes in the forms of efforts and activities that we must turn when in search for the keynotes of the history of mankind."[7] Activities create wants; not wants, activities. Hence, the old em-

---

[6] *Ibid.*, p. 517.
[7] Alfred Marshall, *Principles of Economics*, Macmillan, 1920, p. 85.

phasis of the classicists upon supply was not mistaken, even though it was excessive. Increasing and decreasing cost, and consumers' surplus testified to Marshall's analytical concern with economic welfare.

Because he wished to be useful, he distrusted long chains of reasoning, concealed the mathematical scaffolding of his theory lest it frighten readers, and made his analysis as realistic as possible, as closely allied to business practice as he could manage.

MARSHALL'S ECONOMICS

We divide Marshall's economics into two parts: his systematization of marginal theory and his armory of tools. As a system builder, Marshall combined a marginal-productivity explanation of supply (mostly in the language of his English classical predecessors), with a marginal-utility explanation of demand. The interaction of supply and demand determined price. In Marshall's words, "the general theory of the equilibrium of demand and supply is a Fundamental Idea running through the frames of all the various parts of the central problem of distribution and exchange."[8]

With some qualifications, Ricardo and Mill had argued that, practically if not theoretically, the value of an article tended to reflect the number of hours required to produce it. Different market prices indicated different quantities of labor employed in producing different commodities. Therefore, their analysis centered upon supply. Jevons, Menger, and Walras had reversed the procedure, though their neglect of supply was much less grave than the classicist's neglect of demand. As a marginalist epigram put it, "men dive for pearls because they are valuable; pearls are not valuable because men dive for them."

Marshall conserved both explanations as part of a complete theory of exchange. His theory of supply started with work. Even if work were pleasant to begin with, it became painful in the end. The longer we worked, the more the pain: the marginal disutility of labor was a function of time. Why did anyone

[8] *Ibid.*, p. viii.

work? Because wages assuaged the pain. Why did anyone stop working? At some point, the wages offered failed to compensate the worker adequately for the fatigue of his labor. Thus, Marshall grafted the marginal idea upon the older conception of labor as simple homogeneous pain. His theory could examine degrees of pain. Thus, a time-and-a-half rate of pay for overtime labor presumably compensated the worker for his additional (marginal) fatigue.

Capital, too, was needed to produce goods. Here Marshall adopted, and adapted, Senior's notion of abstinence as the justification of interest. However, the term made him uneasy. He realized that the very rich, who did no abstaining in any usual sense of the word, saved involuntarily large parts of their income. Marshall therefore substituted the ethically colorless word "waiting," and employed it to mean no more than that the "waiter" postponed spending funds which he could have spent. Terminology aside, the supply of both capital and labor depended upon discomfort which money payment overcame. We could presume, said Marshall, that just as higher wages were needed to overcome the fatigue of extra work, higher rates of interest compensated savers for the increasing marginal discomfort of postponing pleasure.

Demand was the other side of the story. Once more the key was the marginal principle. Its application was easy. As we acquired more of anything, money included, the satisfaction it yielded us (its marginal utility), diminished. Correspondingly, the price we offer for additional amounts decreases. The rational consumer was engaged in a never-ending balancing act at the margin. Perpetually he compared the additional satisfaction resulting from expenditure on one good, with the additional satisfaction derivable from an alternative purchase. In equilibrium, the consumer reflected with gratification that no reallocation of his income could increase his satisfaction. If he were not in equilibrium, he would arrange his future purchases so as to maximize his total satisfaction or utility. A condition of equilibrium was proportionality of prices to utilities: a pound of steak at $1.00 a pound should result in ten times as much satisfaction as an ice-cream cone at 10¢, and the ice-cream cone ten times as much satisfaction as a piece of bubble gum at 1¢.

The producer acted like the consumer. Although his object was maximum profit rather than maximum utility, he allocated his funds among the elements of production, much as the thrifty housewife allocated her food budget among the hundreds of items which clamored for her attention. The producer compared the additional product which $100 spent on labor would produce with the additional product the same sum expended on a small machine, or better materials, or increased maintenance, might occasion. He juggled many factors and subfactors with the design of making their marginal products proportional to their prices. The parallel to the consumer's behavior was precise. If the producer spent $100 on labor, $1000 on a machine, and $200 on better materials, he anticipated that the machine would add ten times as much product as the man, and the materials twice as much as the man. Throughout, the great principle of Substitution guided him. For the more expensive, he substituted the cheaper.

Was it utility or cost of production which determined price? Both: "We might as reasonably dispute whether it is the upper or the under blade of a pair of scissors that cuts a piece of paper, as whether value is governed by utility or cost of production."[9] Supply and Demand still determined price, but we now knew what influenced them. Marshall's explanation amplified understanding.

Part of the amplification concerned time, "the center of the chief difficulty of almost every economic problem."[10] How did prices behave over time? How did the forces which determined supply and demand work themselves out? The world, said Marshall, was very complex, and time was continuous. As a mathematician and grudging student of Walras, Marshall was perfectly aware of general interdependence, of the fact that everything af-

[9] *Ibid.*, p. 348.
[10] *Ibid.*, p. vii.

fected everything else. At the same time, he saw how hopeless it was to examine any concrete problem from a general equilibrium standpoint. Therefore he invented one of the fictions which have been referred to, the device of partial analysis. He asked his readers to pretend that we could concentrate our attention upon one industry and, within that industry, upon one business unit, the equally fictitious Representative Firm. Of course, what happened in one industry inevitably altered the sales of other industries, but the fiction misled very little if the industry were small and the firm nearly typical. Marshall described this method, which was at the heart of his procedure, in these words: "The forces to be dealt with are, however, so numerous that it is best to take a few at a time; and to work out a number of partial solutions as auxiliaries to our main study. Thus, we begin by isolating the primary relations of supply, demand and price in regard to a particular commodity. We reduce to inaction all other forces by the phrase 'other things being equal': we do not suppose that they are inert, but for the time we ignore their activity." What became of these segregated "forces"? "In the second stage more forces are released from the hypothetical slumber that had been imposed on them: changes in the conditions of demand for and supply of particular groups of commodities come into play; and their complex mutual interactions begin to be observed." The procedure has a terminus. "Gradually the area of the dynamical problem becomes larger; the area covered by provisional statical assumptions becomes smaller; and at last is reached the great central problem of the Distribution of the National Dividend among a vast number of different agents of production."[11] Like many of his contemporaries, Marshall hoped to move from statics to dynamics.

How did time affect such an industry and such a firm? Employing another useful fiction, Marshall identified three different time periods. Although these periods could be isolated only hypothetically and they shifted from problem to problem, they

[11] *Ibid.*, pp. xiv-xv.

helped us understand the events of real life. The market period was the shortest of these time divisions. In it, supplies were fixed, and demand determined price. In Marshall's spirit, we might suppose that strawberries were brought into New York City in the morning. For the day, supply was fixed. Since sellers cannot save a perishable product for a better market, the price of the strawberries at the day's end must reflect the intensity of demand for the delicacy. But however strong the demand, sellers were unable to increase that day the supply of the berries. Thus if a person stationed himself outside a New York fruit store, he might observe either that the price set moved the strawberries so rapidly that they disappeared before afternoon, or that few were sold initially and, as time wore on and the closing hour approached, the storekeeper lowered his price. In the first instance, sellers correctly estimated equilibrium price, or possibly underestimated it. In the second, they overestimated that price. The overestimate led to sales at different prices, some above, some below equilibrium. Demand controlled the transactions. Marshall was careful to limit his demonstrations to comparatively inexpensive, readily divisible items. In such cases only, could he assume plausibly that the marginal utility of money did not change for individual purchasers as they made their successive purchases.

The second time period, the short-run normal, lasted long enough to enable firms to vary the supply of given products, produced in existing plants. Now supply varied but productive facilities were constant and the law of diminishing returns applied. The forces which influenced supply now took a larger role. If consumer demand rose, producers expanded their output. The expansion continued until the cost of the last unit of output equaled the price at which it sold. If consumer demand fell, the producer contracted his production, again to the point where the cost of the last unit matched the price received for it. If demand dropped off too much, the producer halted operations. "Too much" implied that the businessman failed to cover day-to-day operating costs.[12] When these costs were covered, he operated

---

[12] Marshall's prime costs, our variable costs.

even at a loss, because his fixed costs,[13] rent, property taxes, continued so long as he stayed in business.

Marshall's third period was the long-run normal. Here, he assumed that firms had time enough to expand the plant itself, as well as vary output from existing facilities. They could expand by adding new machines and constructing plant extensions to house them. By failing to replace worn-out equipment, they could contract. Moreover, old firms could drop out completely and new firms could enter. In modern language, the law of returns to scale, with every resource variable, applied. What forces played upon entrepreneurs as they considered such decisions? When demand was so low that total costs were not recovered, firms dropped out or contracted. The survivors earned normal profits. If demand was very high, old producers expanded and new producers entered the industry. In long-run equilibrium, prices covered costs, including normal returns on capital. As this exposition intimated, given enough time, supply, not demand, had the larger influence upon price. So Marshall must have assumed in failing to parallel his careful discussion of time and supply with an equally precise account of the chronological dimensions of demand.

While these adjustments proceeded, many other influences were at work. In a progressive society all firms enjoyed a combination of internal and external economies. The internal economies were a gift from an old friend, the division of labor. As manufacturing operations were subdivided, and increasingly specialized machines substituted themselves for human labor, the cost per unit of output shrank. Education was another influence. As its quantity and quality increased, the intelligence and skill of the average worker improved.[14] Many industries enjoyed increas-

---

[13] Marshall's term was "supplementary costs."

[14] In the light of current tendencies, Marshall's hopes for consumer behavior make grim reading: "The world would go much better if everyone would buy fewer and simpler things, and would take trouble in selecting them for their real beauty; being careful of course to get good value in return for this outlay, but preferring to buy a few things made well by highly paid labour rather than many things made badly by low paid labour." Marshall, *op. cit.*, p. 137.

ing returns to scale, a tendency which warred against continued diminishing returns from land. Although their health was closely related to the energies of their founders, representative firms grew with their industry. Marshall was cheerful about capitalism. He expected it to raise the standard of living of ordinary people. Above all, he looked forward to a higher moral tone, as capitalists and workers learned to behave more honorably toward each other. Ultimately capitalism would put, not riches, but the "noble life" within the reach of all.

Marshall's feats of technique scintillated most dazzlingly in Book V of the *Principles*. Four of these feats can be grouped around the idea of market organization: external economies, the representative firm, internal economies, and the producer's private market. Marshall's concept of the representative firm has not won enduring favor. As he described it, this firm was "one which has had a fairly long life, and fair success, which is managed with normal ability, and which has normal access to the economies, external and internal, which belong to that aggregate volume of production."[15]

These economies were very powerful. Internally, division of labor, specialization of equipment, and economies in buying and selling were the principal gains of scale. The importance of external economies was constantly growing. They included all the benefits to a firm of the increasing efficiency of the industries which supplied it. Thus economies external to one industry were internal to another. Marshall hinted at monopolistic competition when he described each firm's special, local, protected market. At another point, he spoke of the firm's demand curves as sloped.

These ingenuities led to a puzzle. If internal economies and the still more potent external economies combined to lower costs as the scale of enterprise grew, how could competition endure? A declining cost (supply) curve meant that the bigger the firm, the more efficient it was. The logical development was monopoly. The limitations of particular markets, and human mortality,

[15] *Ibid.*, p. 317.

saved competition.[16] It was the entrepreneur of vision and ability who sparked the representative firm. Like the rest of us, such entrepreneurs die. The odds were high against the succession of others as able. New representative firms succeeded the old ones, before the latter could take advantage of all the available internal and external economies. In turn, the new representative firms flourished for a generation, and then flagged with the energies of their directors. In Marshall, death limited growth. In some versions of modern theory, human limitations and the indivisibility of the executive function serve to explain why returns cease to increase.

Marshall made ingenious use of increasing returns as a guide to tax and subsidy policy. If a tax was placed upon an industry subject to diminishing returns to scale, entrepreneurs reduced production. At lower levels of output, efficiency was greater and unit costs declined. If subsidies were granted industries which enjoyed increasing returns to scale, entrepreneurs expanded output, at lower unit costs. The welfare implications were plain. If diminishing-return industries paid taxes, which an intelligent government transferred in the shape of subsidies to increasing-return industries, total output and total consumer satisfactions rose.

Marshall's consumer surplus also centered on welfare. The device was simple but ingenious. The price an individual paid for an item was proportional to its marginal utility. If a consumer bought six units, the law of declining marginal utility taught that he would have paid more for the first than for the second, more for the second than for the third, more for the third than for the fourth, and so on. The differences between what he would have been willing to pay for the six units and what he did pay, constituted consumer's surplus. The discriminating monopolist, who charged different prices for different portions of his sales, appropriated consumer's surplus. These conclusions had tax implications. Proper tax policy diminished consumer surplus as little

---

[16] Partial equilibrium analysis was ill adapted to the problems of expanding scale. At some point, the assumption of insulation from other forces became too unrealistic to maintain.

as possible. By extension, the argument favored income taxes over commodity taxes. The income tax allowed consumers to allocate the expenditure reduction so as to restrict their surplus by a minimum amount.

Marshall did not invent elasticity. Cournot discussed it and Mill hinted at it. But he did refine, amplify, and apply the concept. Point elasticity of demand, cross-elasticity, and elasticity of supply all appeared. Marshall described easy substitution as the prime cause of high elasticity. The *Principles* contained an acute discussion of the difficulties in the way of deriving statistical demand curves. Too many important variables changed, among them the value of money, the size of incomes, the scale of the economy, and the tastes of consumers. These considerations convinced Marshall that long-run elasticity was higher than short-run elasticity.

Marshall made numerous significant contributions to the theory of money. His exposition of the quantity theory of money brought it close to the general theory of value. Somewhat in the manner of Fisher, he distinguished between real and money rates of interest. He identified the chain of events in which an increase in the supply of money reflected itself in an increase in prices. He enunciated the cash balance versions of the equation of exchange. Finally, he invented the chain index number.

There can have been few economists who combined as well as Marshall did the ability to construct a system with the ingenuity to build the tools which equipped it. The problem in reading the *Principles* is to penetrate beneath the style to the matter.

THE AUSTRIANS

Despite specific disagreements, the Austrian school agreed in its major attitudes. The Austrians were anti-historical. As a corollary, they preferred abstract analysis. Marshall was full of ethics; the Austrians were full of metaphysics. Operating, perhaps, on the premise that important phenomena have distinguished origins, they sought the essential, inner meanings of the ideas they cherished. Therefore their explanations tended to concentrate upon the universal. Cunningham's complaints about Marshall's generalizations of economic laws applied much more accurately to Böhm-Bawerk than they did to Marshall. In the concept of capital, Böhm-Bawerk discovered an explanation of economic behavior appropriate to all societies. Wieser's natural value purported to derive profits, rents, and wages from the most general of all economic circumstances, the communist state. The great Austrians were persistently more abstract, general, and timeless than Marshall ever permitted himself to become. Despite obvious differences in aim and manner, the Austrians bore strong resemblances to Marx.

It was somewhat paradoxical that these devotees of generality and abstraction avoided the device capable of generating the broadest conclusions, Edgeworth's "sovereign science," mathematics. The fact was that the Austrians condescended to no trace of mathematics, even diagrammatic illustration. These aids to brevity might have considerably mitigated the school's tedious prolixity. An analytical consequence was the failure of Austrian writings quite to attain the demonstration of interdependence which was the most valuable contribution of the general-equilibrium theorists.

Abstraction had its merits. Wieser was able to survey the controversy between capitalism and socialism from a height denied to the theorists of partial equilibrium. While pressing the marginal principle to its limits, the Austrian carefully distinguished it from hedonism. Jevons, Edgeworth, and Clark were less successful. The high level of abstraction helped them develop the theory of demand as the logic of pure choice, whatever the dispositions or aims of the choosers.

EUGEN BÖHM-BAWERK (1851–1914)

The best-known of this group, Böhm-Bawerk made his leading contribution to capital and interest theory. First, proceeding on Mengerian lines, he produced a clear exposition of value theory. He added to Menger's explanation the notion of marginal pairs, the idea that, out of all the participants in a market, two buyers and two sellers determined price. One pair included the seller just willing to sell at a price and the buyer just willing to buy at the same price. The other pair consisted of the buyer just barely *unwilling* to buy at that price and the seller just barely *unwilling* to sell. In Marshallian diagrams, the marginal pairs were the buyers and sellers either at or close to equilibrium.

Böhm-Bawerk produced a massive history of interest rates as a prelude to his *Positive Theory of Capital*, his major work. The *Positive Theory* itself suffered from verbosity and ambiguity. Nevertheless it contained an exceedingly ingenious and detailed explanation of capital's functions, and two explanations of interest. Its author started with the "fundamental proposition" that "roundabout methods" were more productive than direct methods.[17] Roundabout methods required capital. Capital implied the passage of time, during which the complex of intermediate goods of which capital consisted were processed and directed to the completion of consumer goods. The creation of capital always meant the postponement of present consumption. Lengthening the structure of production invariably increased productivity, but in diminishing degree.

The period of production which entered the exposition at this stage encountered much criticism. Neither Menger nor Wieser adopted it. It was an effort to give precision to roundaboutness. Imagine, asked Böhm-Bawerk, that the production of a certain good required 100 days of labor spread over 10 years. Assume also that 20 days of the labor were expended 10 years ago; 20 days, 9 years ago; 5 days in each year from 8 to 1; and the last 20 days immediately before the completion of the product. If we wished to derive the average period of production, here was how we computed it: we added 20 times 10 (200), to 20 times 9 (180), to 40, 35, 30, 25, 20, 15, 10, and 5. We divided by 100 the 560 which was our total and derived as quotient, 5.6 years as the average period of production. Time expended had been weighted

<hr/>

[17] See Böhm-Bawerk, *The Positive Theory of Capital*, translated by William Smart, 1891, p. 20.

according to its distance from the present: 20 days expended 10 years ago were worth 200. The same number of days expended just before consumption were worth only 20.

Despite its rather spurious precision, the concept was extremely obscure. How could specific inputs be associated with specific outputs? What could be done about the proposition that capital extended in time all the way back to antiquity? Labor expended centuries earlier helped procreate today's capital. Precisely because the labor was expended so very long ago, logical consistency demanded that Böhm-Bawerk grant it very heavy weight.

In an exchange economy, suggested Böhm-Bawerk, we could visualize production as a series of circles. The outermost contained goods ready for immediate consumption. The next contained goods a year away from the consumer's market, and so on. The more highly developed the community, the larger was the number of circles and the greater was the area of the circle furthest removed in chronology from the present. In a stationary economy, the community produced just enough each year to maintain this structure of production. In a progressive economy, enough was produced to lengthen the structure of production and increase the economy's productivity. A retrogressive community consumed more than current production and shortened the structure of production. The disastrous effects of its behavior appeared only in the future.

At the center of the process was saving. When saving increased, the structure of production lengthened. When it diminished, the structure contracted. Why did people save? Why was interest paid? Although Böhm-Bawerk insisted that he made a single answer, most critics divided it into two. We preferred present goods to future goods. For this preference, Böhm-Bawerk advanced three explanations. The first two were logical enough. The third demands interpretation. First, the present and the future corresponded to "different circumstances of want and provision."[18] Like a young professional man starting his career,

18 *Ibid.*, p. 249.

we could reasonably anticipate rising incomes. Because it was more scarce, money in the present was worth more than money in the future. Böhm-Bawerk did not examine cases in which the opposite preferences were plausible: professional athletes preparing for a drop in their income after their careers ended, couples supporting children in college, the middle-aged looking forward to inexpensive retirement in warm climates. Second, we underestimated the future for temperamental reasons. Our imaginations were defective. Future pleasures were less distinct than present pleasures. Moreover, our wills were weak. Even when we knew better, we grasped at the present, in despite of the future. Finally, human life was short and uncertain. *Carpe diem.*

So far, Böhm-Bawerk explained why interest must be paid to evoke saving. The causes did not explain how interest *could* be paid. Böhm-Bawerk had implied the answer. He stated it once more in his notorious "third ground." Capital was productive. Roundabout methods permitted larger output per man and per other resource. Interest could be paid out of the postponed output of capital. No quarrel could be justified with this statement, if Böhm-Bawerk had simply accepted its connection with productivity alone. He insisted on relating it to time preference.

No critical tone should conceal Böhm-Bawerk's achievements in constructing a plausible theory of interest and a vivid conception of the capitalistic process. To the English-speaking reader, the manner of the Austrians does not ingratiate: the Austrian contribution was no smaller for that fact.

FRIEDRICH VON WIESER (1851–1926)

Wieser's major contribution was the concept of alternative or opportunity cost. In pleasant contrast to Böhm-Bawerk, Wieser's exposition was lucid. The contribution of a given productive resource was measured by the maximum addition to output which a unit of that resource could make in another use. If a carpenter, at work on a house, contributed $30 to total output in one day, his wage tended to be $30. An employer who sought a carpenter to build workbenches in a factory would find that the wage he had to pay was determined by the amount the carpenter got elsewhere, say, in building the house. Thus, the value of service *A* in employment *X* was measured by the value of its product in employment *Y*, if it were assumed that employment *Y* made most effective use of *A*.

From this principle of imputation, Wieser inferred an interesting corollary. If the value of the factors of production depended upon the presence of alternative uses, it followed that monopoly was defined as a situation in which there were no alternative uses. As defined by Wieser, payments to the owners of monopolized resources were not costs, they were rents. The point is easy to illustrate. A Mickey Mantle is a monopoly. He has no alternative uses and there are no alternatives to him. If he were not a baseball player, he would presumably earn a great deal less in some other occupation. If his baseball salary were $80,000 and he could earn $5,000 elsewhere, only $5,000 of his salary would be a cost. The remaining $75,000 amounted to a rent paid for a monopolized resource.

In Wieser, opportunity cost was a general principle of imputation. In equilibrium, the prices of products equaled the costs of productive services. Therefore no service was used in one place when it might be more valuable in another. The path to equilibrium was a series of shifts from one employment to another, until prices equaled costs.

Wieser's great book, *Natural Value*, which he wrote in 1884, contained a good deal more than opportunity cost. The title indicated one of Wieser's objectives: to prove that, in an otherwise highly developed community innocent of prices and exchange, rent, interest, and wages would nevertheless manifest themselves. In such a community, prices reflected the relative marginal utility of commodities. At this stage, Wieser implicitly assumed the possibility of interpersonal utility comparisons.

In an exchange economy, this equality between prices and marginal utilities failed to hold. Differences in wealth caused differences in the marginal utility of money.[19] These differences had

[19] Wieser, this is a good place to say, invented the term "marginal utility."

momentous consequences. Now production was so ordered that "instead of things which would have the greatest utility, those things are produced for which the most will be paid."[20] The greater the inequality, the worse the result. Inequality "will furnish luxuries for the wanton and the glutton, while it is deaf to the wants of the miserable and the poor."[21] Where income and wealth were unevenly divided, the poor inevitably paid as much as possible, and the rich paid much less than they could.

Wieser's demonstration made it clear that the logic of choice and its agent, the marginal principle, applied as much to socialism as to capitalism. Marginalism neither presupposed nor endorsed capitalism. By implication at least, Wieser pursued the line of reasoning which Barone, somewhat later, and Lange, considerably later, adopted in proving the feasibility of rational-resource allocation under socialism.

Wieser's conception of the state's appropriate role contrasted interestingly with Mill's painful wrestlings with permissible departures from laissez faire. Weiser was much less attached to this principle and took occasion to castigate the doctrinaire leanings of the English economists. He identified three major reasons for state intervention, dependent on the common difficulty of private calculation. In the first category of cases, the individual was too weak either to defend his country or to maintain a system of courts and police. So far, so familiar. The second category included situations where profit was too small or too uncertain to encourage private action. Because the return from railroad investment was so slow in coming, the state had to act. In the case of public streets, private enterprise impeded wide use. The last justification of state action was most interesting. It reflected something of German economic history. In countries which were backward, capitalists were scarce. It was the state's duty to fill the gap. Little imagination is needed to see Wieser approving

[20] Friedrich von Wieser, *Natural Value*, translated by C. A. Malloch, Stechert, 1893, p. 58.
[21] *Ibid.*, p. 58.

state planning in the world's underdeveloped countries. Moreover, the case for state intervention was strong when private power aroused legitimate fears. Trusts and monopolies were appropriate instances.

Thus, Wieser was far removed from orthodox laissez faire and still further away from the apologetics of which his school was frequently accused. Wieser was a good example of the political neutrality of the marginalist tools.

AMERICAN MARGINALISM

Nothing has been said about American economists up to this point, for the sufficient reason that there was little to say. With the exception of Carey, who disputed Ricardian rent theory, and Francis Walker, who criticized the wages-fund doctrine, American economists, as theorists, imitated Ricardo and Mill. For the rest, they dealt with the practical exigencies of a new, growing economy. Henry George, whose single doctrine has been mentioned, and Thorstein Veblen, who will be examined elsewhere, belonged to the last third of the nineteenth century. The first two major economists who contributed importantly to the mainstream of European economic doctrine were John Bates Clark and Irving Fisher.

Clark's most famous student was Thorstein Veblen. During a year of study in Germany, Clark's own teacher was the eminent Karl Knies, a leader of the historical school. Something of a Christian Socialist, Clark preached the glories of competition. Between his *Philosophy of Wealth*, written in 1885, and his *Distribution of Wealth*, published in 1899, there was a shift of viewpoint as sharp as that between the Adam Smith of the *Theory of Moral Sentiments* and the Adam Smith of the *Wealth of Nations*. Always, however, the guiding concern of his thought was ethical. He shifted his viewpoint after he had changed his mind about how to attain unchanged goals. His distinguished son, John Maurice Clark, believed that his father looked at the economic world in much the same way as Alfred Marshall.[22] Parallels could be drawn, also, between him and John Stuart Mill.

As a person, Clark was generous even in dissent. He wrote an introduction to an American edition of Rodbertus, while disagreeing with the ideas he introduced. Like Marshall, he was a man of a single controversy, the prolonged disagreement with Böhm-Bawerk over the nature of capital. His work emitted a pleasant optimism, not extinct today. This passage was typical: "Better things of every kind come to constitute the world's working equipment: buildings are taller, ships are faster, engines are more economical, railroads are straighter and more level, locomotives are more powerful, trains are longer."[23] As as American with a claim to the independent discovery of marginal productivity, Clark deserved respectful attention.

The Philosophy of Wealth was vigorously written, almost to the point of the polemical. Showing the influence of the German historical economists, it severely criticized English classicists. Clark attacked Ricardo on two grounds. First, Ricardo's view of human nature was erroneous. In fact, "economic science has never been based on adequate anthropological study."[24] No doubt Veblen read this passage. Man was not an independent entity, as Ricardo believed. A person "is made by his relations to others, to be an atomic portion of a higher organism."[25] The Teutonic coloration was unmistakable. Ricardo was wrong about an even more important, second matter, the competitive nature of the market. Writing in 1885, Clark was certain that competition was diminishing. What he saw with transitory gloom was the increasing solidarity of labor on the one side and of capital on the other, a phenomenon certain to cause "blind struggle" and to be settled by the "crudest force and endurance."

For this condition, Clark advanced three remedies, two of them familiar to readers of Mill: arbitration, profit sharing, and full

[22] See "J. M. Clark on J. B. Clark," in Henry W. Spiegel, *The Development of Economic Thought,* Wiley, 1952, p. 604.

[23] John Bates Clark, *The Distribution of Wealth,* Macmillan, 1899, pp. 247–248.

[24] John Bates Clark, *The Philosophy of Wealth,* Ginn & Co., 1903, p. 33.

[25] *Ibid.,* p. 37.

coöperation, "in the direct order of their availability and in the reverse order of their intrinsic excellence."[26] The prescription shared Mill's characteristic defects of vagueness about the means of achievement and uncertainty about the definition of the justice to be sought.

In the course of his analysis, Clark castigated both labor and capital for acting against the public interest. Despite his pessimistic prediction, he could not bring himself, any more than Mill could, to abandon competition as a principle. Too much went with it: "Society does not and will not completely abandon the competitive principle; it is still needed as an agent of distribution, and it is the sole means on which we can rely for the securing of a large product to distribute." The endorsement was not complete: "Yet . . . society should hold this agent in abeyance within limited fields of industry, whenever, within those limits, a better system is available."[27]

Clark's manner in his masterpiece, the *Distribution of Wealth*, was slightly old-fashioned in its emphasis on natural laws and its copious illustrations, which aided comprehension but added length. The opening paragraph served notice that Clark had shifted his opinions: "It is the purpose of this work to show that the distribution of the income of society is controlled by a natural law, and that this law if it worked without friction would give to every agent of production the amount of wealth which that agent creates."[28] The dire forebodings of 1885 had turned into the "friction" of 1899. Clark was to imply that the friction was too slight to disturb seriously the working of the natural law. Clark seemed to say that competitive distribution was not only efficient—his earlier book conceded that much—but also equitable.

Although he too conceived statics to be a prelude to dynamics, Clark's method was static. He was convinced that, even in a static frame, the truths of economics could be adequately displayed.

[26] *Ibid.*, p. 196.
[27] *Ibid.*, p. 207.
[28] Clark, *The Distribution of Wealth*, p. v.

The static society required fixed quantities of labor and capital, constant techniques of production, stable consumer tastes, and unchanging industrial organization. In this society, wages and interest reached the "theoretically natural rates which science has been seeking."[29]

Natural law operated to divide total product among three claimants: laborers who received wages, capitalists who earned interest and rent, and entrepreneurs who worked for profit. Clark merged rent and interest and reduced land to a species of capital. The profits of entrepreneurs were payments for coördinating business activity. Clark's theory of interest rested heavily on productivity.

The wage of the laborer tended to equal the value of his marginal product. Clark took pains to prove that the intramarginal workers were not exploited, even though wages were set by the marginal worker. His ingenious though not entirely convincing argument depended upon the assumption of extreme flexibility of capital form. As additional workers were hired, total capital did not change, but the average amount per worker diminished and entrepreneurs altered the capital to adapt it to a larger number of workers. After the adaptation was complete, the gap between the marginal productivities of the first and last workers employed, disappeared. Capital, it turned out, was responsible for the extra returns from intramarginal laborers. In the determination of the wage rate, there was a zone of indifference within which it made no difference to the employer whether he hired one more worker or not. The marginal worker could be found within this zone.

Clark's theory of capital aroused most controversy. He regarded capital as an "endless succession of shifting goods always worth a certain amount," or "a fund, a sum of active and productive wealth, that continues in industry, as successive instruments of production live, as it were, their industrial lives and die."[30] If there was not something mystical about a constant fund of capi-

---

[29] *Ibid.*, p. vii.
[30] *Ibid.*, p. 121.

tal, shifting in its individual parts, at the least there was an index number problem of heroic dimensions.

Capital came into being because people abstained from consumption. However, once capital had appeared, no new act of abstinence was needed to maintain the existing stock. "Paying interest is buying the product of capital, as paying wages is buying the product of labor. *The power of capital to create the produce is, then, the basis of interest.*"[31]

To Clark, Böhm-Bawerk's period of production missed an essential point. Capital enabled work and finished product to synchronize. "The men keep the stock of capital-goods from failing. Their permanent stock of shifting capital goods—the true capital—keeps the men from waiting."[32] Clark held that the existence of a permanent stock of capital permitted today's work to be rewarded today. Paradoxically, this result was impossible in the absence of capital. All the waiting had been done in the past.

A few special features of Clark's theory conclude this account. Clark extended the Ricardian rent concept so far that he remarked, ". . . all wages and interest . . . [are] . . . surplus that is of the nature of rents."[33] Diminishing returns applied to all cases where one factor was fixed and others were variable. In a dynamic society, profits vanished. Clark's treatment of demand was fresh. Although he endorsed consumer's surplus, he made no attempt to estimate its monetary value. Instead, he dealt with commodities as bundles of qualities. He carefully argued that consumers value the marginal utility of successive qualities contained by commodities, rather than the entire commodity. His diagrams of the disutility of labor and the utility of product were reminiscent of Jevons' constructions.

While the comparison to Marshall was appropriate, Clark was less guarded in deriving ethical conclusions from his theory. In consequence, his former pupil, Veblen, found him a better target than the Englishman. Nevertheless, as in other cases, the ethics

[31] *Ibid.*, p. 135.
[32] *Ibid.*, p. 318.
[33] *Ibid.*, p. 354.

and the analysis are separable. The analysis ranked high among marginalist expositions of productivity theory.

P. H. WICKSTEED (1844–1927)

Wicksteed, a Unitarian minister and fine classical scholar, was an unusually modest man who claimed for himself no originality. His single aim was careful, clear explanation of marginalism. It was an aim he completely accomplished. His *Common Sense of Political Economy* must have been the most painstaking exposition of marginalism ever written. Wicksteed skipped no problems. Like Marshall, his target was the ordinary reader. He achieved this tour de force by borrowing the best features of the Walrasian, Jevonian, and Austrian theories, and combining them in one coherent, nonmathematical account.

Wicksteed did himself an injustice. His mind was original as well as patient and his versatility was exceptional. To each work he added something of his own. His *Alphabet of Economic Science* professed to be only a summary of Jevons, but it incorporated Austrian features including Wieser's term, "marginal utility." His *Essay on the Coordination of the Laws of Distribution,* in appearance a statement of marginal-productivity theory as it stood in 1894, added a new notion, which Wicksteed, possibly mistakenly, later withdrew. This was the proposition that "if each factor is rewarded according to its marginal productivity, the sum of the remunerations of the separate factors will exactly exhaust the product: in other words that the marginal productivity analysis is a *sufficient* explanation of distribution in this sense."[34]

The *Common Sense* was Wicksteed's finest work. In its uncompromising adherence to the marginal principle, it invited comparison to other monomanias: Bentham's and Marx's. Wicksteed insisted that marginal balancing guided aesthetic appreciation, friendship, and religious observation, in short, all aspects of life.

---

[34] Philip H. Wicksteed, *Common Sense of Political Economy,* Routledge, 1935, Vol. I, pp. x–xi.

Strangely enough, the insistence was not crass. It was consistent with the recognition that some choices are better than other, and even with the sophisticated observation that tastes are not necessarily transitive. Even if X prefers A to B and B to C, he may not prefer A to C. Wicksteed's vital point was the central importance of choice. What men chose was their own affair, though as a minister and a classicist, Wicksteed had his own opinions.

Much of this was Jevonian, but the influence of the Lausanne School and of Pareto in particular was strong. Wicksteed managed to deal with general equilibrium, without its mathematics. The intellectual and literary quality of his exposition appeared in passages like this:

. . . through widening circles of remoter and fainter influences, everything that changes the value or significance or any possible application of energies and resources or that changes the terms on which any alternative whatever is offered, may affect the purchase of any single article at a market stall. Primarily it will be affected by its own price, secondarily by the price of the things that are most readily thought of as substitutes for it, and more remotely by the whole range of alternatives open to the individual, or the group, by whom, or from whom, the purchase is to be made.[35]

Wicksteed's general equilibrium preferences led him to a vigorous attack upon the conventional division of the factors of production into land, labor, and capital. There was no scientific principle of division.

He combined Wieser's alternative costs with general equilibrium. His statement could not be improved: "[the entrepreneur] . . . must be able so to arrange the proportions of his factors, and so to combine them, as to make them all worth as much at the margin in his own concern as other people expect them to be in theirs."[36]

Reservation price was his most novel concept. It was a way of dispatching the supply curve as an independent entity and making the entire analysis of price depend upon demand. Wicksteed ad-

[35] *Ibid.*, p. 25.
[36] *Ibid.*, p. 371.

vanced the hypothesis that sellers become buyers at a certain price, which might be called the reservation price. If price fell too low, sellers went home with their product. Or, what amounted to the same thing, at that price the farmer who brought grapes to market bought them from himself and turned them into jam. In every market, sellers were buyers at some prices. Their demand had to be added to that of the declared customers. The case was clearest in a securities market, where sellers instructed their brokers not to sell below a certain price, and below another price might instruct their agents to purchase additional shares. Wicksteed may have exaggerated the usefulness and generality of this concept, out of a desire "to abandon the favourite diagrammatic method by which prices, whether market or normal, are indicated by the intersection of a curve of demand and a curve of supply, or a curve of demand and a curve of cost of products."[37] Theorists still apply the idea.

KNUT WICKSELL (1851–1926)

From the end of the nineteenth century on, Sweden has supported a flourishing school of economists. It has included names like Cassel, Ohlin, Myrdal, and Heckscher, who have played substantial roles in economic thought. Wicksell, the first, may have been the greatest. His were two roles. In the first, he systematized, expounded, and improved marginal theory. In the second, as a monetary theorist, he anticipated many Keynesian doctrines.

Wicksell came to economics late. He was 35 before his mounting interest in social reform and his increasing anxiety about population directed him to economic remedies. In some ways, his attitude toward his subject was like Marshall's: he was more concerned to find the truth than to get credit for the search. Thus his analysis drew freely upon the English classics (unlike other marginalists, he saw much good in them), Austrian value theory, Böhm-Bawerkian capital theory, Walrasian general equilibrium, and the analysis of Wicksteed and Edgeworth. Like

[27] *Ibid.*, p. 8.

Wicksteed, he transformed what he borrowed. His *Lectures on Political Economy*, written at the outset of the twentieth century, taught many novelties.

The most striking quality of Wicksell's economics were their sophistication. His discussion of complementary and competitive goods rivaled Pareto's. He examined the backward-bending supply curve of labor. In handling marginal-utility doctrine, Wicksel stressed all the major criticisms of the theory: discontinuity, indivisibility, mixture of motives, economic friction, and defects in competition. He subjected to acute criticism Walras' proposition that, in free competition, exchange maximized satisfaction. As Wicksell said, Walras himself had proved that many equilibrium positions were possible. How could all of them maximize satisfaction? He made two sharp points. Could we measure interpersonal utilities? He doubted the possibility. But if we could, or if we assumed, after Bentham, that people were equal in their capacities to enjoy pleasure, social differences and unequal income distribution stopped the society short of maximum satisfaction. On these assumptions, government intervention could increase welfare. The intervention might take the form of an increase in minimum wages, or some other redistributionist device.

Wicksell edged closer to monopolistic competition than Marshall. His equivalent to Marshall's private market placed its emphasis upon the ignorance of the buyer and the location of the seller. Neither consideration was trivial. In Chamberlinian fashion, he argued that in some markets costs tend to rise: ". . . the anomaly must remain that competition may sometimes raise prices instead of always lowering them, as one would expect."[38]

In masterly fashion, Wicksell took up the tangled question of whether marginal equilibrium entailed the exhaustion of the product. His answer was affirmative, when one of two conditions held: either small and large producers were equally efficient (proportional returns), or the firms shared the same minimum cost points.

[38] Knut Wicksell, *Lectures on Political Economy*, translated by E. Classen, Routledge & Kegan Paul, 1934, p. 88.

F. Y. EDGEWORTH (1845–1926)

Edgeworth, Fisher, and Pareto were among the most original of the marginalists. Pareto was the author of a general equilibrium system which extended Walras. They were also the most technical of the marginalists, the most mathematical, and the closest to the economics of the mid-1950's. The three share the credit for independent invention of the indifference curve.

Edgeworth's most novel ideas appeared in a little volume entitled *Mathematical Psychics,* written in 1881. It was a strange blend of abstruse mathematics and purple patches of ethical speculation. Edgeworth began his intellectual life as Jevon's most faithful disciple. Later he transferred his allegiance to Marshall. As the title of his book intimated, Edgeworth was a mathematical utilitarian who started with the hope of measuring utility. In an extravagant passage of poetic prose, he made light of the difficulty of interpersonal comparison: "We cannot *count* the golden sands of life; we cannot *number* the 'innumerable smile' of seas of love; but we seem to be capable of observing that there is here a *greater,* there a *less,* multitude of pleasure-units, mass of happiness; and that is enough."[39]

His technical ingenuity demonstrated itself on indifference curves, the path to market equilibrium, and duopoly. Edgeworth was first in time to develop the indifference curve as a set of alternative choices equally satisfactory to an individual, in the familiar shape of a downward-curving figure, asymptotic to both axes. Edgeworth applied his construction to barter. Equilibrium was reached, his analysis demonstrated, when the contract curves of two individuals were tangent to each other.

Edgeworth's solution to the question of how traders moved toward equilibrium in a competitive market was formally complete, but factually unsatisfactory. In examining false (nonequilibrium) prices, Marshall had assumed that each purchase took so minute a part of any individual's income that the marginal utility

[39] F. Y. Edgeworth, *Mathematical Psychics: An Essay on the Application of Mathematics to the Social Sciences,* 1881, pp. 8–9.

of money was unaffected. If the market were well organized and the number of purchases prior to equilibrium few, true equilibrium might imply the exchange of something like equilibrium quantities of goods. Wicksteed had handled the same difficulty by assuming great care and rationality among buyers and sellers. Their mutual explorations, retreats, and transactions finally created the equilibrium price. But it was Walras who, in his approximations, came closest to Edgeworth's answer. Determinate, true equilibrium demanded, said Edgeworth, the privilege of "recontract." Recontract meant that transactions at "false" or nonequilibrium prices were to be regarded as provisional and subject to confirmation at the "true" price. Although the solution was logical enough, it was hard to find markets which actually permitted recontract.

This same ingenuity of theoretical premise and blithe carelessness of empirical notations showed itself in Edgeworth's encounter with duopoly. He assumed that no buyer would deal with more than one seller at a time and that neither seller would learn from experience. Happy in these heroic assumptions, he produced a solution whose main feature was oscillation within two price limits. No single determinate equilibrium could be anticipated.

IRVING FISHER (1867–1941)

Fisher has been called "this country's greatest scientific economist."[40] Nevertheless, his career was marked by neglect at its inception, and ridicule at its close. His highly original *Mathematical Investigations in the Theory of Value and Price* (1892) found few readers. His later years were marred by adherence to a variety of food fads, which confused the public image of the economic scientist.

Fisher emptied the hedonism out of demand theory. His severe economy of assumption directed that "the economist should go no further than is serviceable in explaining economic *facts*. It is

[40] By J. A. Schumpeter in *Ten Great Economists*, Oxford, 1951, p. 223.

not his business to build a theory of psychology. It is not necessary for him to take sides with those who wrangle to prove or disprove that pleasure and pain alone determine conduct. . . . Each individual acts as he desires."[41] He illuminated this pure logic of choice with clearly drawn and ingeniously applied indifference curves. His apparatus included price and income lines. He spoke of inferior and superior goods. There was a subtle discussion of complementarity and substitutability. One of his illustrations of perfect substitutability was an indifference diagram on which a set of parallel straight lines were drawn. A great deal of the modern theory of demand was succinctly compressed in Fisher.

This same talent for exposition helped him achieve reputation in interest theory. His *Rate of Interest* (1907) and *Theory of Interest* (1930) employed the method of successive approximations. He demonstrated, first, how an interest rate emerged in a simple world, ruled by time preference. He showed how in a more complex world productivity influenced the result. Finally, he came to the real world of risk and uncertainty, and explained how it generated many interest rates. The theory was a great deal more than an eclectic combination of elements from Böhm-Bawerk and others. With typical modesty, he dedicated his book to the memory of John Rae and Böhm-Bawerk, "Who Laid the Foundations Upon Which I Have Endeavored to Build."

VILFREDO PARETO (1848–1923)

Pareto, a transplanted Italian nobleman, succeeded Walras in the chair at Lausanne. Although he extended Walras' general economics and developed a more elegant version of equilibrium, he could scarcely have been further away from Walras' reformist politics. An aristocrat and a pessimist, Pareto found in history repetitive cycles, not unilateral progress. In contrast to Marshall and Clark, he stressed the hostility and conflict in social affairs. His massive sociological investigations grimly systematized these misanthropic observations.

[41] Irving Fisher, *Mathematical Investigations into the Theory of Value and Price*, Yale, 1892, p. 11.

However, in his economics he abstracted from actual institutional arrangements, in accordance with his definition of the subject's appropriate boundaries. Much of Pareto is still obscure, particularly the theory of productivity which quarreled with contemporary marginal-productivity theory over the question of the variability of coefficients.[42]

Not all of Pareto was baffling. His discussion of consumer demand surpassed Fisher in one important respect at least, the distinction between income and substitution effects. His complex indifference apparatus made use of three-dimensional figures. In form, the presentation was based on general equilibrium. But, it has been observed, his treatment of market price concentrated on the variation of a single price, Marshall's problem.[43] Pareto translated marginal utility into indifference curves, dropping along the way the assumption that consumers knew by how much they preferred one item to another, and retaining the less stringent requirement that they simply knew that they preferred one collection of items to another. On this basis, Pareto presented the tangency solution between price lines and indifference curves. This solution yields successive points (after translation) on a demand curve, as the price line is rotated.

Pareto made another suggestion which led to the "new" welfare economics. If, as Pareto assumed, interpersonal comparisons of satisfaction were impossible, and pleasure could not be aggregated, definition of the optimum social position appeared unattainable. Governmental intervention represented guess or prejudice.[44] Pareto had a way out. In given circumstances, an optimum position was defined when nobody could be shifted to a higher indifference curve without causing a downward shift for someone else. However, there were an infinite number of

---

[42] Schumpeter commented on Pareto's great feat of forming a school "on the basis of a theoretical structure that was inaccessible not only to the general reader but in some of its most original parts, also to students of economics." *Op. cit.*, p. 119.

[43] See J. R. Hicks, *A Revision of Demand Theory*, Oxford, 1956, p. 2.

[44] As a practical matter, democratic governments especially act as though utility were roughly measurable and interpersonal comparisons feasible. Consider any tax debate.

different institutional arrangements, and each one implied its own optimum position.

CONCLUSION

One of the tests of whether an idea or a method has taken root is the number of its exponents and the difficulty of telling them apart. Although this chapter has looked only at major figures, the impression is justified that similarity of conclusion and analytical method was more pronounced than difference. On the other side, it is only accurate to add that the differences had momentous theoretical consequences. Modern demand theory is constructed with indifference curves. Pareto's welfare observations fathered a new school of theorists. Fisher's return over cost preceded Keynes's concept of the marginal efficiency of capital.

Despite real differences of manner among the rival schools, and despite disagreement about the place of mathematics, everybody accepted the marginal principle. They all applied it to the pricing of consumer goods, producer goods, and productive services. All of the major figures saw in economic life multitudinous adjustment in the guise of individual transactions. Although it was easier to perceive how prices were mutually determined in Pareto, Wicksteed, and Wicksell than in Marshall, even the latter, in his partial equilibrium, seldom lost sight of the larger problem.

Although we have seen how unfair it is to label all of these marginalists defenders of the established order, there is little doubt that the technical concentration of all, and the partiality to capitalism of some, did divert attention from consideration of general economic development, and did give some color to the charges of Veblen and others that they neglected capitalism's really important variables. Eager as they were for improvement, Marshall and Clark imagined its occurrence within the current institutional system.

It is possible to regret that increased analytical precision and impressive theoretical achievements were accompanied by the narrowing to a static framework of the whole subject of economics. In the end, the historical economists could not get along without theory. Some theoretical economists seemed willing, if not able, to live without history. It was also unfortunate that so many marginalists held factual investigation so lightly, in practice if not in preachment. Some of the tangled theoretical questions—fixed versus variable coefficients was an example—demanded more empirical research and less fine-spun logic.

Chapter 12

Historical Economics

INTRODUCTION

In histories of economic thought, analytical techniques are likely to enjoy more appreciative treatment than other working methods. For one thing, it is easier to isolate the analytical novelty, whether of doctrine or representation, marginal principle or graphic drawing. It is harder to deal with a Veblen, whose message was elusive and whose intellectual antecedents were unclear. Moreover, those who work with historical materials tend to be long-winded. Since much of their work is embodied in monographs, it is all the harder to summon the necessary patience to extract the kernels of truth and innovation which may be there. The suspicion does arise that the historical dissertation is out of date about the time it leaves the hands of the printer. For these reasons, the historical economists who are the subject of this chapter have often been underrated, particularly in England and the United States. The home of the school was Germany.

In the early part of the nineteenth century, the intellectual climate of Germany was unsympathetic to the abstract, deductive economics of the Ricardians. Later in the century, it proved equally hostile to the marginalists. In Germany the relatively few followers of the English classical school favored Smith, in whom they found broad philosophical interest and even problems, over Ricardo. Germany's own analytical pioneers, Mangoldt, Hermann, Gossen, and von Thünen, met little response.

In economics the German taste was strong for history and metaphysics, for economics which explained the very basis of economic existence, rather than surface phenomena like prices and incomes.

Like English analytical procedure, English economic policy was not ingratiating. English economists were noninterventionist by general rule. Intervention by the state required special argument, circumstances, and dispensation, as the self-torments of John Stuart Mill on the exceptions to laissez faire demonstrated. But German economists took a much larger view of the state. Although members of the historical school differed among themselves on this point, most of them considered the state an active agent of social and economic improvement. Going further, some regarded the state as the embodiment of that mystic concept, nationality. This emotional preference explained the popularity, in Germany, first of Rodbertus' version of state socialism and then of the Marxist prescription. Neither Rodbertus nor Marx ever achieved firm footing in England.

There was a closely related additional reason why Germans distrusted classical English economics. In their eyes, the group's leading doctrines were associated, if not identical, with English national interests. Free trade was splendid for a country whose industry dominated the world and could only be benefited by still larger markets. What about countries whose industries were now weak and could never be strong if they were left to face, unaided, the chilly blasts of English competition? This was the infant-industry argument for protective tariffs, to be found above all in Friedrich List. It symbolized the German belief in historical relativity. Economic truth was related to time and place. English convenience was not universal revelation.

The most important reason why German economists distrusted their English colleagues was cultural. All their training and intellectual preoccupations persuaded German historical economists that English economics was the superficial examination of the ephemeral phenomenon. With equal conviction, English economists shied away from metaphysics and global theories, in all the embarrassment of a well-bred man in the presence of a bounder.

The historical school spanned the greater part of a century. Its first wave—the major figures were Karl Knies, Bruno Hildebrand, Friedrich List, and Wilhelm Roscher—did its important work in the 1840's and the 1850's. A second group, led by Gustave Schmoller, flourished in the last third of the nineteenth century. It was succeeded by a third group, whose work covered the first three decades of the twentieth century. Its leading names were Max Weber and Werner Sombart.

ROSCHER AND LIST

Roscher has been generally credited with the founding of the first historical school. In contrast with Schmoller and his disciples, his spirit was conciliatory. He did not disdain economic theory. Indeed, in his textbook,[1] he employed a rather simple version of English classical price theory. What he sought was the historical basis of abstract economics. Perhaps it oversimplifies his views to say that he hoped that from the historical monograph could be evolved the generalizations which English economists had accustomed themselves to making deductively. Certainly he tried to discover history's laws and stages, and he was sure that comparative analysis of historical situations was the only safe route to appropriate generalization.

His work exemplified his doctrine. With the awe-inspiring industry of the German scholar, he wrote detailed historical volumes on many subjects, ranging from the age of Thucydides, through socialism and communism, to the practical problems of agriculture, colonies, and the like. He produced a history of economic thought and a textbook. The last was not to the eyes of an English-speaking reader entirely prepossessing. The book was footnoted with horrible profusion, but, still worse, the text flitted from history to analysis to doctrinal exegesis in a manner

[1] See his *Principles of Political Economy*, translated from the 13th German edition, 1877. The first edition appeared in 1854.

which destroyed coherence and obscured the author's purposes. Roscher's writings did make it plain that he was less addicted to state action than most of the historical economists who followed him. His admirer Gustave Schmoller considered his views close to those of the English liberals.

List, who has often been associated with the romantic nationalism of Adam Müller and his followers, invites discussion as an historical economist, because he argued directly from history against the English economists. Although his was history with a purpose, far from the dispassionate investigations of Roscher and Schmoller, history was his favorite weapon and basis of policy.

Friedrich List (1789–1846), a native of Württemberg, was a journalist who, like Karl Marx, was expelled from his native state for excessive forthrightness. He traveled extensively in Europe and spent some years in the United States. His opinions blended fervent nationalism for a Germany not yet in being, ardent democracy for a land then defaced by petty tyrannies, and persistent belief in the efficacy of state action. Although he wrote extensively, the book for which he was remembered was the *National System of Political Economy*.[2] Among other things, the book was a not very fair polemic against Adam Smith, whom List attacked on the grounds of cosmopolitanism and individualism. Parodying Smith, he said, ". . . that may be wisdom in national economy which would be folly in private economy."[3] Smith neglected the nation. List, on the other hand, "would indicate as the distinguishing characteristic of my system, NATIONALITY."[4]

The first section of the book was an historical survey. List passed in rapid review the city states of Renaissance Italy, the Hanseatic League, France, England, Holland, and Germany. As read by List, the teachings of history associated prosperity and decline with four circumstances. Wherever economic progress

[2] Written in 1841, it was translated into English in 1885 and last reprinted in 1928.
[3] List, *National System of Political Economy*, Longmans, Green, 1904, p. 134.
[4] *Ibid.*, p. xliii.

had been substantial, as in England, the nation had been unified and strong. Where, as in Italy or Germany, the state was weak and disunited, prosperity did not long endure. Holland's prosperity was temporary because she was too small a state. If she had prudently united with Belgium and the Rhine provinces, she would not have yielded commercial power to England.

History's second lesson was directed against individualism. The productive powers of individuals did not depend upon their own initiative and abilities. Rather they stemmed from the social conditions and institutions in which people worked. We were the products of our society and our society had, therefore, a right to call upon us to subordinate our own interests to its. The state was not Bentham's sum of individuals. Rather, it was an organism different from and greater than its parts.

List's third finding affirmed that navigation and trade could flourish only when manufacturing prospered. His favorable analysis of English mercantilist restrictions upon trade, while qualified, did, in the end, justify the mercantilist emphasis upon the nation, and did credit mercantilist administrators with protecting and fostering English manufacturing. Smith was wrong when he attacked the Navigation Acts. These acts well and truly promoted English interests. Only because they did so, did England become strong enough to discard them.

Finally, internal freedom was an essential condition of economic advance. With Germany always in his mind, List wanted to end the intricate restrictions upon the flow of trade and the free movement of economic resources which hampered German economic growth. These, then, were the four lessons his tendentious reading of history uncovered.

From the morals of history he drew his policies. If universal peace were the rule, free trade would be a wonderful arrangement. If the facts of national sovereignty and national rivalry were accorded proper importance, it was clear that free trade now would simply extend English dominion. England enjoyed the advantage of having begun her career as a manufacturing nation first. Since only manufacturing fully released the productive powers of the nation, it was these powers that the state should encourage. It could do so by introducing protective tariffs. These tariffs enabled manufacturing to be established against the opposition of nations which had started earlier. Even more important, tariffs developed the productive powers of the nation and encouraged the towns in which civilization flourished. List was not far from Marx's opinion of life outside the metropolis. When manufacturing had developed and universal peace had been attained, then was time enough for free trade. Thus did List prove that free trade was a contingent doctrine and the analytical structure of English economics was most useful to the nineteenth-century English.

GUSTAVE SCHMOLLER (1838–1917)

Schmoller's mode of historical investigation was much better balanced than List's, but at the beginning of his career his methodological views were fiercer than Roscher's, and his social views were more interventionist. The foolish battle between theorists and historians owed much to Schmoller's controversial spirit.

Observing the scant success of efforts to draw laws and generalizations from historical research, Schmoller emphasized the detailed monograph, free of bias and prior conclusions. Although he was influenced by Hegel and his own warm belief in progress, Schmoller endeavored to write dispassionate history. He rejected the idea of economics as a deductive science. On the contrary, he wished to include in economics what the abstract economists took for granted: the genesis of economic institutions, their current mode of behavior, and the psychology of classes. Schmoller aimed to furnish the context within which economic calculation took place.

His activities as a social reformer had no logical connection with his opinions on economic method. Nevertheless, they were an important part of his school's practical influence. The Verein für Sozialpolitik, or Union for Social Policy, in which the historical economists were active, was an organization of the "socialists of the chair." Mild and moderate, it opposed "Manchesterism," a caricatured version of the doctrines of Mill and Ricardo. More positively, it stood for piecemeal study of social institutions and problems in a manner not very different from the work of the Webbs in England, practical reforms in working conditions, social insurance, and factory legislation. Schmoller regarded none of these views as inconsistent with his strong monarchical sentiments.

The struggle of methods which his polemics with Menger had begun was concluded by Schmoller in a major work written in 1900, his two-volume *Grundriss* or *Outline*. In it, he employed with much good will, but very little finesse, Mengerian analysis, in addition to history, in the course of surveying an impressive series of topics. The list included land, population, technology, the social order and the economy, the state and the economy, the division of labor, property, classes, the firm, markets and exchange, competition, money, value and price, capital and credit, labor regulations and conditions, economic progress, and a great many more. That is to say, he covered all that a two-volume contemporary text might include in principles and problems.

With the publication of this massive treatise, the weary struggle ended. It was clear, as it should always have been, that all methods had their value. The battle had been as much for personal precedence as for scholarly principle.

MAX WEBER (1864–1920)

Whether as economist, historian, or sociologist, Weber was an eminent scholar. Sociologists know him for the concepts of ideal types and meant meaning, and for the analysis of bureaucracy. Here he illustrates how the historical approach to economics, in the hands of a master, could produce meaningful though controversial generalizations. Among economists, Weber's best-known work has been *The Protestant Ethic and the*

Spirit of Capitalism.[5] It actually consisted of two long articles which were designed to form a small part of a much more extended examination of the sociology of religion. Weber did not live to complete the larger work. Moreover, these articles did not profess to be a complete description or explanation of capitalism. In them, it was true, the Calvinist religious influence was closely analyzed, but in the later *General Economic History*, Weber listed it last among four factors. The other three were the modern state with its unique bureaucracy and special sense of citizenship, rational law, and modern science and its offshoot, technology.

The argument of the *Protestant Ethic* took the following course. The pursuit of gain was universal. However, what defined capitalism was something else: ". . . the pursuit of profit, and forever *renewed* profit, by means of continuous, rational, capitalistic enterprise."[6] Also new were rationalistic capitalistic organization and free labor.

The historical problem Weber set himself was the origin of the business leaders of the West, the bourgeois class whose behavior exemplified capitalism. Contemporary statistics and past historical analysis proved that business leaders in every country were Protestants. This conclusion held as strongly for countries in which Protestants, as minorities, suffered oppression, as for countries in which, as majorities, they inflicted it. The case was even more striking when it was observed that the commercial leaders at capitalism's beginnings were not merely Protestant, but specifically Calvinist. They were English or Dutch.

Could these glaring facts be ignored? Was there an explanation in specific Calvinist doctrines of these historical truths? One key to understanding was the Calvinist tenet of the "calling," the performance of God's work in this world. Catholicism preached no analogous doctrine. Nor was the Lutheran conception of calling helpful to capitalism. In the spirit of the Middle

[5] Published in Germany in 1904–1905, it was translated into English by Talcott Parsons in 1930.

[6] Weber, *The Protestant Ethic and the Spirit of Capitalism*, Scribner's, 1930, p. 17.

Ages, Luther anathematized money as sterile. For him, calling had a traditional implication: the individual was forced to accept as God's intention the station in life where he found himself. Although Calvinists, like Lutherans and Catholics, burned to save souls rather than make money, there was a congruence between their ethic and capitalism's necessities.

Weber established this congruence with an extended exploration of the ethical doctrines of Calvinism. How were these doctrines connected with the specifically capitalist spirit of profit seeking and worldly success? He wrestled immediately with Calvinism's central belief, predestination. In all its grimness, this article of faith declared that God, of his own mercy, had selected some men for salvation and had condemned the remainder to eternal damnation. Sinners and saints looked alike. They might even seem to act alike. Yet no act of the damned could revoke God's verdict. No sin of the saved could condemn him. Even those not among the elect were, nevertheless, for the glory of God, under the discipline and command of the Calvinist church.

This doctrine, commented Weber, must have created intense loneliness and anxiety. The critically important question in the heart of each Calvinist must have been: Am I of the elect? How can I be certain? In answer, the literal doctrine said: You cannot be sure. But the psychological burden was too great to bear. As described by Weber, the mechanism of relief worked in this way. Calvin himself had no objection to the prosperity of his ministers. Indeed, he considered their prosperity an acceptable tribute to their role. Similarly, worldly success, while it was incapable of "purchasing salvation," was the means of "getting rid of the fear of damnation."[7] In practice, therefore, the good Calvinist bettered himself, out of the necessity to believe that only so would God help him. The godly man, who led an active, energetic, ascetic life, full of good works, purchased nothing with his good works. But he felt that his life was a testimony of God's grace. Hence, idleness was the deadliest of all sins. Indeed, the

[7] *Ibid.,* p. 115.

Calvinist was called in this world to God's work. However, this calling, this work, was something that he had to find for himself; it was not a traditional role. Once he identified his calling, he had to pursue it whole-heartedly, never faltering. The godly man was the Lord's steward. The property he amassed was not his: it was God's and God meant him to pass it on for His good purposes.

Intense, unremitting labor was a relief from anxiety. If worldly success attended the effort, the success was evidence of salvation. It is easy to conjecture the darker side of the doctrine. If success was the mark of salvation, then failure was the sign of damnation. At its most extreme, the doctrine stigmatized charity to the poor and the unfortunate as support of sin. If work was the chief good, then all diversion was waste or worse. The grim Puritan Sunday was a monument to Calvinist logic. What this meant for capitalism was summarized in Weber's conclusion: "A specifically bourgeois economic ethic had grown up. With the consciousness of standing in the fullness of God's grace and being visibly blessed by Him, the bourgeois business man, as long as he remained within the bounds of formal correctness, as long as his moral conduct was spotless and the use to which he put his wealth was not objectionable, could follow his pecuniary interests as he would and feel that he was fulfilling a duty in doing so." The businessman also enjoyed the benefits of docile labor: "The power of religious asceticism provided him in addition with sober, conscientious, and unusually industrious workmen, who clung to their work as to a life purpose willed by God." And the ethic relieved him of any guilts about the less fortunate: "Finally it gave him the comforting assurance that the unequal distribution of goods of this world was a special dispensation of Divine Providence, which in these differences, as in particular grace, pursued secret ends unknown to man."[8] Right or wrong, the argument was powerful.

Since Weber wrote the *Protestant Ethic*, scholars have made many criticisms of its thesis. Some have suggested that the capi-

[8] *Ibid.*, pp. 176–177.

talist spirit could be located in the Catholic cities of the Mediter-
ranean and in Antwerp. It was alleged that Weber neglected
economic factors and ignored changes in Calvinist doctrine. One
of the more imaginative criticisms, that of his contemporary,
Werner Sombart, will be shortly discussed. The criticisms left
Weber the unrivaled explorer of *one* part of the story of capitalism's emergence.

WERNER SOMBART (1863–1941)

Sombart was a brilliant man of idiosyncratic method. Unlike
Schmoller, whose meticulous research produced limited conclusions; unlike Weber, whose original research was the basis of
sweeping generalizations, Sombart employed secondary materials to derive very large conclusions. His major work, *Der
Moderne Kapitalismus*, or *Modern Capitalism*,[9] traced in several
thousand pages the history of capitalism from its beginnings to
what Sombart called the period of "high capitalism," 1760–
1914.

Capitalism was a "historical individual," important only during
a part of human history. The passion for moneymaking, while
central to capitalism, was not a universal trait in time or space. It
was not even universal during capitalism's ascendancy. A relatively few men were overcome with the passion to make money.
(We shall see who they were later.) Because this passion drove
this small group, populations exploded, cultures changed, and
the face of the world altered out of recognition. The change began in England, spread to Western Europe and the United States,
and now threatened to engulf the remainder of the world.

For all of this, an idea, the passionate yet rational pursuit of
gain, was responsible. In Sombart, however, there was no direct
link between idea and actuality. Accident supplied the connect-
ing element. Some of the major events which had stimulated capitalism were historical accidents. Nevertheless, they fitted snugly

---

[9] It was published in 1902, expanded in 1916–1917, and still further enlarged in 1927. Its size has evidently discouraged English translation.

the capitalist premise of the pursuit of gain. Thus what Weber regarded as causes, Sombart labeled accident. Among the accidents were the new kind of man who assumed economic control, the new type of state, and the novel techniques which came to dominate industry. What capitalism needed with desperate urgency was capital, labor, and markets. Accident, once more, supplied the capital in the enormous gold deposits discovered by Spanish exploration and conquest. Aided by these events, capitalism rationalized more and more economic activity in its spirit. For Sombart, as for Weber, the spirit was above all rational

Sombart's characteristic boldness was displayed in *The Jews and Modern Capitalism*,[10] which examined Weber's hypothesis about the rise of capitalism, from another angle. For Weber's Calvinists, Sombart substituted the Jews as the operating force in the creation of the impersonal and rational spirit of contemporary capitalism. It turned out, therefore, that the Jews were the handful of men who introduced the spirit of passionate acquisition which was at the center of capitalism. The temerity of the venture was the more striking when it is observed that Sombart knew no Hebrew. Therefore he was unable to read the literature which might have altered or strengthened his theory.

The argument was ingenious. During the fifteenth and sixteenth centuries, the Jews were expelled from Spain (1492), Portugal (1495 and 1497), Cologne (1424), other German cities in the remainder of the century, and some Italian cities From the south, they moved north to Frankfort, Hamburg, Amsterdam, and England. Finally, in the seventeenth century, the center of commercial activity shifted from the south to the north. Could it be sheer coincidence that the countries and the cities left by the Jews declined in prosperity, and those entered by the Jews gained in economic strength? Of course not. In fact, the Jews were responsible for both the "outward form" and the "inward spirit"[11] of capitalism.

---

[10] Written in 1911, the book was translated in 1913, and reprinted by the Free Press in 1951.
[11] Sombart, *The Jews and Modern Capitalism*, Free Press, 1951, p. 21.

Take "outward form" first. In the seventeenth and eighteenth centuries, the Jews almost monopolized the luxury trade in jewelry, silks, and precious stones. They were powerful in the major export trades and they took care to sell to countries, Spain and Portugal, which could pay in the precious metals. Their role in colonization was substantial. Not only did Jews finance Columbus, but some went with him, and Columbus himself may have been Jewish. Jews swarmed into America and played a leading part in its history. "What we call Americanism is nothing else, if we may say so, than the Jewish spirit distilled."[12] Jews were indispensable in the founding of the modern state. As its financiers and purveyors, they loaned it money and sold its weapons and food. "Arm in arm, the Jew and the ruler stride through the age which the historians call modern."[13]

With characteristic ingenuity, the Jews invented a whole armory of capitalist devices. Among them were securities markets, international stock dealings, modern credit instruments, nine-teenth-century stock promotion, installment selling, advertising, and the modern newspaper. "The attitude of the Talmud . . . is friendly . . . towards exchange, and the Jews adopted it throughout the Middle Ages."[14]

How could the Jews, a small, physically weak people, accomplish so much? Four objective circumstances assisted them. They were widely dispersed, treated as strangers, given only quasi-citizenship, and well endowed with worldly goods. In other words, they were everywhere and, consequently, could always find fellow Jews with whom to negotiate. At this juncture, Sombart asked whether what Weber ascribed to the Puritans might not better be attributed to the Jews. His answer read: "Nay, it might well be suggested that that which is called Puritanism is in reality Judaism."[15]

More important than these outward Jewish qualities was Jewish religion, which molded the Jewish spirit and, through it, the

[12] *Ibid.*, p. 44.
[13] *Ibid.*, p. 49.
[14] *Ibid.*, p. 82.
[15] *Ibid.*, p. 192.

spirit of capitalism. As Sombart interpreted it, the Jewish religion "has the same leading ideas as capitalism."[16] The Jewish religion was a contract between man and God in which appropriate behavior brought proper reward. As in any commercial contract, the accounts were carefully kept, and penalties applied to the man who failed to fulfill his bond. The Jewish religion rationalized all of life. It prepared the way naturally for capitalist transactions. Restraint and asceticism marked all its teachings. Thus, Judaism and Puritanism were very close here again. "Puritanism *is* Judaism."[17] Jewish religion promoted four special Jewish characteristics. Jews were intellectual. Although the intellectuality was shallow and narrow, Jews reasoned closely and accurately in all commercial matters. Jews believed in teleology: every thing, every act must have its purpose. They were mobile and they were energetic. Thus, there was a triple parallelism between Jewish character, Jewish religion, and capitalism.

There were many flaws in these arguments. Sombart overestimated the importance of Jews in the shift of commercial activity from south to north. He ignored or was unfamiliar with the strong vein of mysticism which was also part of the Jewish tradition. He neglected to explore the question of how far Jews had adapted themselves to capitalism, rather than the other way around.

Sombart lived long enough to become a Nazi. The inevitable question is the degree to which anti-Semitism influenced his opinions. What he became in 1933 does not necessarily prove what he was in 1911. Nevertheless, Sombart's discussion of specifically Jewish qualities was scornful, and his passages on Jews as a race were ambiguous at best. There were intimations, finally, that he reversed his own argument when it was convenient to do and declared that if certain activities were pursued, then Jews *must* be at their head, even if no Jews were in evidence. He appeared to believe that once a Jew always a Jew, even to the second and third generation.

[16] *Ibid.*, p. 205.
[17] *Ibid.*, p. 249.

ENGLISH HISTORICAL ECONOMICS

If the term "historical school" means a determined assault upon theoretical analysis by desperate partisans of historical method, England lacked such a school. The moderation, or perhaps the muzziness, of English controversy evoked nothing worse than occasional sharpness. In his pioneer exploration of the *Industrial Revolution*, Arnold Toynbee[18] commented mildly on the relative claims of deductive and historical method: "There is no real opposition between the two. . . . The right method in any particular case must be largely determined by the nature of the problem."[19] He proceeded to say that it was hopeless to expect history to produce general laws, when so many facts must remain unknown. History, sensibly conceived, could check the conclusions of deductive analysis and demonstrate their relativity. He devoted much effort to fleshing out Ricardo and Malthus with historical facts, so that the valid portions of their theories might be identified. History was capable of adding life and point to theory: it was no substitute.

William Cunningham, whose brush with Marshall was described above, while strongly critical of deductive economics, centered his attack upon its excesses. It erred in thinking capitalism universal. It should not, therefore, apply to precapitalist times the generalization applicable to contemporary society.

The fiercest attacks upon deductive economics were made by Cliffe Leslie, whose writings showed the strongest evidence of German influence. Written in 1879, his criticisms appeared in two articles.[20] He attacked the Ricardians for oversimplifying human motives and ignoring their alterations over time. He cited with approval Bagehot's limitation of political economy's applicability to contemporary England, and to the male sex exclusively. Deductive economics, he charged, ignored the activity of the

---

[18] These lectures were published in 1884. Arnold Toynbee was the uncle of his contemporary namesake, the noted historian. The term "industrial revolution" was the first Toynbee's coinage.

[19] *Ibid.*, p. 3.

[20] *Fortnightly Review*, 1879, Vol. 13, pp. 25–46, 934–949.

community, carried on "through its positive institutions as an organized political body or state" and the "social environment with which it encompasses every man and woman within it from the cradle to the grave."[21] Finally, he attacked the Ricardian assumptions that the relative advantages of occupations were known, that competition equalized wages and profit, and that cost of production determined price. Not only did such assumptions depend upon an erroneous view of human nature; they also neglected the growing complexity of the economic universe.

The English economists closest in spirit to the German school were the Webbs, Sidney (1859–1947) and Beatrice (1858–1943), his wife. This formidable couple,[22] among much else, helped found the Fabian Society, established the London School of Economics, renovated the Poor Laws, influenced the London County Council to act as an efficient implement of social welfare, and more than anyone else gave its official ideology to the British Labor Party. Theory, they both scorned. According to a sympathetic biographer,[23] Sidney felt that if a theory of value were essential (which he doubted), Jevons was to be preferred to Marx. However, the subject failed to interest him.

Their work was "the study of social institutions with a view to transforming them."[24] In the eyes of the Webbs, transformation was a judicious blend of social reform and state ownership. Only at the end of their lives did they embrace the central planning practiced by the Russians. Their massive work on English local government, socialism, Poor Laws, and labor unions was never an end in itself. Although their attitude toward their materials was scholarly and their work was highly original, they thought of it as prelude to social change.

[21] *Ibid.,* p. 37.

[22] H. G. Wells's novel *The New Machiavelli* included an amusing, though unfair, caricature of the pair. Wells was, for a short time, a member of the Fabian Society. For a much longer period, George Bernard Shaw was active in its affairs.

[23] See "Tawney on the Webbs," in Henry W. Spiegel, *The Development of Economic Thought*, Wiley, 1952, pp. 342–359.

[24] *Ibid.,* p. 343.

Chapter 13

Institutional Economics

INTRODUCTION

In its distaste for conventional price theory, willingness to contemplate social change, and preference for the materials of history and sociology, the American institutionalists resembled the German historical economists. However, these were the only major points of similarity. The institutionalists put history to their own uses and advocated more drastic changes than the German socialists of the chair envisaged. A school only by grace of the necessities of classification, institutional economics was the first indigenous American grouping of genuine importance. Appropriately enough, its founder, that most original of American economists Thorstein Veblen, was the son of Norwegian immigrants. Through John R. Commons, institutional doctrine attracted a generation of economists at Wisconsin, including Hoxie and Perlman. Through Mitchell, Veblen's student, it won still more supporters at Columbia University. Yet institutionalists have differed so much among themselves, and Veblen took such successful pains to mislead his readers, that it is difficult to be coherent about the institutionalists.

THORSTEIN VEBLEN (1857–1929)

What was Veblen like? Born on a Wisconsin farm, the fourth son of Norwegian immigrants, he moved with his family, in 1865, to another farm in Minnesota. At home Veblen usually spoke Norwegian, and when, in 1874, he entered Carleton College, his English betrayed his foreign origin. At Carleton, John Bates Clark, the leading American marginalist, was one of his teachers.[1] After teaching briefly at Monona Academy, a Norwegian school, Veblen went east to Johns Hopkins in 1881. There he studied economics with Richard T. Ely, and logic with Charles Peirce, the famous philosopher and precursor of John Dewey. The next three years he passed at Yale, studying philosophy under President Noah Porter, and economics under the ferociously laissez-faire William Graham Sumner. His doctoral dissertation was entitled *Ethical Grounds of a Doctrine of Retribution*, an odd subject for a future economist.

At a time when almost all teaching jobs in philosophy were clerical perquisites, the constitutionally skeptical Veblen could not find a post. Therefore, for want of occupation he returned to the family farm in 1884. Four years later he married Ellen Rolfe, whom he had met at Carleton. After seven years of semi-idleness and complete intellectual isolation, in desperation he traveled east again to Cornell for further study. The year was 1891 and Veblen was 34. In 1892, Laughlin, the head of the Cornell economics department, took Veblen with him to the University of Chicago, just founded with Rockefeller money. At first, all that Veblen had was a small fellowship, very little for a man of 35 equipped with a doctorate. Moving at his accustomed snail's pace, he was promoted four years later to instructor. Finally, in the last years of the nineteenth century, he began to write for publication.

His first book, the *Theory of the Leisure Class*, apparently a nasty attack upon the habits and manners of the rich, appeared in 1899. The hostility of most reviews was not astounding, for the style was involved, the economics concealed, the tone unpleasant, and the conclusions ambiguous. Nevertheless, the book became something of a sensation when William Dean Howells, the most influential critic of the age, reviewed it glowingly as a masterpiece of social satire. Certainly it bore little resemblance to an economic treatise.

[1] See pp. 283–287.

In 1900 Veblen was made an assistant professor, and in 1904 he published a second major book, the *Theory of Business Enterprise*. Never able to find a permanent resting place, Veblen moved in 1906 to Stanford as an associate professor (the highest rank he ever attained), but marital troubles and rumors of affairs with students forced him to resign in 1909. In 1911 he wandered to the University of Missouri, where a former student, Davenport, himself a successful price theorist, aided him. Here, as elsewhere, Veblen, to most tastes, was a poor teacher, a mumbler who gave only C's, and a faculty member who ignored his colleagues when he didn't covertly insult them. What he thought of the academic community was revealed in his threat to subtitle his book on American colleges *A Study in Total Depravity*.

He wrote, he momentarily held a government job, and just as briefly joined the editorial staff of the *Dial*. For a time he was a member of that remarkable New School for Social Research staff which, in 1919, included James Harvey Robinson, Charles Beard, and Wesley Mitchell. In 1924 the American Economic Association belatedly offered him its presidency. He coldly refused it. In 1929 he died, having eked out his last years as a dependent of a former student.

These were the outward events of an unhappy life. What was the man really like? Central to his nature was a strange isolation. Never was Veblen a member of a group. At Carleton he was the rustic Norwegian, unbecomingly attired in homespun, too poor to attend dances, and forced to live in a frame house his father built for him and his brothers on the outskirts of the campus. Even in his own family he was something of an outsider, little inclined to act the good Norwegian farmer, much more ingenious in avoiding manual labor than in doing it. Some clue to his personality can, perhaps, be found in his essay on the intellectual preëminence of the Jews. In that essay he alleged that the Jews, having lost faith in their ancient beliefs, and being unable to accept newer Western doctrines, adopted instead a skeptical, critical attitude which sharpened their apprehensions and multiplied their achievements (a much more flattering estimate than Sombart's). Possibly he thought of himself as he wrote that essay. With the substitution of Norwegians for Jews, the essay well described Veblen's characteristic outlook upon life.

Not only was Veblen an outsider, he was also a tease. This is more than a trivial comment. As a child, he labeled his elders with devastating nicknames, far too accurate for polite usage, far too apt to be forgotten. At Carleton he dubbed the unpopular dean of women "Mater Dolorosa." This teasing propensity showed up in his writing and tended to unsettle audiences who were not quite sure whom Veblen was teasing. Think of the language which he invented, terms like "conspicuous consumption," "vicarious leisure," and "pecuniary emulation." Think of some of the stories he solemnly told, like the one of that King of France who, Veblen claimed, burned to death in front of a fire because the servant who should have moved his royal person was absent and his dignified sense of status did not allow him to move himself. Could such a man be taken seriously? Worse, if he was not serious, was he not deliberately poking fun at the more sacred cows of his society?

The pyrotechnics may have concealed the undercurrent of deep earnestness in Veblen. What made him a stranger in modern life, as much as anything else, was its wastefulness. What he admired above all else was workmanlike efficiency, the proper adaptation of appropriate means to seemly ends. Nowhere did he define these terms closely. Probably, like all the things in which men believe most sincerely, he took them for granted. His Norwegian heritage taught him that the simple work of the farmer, the honest craftsmanship of the local carpenter, and the necessary tasks of spinning and weaving, little as Veblen was inclined to share them, still represented honorable human activity. They were an honest expression of the deep desire to produce useful objects which Veblen supposed everyone to possess, much as modern life perverted it.

In an important sense, Veblen was a man of a single idea, a key distinction which ran through all his books, even when, as in the *Theory of the Leisure Class*, the ostensible subject was quite different. This master notion was the sharp contrast between business enterprise and the machine process. By the latter, he meant the technical methods used in producing goods, the relations of these methods to each other in the factory, and, most of all, the habit of thought which working with machines and directing their operations formed. Through its reasoned procedures, standard measurements, and intelligent arrangements, the machine process offered an outlet for the instinct of workmanship. In Veblen's words, "wherever manual dexterity, the rule of thumb, and the fortuitous conjunctures of the seasons have been supplanted by a reasoned procedure on the basis of a systematic knowledge of the forces employed, there the mechanical industry is to be found, even in the absence of intricate mechanical contrivances."[2] Serviceability was the object of the machine process: gratification of man's biological needs to eat, stay warm, work constructively, and satisfy his idle curiosity. Though the emphasis would have been different, Veblen, if he had stopped here, would have approximated Weber's definition of capitalism as rational activity in the pursuit of profit.

But he did not stop. The other half of capitalism was business enterprise. It was severed from the machine process by a direct opposition of aim. The businessman was interested only in pecuniary gain, profits. Serviceability was secondary, though, other things equal, businessmen preferred the serviceable to the useless, or, as Veblen unpleasantly put it, "the officials of a railway commonly prefer to avoid wrecks and manslaughter, even if there is no pecuniary advantage in choosing the more humane course." He hastily withdrew this minor concession, for "the captains of the first class necessarily are relatively exempt from these unbusinesslike scruples."[3] Was he serious? Probably. For the point to which he incessantly returned was businessmen's indifference to serviceability and their exclusive concentration upon vendibility. Their question was always: Can it be sold at a

---

[2] Thorstein Veblen, *Theory of Business Enterprise*, Scribner's, 1904, p. 6.
[3] *Ibid.*, p. 43.

profit? Necessarily, therefore, the businessman made no objection to selling the meretricious rather than the useful. Indeed, he might prefer the former because it would displease customers sooner and stimulate profitable replacement. For such reasons, women's fashions changed every year, and each season's style looked better than its predecessors, because it was a relief from the specific ugliness of the season before. Not for a moment did Veblen share the useful and soothing assumption made by most economists, that vendibility and serviceability ran parallel to each other.

The businessman was not always best off when the economy ran smoothly. Frequently, profits were larger when the economy was properly disturbed. Bearing in mind the events of his time, Veblen instanced the formation of the United States Steel Corporation as a triumph of business maneuver which accomplished no industrial end, caused much incidental uncertainty in financial markets prior to its completion, and profited only the promoters. Among the latter was J. P. Morgan and Company, which received some $65 million for its efforts in putting the company together. Bluntly put, the businessman's pursuit of gain frequently caused unemployment, higher prices, decreased industrial efficiency, and delayed innovation. Such, said Veblen, was business enterprise.

The business cycle itself was the result of business enterprise. Depressions were "a malady of the affections. The discrepancy which encourages businessmen is a discrepancy between that normal capitalization which they have set their hearts upon through habituation in the immediate past and that actual capitalizable value of their property which its current earning capacity will warrant."[4] Much simplified, Veblen's description of the business cycle went something like this: Businessmen borrowed on the basis of expected earnings and specific collateral. Their borrowing bid prices up, and the value of the collateral which secured their loans increased. To do the same physical volume of business, they had to, and could, borrow still more. At some point, un-

[4] *Ibid.*, p. 237.

specified by Veblen, uneasiness about the continuance of the high profits necessary to support the credit structure spread through the business community. The uneasiness started, perhaps, because some small group glimpsed a profit in contraction. Then loans were called in, liquidation began, big businessmen swallowed their smaller brethren, and depression continued until the readjustment of capitalization to profits was completed. None of these events was the consequence of the machine process: all flowed from the normal routine of business enterprise. In some respects, the similarity to Marx was striking. The events were inevitable. Crises were recurrent. The scale of enterprise ever increased.

The differences between the two were still more striking. Marx's crises occurred, in part, because capitalists created too many goods. Veblen was convinced that the excesses of business enterprise might actually diminish output, at least of serviceable items. Their forecasts also differed. In Marx, revolution came because the conflict between the material interests of owners (capitalists) and nonowners (proletarians) sharpened. Revolution was the consequence of workers' rational pursuit of their own interests.

Veblen's conflicts were another matter. The future would evolve from the struggle of three different cultural tendencies: business enterprise, the machine process, and a third contender. This third set of beliefs was connected with warlike or predatory activities, going back archaically to the Middle Ages or earlier. These radically dissimilar strains of thought were inescapably hostile to each other. Thus the struggle was not between the owners and the nonowners of property, but between ways of thinking. Business enterprise, said Veblen, was founded on natural-rights concepts. The businessman believed that the natural order validated titles to property. Philosophical support for this proposition went all the way back to John Locke. In modern times, businessmen converted this proposition into the opinion that each businessman was the "putative producer of whatever wealth he acquires." The businessman concerned himself with legal rights, inheritance, judicial precedent, none of them relevant to industrial efficiency, all directly related to pecuniary accomplishment. In this work, his ally was the lawyer who was "exclusively occupied with the details of predatory fraud," one of literature's more unflattering descriptions of this maligned profession. The businessman ignored the industrial process just as much as he could.

The frame of mind of the skilled workmen and engineers, who were devoted to the machine process, was radically different. Because these men valued efficiency or serviceability, they tended to view their work and their life in matter-of-fact, step-by-step fashion. They saw everything in terms of scientific cause and effect. Understandably, therefore, they became impatient with the natural-rights, paper-cherishing habits of businessmen. The rights of property aroused no emotion in them, and pecuniary aims in general struck them as irrelevant. They cared little for the preoccupations and pastimes of the business classes, religion, sport, and government.

If the conflict were simply between these two groups, its outcome could readily be predicted. The devotees of the machine process must win. They could readily dispense with businessmen, who annoyed them more and more as they meddled with industrial processes. But the businessman could never dispense with them. After all, the machine process supplied the products which earned their profits. Indeed, in his last important work, *The Engineers and the Price System*, written during the 1920's, Veblen almost flatly predicted that engineers and skilled workmen, the guardians of the machine process, provoked beyond endurance by the inefficiency of the business proceedings, would take into their own hands the operation of the industrial system, and operate it solely in the interests of mechanical efficiency and biological serviceability. It was ironical that a crackpot movement, Howard Scott's Technocracy, found in this book its manual, and more ironical still that, for a time, its headquarters were in a building of the highly respectable School of Engineering at Columbia University. Quite possibly, this was as close to revolution as Veblen's engineers will ever come.

In the bulk of his work, Veblen left the issue open, in deference to the third entrant in the race for power, the remnants of still "older conventions," in the intellectual activity of "soldiers, politicians, the clergy, and men of fashion." These were the groups whose habits of thought were formed long before the natural-rights philosophy of business enterprise was born. Soldiers, in particular, were drawn into the area of conflict by the expanding operations of business enterprise. As these operations spread over the world, the businessmen of different nations, backed by the governments which represented them, conflicted with each other's markets. Wars required soldiers, and their generals led us back "to a more archaic situation that preceded the scheme of natural rights . . . absolute government, dynastic politics, devolution of rights and honors, ecclesiastical authority, and popular submission and squalor."[5] Conceivably, Veblen might have accorded the honor of embodying these "archaic" virtues to the late General George Patton or General of the Army Douglas MacArthur, insofar as they both sought glory and victory rather than profit like businessmen, or efficiency like engineers.

Of one result, Veblen was certain. Business enterprise was doomed, even if the identity of its executioner had not been revealed. This conclusion Veblen stated in a passage of unusually opaque prose: "Natural rights being a by-product of peaceful industry, they cannot be reinstated by a recourse to warlike habits and a coercive government, since warlike habits and coercion are alien to the natural rights spirit. Nor can they be reinstated by a recourse to settled peace and freedom, since an era of settled peace and freedom would push on to the dominance of the machine process and the large business which break down the system of natural liberty."[6] Business enterprise faced the grim choice between reversion to archaic absolutism under military domina-

[5] *Ibid.*, p. 394.
[6] *Ibid.*, p. 316.

tion, or submission to the impatient partisans of mechanical efficiency. In 1915 Veblen cited Germany[7] as an illustration of reversion to archaic modes of thought. As later events turned out,
he was prescient in placing Japan in the same category.

What had all this to do with institutionalism? In Veblen's
sense, everything so far written had been about institutions. Veblen's institutions were "prevalent habits of thought with respect
to particular relations of the individual and of the community."[8]
This analysis of Veblen's world has centered upon the definitions
and conflicts of habits of thought.

Veblen's psychology emphasized instinct rather than rational
calculation. He invented his own collection of instincts, among
them idle curiosity and workmanship. His was a Darwinian conception of the development of institutions. It was this belief in
evolutionary change which furnished him with his principal
ground of complaint against classical and contemporary economics. In his opinion, they ignored the whole process of change,[9]
in favor of a barren system of static classification—taxonomy.

Veblen's occasional, guarded confidence that, in the end, the
machine process was fated to triumph, was an easy inference
from the evolutionist's proposition that variations favorable to
the survival of the species were passed on from generation to
generation, while those unfavorable to survival disappeared. If
human ends were defined as biological survival and biological
improvement, the machine process supported them infinitely better than either business enterprise or more archaic forms of organization. Therefore, on the evolutionary grounds where Veblen's musings often rested, the machine process deserved to win.

This line of thought was exceedingly un-Marxist. Veblen and
Marx both looked forward to the expropriation of the capitalist.
However, causes and results were both quite different. In Marx,
capitalists and proletarians fought because the first owned every-

[7] See his *Imperial Germany and the Industrial Revolution*, Viking, 1939.
[8] Thorstein Veblen, *Theory of the Leisure Class*, Modern Library, 1931,
p. 190.
[9] As Veblen put it, "everything that is, is wrong."

thing and the second owned nothing. Ownership was the central legal relationship. When the proletarians came to own the means of production, the organization of the factory did not have to change. Its products would simply flow to the workers who produced them. In Veblen, the ground of the quarrel was the difference in habits of thought and the various classes thought differently because their work induced habitually divergent bents of mental activity. Many employees who owned nothing nevertheless responded like businessmen because they lived by pecuniary rather than mechanical symbols. Lawyers, accountants, and economists were three illustrations. On the other side, there were some businessmen who resembled workers, because they were addicted to mechanical processes. If Veblen forecast the victory of mechanical processes, perhaps it was as much because he was a Norwegian boy trained in the skillful, reverent handling of tools, as because he reasoned his way to inevitable conclusions.

JOHN R. COMMONS (1862–1945)

At their best, Veblen's economics was a brilliant series of insights into the nature of society. For their effect, these insights depended less upon evidence and more upon the immediate conviction which flashed into the mind of the receptive reader. But how could a school move on from a series of intuitions, however scintillating? Presuming it were formed, how could such a school overcome the opposition of professional economists, who dismissed Veblen's work as either wrong or sociology? Veblen had ostentatiously snubbed the problems of conventional economics: prices, wages, rents, and profits. Instead, he had deliberately written about the very subjects most economists took for granted: the legal arrangements of his society, the institution of private property, and the pecuniary character of economic activity. A fruit of Veblen's evolutionary bias was the question: Why worry about today's prices when today is already obsolete and tomorrow is upon us?

The questions answered themselves. Institutional economics did not convert many economists. The profession continued to concentrate upon the problems of equilibrium and to take for granted existing social arrangements. Even today, Veblen is probably more admired by sociologists than by economists. Moreover, institutional economics changed its character. Economists like Commons carefully gathered the facts about institutions. In doing so, they insensibly shifted from habits of thought to measurable characteristics.

John R. Commons was born in Indiana in 1862, the son of a Presbyterian mother and a Quaker father. Like Veblen, his academic career was checkered. As a student at Oberlin, he was less than a success, and he flatly failed in his first efforts at teaching. He drifted from job to job, partly because he was a wretched lecturer incapable of systematic presentation, partly because his political opinions were heterodox. As one of the pioneer experimenters with field-work supplements to lectures, he took his students to factories, courts, and prisons. In the end, Commons' luck was better than Veblen's. In 1904 an old teacher, Richard T. Ely, made a place for him at University of Wisconsin. There he stayed, happy in his work and the sympathy it evoked.

His accomplishments at Wisconsin highlighted the difference between lonely thought and constructive action. He came at the precise moment when a reform governor, the elder Robert La Follette, needed help in drafting and administering a new program of reform and social legislation. On the state level, his contribution closely resembled the work of the Webbs. He wrote a civil-service law, helped extend public-utility regulation, promoted a small-loan measure, and, in 1932, drafted Wisconsin's unemployment reserve act.

He wrote extensively and his publications again approached the spirit of the Webbs. He compiled a ten-volume *Documentary History of American Industrial Society* and a history of labor. Although he called his major theoretical production *Institutional Economics*, his definition of institutions was not Veblen's. It was "collective action in control of individual action." The definition exemplified his beliefs. He emphasized the mutual dependence of men, their need to coöperate, the conflicts of interest which private property created, and the necessity of collective action to reconcile these conflicts in the general interest.

Because he believed that the courts took a crucial part in the actual settlement of social arrangements, he traced their influence in his *Legal Foundations of Capitalism*. In his opinion, by concentrating on market transactions economists missed the significance of two other, extremely important varieties of transaction. The first was the managerial transaction between superiors and citizens. Examples were the relations between supervisors and subordinates, or police officials and ordinary citizens. And in the background, always, was the transaction's third participant, the controlling authority. The second neglected transaction was rationing. Superiors, inferiors, and courts again participated in it. Corporate declarations of dividends and union collections of dues were rationing transactions. The three kinds of transaction converged upon the going concern, which was at the center of Commons' analysis. Much of his painstaking work was a detailed effort to understand, first, the nature of these transactions and, second, how courts came to hold their opinions of them. The bulk of his work was descriptive and historical.

WESLEY CLAIR MITCHELL (1874–1948)

Personal links are indispensable in the spread of ideas. Wesley Clair Mitchell was a student, admirer, and friend of Veblen, but he fell far short of blind discipleship. Almost from the first, Mitchell's concept of research centered upon quantitative measurement. Although he continued to share Veblen's judgment of conventional theory's inadequacy, his reaction to its shortcomings was not Veblen's. To Mitchell, statistics had the advantages of comparability and weighting over economic description. Mitchell's classic 1913 volume, *Business Cycles and Their Causes*, illustrated his technique. Employing the most meticulous of procedures, he gathered a mass of statistical series and from them distilled a tentative explanation of the business cycle. In so doing, he adopted a drastically transformed conception of institutional economics. No set of statistics could have yielded Veblen's results. Statistics, in fact, yielded nothing comparable in scope to Mitchell, who, with the instinct of the scientist, confined himself rigorously to his materials. For Veblen, facts had been trimmings. When he wrote his early book, he might conceivably have plucked a few illustrations from Mitchell's statistical series, if they had been available. It was highly improbable that he would have allowed facts to alter his conclusions. These were probably more a part of him than of the society he analyzed.

The nudge that Mitchell gave to institutional economics proved decisive. Right after the First World War, Mitchell organized the National Bureau of Economic Research, the organizational cloak of the new institutionalism. The profusion and superiority of American statistics owe more to the Bureau than to any other agency. The profession has been indebted to Mitchell and his adroit colleagues for pioneering investigations of national-income measurement, business cycles, productivity changes, price analysis, and many other topics. Economists of every persuasion have benefited.

However sympathetic Mitchell was to his old teacher's aims, however honorable the place he accorded him in his famous Columbia course in the history of economic thought, he retreated, under the influence of his statistical achievements, further and further from the large-scale analysis of habits of thought which had delighted Veblen. It is easy to identify the steps in this retreat. In 1913 he had propounded an interesting theory of the business cycle, which is still of more than historical interest. Fourteen years later he published a magnificent study, significantly entitled *Business Cycles: The Problem and Its Setting*. As the title hinted, a decade and a half of devoted work had convinced Mitchell that he no longer possessed an adequate theory of the business cycle. The book described the array of methods which, one day, might conceive such a theory. Undoubtedly, Veblen's influence lingered on in Mitchell's discussion of the monetary system, his summary of business records, and his appreciation of the evolving characteristics of the phenomena which he examined.

But these pursuits tended to diminish in importance as Mitchell's concentration upon statistical measurement increased. In 1946, in collaboration with Arthur F. Burns, he published *Measuring Business Cycles*. This was a patient, admirably clear account of the techniques which the National Bureau of Economic Research had evolved for the partial decomposition, analysis, and averaging of the business cycles of experience. In technique and conclusion, the book was a far cry from Veblen. One of the few general judgments the authors tentatively allowed themselves found that the business cycle, so far as their measurements showed, was stable over time. The vast changes pointed out by the authors themselves, which had occurred in population, land settlement, industrial combination, labor organization, banking, and financial institutions had not sufficed to produce a business cycle statistically different from the cycle of half a century earlier.

The heirs of the man who had said, on the best Darwinist principle, "everything that is, is wrong," could only conclude that change in the phenomena that involved them most had been too slight to invalidate their averaging procedures. No quarrel with these conclusions was necessary in order to recognize that these distant descendants of Veblen had moved to a world of new techniques, objectives, and conclusions. Institutional economics' paradoxical end was not a science of change but a science of measurement—an odd monument to Veblen.

PART IV

Contemporary Economics

Chapter 14

John Maynard Keynes

> Soon or late, it is ideas, not vested interests, which are dangerous for good or ill.
>
> *John Maynard Keynes*

INTRODUCTION

John Maynard Keynes has been the twentieth century's most influential economist. In fact, it is necessary to go back to Alfred Marshall to find an economist equally effective with professional colleagues, and to David Ricardo for an illustration of equal impact upon public policy. In this state of affairs, an element of paradox was mingled, because the Keynesian explanation of the size of national income and employment was clothed in severely technical language, addressed originally to economists, and applied in explicit form to short-run situations only. Nevertheless, Keynesian economics have altered the actions of politicians, trade-union leaders, government officials, and even bankers, many or most of whom have never read Keynes's central work, *The General Theory of Employment, Interest, and Money*. After all, the paradox was slight. Like Ricardo, with whom he has often been compared, Keynes triumphed because of his intellectual virtuosity and his supreme relevance to the events of his own day. The problems of full employment, upon which Keynes centered the force of his mature abilities, had, by the 1930's, fascinated every political party and every organized economic group. Because Keynes's analysis, however abstruse, met

331

the problems head-on and appeared to solve them, his ideas have been taught in the schools and debated in the parliaments of the West. From them has been derived not alone a set of short-run policies, but also a diagnosis of capitalist ailments. He has stimulated research in economics and opened new avenues of coöperative study for sociologists, psychologists, and economists. In his inaugural lecture as Regius Professor at Oxford, the distinguished historian Hugh Trevor-Roper cited Keynes among the major contributors to historical method.

Keynes was a major economic innovator. What he borrowed, he altered. He extended Wicksell's emphasis upon the central importance of the saving-investment relationship. He denied Say's Law. He made much of psychology in explaining investment, speculation, saving, and consumption. New constructions included the consumption function and the liquidity preference analysis. Derived from all of these was a forceful emphasis upon the positive role of the state in compensating for deficiencies in employment and income. This last point caught the fancy of his time. It convinced economists because exact technical analysis had preceded the conclusion.

KEYNES'S LIFE

Keynes's intellectual outlook and even the nature of his economics reflected some strategic facts. Keynes was the son of members of that high intellectual bourgeosie who, by their intermarriages and friendships, have sometimes given the impression of monopolizing the supply of brains. The charmed and envious American can stimulate his envy by reading Noel Annan's *Leslie Stephen* and Gwen Raverat's *Period Piece*. There have been no American analogues to the Bloomsbury Group. Moreover, Keynes belonged to a Cambridge family. His father, John Neville Keynes, was a distinguished economist, logician, and college administrator. For some years, his mother was mayor of Cambridge. Cambridge has long been host to English rationalism, just as Oxford is the English home of aestheticism and philosophy. Inevitably, Cambridge fostered economists.

Keynes went to Eton and, in due course, to Kings College, Cambridge, in 1902. Here Alfred Marshall taught him, and, although Keynes thought Marshall in private life rather silly, he conveyed Marshallian economics for many years to his own students. Never narrowly an economist, Keynes was much impressed at Cambridge by the philosophy of G. E. Moore and its hymn to beauty and personal relationships as the enduring verities of life. He became a member of Cambridge's most exclusive club, the "Society." Other members were Lytton Strachey and Leonard Woolf. Through the Society, Keynes met Virginia Stephen (later Virginia Woolf), Roger Fry, E. M. Forster, Duncan Grant, and Clive Bell. This group of writers, critics, and painters acquired the title of the Bloomsbury Group. For a generation, its influence on literary and artistic pursuits was substantial.[1] Throughout his life, Keynes was a logician, financier, book collector, art lover, and journalist, as well as economist.

After he received his degree, Keynes entered the India Office, where he spent two years, returned to Cambridge in 1908 as a lecturer, assumed the editorship of the *Economic Journal*, the leading technical periodical, in 1911, and published his first book, *Indian Currency and Finance*, in 1913. During the First World War, he served in the Treasury, concentrating on problems of external finance. As the war approached its end, he shifted to the subject of German reparations. At the 1919 Versailles Conference, he participated in the reparations negotiations. When it was clear that his own moderate estimate of the amount that Germany could pay stood little prospect of adoption, he resigned. In two months he wrote his influential and exceedingly readable polemic, the *Economic Consequences of the Peace*. What sold the book was the vitriolic portrait of the conference's leading actors, Wilson, Clemenceau, Lloyd George, and Orlando. However, its

---

[1] An account of the sect is available. See J. K. Johnstone, *The Bloomsbury Group*, Noonday Press, 1954.

core was a closely reasoned argument that Germany could neither produce the goods to pay the reparations demanded nor sell them abroad, if, by chance, she produced them. The book attracted many converts. It undoubtedly led to the modification of reparations schedules during the 1920's.

When the war ended, Keynes sought a supplement in activity and income to university teaching. He accepted the chairmanship of a life-insurance company, and, at the same time, began to speculate heavily upon his own account. It was a comment on his capacity to turn economic theory to practical profit that when he died his estate was valued at £450,000.

During the 1920's he wrote frequently for the Liberal periodical, the English *Nation*. His articles favored a larger role for the state in the mitigation of economic adversity. During the decade Keynes matured as an economist. In 1923 he published his *Tract on Monetary Reform*. In part, this book restated Cambridge monetary theory. In its policy proposals it went much further. Anticipating by ten years or more the conclusions of economists and men of affairs, Keynes attacked the gold standard, advocated a managed currency, and sketched a much larger role for central banking policy.

In 1925 his marriage to Lydia Lopokova, the star of the Russian ballet, coincided with increased concentration upon his role as an economist and diminished association with his Bloomsbury friends. In 1930 he produced an ambitious, two-volume *Treatise on Money* which focused upon the saving-investment relation as an explanation of economic fluctuations, amplified Keynes's banking recommendations, and contained excellent technical descriptions of financial markets and institutions. A masterly performance, the *Treatise* had the misfortune to be blanketed by the fame of the *General Theory*. Yet it foreshadowed many of the ideas in the later book, showed off Keynes's most ingratiating literary style, and merged fact and theory as the *General Theory* did not.

As the *Treatise* was published, economic depression descended upon England. England in 1930 was still coping with problems of foreign markets, currency valuation, and unemployment left over from the First World War. Ever a patriotic Englishman, Keynes turned more and more to the analysis and solution of unemployment. He served in 1930 on the Macmillan Committee on Finance and Industry, and signed a minority report which advocated public works. Until this time a free trader on good traditional grounds, he now supported some degree of protection. In other words, he concentrated upon England's special problems. His 1933 pamphlet, *The Means to Prosperity*, supported capital budgeting, public works, and increased government intervention. It employed the novel concept of the multiplier, the arithmetic relation between increases in investment and increases in income, which had been invented by Keynes's colleague and friend, R. F. Kahn.

During this period, he was working on the *General Theory*, which he expected to revolutionize economics: Keynes usually appraised himself realistically. In his endeavors he was assisted by colleagues who read and criticized successive drafts, among others D. H. Robertson, R. G. Hawtrey, Joan Robinson, and Roy Harrod.[2] In January, 1936, the book appeared. As the next section of this chapter will suggest, Keynes's anticipations were realized.

In a sense, the remainder of Keynes's life was anticlimax, even though he gave England valuable public service. Despite a heart attack in 1937 which impaired his health and caused his death nine years later, he worked actively in the Treasury during the Second World War, took a major part at Bretton Woods in establishing the International Monetary Fund and the World Bank, and employed his powerful arts of advocacy in negotiating the British Loan of 1945. When he died in 1946, general opinion recognized the loss of England's greatest economist and one of its wisest men of affairs.

---

[2] The best source of biographical information is Harrod's *Life of John Maynard Keynes*, Macmillan, 1951.

THE *GENERAL THEORY*

A central text in the canon of economics, the *General Theory* was often an unnecessarily difficult book. The style lapsed from its author's usual clarity. At times, it was even shockingly reminiscent of Ricardo. In it, nevertheless, there was a vision of capitalist society no longer able to employ all of its members or furnish adequate investment outlets, but much too able to induce savings.

What were Keynesian economics like? Alfred Marshall had analyzed in marvelous detail individual price formation. For fluctuations of aggregate income or employment, his *Principles* had little space. Aggregates could take care of themselves. Built into capitalist economies was a mechanism for the maintenance or, at least, the restoration of high levels of economic activity—Say's Law. In effect, Marshall assumed full employment. Keynes reversed Marshall's assumptions and concentrated upon the analysis of income and employment, the aggregates Marshall had accepted as data.

Employment and income were variable. There was no assurance that, except by accident, equilibrium would coincide with full employment. There are many possible ways to summarize the powerful theory which Keynes erected upon these assumptions. What follows is no more than one convenient version.

There are two important ways of classifying national income. National income may be the sum of salaries, wages, rents, interest, and profits, which individuals earn for services performed. People either spend or save these incomes. From this point of view, National Income is equal to Consumption plus Saving. National Income can also be the value of, or the prices paid for, total new output. Output can be divided into goods and services destined for the direct consumption of individuals and those machines, buildings, and inventories deployed by businessmen in the production of other commodities. Regarded in this manner, National Income is the sum of Consumption plus Investment. The two totals must be identical, since the sum of the prices of goods flows into the hands of individuals in the character of the salaries, wages, rents, and interest which were the parts of the first definition. Since Consumption and National Income appear in both classifications, Savings and Investment, the residual items, must actually always be equal.

A series of definitions facilitates the story. Consumption includes expenditures on food, clothing, rent, etc. It is frequently useful to classify consumer goods according to the length of time during which they yield their services. Thus automobiles are durable goods, clothing is semidurable, and food is perishable. Saving is the portion of income not spent on consumption. Investment entails the acquisition of a machine, a building, or an addition to inventories. In every case, the test of investment status is whether the item is directly consumed or used to produce other goods. Speculation is the purchase of titles to wealth, primarily stocks and bonds. A casual examination of any income distribution—and common sense—prove that an individual may play two or more economic roles. Keynes's theoretical discussion runs almost entirely in terms of pure consumers, pure investors, and pure speculators.

The definitional identity of saving and investment neither implies that savers and investors *plan* to save and spend equal amounts nor explains the size of the National Income, out of which savings and investments are made. Savers and investors are different individuals, possessed of different aims. This divergence in objective had important consequences to the economic system, because it started an economic process which reconciled the plans and determined a new level of income.

An arithmetic example illustrates this process. Assume an economy in which the starting National Income is 100. Assume further that out of this income consumers spend 90 and save 10. Investment must also be equal to 10. Now, assume a change: investors increase their commitments to 20, for reasons which will emerge later. For the moment a contradiction threatens: investment apparently exceeds saving. The contradiction can be resolved. Increased investment entails increased spending by businessmen and larger incomes for their employees. Out of these expanded incomes, individuals increase both consumption and saving. For simplicity's sake, imagine that for every additional dollar of income, consumers increase consumption and saving 50¢ each. The sums which consumers spend become income to other individuals, who in turn spend and save equal shares. Thus the original increases in investment foster a series of increases in consumption and saving, as follows: 5, 2½, 1¼, etc. The sum of each set of increases is 10. The eventual result is a new National Income of 120, out of which consumption is 100 and saving 20. Saving is once more equal to investment, and this new level of National Income will last just as long as investment remains 20.

Thus *actual* saving and *actual* investment are always equal. It is easy to see why. Suppose that consumers save 20 and investors plan to expend only 10. Then goods to the value of 10, which businessmen had expected to sell, remain unsold. Consequently, they are added to inventories. It will be recalled that this addition has been defined as a part of investment. Therefore, 10 planned investment plus 10 unplanned investment equal 20, the amount consumers save, and actual saving and actual investment match each other. Or, as another example, investors might plan to invest 20 and savers to save only 10. To their pleasant surprise, businessmen discover that they sell 10 more goods than they had expected. Hence their stock of inventories declines by 10. This decline is a deduction from their total investment, a disinvestment of 10. Therefore net investment at 10 is equal once again to saving. Planned investment and planned saving, on the contrary, are unequal except in equilibrium.

Thus far the tale proves that the total spending of the community can be enlarged by the activities of investors. Can it not also be increased by additional spending by individuals out of their incomes? Although the numerical answer was obviously affirmative, Keynes attached little theoretical importance to this type of change. For him, consumer behavior, in the short run, was rather stable, and alterations in consumption derived from alterations in the size of the National Income. Consumers react to, rather than initiate, new levels of National Income. Disturbing circumstances aside, their tastes are stable. Should their incomes increase, their actions are also predictable: their consumption will rise, but by an amount smaller than the increase in their incomes. In recent years this aspect of the Keynesian apparatus has received the severest attacks.

The preceding paragraph rested upon several definitions. The relation between National Income and consumption is termed interchangeably the consumption function and the propensity to consume. The relation between *additions* to consumption and *additions* to National Income is the marginal propensity to consume. The ratio between an increase in income and an increase in investment is called the investment multiplier. The investment multiplier of our example was 2, and the marginal propensity to consume was ½. The higher the value of the marginal propensity to consume, the larger is the multiplier and the more substantial is the effect of a change in investment on National Income. In the summer of 1955 consumers were saving only about 6 percent of their incomes. If marginal and average propensities were equal, the multiplier was in the neighborhood of 16.

The central issue consequently discloses itself as the determination of investment. If the consumption function is stable, it must be changes in investment alone which occasion changes in National Income and employment. What determined the businessman to invest? Businessmen (or entrepreneurs) who make investments compare as well as they can the rate of profit[3] expected from the use of a machine during its productive life, with the rate of interest[4] which must be paid to secure the funds needed to

[3] This is an inexact but approximate definition of Keynes's marginal efficiency of capital, which is more correctly defined as the highest rate of return over cost obtainable in given economic circumstances. As Keynes himself pointed out, the concept bears a close family relationship to Irving Fisher's return over cost.

[4] "The" rate of interest in Keynes usually refers to the rate paid on long-term government securities, a nearly riskless bond. All other rates exceed this one by amounts which vary according to the differences in risk which are assumed. Keynes assumes the existence of a sensitive structure of interest rates, change in any one of which will cause tremors and readjustments in all the others.

purchase the investment good. An investment will appear profitable only when the marginal efficiency of capital exceeds the rate of interest. In promoting investment, a drop in the rate of interest brings the same result as an increase in the marginal efficiency of capital.

The result is simple but incomplete. We have seen that investment dominates National Income and, in turn, is influenced by two groups of influences, summarized in the marginal efficiency of capital and the rate of interest. An explanation of the rate of interest and the marginal efficiency of capital completes the account. Once more, Keynes's answers permit concise statement. The expected rate of profit or marginal efficiency of capital depends on one objective cause, the price of capital assets or machines, and on one subjective factor, the expectations held by investors of the total dollar profits their investments will earn. A shift either in the dollar amount of profits expected or in the price of a capital asset alters the marginal efficiency of capital. Similarly, two forces account for shifts in the rate of interest: the existing stock of money, an objective influence, and individuals' attitudes toward the holding of money, a subjective influence. Money is desired to facilitate transactions and to provide prudently for the future. In these uses, its holders have little effect upon interest rates. The strategic group consists of speculators who divide their liquid assets between cash and securities.[5] When all of them are satisfied with this division, no change in interest rates occurs. But if speculators expect interest rates to drop and security prices to rise,[6] they will endeavor to shift from cash to securities. Should this expectation be general, security prices will

[5] Keynes argued that the existence of any rate of interest derives from the natural preference of individuals to hold their liquid assets in the safest of all ways, in cash. Interest becomes the payment made to them for holding their resources in less safe and less liquid forms. It is not a payment for abstinence, as Senior put it, or for waiting, as Marshall proposed. Income, not interest rates, determines the amounts which are saved rather than consumed.

[6] Yields and security prices are inversely related. Thus, if a fixed payment bond, say a 5% security, sells at 100, its purchaser truly earns 5%. If he sells it at 125, the new holder, entitled only to the contractual $5, will earn a yield of only 4%.

rise and the rate of interest will decline *in the present*. In the same manner, if speculative expectations are of higher interest rates, security prices will decline and the rate of interest will rise *in the present*. In Keynesian language, liquidity preference declined in the first example, and increased in the second. In other words, interest rates change *now*, because speculators expect them to change *later*.

The apparatus is complete. To recapitulate briefly: Investment determines income and employment, and is itself derived from the comparison of the marginal efficiency of capital and the rate of interest. The price of capital assets and the state of long-term expectations combine to explain the marginal efficiency of capital. The stock of money and the state of liquidity preference explain the rate of interest.

For the devotees of pictorial representation, it is easy to offer a diagrammatic supplement.

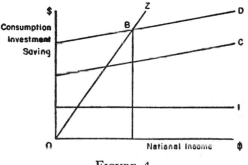

FIGURE 4

In Figure 4 the investment curve is drawn parallel to the X-axis in order to indicate that investment is independent of current levels of income. Consumption increases as income increases, but by a smaller amount. The D-curve represents the total demand for goods. The Z-curve is the supply curve of income and, by extension, of employment as well. Drawn at a 45-degree angle to the axes, it indicates that businessmen at large will pay out incomes no larger than the sum of the prices they expect to receive. Where the two curves intersect, income is at an equilibrium level. It will remain there in the absence of shifts in investment.

The shape and position of the investment demand curve in Figure 5 indicate that there are a few opportunities which promise high returns, others which promise moderate returns, and so on down to investment possibilities which point to little or no return. Should businessmen become more optimistic about the future, the whole curve shifts upward and to the right.

Figure 6 describes how speculative expectations which determine the shape and position of the liquidity preference curve, when combined with a given stock of money, determine the cur-

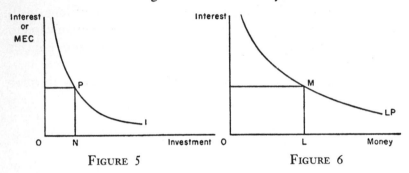

FIGURE 5   FIGURE 6

rent rate of interest. Given the stock of money *OL*, and the expectations embodied in the *LP*-curve, the rate of interest will be *LM*. Given an interest rate of *LM* and the profit expectations pictured in Figure 5, the level of investment will be *ON*. Given investment *ON* and the attitudes of consumers embodied in the *C*-curve of Figure 4, the level of income will be *OA*.

Not the least of the construction's charms are in its uses. A simple example will demonstrate how one change introduced into the system can produce large results. Assume a downward shift in liquidity preference. Then the rate of interest falls, investment rises, income increases by some multiple of the change in investment, and the multiple itself can be discovered by examination of the consumption function. The same effect on income follows from a drop in the price of investment goods, an increase in the supply of money, or an upward shift in the marginal efficiency of capital.

With varying success, this array of concepts has been used by economic forecasters. If the forecaster can form an enlightened estimate of investment plans from business surveys, he can, in this unsophisticated illustration, go on to predict the size of National Income, consumption, and saving. Saving must equal investment. The level of National Income with which such an amount of saving is associated can be deduced from the consumption function. Subtract saving from National Income and the remainder is consumption. If the predicted level of National Income falls short of full employment, the community is warned that government action is indicated.

How original was the *General Theory?* In terminology, early readers found a bewildering array of multipliers, propensities, functions, and marginal efficiencies. Yet, in important respects, Keynes's work demonstrated deep continuities with his English predecessors. Very much in Marshall's tradition, his analysis addressed itself to the location of equilibrium. His favorite categories were Supply and Demand, even if they were made to contain much more than Marshall had put into them.

Anticipations of specific doctrines were numerous. Knut Wicksell and Dennis Robertson had both emphasized the relationship between saving and investment. The marginal efficiency of capital came from Irving Fisher. R. F. Kahn invented the multiplier. However, specific parts of the theory were highly original. Two important examples were the relation between consumption and income, and the theory of interest. Keynes's most striking originality was his combination of elements, new and old, into a freshly created structure. Keynes's reading in his predecessors was not wide: Gunnar Myrdal was probably justified in mocking Keynes's "unnecessary originality." At Cambridge, economists have long preferred to think things up, rather than look them up.

PUBLIC POLICY

Strictly speaking, the *General Theory* can be applied with equal facility to situations of inflation and excessive demand and to conditions of unemployment and deficient demand. Both can be described in income terms. The problem of public policy is so to manipulate the determinants of income as to dampen inflation, or to increase employment and demand. In hypothesis, if not in practice, the policies are perfectly reversible.

We ignore the context of theory, if we rest on this truth. Keynes wrote during a depression which deeply worried him. The depression influenced the shape and, perhaps, caused the existence of the *General Theory*. The book's dicta all apply to depression. Not amazingly, Keynes has been interpreted by the general public and by many of his colleagues as a "depression economist."

How, then, was the *General Theory* to ameliorate depression? Logically, income would rise in response to either an increase in consumption or investment. The change in investment could result from government action which stimulated private investment. It might be the effect of direct government spending on public works or state operation of selected enterprises, nationalization. Or there might be a combination of these measures.

Through the *Treatise*, Keynes had reposed great confidence in central banking policy as an investment stimulant. In the *General Theory* he went further. He doubted the adequacy, though not the propriety, of interest rate manipulation via the central banking techniques of open market operations and discount rate variation. Here were his grounds: "I am now somewhat skeptical of a merely monetary policy directed towards influencing the rate of interest. I expect to see the State . . . taking an ever greater responsibility for directly organizing investment; since it seems likely that the fluctuations in the market estimation of the marginal efficiency of capital . . . will be too great to be offset by any practicable changes in the rate of interest."[7] Much of the importance of interest rate policy was as a superior alternative to wage policy. Lowering interest rates had much the same effect as lowering wages. Either action increased the funds available for speculative purposes, lowered interest rates, and increased investment.

---

[7] John Maynard Keynes, *The General Theory of Employment, Interest, and Money*, Harcourt, Brace, 1936, p. 164.

It was fairly clear in the *General Theory* that Keynes's minimum program called for public works and that he was not over-solicitous about their usefulness or nature. Keynes's remarks about pyramids and treasure hunts made the point with a touch of fancy added:

If the Treasury were to fill old bottles with banknotes, bury them at suitable depths in disused coal mines which are then filled up to the surface with town rubbish, and leave it to private enterprise on well-tried principles of *laissez-faire* to dig up the notes again . . . there need be no more unemployment, and, with the help of the repercussions, the real income of the community, and its capital wealth also, would probably become a good deal greater than it actually is. It would, indeed, be more sensible to build houses and the like; but if there are political and practical difficulties in the way of this, the above would be better than nothing.[8]

History offered Keynes good examples: "Ancient Egypt was doubly fortunate, and doubtless owed to this its fabled wealth, in that it possessed two activities, namely, pyramid-building, as well as the search for the precious metals the fruits of which since they could not serve the needs of man by being consumed, did not stale with abundance. The Middle Ages built cathedrals and sang dirges. Two pyramids, two masses for the dead, are twice as good as one; but not so two railways from London to York."[9] Public works at least, nationalization if necessary, seem to summarize this aspect of Keynesian policy.

An appropriate supplement was the stimulation of the propensity to consume. "Whilst aiming at a socially controlled rate of investment with a view to a progressive decline in the marginal efficiency of capital, I should support at the same time all sorts of policies for increasing the propensity to consume."[10] This second line of action led Keynes to favor redistribution of income. If the rich saved a larger proportion of their incomes than the poor, then redistribution of income in favor of greater equality, should, other things equal, diminish saving and increase income.

[8] *Ibid.*, p. 129.
[9] *Ibid.*, p. 131.
[10] *Ibid.*, p. 325.

In all of his proposals, Keynes was an empiric. The needs of the community determined the policies to be applied. Little in Keynes exalted, *on principle*, one policy rather than another. The test was always effectiveness in lessening depression. Consumption and investment measures marched hand in hand.

The world around us testifies that the Keynesian lesson has been learned. Many American policies support the propensity to consume by protecting various groups against economic adversity. Manual workers enjoy the benefits of Fair Labor Standards legislation, frequently strengthened by state laws. Their unions, aided by the Wagner Act, have been hampered only moderately by the Taft-Hartley Act. Federal and state laws regulate workmen's compensation and the conditions of employment. An impressive collection of union welfare funds and company pension programs guards the worker against indigence in old age, and encourages him to spend his income—and more. Directly or indirectly, these features of the economic landscape are brakes against income decline. They are reinforced by agricultural legislation which places a floor under farm income. Pressure to increase the scope and amount of such legislation increases during every recession. No theoretical barrier remains to stem the demand.

Moreover, as income taxes have become more progressive, the proportion of income retained by income recipients goes up as total income goes down. The increase in progression itself is reflected in upward shifts in the consumption function. Consumer credit and guaranteed annual wage plans can be expected to stimulate larger percentages of spending out of given incomes.

Many government actions influence the level of investment. Direct government investment has expanded, not alone in atomic energy and other defense industries, but in water power and roads as well. In recent years, tax laws have been designed to promote investment, by, among other techniques, more liberal depreciation policies. The Federal Reserve System has taken care to maintain the flow of credit to businesses. Government guarantees protect important classes of investment. A major instance has been the sustained guarantees of bank mortgage loans by the Federal Housing Administration, which have made possible the post-World War II housing boom.

No assurance can be given that these measures have ended the threat of depression. What is fairly probable is the statement that no intellectual barrier prevents a modern government from taking the additional steps to prevent such a depression from becoming too deep or lasting too long. Old attitudes do not die and many influential conservatives still regard deficits with something akin to horror. Economists differ widely about the timing and combination of the government's moves in recession. But wide agreement in every sector of the community appears to favor ultimate government intervention in economic foul weather.

THE LONG RUN

Running through the *General Theory* was a conception of capitalism's future. Although Keynes's formal economic analysis was limited by an array of short-run assumptions,[11] the emphases and policy proposals all emerged from a particular historical outlook and a firm conception of desirable social change.

Keynes perceived that in the making of current institutions, problems, and policies, many irrational forces participated, among them emotion, wrong-headedness sanctified by tradition, insensate greed, and sheer stupidity. Keynes never admitted that these influences were controlling. Nor does the reader discover that perception of "inevitable" trends, hardly to be altered by human will, that is the quality of a Marx, or even of a Schumpeter, a Sorokin, or a Toynbee. To Keynes, if post-World War I England suffered from unemployment, dwindling markets, and unfavorable trade balances, it was not the result either of long-run changes which had fatally undermined her economy, or of the

[11] "We have taken as given the existing skill and quantity of available labor, the existing quality and quantity of available equipment, the existing technique, the degree of competition, the tastes and habits of the consumer, the disutility of different intensities of labor and of the activities of supervision and organisation, as well as the social structure including the forces other than our variables set forth below, which determine the distribution of the national product." *Ibid.*, p. 245.

destruction of the tenuous balance of English class relationships. English problems were the result of "muddle"—unclear thought and hesitant action.

Here was the clue to Keynes's historical outlook: history at its simplest presented to the intelligence a series of problems, some of them economic, some of them social, and all of them intellectual. At least for the England which he addressed, Keynes never entertained the hypothesis that the failure of intelligence might be symptomatic of other social failures. For him, the line of causation ran in the opposite direction.

Keynes was a man happily wedded to an intellectual heritage, that "English tradition of humane science," which included Locke, Adam Smith, Hume, Jeremy Bentham, and John Stuart Mill. To its past exponents he attributed a decisive influence on English history. In their descendants, the "educated bourgeosie," Keynes reposed his hopes of English progress and rational social control. This group alone can be expected to formulate policies at once clear-headed and disinterested, novel enough to cope with new circumstances, and reverent enough to respect useful tradition.[12]

This vital intelligence was unevenly distributed among Keynes's major social groups. Consumers were guided in their spending by habit and income in the short run, and by a set of unanalyzed institutional shifts in the long run. In the case of investors, emotions, "animal spirits," were often decisive. As for manual workers, they suffered from an aggravated case of "money illusion" which persuaded them to combat reductions in money wages, but to submit to the rising prices which had identical effects on their real incomes.[13] Even the accumulations of capitalists were guided less by the economically rational motive of enjoy-

---

[12] See Keynes's essay "The Villiers Connection," in *Essays in Biography*, Macmillan, 1933. In that volume Keynes placed notable emphasis on blood relationships and on intellectual lineage where other ancestry failed. The point was clearest in the essays on Malthus, Marshall, and Edgeworth.

[13] This is one of the many Keynesian observations which labor unions have taken to their hearts. Large numbers of wage contracts, in England and the United States, are tied to changes in cost-of-living indices.

ment than by the wish to achieve prestige or pass on a fortune. Amid all this unreason, Keynes remained confident of the manipulative capacity of that small group which does guide its actions by conscious intelligence. "Ideas," not "vested" interests, always win.

Because Keynes trusted in the power of truth to overcome error, he was not disheartened by his own gloomy diagnosis of the state of capitalism. Keynes argued that the nature of capitalism had changed from the apparent durability of the nineteenth century to the growing instability of the twentieth. In 1920 he commented that "very few of us realise with conviction the intensely unusual, complicated, unreliable, temporary nature of the economic organization by which Western Europe has lived for the last half-century."[14] As he saw them, many of Europe's troubles were institutional: the list included maintenance of a precariously poised gold standard, and the increasingly complex division of labor and national specialization. Here was Keynes's description of Europe's greatest instability, her twisted psychological condition: "While there was some continuous improvement in the daily conditions of life of the mass of the population, Society was so framed as to throw a great part of the increased income into the control of the class least likely to consume it." The truth was not in these arrangements: "This remarkable system depended for growth on a double bluff or deception. On the one hand, the laboring classes accepted from ignorance or powerlessness, or were compelled, persuaded or cajoled by custom, convention, authority, and the well-established order of Society into accepting a situation in which they and Nature and the capitalists were cooperating to produce. And on the other hand the capitalist classes were allowed to call the best part of the cake theirs and were theoretically free to consume it, on the tacit underlying condition that they consume very little of it in practice."[15]

"This remarkable system" operated, in part, spontaneously. Its

[14] John Maynard Keynes, *Economic Consequences of the Peace,* Harcourt, Brace, 1920, p. 3.
[15] *Ibid.,* pp. 18–20.

success depended also on the astute men who sat at the central banking controls in each nation, and played an economic game according to a set of rules which they, if no one else, completely understood. After the First World War, it was a different game. The gold standard vanished for a decade, and returned only a ghost of its former self. The Peace of Versailles distorted the complex division of labor, of which Germany had been an indispensable part. That same treaty, born in emotion and nurtured in stupidity, fostered an inflation which destroyed the incentives to accumulate and revealed the nature of the double bluff which had supported prewar capitalism.

From such a picture, the faint-hearted might have concluded that the case of capitalism was hopeless. Keynes, on the contrary, remained steadfastly confident of the creative potentialities of the human mind. There was nothing here that intelligence could not mend, he stoutly affirmed, and, in proof, proposed an armory of ingenious expedients. If inflation threatened, let the currency of England be managed. If the gold standard impeded English recovery, either dispose of it or amend it into tractability. If the Treaty of Versailles threatened all Europe, men of reason could revise it. Not revolution but stupidity was the enemy.

As the 1920's merged into the even more troubled 1930's in England, Keynes's diagnosis deepened. He became convinced English capitalism's great disease was oversaving. Partly, it was England's time of life. "Great Britain is an old country. . . . The population will soon cease to grow. Our habits and institutions keep us, in spite of all claims to the contrary, thrifty people."[16]

In the *General Theory* the theme was unmistakable: "Today and presumably for the future, the schedule of the marginal efficiency of capital, is for a variety of reasons, much lower than it was in the nineteenth century. The acuteness and peculiarity of our contemporary problem arises, therefore, out of the possibility that the average rate of interest which will allow a reasonable average level of employment is one so unacceptable to the wealth-

[16] John Maynard Keynes, *Treatise on Money*, Macmillan, 1930, Vol. II, p. 428.

owners that it cannot be readily established by manipulating the quantity of money."[17]

This was the germ of the secular-stagnation hypothesis, to be discussed shortly. In 1935, as in 1920, Keynes pointed to a massive structural change in capitalism, a shift which occasioned new difficulties and demanded new solutions. Nevertheless, he curiously limited the effects of the development. He identified no substantial changes in class relationships and no mortal wound to the institutional structure with which capitalists lived. No one was to conclude with the Marxist that capitalism's irreconcilable conflicts were ending as foretold in proletarian triumph, nor with Schumpeter that socialism would win by default and capitalism disappear without a whimper. Keynes did not always agree even with the more moderate opinions of the English Labor Party.

He could accept none of these plausible inferences, for they all smacked to him too much of intellectual abdication in favor of a rigid creed. Moreover, his attachment to nineteenth-century individualism was far too strong to purchase security with the price of variety. How eloquently he put the virtues of individualism: "Let us stop for a moment to remind ourselves what these advantages are. They are partly advantages of efficiency—the advantages of decentralisation and of the play of self-interest. The advantage to efficiency of the decentralisation of decision and of individual responsibility is even greater, perhaps, than the nineteenth century supposed; and the reaction against the appeal to self-interest may have gone too far." However, individualism's greatest virtue was none of these:

But, above all, individualism, if it can be purged of its defects and abuses, is the best safeguard of personal liberty in the sense, that, compared with any other system, it greatly widens the field of personal choice. It is also the best safeguard of the variety of life, which emerges precisely from this extended field of personal choice, and the loss of which is the greatest of all the losses of the homogeneous or totalitarian state. For this variety preserves the traditions which

[17] Keynes, *General Theory*, p. 309.

embody the most secure and successful choices of former generations; it colors the present with the diversification of its fancy."[18]

SECULAR STAGNATION

Keynes's American followers took his estimate of capitalism, expanded it, and applied it to American conditions. The result was the popular theory of the 1930's, now in disrepute, secular stagnation. Economists of this persuasion believed that the very severe depression of the 1930's exemplified a graver disease than the chronic business cycle. This malady was a persistent decline in investment opportunities to the point where equilibrium between savings and investment tended to occur, persistently, at income levels well below full employment. Like Keynes, the secular stagnationists were alarmed by the declining marginal efficiency of capital.

What had caused this decline? In the United States, the vast expansion of the nineteenth century had been the consequence of a glorious investment boom. The three pillars of the boom were rapidly increasing population, the effect of natural increase and unlimited immigration; tremendous technological change; and the taming of the country's large, shifting frontier. In the United States, economists, like historians, find it hard to forget the frontier.

In the twentieth century, something happened to all three of these props to investment. The rate of population increase has been falling.[19] When the birth rate falls, the tremendous investments in schools, houses, and furniture decline with it, and the tone of the business community becomes less optimistic. It is one thing to build too large a plant, when an expanding population in the next decade will surely supply the customers to justify its size. It is quite another to build a plant and wait vainly for customers who do not plan to be born.

[18] *Ibid.*, p. 380.
[19] One reason for the brooding silence of stagnationists in the 1950's has been the apparent reversal of this trend. The Census of 1950 revealed an upsurge in births, and interim samplings since then indicate no return to lower rates.

When Americans hacked a civilization out of the western wilderness, they incidentally created extensive opportunity for capital investment. The frontier settlements needed roads, schools, houses, railroads, and the remainder of the material fabric of a new society. Now the frontier is gone. With it passed a second major outlet for capital investment.

About technological change, the theorists of secular stagnation were more cautious. As they recognized, significant inventions were rare, unheralded, and unpredictable. However, even here the outlook was darkened by the fact that so many inventions tended to be capital-saving: they replaced more expensive with less expensive equipment, in the fabrication of identical outputs.

Among the criticisms which the theory attracted were both the statistical and the historical. It has been pointed out, for example, that population growth began to decline before the end of the nineteenth century. The frontier also disappeared before the twentieth century began. Why did secular stagnation take so long in manifesting its effects? One answer pointed to the First World War and its aftermath. Some stagnationists conceivably might use the Second World War for the same purpose.

CONCLUSION

Keynesian economics are modern economics. This does not deny the extensive revision, amendment, correction, and supplements of critics and admirers. The point to preserve is that all parties use the same language. That language is Keynes's.

What will become of Keynesian economics is no business of a historian of economics. Some econometricians have battened upon Keynes, although Keynes himself used little mathematics. His principal variables—income, saving, consumption, investment—could readily be quantified and analyzed mathematically. Combining economics, statistics, and mathematics, the econometricians have created equation systems designed to predict income and employment.

Keynes has also stimulated survey research. The Survey Research Center at the University of Michigan annually surveys consumer finances in an attempt to discover how consumers spend their money, what the structure of their assets is, and what they plan to do with their income in the near future. Franco Modigliani and others have attempted similar work in the field of investment expectations. This research has followed leads given by the *General Theory*. As economists have looked more closely at Keynes's variables, they have inevitably concluded that things were more complicated than Keynes believed. Theoretical and statistical examination suggested that each of the important variables was better explained by more forces than Keynes had discussed. Age, family status, asset holdings, income history, geographical location, these are among the influences upon consumer income.

Undoubtedly, continued research will reformulate the Keynesian theories of income, consumption, and investment. At this moment, the categories are still Keynesian.[20]

---

[20] A list of Further Readings for Part IV appears on pp. 412–414.

Chapter 15

Business-Cycle Theories

INTRODUCTION

In the development of economic ideas, theories of industrial fluctuations—business cycles—have had an odd fate. In the nineteenth century and even the first part of this century, business-cycle theory took a position of minor importance in the works of major writers. A brief chapter sufficed for Ricardo, and Mill's suggestive comments had no organic connection with the remainder of his theory. What characterized the classicists was even more true of the marginalists. Jevons' statistical investigations were unrelated to the value theory which he prized, and a similar emphasis marked the works of his peers. Implicitly or explicitly, writers in the main tradition of political economy assumed that capitalist economies tended toward equilibrium at full employment. They joined to this endorsement of Say's Law the corollary that wage and price flexibility in competitive markets reduced unemployment to the frictional and, therefore, the temporary. Free of concern for these aggregates, economists could concentrate upon value and distribution.

Major theories of the business cycle were generally the angry product of economists who deeply suspected capitalism. Sismondi's emphasis upon underconsumption early in the nineteenth century was sufficiently heterodox, but Marx's pioneer empirical investigations (he assumed a ten-year cycle) and his theoretical explanation of business cycles were joined to a bitter critique of industrialism and a pleased prophecy of its ultimate destruction.

Veblen's emphasis upon loan credit as an explanation of business fluctuations accompanied his sharp criticism of the wastes of business practice and his forecast of revolution by technicians. Proper practitioners admitted neither Marx nor Veblen to their guild.

In this century, business-cycle theorists and their theories became respectable, partly because respectable economists specialized in the subject. But the struggle of these theories to central place in economics was frustrated by the Keynesian line of analysis. The Keynesian theory was not a business-cycle theory. Rather, it was an explanation of how aggregate income was determined. However, its predictive possibilities were so seductive, and promises of social control were so enticing, that many economists deserted their old love for the new.[1] It may have been the sad fate of business-cycle theory to place second initially to value theory, and then, to income analysis.

This is something of an injustice. Business-cycle theory has tasks of explanation of its own. The two upon which it has concentrated are the description of the cumulative process by which an upturn or downturn, once begun, feeds upon itself; and the meaning and location of the turning points. Why do neither expansion nor contraction last forever? Most theories have done rather better with the first problem than with the second. By now, most theories agree upon the principal features and order of events of the cumulative process.

The important business-cycle theories of the twentieth century can be classified in various ways. No single classification completely satisfies, because the best theorists have combined the features of several categories. Very loosely, theories of the cycle emphasize either overinvestment, monetary disturbance, or underconsumption. However, two of the most plausible theorists, Schumpeter and Mitchell, were so original in approach that labels on their work must mislead. They will be discussed separately.

---

[1] With one considerable exception. A popular theory emphasizes the production of a cycle from the interaction of the multiplier and the acceleration principle.

UNDERCONSUMPTION

This line of analysis has a long history. Although Malthus advanced no complete theory, his *Principles of Political Economy* stressed inadequacies of demand. In Marx's extensive musings on the cycle, there was an underconsumptionist element, based upon a maldistribution of income which posed perpetual contradiction between the broad powers of production and the narrow possibilities of consumption. Hobson's business-cycle theory, again a corollary of distorted distribution of income, found the villain in oversaving.

However, no underconsumptionist theory could win general acceptance so long as most students believed in wage and price flexibility. The interest-rate mechanism guaranteed, apparently, that if saving increased, interest rates fell and investment increased. Whatever individuals did not spend on their personal gratification, they used, directly or otherwise, to purchase investment assets. Thus the high rate of saving which attended an unequal distribution of income simply promoted low rates of interest. Since low rates of interest encouraged investment, and investment measured the degree of economic progress, much could be said for the unequal distribution of income. Say's Law, in ever more sophisticated form, debarred that modern successor to general glut, the depression.

Before Keynes, the best answer that the underconsumptionist could make to such criticism was the plaintive plea that events never turned out after this fashion. Depressions did exist. Idle men and idle factories continued to blot capitalism's copybook. If it had been valid, Say's Law had been repealed. The critics were unshaken in their conviction that, when the mechanism worked properly, wage and price reductions limited the duration and amplitude of contractions.

Rescue by Keynes came too late and offered too much, no less than a complete theory of income determination which swamped business-cycle specialists. Keynes, however, performed one enormous service for the underconsumptionists: he demonstrated that equilibrium at less than full employment was possible and likely. Although a learned discussion raged for years afterwards about whether or not Keynes had reintroduced rigidities in arriving at his underemployment solution, the underconsumptionist could at last climb out of Keynes's underworld, where the respectable had confined him.

MONETARY THEORIES

The most persuasive exponent of the monetary system's primary explanatory role has been R. G. Hawtrey.[2] Hawtrey started with some unusual definitions. His "consumer outlay" included expenditures by *both* consumers and investors. The "unspent margin" represented the means of payment in the hands of individuals. The theory hinged on changes in the unspent margin, for consumers' income and outlay could rise or fall only with similar changes in the unspent margin. The margin changed because there was an agency capable of expanding it, and a group eager to lay its hands on additional funds. The agency was the banking system which created, as it loaned, money. This money represented additions to the unspent margin. Hawtrey's borrowing group consisted of "traders," or wholesalers, in this country. When traders set out to increase their stocks, or inventories, the amount they borrowed to do so was added to consumers' outlay.

If the chain of events were traced further, it became apparent that, in expansion, life was a series of pleasant surprises for traders. They borrowed to expand their stock of goods. Their very borrowing created a "new consumers' demand, which tends to deplete their stocks almost as fast as they are replenished."[3] Encouraged, traders increased their orders. However, there were limits to the capacity of the manufacturers who fabricated the stocks of

[2] See his "The Trade Cycle," in *Readings in Business Cycle Theory*, edited by Gottfried Haberler, Blakiston, 1944, pp. 330–349.
[3] *Ibid.*, p. 339.

goods. When these limits were approached, producers raised the prices they charged traders, and traders raised their prices to their customers. Here was a characteristic event of expansion.

The contraction process was the simple reverse of these events. When the trader sought to reduce his stocks because further credit was unavailable, the reduction in the unspent margin which this effort necessitated led to reduced spending, and a refusal of the stocks to shrink. Still further reduction in traders' orders led to reduced prices.

Why did such cycles in bank credit occur? Hawtrey advanced two reasons. One was related to the gold standard. Gold and the supply of credit were closely linked. As gold flowed into a country, credit expansion was encouraged and prices tended to rise. But unless credit expansion in the leading commercial countries proceeded simultaneously (and how could gold flow to all countries at once?), the country which expanded most vigorously suffered an inevitable check. The balance of trade turned against it, as its citizens spent more on relatively cheap imports and could find customers abroad for fewer of their own higher-priced goods. The sequel was credit contraction.

The second explanation of the upper turning point centered upon the concept of the cash drain. By cash drain, Hawtrey meant the flow of currency into the hands of individuals, for their daily needs. This definition approximated Keynes's later transactions motive for holding cash balances. As wages rose during expansion, ordinary workers, who, Hawtrey assumed in England in the mid-1920's, had no checking accounts, withdrew more and more of their wages from the reserve balances of the banks. The latter were affected in much the same way by cash drain, as by the adverse situation of the balance of payments. In both instances, they could lend less.

Hawtrey's explanation of the lower turning point was less complete. As he put it, "the pressure of unemployment and inadequate wages has to drive the working classes to draw upon their supplies of cash, or at any rate to prevent them increasing those supplies, while the new gold from the mines flows into the banks."[4] Which seemed to say that gold flows had the ultimate voice in recovery.

OVERINVESTMENT

The common thread of explanation here was a conviction that prosperities drew to their conclusions because a necessary level of investment could not be maintained. In contrast to the underconsumptionist, members of this school located the trouble in undersaving, not oversaving. Some of the group stressed "real" overinvestment. One of the most persuasive advocates of this line of reasoning, Dennis H. Robertson, has pointed to the lumpiness of investment, the indivisibilities which make a smooth flow of investment impossible. No one can add a quarter of a track to a single-track railroad. Nor is it possible to add a tenth of a blast furnace, or a fifth of a newspaper press. Investment does not describe the smooth course of a sine curve. It moves, inevitably, in leaps and jumps.

One of the more intricate hypotheses, rooted in Böhm-Bawerk's notion of the period of production, was F. A. Hayek's monetary overinvestment explanation. According to Hayek, business cycles could not occur in the absence of an elastic money supply, that is, if the banks were unable to create new money and new credit as supplements to the normal savings of individuals. Although the primary trouble was monetary and the primary cure also monetary, the malady's effects were real. The structure of production was closely related to the state of credit, the quantity of money, and the rate of interest. By the structure of production, Hayek meant the number of stages through which raw materials moved until they assumed their ultimate shape as consumer goods. The number of these stages depended on the rate of interest. More efficient processes and better machines always exist. All of them cost money and involved some postponement of current consumption in deference to future consumption. When the rate of interest was high, business men limited investment. When it was low, they expanded investment, dimin-

4 *Ibid.*, p. 344.

ished the flow of consumers' goods, and lengthened the structure of production.

Hayek's explanation of the upturn started with a definition of equilibrium. In equilibrium, individuals voluntarily saved enough money to maintain the existing structure of production. Similarly, they spent as much as they wished out of their limited incomes. If they wished to alter permanently their division of income into consumption and saving, in favor of more saving, then investment rose, the structure of production was permanently lengthened, and a new equilibrium ensued. Prices of goods in the higher stages of production rose, because of the increased flow of savings which bid for them, and prices of goods in the lower stages, consumer goods and products nearest consumer goods, fell.

Unfortunately, said Hayek, this was not the way of events in contemporary credit economies. In an elastic credit system, banks interfered with the attainment of equilibrium. When they increased their loans, the central fact was that these loans did not represent voluntary saving. Borrowers used this new money to bid for the limited resources available, the original means of production and intermediate products. In doing so, they deprived consumers of some of the goods and services for which they had planned. This phenomenon Hayek labeled forced saving. Prices of producers' goods rose, prices of consumers' goods fell, and resources were reallocated accordingly.

Why did the upturn end? In part, because consumers were discontented with the deprivations of forced saving. In part, because bank credit was limited. Consumers were able to rectify their injustices in this way. As expansion swelled, workers in the higher stages of production enjoyed larger incomes. These incomes they used to swell the demand for consumer goods. This action halted expansion and began recession. For consumers' goods prices now rose and the prices of producers' goods fell. Parallel to this event were increases in cost. As a result, the makers of producers' goods began to suffer losses. In a familiar way, their troubles spread to the remainder of the economy. Features of the recession were curtailed credit and unfinished capital projects.

What happened during the depression phase was less clear. The most literal interpretation suggested that some projects begun in prosperity would be abandoned. The dramatic evidence of depression would include a trail of abandoned improvements, roads leading nowhere, machines rusting in windy buildings, and unsold houses in brave new subdivisions. Alternatively, producers might complete their plants, but falling demand might preclude their operation. A still less drastic interpretation of events suggested that the major effect would be a halt to the lengthening of the structure of production.

How did revival start? Consumers, finally, were able to allocate their incomes according to their own preferences. The rate of voluntary saving once again influenced the equilibrium interest rate. Finally, a renewal of investment followed. Hayek's theory suggested a number of practical questions. Could we define the structure of production well enough to measure it? If we could, did the structure of production actually lengthen in prosperity and shorten in depression? Did consumers' goods prices fall in relation to producers' goods prices in the upswing, and was the reverse true during contraction? How important were interest rates? Did they vary as Hayek assumed?

Hayek's analysis implied some public policies. If depressions were to be averted, the phenomenon of forced saving had to be avoided. Since the devil was the banking system, one solution contemplated limiting the function of banks to service as intermediaries between savers and investors. Thus they could not independently increase the money supply. If banks continued to operate, they had to be controlled, with a view to preventing a rise in prices. If an economy were to remain in equilibrium, prices must fall as industrial efficiency increases.

JOSEPH ALOIS SCHUMPETER (1883–1950)

Schumpeter's massive two-volume *Business Cycles* endeavored to present not so much an explanation of the business cycle as a theory of capitalism itself. With tremendous virtuosity, the ambitious work combined statistical, theoretical, and historical techniques. Schumpeter sought to measure cycles, describe the historical features of every fluctuation since the end of the eighteenth century, and derive a common ground of explanation. The key to the explanation was the activity of the entrepreneur. On his role, more will be said shortly. A noteworthy feature of the analysis was a three-cycle schema. There was a very long wave in economic activity, a hypothesis with which Schumpeter credited Nikolai Kondratieff.[5] The first long wave, beginning in the late 1780's and ending in the 1840's, Schumpeter identified with the development, in England, of steam power and textile manufacturing. The second, extending to the end of the nineteenth century, he associated with railroads, and iron and steel. Electricity sparked the third long cycle. In addition to these long waves were shorter ten-year cycles named, after their inventor Clement Juglar, juglars, and the still shorter 40-month cycle, the kitchin, named after Claude Kitchin. These cycles revolved around each other simultaneously in time. The Kondratieff was the trend of the juglars, and the juglars were trends for the kitchins. Juglars in the upswing of a Kondratieff carried the system further up than in the long downswing. When, as in the 1929–1933 contraction, lows in all three cycles coincided, depression was unusually severe.

Schumpeter distinguished three influences upon the values of economic quantities. The first was the circular flow: the interchange of productive services for incomes, and of goods for money which characterized a stationary economy. All the events in the stationary economy were repetitive. The second factor was economic growth. The third was the external event: wars, revolutions, earthquakes, and gold discoveries. These two last categories caused changes in the unvarying course of the circular flow. But the activating agent in the business cycle was the innovation. The innovation is a "historic and irreversible change in the way of doing things." It can take the form of alterations in

[5] See Kondratieff's "Long Waves in Economic Life," in *Readings in Business Cycle Theory.*

techniques, conquest of new markets, permissive legal devices, and novel modes of organizing distribution.

The innovator was the bold spirit who forced himself onto the industrial scene and disturbed the routine methods of conducting business which satisfied the administrative type of executive. Innovation itself could generate a simple model of the business cycle. Suppose, asked Schumpeter, we started from a neighborhood of equilibrium and examined a disturbance, an innovation. The immediate impact upon goods and services was slight, a small decrease in the output of consumers' goods. Still, the effect of the innovation was to increase expenditure in excess of the current flow of goods. This increase of expenditure and the adjustment of noninnovating sections of the economy to it was the prosperity phase. The downswing displayed a paradoxical aspect. It began when new products, the result of innovation, reached their markets. Displacing other products and services, they compelled liquidation, readjustment, and absorption into the system of the new item. Here was depression. The cycle did not touch either employment or total output. It was purely in producers' goods and consumers' goods. The new equilibrium was at a higher total output than the old one.

This was only a first approximation. In the cycles of reality, fluctuations were more extreme, and they included both credit and employment. Secondary phenomena explained this depth and violence. Among the secondary phenomena were errors of pessimism and optimism on the part of businessmen and overexpansion of credit and speculation. These excesses caused additional phases of the cycle, depression and revival. As a pure concept, the cycle depended upon innovation, even though, granted Schumpeter, most observable cyclical features stemmed from the secondary phenomena.

If juglars as well as Kondratieffs were associated with the rise of specific industries, and if innovation explained the appearance of these industries, Schumpeter still had to explain why innovations clustered instead of distributing themselves evenly over time. Schumpeter's not completely satisfactory answer[6] was this. Undoubtedly, the first innovator was a person of exceptional force, courage, and determination, not to mention imagination and good fortune. The success of one innovator smoothed the path for others in whom the entrepreneurial characteristics were less highly developed. New waves of innovation could not start until the effects of the last wave had been absorbed.

WESLEY CLAIR MITCHELL

Mitchell was the leading empirical student of the business cycle. It has been a pleasant irony of the relations of ideas that conservative teachers like Ricardo sometimes have radical students like Marx, and radical teachers like Veblen produce conservative heirs. Mitchell's admiration for Veblen did not distort his judgment:

What drew me to him was his artistic side. I had a weakness for paradox—Hell set up by the God of Love, but Veblen was a master developing beautiful subtleties, while I was a tyro emphasizing the obvious. He did have such a good time with the theory of the leisure class and then with the preconceptions of economic theory! And the economists reacted with such bewildered soberness! There was a man who could really play with ideas. If one wanted to indulge in the game of spinning theories who could match his skill and humor?[7]

But what did one have at the end of the display? ". . . if anything were needed to convince me that the standard procedure of orthodox economics could meet no scientific tests, it was that Veblen got nothing more certain by his dazzling performances with another set of premises."[8]

Basing his theory of the cycle on solid information, Mitchell

[6] Simon Kuznets made the most effective criticism of innovation's periodicity. See his collection of essays, *Economic Change*, Norton, 1953.

[7] Cited by Arthur F. Burns, *The Frontiers of Economic Knowledge*, Princeton, 1954, p. 66.

[8] *Ibid.*, p. 66.

sought demonstrable statements, not brilliant hypotheses. He started his description of a typical cycle, after revival had set in, although, in his view, it made no difference where the analyst broke into the ceaseless round of economic activity. A mark of revival was an increase in the physical volume of purchases. Once begun, this recovery grew cumulatively. The improving state of trade produced a more cheerful frame of mind among businessmen, and the more cheerful frame of mind gave fresh impetus to the revival. It was only a question of time before such increases turned dullness into activity. Increases in physical volume usually preceded price changes. As facilities approached capacity, prices too began to rise. Like the increase in the physical volume of business, the price changes spread rapidly. Every advance of quotations put pressure upon someone to recoup by making a compensatory advance in the prices of what he sold.

Because of its empirical foundation, Mitchell's explanation could distinguish differences in how the process worked. In most cases, retail prices lagged behind wholesale prices. Similarly, finished goods prices lagged behind raw material prices. Among raw materials, the prices of mineral products reflected changed business conditions more regularly than did the prices of animal, farm, or forest products. Wages sometimes rose more promptly, but nearly always less steeply than wholesale prices. Discount rates rose sometimes more slowly than commodities and sometimes more rapidly. In the early stages of revival, interest rates on long loans moved sluggishly, while the prices of stocks generally preceded and exceeded commodity prices.

Mitchell located the causes of these distinctions in timing and amplitude in three places. Markets, first of all, were differently organized. Also, the technical circumstances surrounding the relative demands and supplies differed case by case. Finally, practice varied in the adjustment of selling prices to changes in buying prices. In revival, these attributes of markets combined to increase profits for the majority of enterprises. Both wages and overhead costs lagged behind selling prices: the difference between costs and prices, profits, inevitably grew larger. Larger profits, added to spreading optimism, sparked an investment expansion. Thus, heavy orders for machinery and larger contracts for new construction further swelled business volume. Every increase in the physical volume of trade caused other increases. Every convert to optimism encouraged others. Every advance of prices offered the incentive for fresh advances. The growth of trade helped to spread optimism and raise prices: optimism and rising prices both supported each other and stimulated the growth of trade. These events joined to swell profit and encourage investment. High profits and heavy investment reacted by augmenting trade, justifying optimism, and raising prices.

Thus far, four characteristics of the analysis stood out. All of the processes occurred within the business system. Neither outside events nor innovation was essential. The system itself produced oscillation. A second feature was the stress on profits. The argument followed the changing differences between costs and prices. Third, the emphasis was upon competition, though Mitchell was aware of combination. Finally, the state contributed little to control, although its potential command of the money supply was important.

A number of stresses brought the happy phase of expansion to its close. The cost of doing business gradually rose. Overhead costs per unit of output ceased to decline when enterprises approached capacity. As old contracts expired, enterprises faced higher rents, interest, and salaries. Antiquated equipment and ill-located plants were brought into operation. As standard wage rates ascended and overtime payments became more common, the price of labor rose. Moreover, labor efficiency declined: overtime caused fatigue, the quality of new workers dropped, and labor morale and discipline sagged. Meanwhile, managerial wastes accumulated.

Tension in investment and money markets was a second stress. The supply of funds fell behind the demand. New issues of securities could be negotiated only upon onerous terms. Limitations of reserves prevented adequate expansion of bank loans, just when the demand for them grew, not alone with the physical volume of trade, but also with the rise of prices and the desire of men of affairs to control as many business ventures as possible. Financial stringency checked expansion, forced the relinquishment or postponement of many projected ventures, and rendered delusory the appearance of enhanced prosperity. For the credit expansion cloaked the failure of physical output to expand further and concealed the rise of inadequately secured debt.

Producers of capital goods were the first to suffer a serious check. In the later versions of his theory, Mitchell made use of the acceleration principle which his colleague at Columbia, John Maurice Clark, had proposed. Suppose that the physical quantity of a certain product varied over five successive years as follows:

Year	Quantity
1	100,000
2	95,000
3	100,000
4	110,000
5	115,000

Assume next that each machine turned out 100 per year. In successive years, the number of machines needed would be 1000, 950, 1000, 1100, 1150. If the machines wore out evenly, at the rate of 100 per year, replacement demand was also 100 per year. however, the demand for additional machines was much more variable. Ignoring the first year, we get 0, 0, 100, 50. The totals were 100, 100, 100, 200, 150. The familiar illustration proved one point: a slackening in the *rate* of growth in the demand for final output caused an *absolute* drop in the demand for investment goods.

These accumulated stresses could be resisted only if selling prices could be raised without limit. For numerous reasons, this alternative was closed. Inelasticity of credit was the ultimate limiting factor. But, long before it operated, other causes did their damage. In some instances, law, custom, public regulation, or long-term contract prevented price rises. In others, the hazards of the harvest determined prices, regardless of costs. In some industries, overcapacity restrained price increases. Finally, the very success of some enterprises in raising their prices aggravated the troubles of others who bought from them. Thus, near the peak of prosperity different enterprises face highly divergent immediate prospects. A majority perhaps enjoy profits higher than at any other point in the cycle. However, a significant minority feel the threat of declining profits, and, as prosperity increases, so also does the size of this menaced group. Sharp readjustment, under the circumstances, is only a matter of time. This decline in profits inevitably arouses the apprehensions of creditors. Inasmuch as business credit depends upon the capitalization of both present and anticipated profits, the time is ripe for liquidation.

Mitchell's exposition of how recession merged into depression and how, in time, revival supervened, was equally meticulous. Here, it must suffice to say that the guiding thread was still profit —the principle of change in the delicate balances and tensions of an intricate system. Nearly a half century later, Mitchell's theory of the business cycle is still the most sensible of business-cycle theories.

Chapter 16

Price Theorists

Modern price theory analyzes a larger number of situations than Marshall and Pigou considered necessary. Market reclassification and reformulation of utility theory are its major advances over previous theory. In the understanding of the new markets, monopolistic competition, and oligopoly, the major names are Joan Robinson in England, and Edward Chamberlin and Paul Sweezy in the United States. Since this theory complements Keynesian income analysis in contemporary teaching, discussion here can be brief.

NEW MARKET CLASSIFICATIONS

The new theories of monopolistic competition, or, in Mrs. Robinson's version, imperfect competition,[1] were designed to fulfill two missions: to meet some of the theoretical problems which the Marshallian and the Pigovian use of increasing and decreasing returns had posed, and to impart a more realistic tone to the theory of price determination in the markets of the real world.

[1] Mrs. Robinson's *Economics of Imperfect Competition* and Professor Chamberlin's *Theory of Monopolistic Competition* appeared in 1933. Both writers, especially Professor Chamberlin, have endeavored to distinguish their respective contributions. Mrs. Robinson started much more clearly from the controversy over the laws of return, discussed below. Her analysis was couched in marginal terms. Although she has been frequently credited with the invention of the marginal revenue curve, she generously gave priority to a number of other economists, among them Harrod and Yntema. Despite these and other important differences, the profession has overruled both disputants and credited them with the simultaneous invention of the same theory.

Much of Pigou's analysis in the *Economics of Welfare*[2] had rested upon the abstract classification of industries as subject to increasing or decreasing returns to scale. The divergence between marginal social net product and marginal private net product which so frequently justified government intervention stemmed from the subtle analysis of these two cases. In industries which enjoyed increasing returns, marginal social net product tended to exceed marginal private net product. The opposite was true of industries which suffered from decreasing returns. Government policy should favor industries which enjoy increasing returns and discountenance industries subject to decreasing returns.

The first major attack upon this apparatus centered upon its realistic applications, not any theoretical inadequacy. In 1922, J. H. Clapham's famous essay "Of Empty Boxes"[3] attacked the classification. The burden of the assault was upon the lack of empirical content in the theory and the improbability that such content could ever be supplied. Clapham made some shrewd thrusts at Marshall and Pigou for their failure to illustrate their categories. He identified some of the ambiguities in the notion of an industry, and he suggested that the various social inferences which Pigou drew from his analysis lacked application in the absence of clearer definition and better classification. Answered with some heat by Pigou, Clapham's provocative essay proved a preliminary skirmish rather than a damaging encounter, largely because Clapham had suggested no real alternative line of investigation. In economics, and no doubt in other subjects also, bad theory has always been held in higher esteem than no theory at all.

The next episode was no skirmish. It was the opening gun of the major assault. Sraffa's article on "The Laws of Returns under Competitive Conditions"[4] vigorously attacked the Marshallian-Pigovian apparatus of diminishing and increasing returns, and

---

[2] See Chap. 17, pp. 387–393.

[3] Reprinted in *Readings in Price Theory*, edited by Kenneth Boulding and George Stigler, American Economic Association, 1952.

[4] *Ibid.*, pp. 180–197.

proceeded to indicate an alternative line of theoretical investigation. Some of the novelty in Sraffa's conception of the way in which real markets differed from theoretical markets appeared in this quotation: "These two points in which the theory of competition differs radically from the actual state of things which is most general are: first, the idea that the competing producer cannot deliberately affect the market prices, and that he may therefore regard it as constant whatever the quantity of goods which he individually may throw on the market; second, the idea that each competing producer necessarily produces normally in circumstances of individual increasing costs."[5] The actual experience of businessmen, said Sraffa, indicated that the barrier to increased sales was not higher unit cost, but the necessity of lowering price in order to increase sales. Anticipating Chamberlin's emphasis upon selling costs, Sraffa added: ". . . the marketing expenses necessary for the extension of its market are merely costly efforts (in the form of advertising, commercial travelers, facilities to customers, etc.) to increase the willingness of the market to buy from it—that is, to raise that demand curve artificially."[6] Buyers preferred particular firms for a long list of reasons, among them "long custom, personal acquaintance, confidence in the quality of the product, proximity, knowledge of particular requirements and the possibility of obtaining credit . . . the reputation of a trade-mark, or sign, or a name with high traditions . . . such special features of modeling or design in the product as—without constituting it a distinct commodity intended for the satisfaction of particular needs—have for their principal purpose that of distinguishing it from the products of other firms."[7] Sraffa then explicitly identified the downward-sloping demand curve of changing elasticity.

So much has been said to indicate how original Sraffa's analysis, in 1926, was. Implicit in his essay was a prescription for a revised theory of price. Since normal circumstances in business

[5] *Ibid.*, pp. 188–189.
[6] *Ibid.*, p. 189.
[7] *Ibid.*, pp. 190–191.

now meant that the supply curve of a seller confronted a particular demand curve, the typical case was the monopolistic, not the purely competitive. Sensible, realistic progress, therefore, demanded a reorientation of the theory of value from competition to monopoly.

CHAMBERLIN

Rather than summarize either Mrs. Robinson's or Professor Chamberlin's book, we shall make a few comments upon the latter. A key demonstration in the *Theory of Monopolistic*

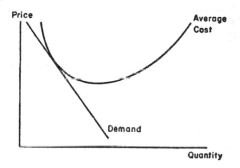

FIGURE 7

Competition was the tangency between the individual demand curve of a monopolistic competitors and his average cost curve. In a situation where sellers were free to vary the nature of their product, the selling costs designed to increase the demand for it, and the price at which it sold, equilibrium for the individual firm[8] tended to occur when excess profits had been squeezed out. If it were assumed that demand and cost curves were identical for members of the group, Chamberlin's symmetry assumptions, then equilibrium for group members would be also identical.

[8] As soon as differentiation characterizes sale, the industry ceases to have a precise meaning. Chamberlin substituted the group, a number of firms producing similar but distinguishable products. Since the products were different, quantities on the horizontal axis could not be aggregated and, somewhat awkwardly, changes in the behavior of the group occurred mysteriously off-stage.

One of the solution's implications was plain. Monopolistic competition implied inefficiency. Firms inevitably operated at outputs smaller than their most efficient possibility. The number of firms, therefore, tended to be too large, and excess capacity was a serious problem. In this market, there were no gainers. Consumers paid higher prices because producers' costs were higher than they would have been in pure competition. But the producers failed to benefit, since, in equilibrium, their high prices just covered their high costs. The pressure of differentiation induced socially wasteful uses of resources in the shape of advertising, technically trivial variations in the product, duplication of services, and frivolous packaging.

CLARK

How serious were these social losses? One critic of Chamberlin's conclusions pointed out "that much of the apparent seriousness of Professor Chamberlin's results derives from what I believe to be the exaggerated steepness of the curves he uses to illustrate them."[9] If the normal degree of differentiation were slight and the cost curves, over a wide range, flat or nearly so, then monopolistic competition would not imply substantial inefficiency. The tangency between cost and demand curves might well occur at prices and outputs little different from those of pure competition. Figure 8 represents such a result. The output OA and the price AB differ little from the output OC and the price CD which are the equilibrium consequences of pure competition.

Was it more sensible to assume sharply sloped demand and cost curves or a gentler variant? Clark argued that if proper account were taken of time, the elasticity of demand would likely be quite high. Potential competition and substitution insured this result. When businessmen, in apparent disregard of maxi-

---

[9] John Maurice Clark, "Toward a Concept of Workable Competition," in *Readings in the Social Control of Industry*, edited by Joel Dean, American Economic Association, 1942, p. 460.

mum short-run profit, endeavored to maintain and increase output, they did so out of a regard for potential competitors. As for product rivalry, "it seems that the differences between substitute products, in cost of production and service value, are nowadays often no more serious than similar differences between different varieties of what we think of as the 'same' product."[10] Both of these circumstances operated to flatten demand curves.

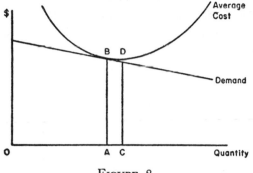

FIGURE 8

As for the shape of cost curves, in the long run, output was expanded not by more intensive use of existing facilities, but by additions to them. Even in the short run, available evidence suggested that, over a considerable output range, average costs varied very little. Such were Clark's conclusions.

Pursuing a different line of criticism, Schumpeter argued that the hope of monopoly was economically beneficial. The prospect of monopoly gained spurred the ingenious inventor and the dynamic organization. In any attempt to understand how capitalism evolved, this quest for advantage was the spring of progress. Inevitably, the advantage was temporary: new enterprisers succeeded old, old monopolies yielded to new, and formerly successful entrepreneurs lost their élan. In Schumpeter's view, monopolistic competition could be thought dangerous only by those who overemphasized the short-run and the static.

[10] *Ibid.,* p. 461.

OLIGOPOLY

The theory of monopolistic competition applied best to retail trade and a limited number of manufacturing industries. The bulk of manufacturing, in recent years, has required other explanations. A favorite hypothesis, by no means undisputed, has been that of oligopoly as the ruling form of organization in manufacturing. As explanation of the alleged price rigidities of oligopolized industries, the kinked-demand curve has enjoyed considerable success. This explanation addressed itself to this diagnosis. By some definitions, most American manufacturing industries are dominated by a few large firms, which produce the bulk of the industry's output. If the managers of these firms behave rationally, they recognize their mutual interdependence and avoid price competition. But rational maximization demands more than brotherly behavior. Monopolists, or oligopolists acting like monopolists, maximize profits when they adjust their prices for shifts in either costs or demand—changes in either marginal cost or marginal revenue. The statistical record, however, demonstrates that oligopolists alter their prices infrequently. Do they behave irrationally? Is there a sensible explanation?

Paul Sweezy's answer to the questions was embodied in Figure 9.[11] If the existing market price was directly above the discontinuity between the branches of the marginal revenue curve, then two consequences followed. Marginal costs could vary by the height of the discontinuity without altering the output at which marginal cost and marginal revenue intersected, or inducing a different price by altering the location of the "kink." The elasticities of the revenue curves told this story. If the oligopolist raised his price, he would lose money, on the assumption that his rivals would not follow him. If he reduced his price, he lost again because other oligopolists matched his reduction. The construction implied that the elasticity of demand for the industry was less than one. In the absence, therefore, of substantial

[11] See his "Demand Under Conditions of Oligopoly," *Readings in Price Theory*, pp. 404–409.

shifts either in demand or cost, price tended to remain at the height of the kink. Unanswered were such questions as how oligopolists arrived at the kink, and how they moved to a new kink when costs or demand substantially changed. How well did the

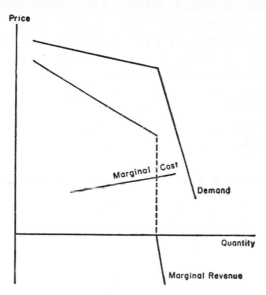

FIGURE 9

theory explain the facts of oligopoly behavior? The evidence was not conclusive. The most substantial attempt to test the theory empirically produced a negative conclusion.[12]

DEMAND THEORY

Modern demand theory substitutes indifference curves for marginal utility. More than any other single person, J. R. Hicks rehabilitated and extended the indifference curve apparatus. Hicks's *Value and Capital*, written in 1939, contains in its first 52 pages the best exposition of the contemporary theory.

[12] See George J. Stigler, "The Kinky Oligopoly Demand Curve and Rigid Prices," in *Readings in Price Theory*, pp. 410–439.

As stated in Book III of his *Principles*, Marshall's theory of demand contemplated a rational consumer with a fixed income, calmly choosing among various commodities whose prices were known to him. His problem was to maximize his utility. When he succeeded, no shift of purchase could improve his position. The solution demanded that prices be proportional to marginal utilities. To the consumer, successive units of a given commodity yielded diminishing marginal utility, and he was aware of the money value of these differences.

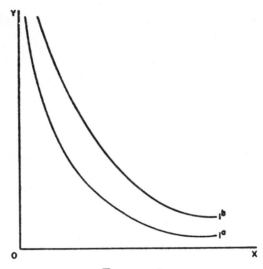

FIGURE 10

Hicks's theory of demand discarded total utility, marginal utility, and diminishing marginal utility. It was an attempt to erect a pure theory of choice. independent of quantitative measurement. Imagine a consumer choosing between two commodities, X and Y. All we need assume is his knowledge that certain combinations of X and Y give him equal satisfaction (he is indifferent between them) and still other combinations of X and Y, equal to each other, yield greater satisfactions. Figure 10 represents such a situation. All combinations of X and Y on I_a are equally satisfactory. All combinations of X and Y on I_b are preferable to the combinations of I_a. Ordinal is substituted for cardinal utility. Then Hicks generalized the analysis. If Y represents general purchasing power or money, and X remains a single commodity, indifference curves can never intersect the X-axis, for this would imply that the consumer would give up everything else to get more X; or the Y-axis, for this would imply no interest in X. Nor can indifference curves ever intersect. If they did, the illogical result would be that one combination of X and Y was both better than certain other combinations and also equal to them.

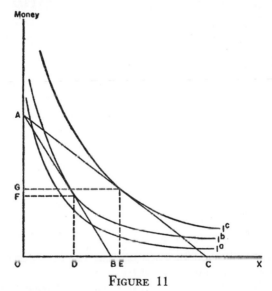

FIGURE 11

From indifference curves, Hicks derived a demand curve. Assume that OA is the money income of the consumer and that the price of X permits him to purchase with OA of income, OB of X. All possible combinations of Money and X fall along the price line AB. Three of these combinations also fall on indifference curves, two at the intersections of AB and I_a and the third at the tangency of AB and I_b. Since I_b represents greater satisfaction than I_a, the consumer will choose to divide his resources between X and everything else in the proportions indicated by this position of tangency. The equilibrium combination is OG of money and OD of X. Next, suppose that the price of X drops in in such a way that OA of money purchases OC of X. The consumer increases his purchases of X from OD to OE and touches a higher indifference curve, I_c. By rotating the price line, it is easy to generate choices of different commodities. A conventional downward-sloping demand curve can be derived by taking one more simple step:

Price	Quantity
OA/OB	OD
OA/OC	OE

and so on. The successive points can be plotted on a diagram whose Y-axis is price and whose X-axis is quantity. The resulting demand curve is free of the taint of marginal utility. It is the consequence of considering the subjective preferences of the consumer, independent of price, in conjunction with his income, and the price of the commodity.

As a matter of pure logic, it is most satisfactory to reach a conclusion with the fewest possible assumptions. But the apparatus has other advantages as well. It is possible to consider simultaneously income and substitution effects and to prove that an increase in purchases consequent upon a shift of the price line is divisible into an income effect (a price reduction, in a sense, increases the consumer's real income) and a substitution effect (the now cheaper good is substituted for more expensive goods). The apparatus can handle elegantly questions of substitution and complementarity which marginal utility cannot. Figures 12 and 13 represent perfect substitution and perfect complementarity, respectively.

Nickels and dimes, in the ratio of two for one, are perfect substitutes, whose relation does not change as one acquires more of one and less of another. The curvature of the more conventional indifference curve reflects the declining marginal rate of substitution which makes the commodity in relatively scarce supply more desirable than the commodity in relatively plentiful supply. I_b reiterates the truism that more nickels or more dimes are prefer-

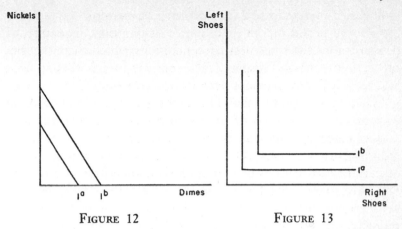

FIGURE 12   FIGURE 13

able to fewer. In Figure 13, left shoes and right shoes are perfect complements. The consumer fails to benefit from additional right shoes, if he is limited to the same number of left shoes. Again, I_b asserts the unstartling truth that, to the wearer of shoes, two pairs are better than one. Obviously, most real-life choices fall between these two cases. Ordinarily the purchaser decides between imperfect substitutes and partial complements.

Indifference curves have been applied to various interesting questions in public finance and international trade. It can be demonstrated, for example, that an income tax will leave a consumer on a higher indifference curve than an excise tax which reduces his actual income by the same amount. Some of the criticisms of the indifference-curve apparatus have centered on the plausibility of separating consumer preferences from market prices. Some critics have wondered whether this complicated apparatus has produced results so very different from marginal utility and even whether measurable utility has not in the end smuggled itself back into the picture.

CONCLUSION

One of Parkinson's laws of public administration concludes that organizations acquire their most magnificent permanent headquarters shortly before they collapse. Price theory is an elegant structure. As intellectual performers, economists have every right to be proud of the precision of assumption, ingenuity of demonstration, and neatness of conclusions which their theories of market behavior display. The contemporary theory is a vast technical improvement over its predecessors.

What doubts can remain? The doubts stress an old question in economics, the closeness of theory to reality. Are even the new market categories adequately devised to cover the varieties of industrial organization? What, indeed, are the factual foundations of current explanations of monopolistic competition and oligopoly? Are there more boxes, mostly empty, than there used to be? Has not the theory of demand, never simple to handle empirically, become still more remote from human behavior? Is there much hope of empirical derivation of indifference curves, except under the highly limited assumptions which characterize the few attempts to construct such maps of human attitudes?

There is a conventional answer to such carping: What is there better? In 1958, nothing whatever. What, then, are the lines of possibility? One approach toward a better understanding of business and consumer behavior implies rapprochement among economists, sociologists, and social psychologists. For decades, economists have cheerfully admitted the probability that the businessman's motives were more complex than the single assumption of profit maximization granted. Hard upon the heels of the admission followed a return to the single assumption. Recent institutional developments make it still more imperative that a less simple assumption, based upon understanding, should be applied. Does profit maximization really help very much to understand the giant organization, whose growing complexity of aim and responsibility, and galloping tendency to substitute committee for individual judgment, have made the single assumption less and less plausible?

Another possibly promising approach attempts to interpret oligopoly behavior by analogies to the strategies of war and games. These and other mathematical diversions, horrible for the nonmathematician to contemplate, grapple, at least, with some of the complexities of experience.

There is no shortage of industry studies. However, few of them employ the categories of economic analysis beyond a primitive level. Such, also, was Sir John Clapham's complaint in the 1920's. Perhaps, in time, ingenious souls will apply our currently intractable theory to their industrial investigations, or out of such investigations will emerge a better theory. The interplay between theory and empirical investigation is now far from satisfactory. Out of such endeavors may come a better dynamic price theory. Its excessively static nature is one of current theory's severest weaknesses. In one of his roles, the economist frequently insists on the progressive character of capitalism; in another, he carefully empties most of the change out of his categories. Weak as their theories may be, both the Marxist and the institutionalist at least center their attention upon what happens next. This focus was Schumpeter's great strength.

The lament sounds like and, indeed, is one more cry for a return to broader concepts, unashamed value judgments, and social concerns. In income theory, economics has done so. Here the prestige of economics is high. In fact, whenever economists have held their proudest place in the community, they have worried about the community's problems. Poverty, overpopulation, Poor Laws, and unsound currency were Ricardo's problems. He did not scamp them. Perhaps the delights of pure theory are dangerous to the health of economics.

Chapter 17

The Analysis of Capitalism

> The economic welfare of a community of given size is
> likely to be greater the larger is the share that accrues to
> the poor.
>
> *A. C. Pigou*
>
> There is no way of comparing the satisfactions of differ-
> ent people.
>
> *Lionel Robbins*

It is surely legitimate for the concluding chapter of a history of economic thought to examine economists' prognoses of
capitalism's future. It has been within capitalism that the study of
economics has matured. Yet there is little general agreement
among economists on long-run change and some question about
the propriety of examining the subject. The larger questions of
capitalist organization and capitalist development have been, on
the whole, neglected in favor of the more technical problems of
price and, even, income theory. This condition explains why
the categories of this chapter are miscellaneous: a theory of welfare economics which may apply to all societies or none; socialist
economics which describe no socialist economy; and various
programmatic discussions of capitalism in which economics, history, and sociology uneasily mingle.

THE OLD WELFARE ECONOMICS

Welfare economics is hard to define. Subject matter and
method have been the two criteria of definition and, historically,

emphasis has shifted from the first to the second. On the assumptions that economic welfare is a large part of total welfare, and that changes in per capita wealth affect economic welfare, the subject begins with the familiar name of Adam Smith. Smith assumed that larger total product and larger per capita product were the twin effects of free competition. The latter he considered an index of economic welfare and, through it, of general welfare, little though the *Wealth of Nations* uses the terms. Wealth and welfare at the beginning of systematic analysis were closely linked.

To the development of this strand of welfare theory, the utilitarians made a major contribution. Borrowed from Francis Hutcheson, Bentham's rule, "the greatest happiness of the greatest number," was muddled and equivocal. How could we choose between a hundred people moderately happy and fifty ecstatic? However, Bentham insisted upon the inseparable connection between ethics and economics. His human beings were all pleasure machines of varying efficiency. Education and environment, not natural endowment, determined the degree of efficiency. If men at birth were equal, as Bentham believed, equal training would keep them equal through life. A modern economist once asserted that equilibrium was just equilibrium, devoid of ethical overtones. To Bentham, pleasure was pleasure, differing in quantity, indifferent as to quality. Bentham, who never lost hope in the possibility of measuring utility, was responsible for the identification of money as the appropriate tool of measurement. He pushed his argument far enough to see that some income redistribution increased total utility, since first units of money, as of other joys, produced more satisfaction than additional units. Only his respect for the security of property prevented him from taking the next step to egalitarian distribution of income.

Mill's version of utilitarianism dropped the conception of measurement and abandoned the idea that pleasures were equal in merit. The hierarchy of utilities which he created represented the preferences of the educated: the intellectual over the sensual, and the public-spirited over the personal. Utility, in Mill, was fastidious enough to win the approval of most ascetic intellectuals.

The last utilitarian to cling to the possibility of measuring utility was Edgeworth. It was a hope he stated but never fulfilled. Somewhat paradoxically, his major contribution to welfare theory was the construction of indifference curves, independent of interpersonal comparisons of satisfaction and free of cardinal implications.

Even though his *Principles of Economics* was an engine of analysis, not a program of social reform, Marshall, in his anxious wish to do good, was a welfare economist. His discussion of consumption took pains to differentiate between objects of consumption which improved their users and those which did not. His emphasis upon production reflected his conviction that the activities of their working lives form the characters of men. Consumer surplus is a measure of the welfare gains of individual consumers. The tax and bounty proposals were directed to the aim of increasing consumer surpluses.

PIGOU AND HOBSON

The major work in welfare economics was Pigou's *Economics of Welfare*, written in 1920. It stands alone in completeness, concentration upon the central problems of welfare, and analytical finish. Before examining it, a word can be spared for one of economics' more appealing heretics, John Hobson. Hobson's *Work and Wealth*, which appeared in 1914, was also an explicit treatment of welfare economics. Its author dealt many shrewd blows at contemporary economics. He charged its leaders with overemphasis upon production and neglect of production's aims, the personal development of the individual and the improvement of the community. Economists neglected to examine the human costs of capitalist organization: they treated men like machines. His aim was to "seek some intelligible and consistent method of human valuation for economic goods and processes."[1]

The key was the notion of organic welfare, covering the en-

[1] John A. Hobson, *Work and Wealth*, Allen and Unwin, 1933, p. vii.

tire "physical and spiritual structure of human society." Then Hobson examined in detail the costs as well as the benefits of all varieties of human labor, and all kinds of consumption. As might have been anticipated, he discovered monotony, danger, and oppression in many kinds of labor, and considerable harm in many articles of consumption. Quoting approvingly Ruskin's "there is no wealth but life," Hobson discarded monetary in favor of human measures.

By no means all of Hobson's criticisms were unjustified. In J. M. Clark's "overhead costs" and Pigou's divergences between marginal social net product and marginal private net product, these criticisms were incorporated into a method of analysis. Hobson's fatal weakness was the absence of an alternative conceptual scheme to justify his quantitative aggregation of human costs and his qualitative interpretation of their meaning. Indignant, vague, and partisan, his writings were readily discounted. Because Pigou played the technical game with singular virtuosity, no one could discount his opinions.

The *Economics of Welfare* was a treatise carefully organized, gravely and temperately argued. The central proposition of its first part associated the economic welfare of the community with the size of the national dividend and with the share of dividend which reaches the hands of the poor. Part II discussed a great many general influences on the size of the national dividend. Part III specifically examined labor. Part IV tackled the critical problems of transfers from the rich to the poor. Pigou's assumptions were utilitarian: men endeavored to maximize satisfaction; they pushed their purchases to the point at which marginal monetary outlays yielded identical satisfactions in different uses; and the marginal utilities of goods were, in equilibrium, proportional to their prices.

Men might not now be equal in their capacity for enjoyment; they were, nevertheless, closer to each other than might appear. Moreover, time and increased income worked to narrow human differences. Pigou made the point eloquently: "The root of the matter is that, even when, under existing conditions, the mental constitution of poor persons is such that an enlarged income will at the moment yield them little benefit, yet, after a time—more especially if the time is long enough to allow a new generation to grow up—the possession of such an income will make possible the development in them, through education and otherwise, of capacities and faculties adapted for the enjoyment of the enlarged income." The tendency of the position was egalitarian: "Thus in the long run differences of temperament and taste between rich and poor are overcome by the very fact of a shifting of income between them. Plainly, therefore, they cannot be used as an argument to disprove the benefits of a transference."[2]

Pigou's discussion of national income and index numbers was careful. Economic welfare and other aspects of welfare might move in opposite directions, but, in the absence of "specific evidence," it was unlikely. Although desires and satisfaction ran parallel, there was an important exception: we tended to undervalue the future because "our telescopic faculty is defective, and . . . we, therefore, see future pleasures, as it were, on a diminished scale."[3] As a result, investment was smaller than it should have been. Public policies which discriminated against saving diminished economic welfare. Taxes or other measures which encouraged saving increased economic welfare. All economic causes affected economic welfare through the mediation of the national dividend, which Pigou defined as "that part of the objective income of the community, including, of course, income derived from abroad, which can be measured in money."[4]

Part II made several strategic assumptions. Employment was high. Resources were not automatically used in ways which maximized economic welfare. The central problem, then, was to understand the departures from ideal use. Here Pigou defined two powerful concepts, the marginal social net product, and the marginal private net product. The marginal private net product (MPNP) Pigou defined as "that part of the total net product of

[2] A. C. Pigou, *Economics of Welfare*, Macmillan, 1932, p. 92.
[3] *Ibid.*, p. 25.
[4] *Ibid.*, p. 31.

physical things or objective services due to the marginal increment of resources in any given use or place which accrues in the first instance—i.e. prior to sale—to the person responsible for investing resources there."[5] The marginal social net product (MSNP) was a wider and less precise notion: ". . . the total net product of physical things or objective resources due to the marginal increment of resources in any given use or place, no matter to whom any part of this product may accrue."[6]

Thus the damage to a forest from the sparks sprinkled by a passing locomotive was a deduction from marginal social net product, though not from marginal private net product. A condition of maximum output was equality of result from the employment of equal resources in every line. MSNP's, in equilibrium, were everywhere the same. Private self-interest maximized the national dividend and economic welfare, only when MSNP and MPNP coincided. Frequently they diverged. When tenants made investments whose benefits flowed partly to landlords, MSNP exceeded MPNP. More broadly, whenever, in the course of rendering a paid service, an individual also rendered services or disservices to others, which were not susceptible to payments for benefits or compensation for damages, a discrepancy between the two marginal products arose. Thus the rich person's private park improves the area's amenities for the rich person's neighbors. Scientific research yields social benefits which exceed those earned for the scientists themselves. On the other hand, the production and sale of liquor causes unwholesome effects upon purchasers which reduce social net product below private net product. Alcoholism may profit the distillers. Novelty may be the occasion of new divergences. A friend's purchase of a new automobile may diminish an individual's pleasure in his older model. Intelligently deployed, taxes and bounties can diminish the divergences between social and private net products. Subsidies to agriculture and taxes on liquor and cigarettes might be justified in this way.

[5] Ibid., pp. 134–135.
[6] Ibid., p. 135.

Much of advertising is wasteful. It diminishes marginal social net product. Some modes of industrial organization create incidental social benefits, others do not. When there are many small enterprises in an industry, workers can readily set up their own businesses. These businesses produce not only goods for profit, but abilities for their operators. Marginal social net product includes the enhanced powers and abilities of these small enterprisers. When the large enterprise dominates an industry, men of potential capacity are forced to work at jobs which are below their abilities. A third sort of divergence between private and social effects occurs when supply price decreases. When increasing returns to scale obtain, MSNP will exceed MPNP. Finally, there was the case of monopolistic competition.[7] Pigou flatly concluded that monopolistic competition must prevent investment of the amounts required to make marginal social net product equal to marginal social net product in competitive industries.

What could the state do to increase the welfare of labor? This was the leading question of Part III. Here the discussion veered toward the institutional. Pigou examined carefully arbitration, mediation, and coercive intervention. What, he asked, would be the effect on the national dividend of working days of different length, and of different modes of paying labor? He answered: "No general statement as to the relation between hours of labour and the national dividend can be made. The relation will be different for different types of workpeople and different kinds of work."[8] There was, Pigou observed, a tendency for people to work too long hours. Pigou believed that there was a prima-facie case for state intervention.

Were piece rates or hourly rates to be preferred? When payment was directly related to performance as payment by the piece assumed, output was higher, provided that employers did not lower rates as workers increased their output. One of the functions of collective bargaining was the prevention of employer

---

[7] In Pigou, monopolistic competition existed whenever two or more large sellers appeared in a single market.

[8] *Ibid.*, p. 463.

pressure of this variety. Pigou concluded that "the interest of the national dividend, and, through that, of economic welfare, will be best promoted when immediate reward is adjusted as closely as possible to immediate results . . . this can, in general, be done most effectively by piece-wage scales controlled by collective bargaining."[9]

What was the best distribution of persons among jobs? The gap between marginal social net product and marginal private net product eliminated the easy solution which held that the national dividend was maximized when the values of marginal private net products were equal in all uses. "When the incidental advantages and disadvantages attaching to different occupations and places are not fully realised and taken into account by workpeople entering employment, this fact causes labor to be distributed in a way that makes the values of marginal net products *more nearly equal* than in the interest of the national dividend they ought to be."[10] The danger was neglect of the marginal social net product. Pigou proceeded to maintain that, where wages were very low, raising them might increase the national dividend, partly because the physical capacity of the workers increased, partly because new hope lifted their spirits and increased their application to their work.

Finally, in Part IV, Pigou offered an extremely ingenious analysis of income redistribution. His conception of the problem was this: ". . . while, in general and apart from special exceptions, anything which either increases the dividend without injuring the absolute share of the poor, or increases the absolute share of the poor without injuring the dividend must increase economic welfare, the effect upon economic welfare of anything that increases one of these quantities but diminishes the other is ambiguous." The analyst must discriminate: "Plainly, when this kind of disharmony exists, the aggregate effect upon economic welfare, brought about by any cause responsible for it, can only be determined by balancing in detail the injury (or benefit) to

9 *Ibid.*, p. 487.
10 *Ibid.*, p. 490.

the dividend as a whole against the benefit (or injury) to the real earnings of the poorer classes."[11]

What happened to economic welfare when resources were directly transferred from the rich to the poor? If employers voluntarily increased their contributions to educational and cultural schemes designed to benefit their employees, then the national dividend rose. Was the result the same when the transfers took the compulsory form of taxes? The effects, said Pigou, were "nebulous." While equality of sacrifice demanded progressive taxation, uncertain effects upon incentives urged moderation. Would the promise of redistribution stimulate the poor? No general answer could be made. It all depended whether the transfers favored the idle, benefited the industrious, or failed to discriminate between the two. Increased poor relief to the thrifty favored industry. Poor laws which assisted only the destitute helped the idle. Universal pensions or bounties for children were neutral. While the effect of general transfers was uncertain, Pigou was confident that selected transfers, competently managed and prudently aimed at the poor, increased the national dividend and economic welfare.

In principle, if not in practice, welfare was measurable. Except in unusual circumstances, redistribution of income in the direction of equality increased welfare. Pigou made interpersonal comparisons and assumed the cardinality of utility. Such comparisons and assumptions were essential to his analysis and conclusions. Pigou, then, was a culmination of the old line of welfare economics. As nearly as it could be said of a book, this treatise was perfect of its kind.

THE NEW WELFARE ECONOMICS

Although the new welfare economics traces its ancestry back to Pareto, it is only in the last 20 years that it has flowered. Many eminent contemporary economists have done work in this subject, among them J. R. Hicks, Paul Samuelson, Lionel Rob-

[11] *Ibid.*, p. 645.

bins, Roy Harrod, Abram Bergson, Nicholas Kaldor, and Harold Hotelling. In elegance and precision, it is outstanding. In applicability to practical policy, it is extraordinarily arid.

Why a new welfare economics? What was wrong with Pigou's work? One critic, J. R. Hicks, identified three critical weaknesses.[12] Pigou had correlated economic and general welfare. He had freely made interpersonal comparisons. He had identified the sum of consumer surpluses with the real value of the national dividend. What could be done to rectify the weaknesses? Hicks, and others, advocated "reorganization" and "compensation." A reorganization was any alteration in economic circumstances: changes in the tax structure, alterations in tariff schedules, and so on. A change in taxes which helped someone without hurting anyone else, improved welfare: it was an ideal reorganization. Although this principle seemed logically irreproachable,[13] it was exceedingly difficult to imagine actual situations in which the only change was favorable. At this point, the second principle was put into play. If it were possible for those who gained from a reorganization to compensate those who lost and still retain some net advantage, the economic possibilities were more numerous. Thus, if the gainers from a tariff reduction compensated the losers, and the former were still better off than before the reduction, economic welfare increased, and, incidentally, tariff policy was easier. However, the illustration implied some of the difficulties of translating these principles into policies. Appropriate compensation demanded that gainers and losers be identified. But who was hurt? How great was the damage? How should the compensation be collected? Who had benefited?

One of the achievements of the new welfare economics was precise identification of the conditions of maximum welfare. As Melvin Reder put it: ". . . If welfare is to be a maximum, it must be impossible to increase it by varying the output of any product consumed by a consumer (including variations from zero);

[12] See his "Foundations of Welfare Economics," *Economic Journal*, December, 1939, pp. 696–712.

[13] Until an astute critic, Kenneth Arrow, pointed out that those who were unhelped might envy those who were helped.

by varying the amount of any product consumed by any consumer (including variations from zero); or by varying the amount of any factor unit used to yield direct service to any individual (including variations from zero)."[14]

SOCIALIST ECONOMICS

The modern theory of economic planning is another act in the curious interplay between Marxism and classical economic theory and its intellectual descendants. In *Capital*, Marx borrowed and extended the labor theory of value. The class struggle, which he thunderously preached, lived implicitly in Ricardo's quiet pages about the antagonism between worker and capitalist over what the landlord left of the national output. The apocalypse according to Marx came at the end of a route planned and graded by Ricardo. But Marx's emphases upon capitalist development and the shape of impending crisis gave no notion of how the future socialist society would be organized. In the *Critique of the Gotha Program*, his vague remarks about the withering of the state represented aspiration, not prescription.

When, at the beginning of the twentieth century, the eminent Dutch economist N. G. Pierson challenged Marxists to describe how goods would be priced and resources allocated in the social community of the future, the best answer that Karl Kautsky, a leading Marxist theoretician, could give was vague and unsatisfactory. There was little meat in this typical statement: "Thus the problem of the distribution of the social product among the individual workers will not be determined according to the principles of justice, however they may be formulated, but by the conditions and requirements of production."

The conservative Italian economist Enrico Barone made an essential advance in 1908, when he proved the mathematical possibility of an equation system which, when solved, distributed resources and incomes efficiently in an economy directed by a

[14] Melvin W. Reder, *Studies in the Theory of Welfare Economics*, Columbia, 1947, p. 38.

central authority.[15] At the time, the prospect of solving millions of equations condemned the solution to the theoretical.

Even as theory, the solution did not suffice. In the eyes of such critics of socialism as Ludwig von Mises and Friedrich Hayek, the hardest part of the problem lingered on. How could human beings—efficiently—make the multitude of actual decisions which a complex of final and intermediate markets made automatically under capitalism?

One Marxist answer was authoritarian. As Maurice Dobb saw the issue, "either planning means overriding the autonomy of separate decisions or it means nothing at all."[16] Any scale of priorities would suffice to facilitate economic calculation. Costs could be determined by technical considerations of productivity, rather than the financial results of monetary calculation. To Dobb the problem did not seem terribly difficult:

In an economy where every detail in the allocation of resources including labour-power was planned, the way in which costs were calculated for purposes of accounting would, therefore, seem to be of no importance. To decide whether resources would be better employed elsewhere than in the place in question, one would need to know the relative productivities of such resources there and elsewhere. To compare the inefficient management with the efficient one would need simply to know the amount of product and the amount of resources allocated and to compare the result with some similar factory, or to compare the product with past experience or what had been estimated."[17]

On the fate of the consumer, Dobb hedged. Although he saw no reason why, after a period of transition, considerable consumer sovereignty should not exist, he tended to deprecate its importance. Consumers, after all, saw only a limited number of the available alternatives. Experts could often make choices which increased the ultimate satisfaction of consumers. The con-

[15] See F. A. Hayek (ed.), *Collectivist Economic Planning*, Routledge & Kegan Paul, 1935.
[16] Maurice Dobb, *Political Economy and Capitalism*, International Publishers, 1945, p. 276.
[17] *Ibid.*, p. 304.

sumer himself might ultimately admit the superior judgment of those who made his choices for him.

As one of Dobb's severer critics, A. P. Lerner, sharply asked,[18] how could the productivities of different industries be compared in the absence of a price system, even if it were granted that intra-industry comparisons could be as easily made as Dobb assumed? How could the productivity of investment be estimated? How much freedom could the consumer be allowed? Did convention, ignorance, and advertising completely destroy the case for free allocation by the consumer of his own income?

A much more plausible line of reasoning employed rather than ignored the price system. In his essay "The Guidance of Production in a Socialist State,"[19] F. M. Taylor sketched a simple trial-and-error procedure for the solution of the price equations which so afflicted the contestants. In Taylor's system, the state assured money incomes to all citizens, and allowed them to spend the incomes freely. The obligations of the citizens were only to work a set number of hours and obey a few simple rules. The managers of state enterprises would charge prices designed to cover their total costs. Taylor proposed to handle the critical question of cost determination in five steps. The first contemplated the promulgation of a factor valuation table based on existing prices, presumably those last charged before socialism superseded capitalism. Managers of productive enterprises scheduled their operations on the assumption that these prices were absolutely correct. However, the managers at the same time watched alertly for signs of incorrectness in the factor prices, as signalized by either a surplus or a scarcity of the relevant factor. In such cases, managers adjusted by using larger quantities of factors in oversupply and smaller quantities of factors in undersupply. The procedure continued until shortages and surpluses vanished.

Oskar Lange extended this sketch. He proved that a Central

---

[18] See Abba P. Lerner, "Economic Theory of a Socialist Economy," *Review of Economic Studies*, October, 1934.

[19] See Oskar Lange and Fred M. Taylor, *On the Economic Theory of Socialism*, Minnesota, 1938.

Planning Board could impose rules upon socialist managers which allocated resources and set prices as efficiently as a capitalist society of the purest stripe, and much more efficiently than the capitalist communities of experience. The advantages of the socialist solution included elimination of monopoly, business cycles, and distortions of demand.

The conditions of equilibrium could be described. Every industry attained its best position on the basis of equilibrium prices. Equilibrium prices, themselves, were determined by equality between supply and demand for every commodity. Each consumer's income equaled his receipts from the sale of his own productive services. In Lange's socialist community, individuals endeavored to maximize utility, profit, or income. They maximized utility by equalizing the marginal utilities of their purchases. Managers achieved maximum profit, according to their instructions, by combining factors as efficiently as possible on the basis of existing prices. Workers maximized their income by selling their labor to the highest bidders.

Some set of prices satisfied all these conditions simultaneously. This was the equilibrium set. The Central Planning Board determined the rate of accumulation. The value of labor in different industries differed not only according to the value of its product, but also according to the varying disutility of the work. Leaders could impart an egalitarian tendency by distributing identical social dividends to all citizens.

It need scarcely be said that economic planning in Russia, or anywhere else, fails rather completely to conform to this model.

SCHUMPETER

In the chapters on Marx and Veblen, the leading dissenting accounts of capitalism's future, by its ill-wishers, have been summarized. Among recent economists, Schumpeter advanced the most nearly complete theory. One of the great economists of the twentieth century, Schumpeter made important contributions to business-cycle explanation, the pure theory of the competitive economy, and the understanding of capitalist change. His pessimistic outlook was not the effect of a dislike of capitalism. On the contrary, Schumpeter was an almost romantic admirer of capitalism, and an acute critic of the socialism which he feared and expected would triumph. Neither inefficiency nor social injustice doomed capitalism. Paradoxically—no one loved a good paradox better—the key to capitalism's demise was its great success, a clear case of a cat choked by an excess of cream.

What was the explanation? The unique element in capitalism was change. Capitalism's glory had been the tremendous improvement in technique and per capita output which had accompanied change. The entrepreneur, as has been observed, was the key figure. Unlike businessmen, entrepreneurs were scarce. Heroes are likely to be.[20]

Why could not capitalism continue as it had begun? Many new products surrounded us. Did they not testify to the present activity of entrepreneurs? Schumpeter's answer was sad. Something had happened to capitalism which blurred and weakened the entrepreneur's role. If he were superseded, then capitalism would lose its defining feature and yield, with scarcely a whimper, to socialism. Schumpeter identified four major changes in capitalism, all of them the by-products of success. Increasingly, corporate bureaucracy had substituted itself for the entrepreneur. This was the most important change. Invention had become a social process, the product of group research supported and controlled in great laboratories, administered by large corporations. Since inventions could be made to order, routine cost-accounting calculation regulates their introduction. The bold spirits who used to disturb existing arrangements with novel ideas and methods can find no scope in a world dominated by the large corporation. With the replacement of the entrepreneur by the salaried employee, the organization man, the dynamic of capitalism van-

---

[20] In a moment of impatience, a colleague called Schumpeter a "feudal remnant." He worshiped heroes and enjoyed life. A story, possibly apocryphal, has it that in his sixties he identified his ambitions as a young man to be the finest horseman, lover of beautiful women, and economist of his time. Two of these three ambitions, said he, he had achieved.

ished. For the salaried administrator will work just as readily for the state after industry has been nationalized. He may scarcely know the difference.

Three other historically unfavorable circumstances reinforced this one. Mature capitalism tended to destroy the small capitalist. Since the small capitalist's emotional commitment has been one of the system's strengths, his disappearance must reduce the number of persons ideologically attached to capitalism. Moreover, a third point, capitalism has tended to destroy the social groups which protect it. In Schumpeter's opinion, businessmen cannot govern well.[21] Historically, they have fared best when other classes ran the state and they were free to pursue their business interests. The point was clearest in England where during the nineteenth century the landed aristocracy governed the country, while industrial capitalists enriched themselves and the community. Finally, capitalism in its later stages has grown rich enough to support in idleness a class with nothing better to do than criticize. These are the intellectuals, who, because they make their living by words, suffer from the feeling that they lack any useful function. They take their resentments out in carping criticism.

Thus, successful capitalism has destroyed the basis of its continued existence. The large corporation is a monument to *past* innovation, to the ingenious souls who invented not only mass-production techniques, but also refined methods of corporate controls. However, their monuments can be administered by men of smaller scale, curators in place of builders. Such was private bureaucracy. How far behind it could public bureaucracy be? How long can capitalism endure? In his more cheerful moments, Schumpeter spoke of a generation or even two, one more run for the system. The end was almost certain. "Can capitalism survive? No. I do not think it can."[22]

---

[21] Democrats, at least, might find support for this position in recent political events.

[22] Joseph A. Schumpeter, *Capitalism, Socialism, and Democracy*, Harper, 1950, p. 61.

Further Readings

Further Readings

The books in this list direct the curious to several sources of information: some of the outstanding commentaries on the history of economic thought; the works of economists discussed in the text; and the contributions of economists neglected in the text. Although the list is selective rather than complete, a student who begins with it can move from it to as detailed an understanding of an aspect of the subject as he chooses.

The work of a great economist, Joseph A. Schumpeter's *History of Economic Analysis* (Oxford, 1954) is the most authoritative and advanced, not to say encyclopedic, account available. Part II of Jacob Viner's *The Long View and the Short* (Free Press, 1958) contains distinguished essays on a number of topics in the history of economic thought, including an erudite evaluation of Schumpeter's *History of Economic Analysis.* Henry W. Spiegel's *The Development of Economic Thought* (Wiley, 1952), frequently cited below, contains a fascinating series of essays by eminent economists about other eminent economists. Joseph Dorfman's *The Economic Mind in American Civilization* (Viking, 1946–1949) is a complete history of economic thinking in this country from the beginning to the end of the First World War.

CHAPTER 1

Plato, *The Republic*, trans. by Benjamin Jowett, Random House, 1937.

Aristotle, *Politics*, trans. by Benjamin Jowett, Modern Library, 1942.

A. E. Monroe, *Early Economic Thought*, Harvard, 1924. Contains translations of early economic classics.

Karl Polanyi, *et al.*, *Trade and Markets in the Early Empires*, Free Press, 1957. Chap. V is a fresh and controversial interpretation of Aristotle's economics.

M. I. Rostovtzeff, *Social and Economic History of the Hellenistic World*, Oxford, 1941. A leading history.

CHAPTER 2

Monroe, *op. cit.*

Nicole Oresme, *The De Moneta*, ed. and trans. by Charles Johnson, Nelson, 1956. An important medieval text.

C. G. Coulton, *Medieval Panorama*, Meridian, 1955.

Jacques Maritain, *St. Thomas Aquinas*, Meridian, 1958. A biography by a leading contemporary Thomist.

R. H. Tawney, *Religion and the Spirit of Capitalism*, Pelican, 1937. The opening chapter is a brilliant summary of the medieval spirit.

Max Weber, *The Protestant Ethic and the Rise of Capitalism*, Scribner, 1930. A still controversial analysis of how the Middle Ages yielded to rational capitalism.

CHAPTER 3

Richard Cantillon, *Essai sur la nature du commerce en général*, ed. by Henry Higgs, Macmillan, 1905. An important precursor of Adam Smith.

David Hume, *Writings on Economics*, ed. by Eugene Rotwein, Nelson, 1955. Relatively brief essays written in something of the same spirit as the *Wealth of Nations*.

John Locke, *Of Civil Government*, Everyman, 1943. The major philosophical support of the labor theory of value.

Thomas Mun, *England's Treasure by Forraign Trade*, Blackwell, 1949. Perhaps the best-known and most nearly typical mercantilist tract.

Sir Dudley North, *Discourse upon Trade*, Johns Hopkins, 1907. An early expression of free trade doctrine.

Sir William Petty, *Economic Writings*, Vol. I, Cambridge, 1899.

Adam Smith, *Wealth of Nations*, Modern Library, 1937. Bk. IV roughly massages mercantilist doctrine.

Lord Edmund Fitzmaurice, *Life of Sir William Petty*, Murray (London), 1895.

Eli Heckscher, *Mercantilism*, Macmillan, 1955. The standard history.

J. M. Keynes, *General Theory of Employment, Interest, and Money*, Harcourt Brace, 1936. Chap. 23 argues that the mercantilists were premature Keynesians. An attack upon this position is in Heckscher, *op. cit.*

Jacob Viner, *Studies in the Theory of International Trade*, Harper, 1937. The most authoritative study of mercantilism's trade doctrines.

CHAPTER 4

Adam Smith, *Lectures on Justice, Police, Revenue and Arms*, edited by Edwin Cannan, Macmillan, 1896.

Adam Smith, *Moral and Political Philosophy*, Hafner, 1948.

Adam Smith, *Wealth of Nations*, Modern Library, 1937.

J. H. Clapham, *A Concise Economic History of Great Britain from the Earliest Times to 1750*, Cambridge, 1951.

J. M. Clark, *et al.*, *Adam Smith, 1776–1926*, University of Chicago, 1928. Evaluations by several distinguished economists of Smith's continuing influence.

W. H. B. Court, *A Concise Economic History of Britain from 1750 to Recent Times*, Cambridge, 1954.

Gide and Rist, *A History of Economic Doctrines*, Heath, 1949. Chap. 1 examines from a sympathetic French view physiocratic doctrine.

Henry Higgs, *The Physiocrats*, Macmillan, 1897.

W. C. Mitchell, *Lecture Notes*, Kelley and Millman, 1954. A wonderfully fresh evocation of the circumstances which surrounded the writing of the *Wealth of Nations*.

John Rae, *Life of Adam Smith*, Macmillan, 1895. An old-fashioned biography which is still the standard source of personal information about Smith.

W. R. Scott, *Adam Smith as Student and Professor*, Glasgow, 1937.

CHAPTER 5

Jeremy Bentham, *Economic Writings*, ed. by W. Stark, Burt Franklin, 1952.

Jeremy Bentham, *Fragment on Government*, Macmillan, 1948.

Jeremy Bentham, *Introduction to the Principles of Morals and Legislation*, Hafner, 1948.

John Stuart Mill, *Autobiography*, Oxford, 1924. The opening chapters describe a complete Benthamite education.

John Stuart Mill, *Utilitarianism*, Everyman, 1944. The later views of a young utilitarian.

William Paley, *Works*, Vol. III, Crissy and Markley (London), 1838. An early Christian version of utilitarianism.

Eli Halevy, *The Growth of Philosophic Radicalism*, Augustus Kelley, 1949. A closely reasoned interpretation of utilitarianism's meanings and inconsistencies.

C. W. Everett, *The Education of Jeremy Bentham*, Columbia, 1931. A demonstration that Bentham's reputation for oddity was unjustified.

W. C. Mitchell, *The Backward Art of Spending Money*, Augustus Kelley, 1950. Chap. 10 is a sympathetic interpretation of Bentham's felicific calculus.

Leslie Stephen, *The English Utilitarians*, London School of Economics, 1950. A nineteenth-century utilitarian's lucid and favorable account of the school.

Graham Wallas, *Life of Francis Place*, Burt Franklin, 1951. A charming tribute to one of the English Radical leaders of the first part of the nineteenth century.

CHAPTER 6

William Cobbett, *Tracts*, Vol. I, London, 1831. Virulent attacks upon Malthusian doctrine by one of its most eloquent critics.

William Godwin, *Political Justice*, ed. by F. E. L. Priestly, University of Toronto, 1946. One of the books whose "errors" spurred Malthus to the writing of his famous *Essay on Population*.

Thomas Robert Malthus, *Essay on Population*, Everyman, 1933.

Harriet Martineau, *Weal and Woe in Garveloch*, London, 1832. One of the novels, based on Malthusian principles, in her influential *Illustrations of Political Economy*.

James Bonar, *Malthus and his Work*, Allen and Unwin (London), 1924.

Kenneth Smith, *The Malthusian Controversy*, Routledge and Kegan Paul (London), 1951.

J. M. Keynes, "Thomas Robert Malthus," *Essays in Biography*, Macmillan, 1933.

CHAPTER 7

John Barton, *The Condition of the Labouring Classes of Society*, Johns Hopkins, 1934. The pamphlet which induced Ricardo to revise his view that machinery inevitably favored the working class.

Thomas Robert Malthus, *An Inquiry into the Nature and Progress of Rent*, London, 1815. The pamphlet which led Ricardo to accord Malthus priority in the discovery of differential rent.

Robert Owen, *A New View of Society*, Everyman, 1927. An eloquent expression of Utopian socialism.

David Ricardo, *The Works and Correspondence*, ed. by Piero Sraffa, Cambridge, 1951–1955. These magnificent ten volumes include everything Ricardo wrote for publication and an enormous quantity of letters.

William Thompson, *An Inquiry into the Principle of the Distribution of Wealth*, London, 1824.

William Thompson, *Labour Rewarded*, London, 1827. Thompson's two essays extended Ricardian theory to justify greater equality of income distribution. Thompson seems to have influenced Marx.

Robert Torrens, *Essay on the External Corn Trade*, London, 1826.

Mark Blaug, *Ricardian Economics*, Yale, 1958. Especially valuable for its discussion of the Ricardian school.

Henry Thornton, *Enquiry into the Nature and the Effects of the Paper Credit of Great Britain*, Farrar and Rinehart, 1939. First published in 1803, this book is an amazingly modern interpretation of English monetary institutions.

Edward West, *Essay on the Application of Capital to Land*, London, 1815. One of the four nearly simultaneous discoveries of the principle of differential rent.

E. M. Forster, *Marianne Thornton*, Harcourt Brace, 1956. Henry Thornton plays a role in this biography.

Elie Halèvy, *Thomas Hodgskin*, Benn, 1956. A biography of another Ricardian Socialist.

Frank Knight, "The Ricardian Theory of Production and Distribution," *Canadian Journal of Economics and Political Science*, May, 1935. A leading critical examination of Ricardo's economics.

Esther Lowenthal, *The Ricardian Socialists*, Columbia, 1911.

Lionel Robbins, *Robert Torrens and the Evolution of Classical Economics*, Macmillan, 1958.

CHAPTER 8

John Stuart Mill, *Autobiography*, Oxford, 1924.

John Stuart Mill, *Essays on Some Unsettled Questions of Political Economy*, London School of Economics, 1948.

John Stuart Mill, *Principles of Political Economy*, ed. by W. J. Ashley, Longmans, Green (England), 1909.

Nassau Senior, *An Outline of the Science of Political Economy*, Augustus Kelley, 1951. One of the major figures between Ricardo and John Stuart Mill.

Marion Bowley, *Nassau Senior and Classical Political Economy*, Augustus Kelley, 1949.

Edwin Cannan, *A History of the Theories of Production and Distribution in English Political Economy*, Staples Press, 1953. Not much is left of economics between 1776 and 1848 after Professor Cannan is done.

Abram L. Harris, *Economics and Social Reform*, Harper, 1958. Chap. II is an excellent account of Mill's social and political opinions and their evolution.

Robert G. Link, *English Theories of Economic Fluctuations*, Columbia, 1959.

Michael St. John Packe, *Life of John Stuart Mill*, Macmillan, 1954. An excellent modern life.

Lionel Robbins, *The Theory of Economic Policy*, Macmillan, 1952. A balanced statement of the interventionist and noninterventionist leanings of the classical economists.

Leslie Stephens, *The English Utilitarians*, London School of Economics, 1950.

CHAPTER 9

Friedrich Engels, *Condition of the Working Class in England in 1844*, Allen and Unwin (London), 1926.

Friedrich Engels, *Herr Eugen Dühring's Revolution in Science*, International Publishers, 1939. The standard Marxist source of dialectical inspiration.

Friedrich Engels and Karl Marx, *Selected Correspondence*, International Publishers, 1942.

Friedrich Engels and Karl Marx, *The Communist Manifesto*, Appleton-Century-Crofts, 1955.

Karl Marx, *Capital*, Modern Library (no date). English translation 1906.

Karl Marx, *Critique of the Gotha Program*, International Publishers, 1938. The major source of Marx's forecast of life in the future Communist universe.

Eugen von Böhm-Bawerk, *Karl Marx and the Close of his System*, Augustus Kelley, 1949. A leading marginalist criticism of Marxist economics.

Harris, *op. cit.*, Chap. III.

Franz Mehring, *Karl Marx, His Life and Work*, Covici Friede, 1936.

CHAPTER 10

Augustin Cournot, *Researches into the Mathematical Principles of Wealth*, trans. by N. T. Bacon, Macmillan, 1929. A remarkable anticipation of the marginalism of the 1870's.

W. E. Hearn, *Plutology*, Macmillan, 1864. One of the influences upon Jevons.

W. S. Jevons, *Letters and Journals*, Macmillan, 1886. The major source of biographical information.

W. S. Jevons, *The Theory of Political Economy*, Macmillan, 1911.

Carl Menger, *Principles of Economics*, trans. by James Dingwall and Bert F. Hoselitz, Free Press, 1950.

Léon Walras, *Elements of Pure Economics*, trans. by William Jaffé, Irwin, 1954.

T. W. Hutchison, *A Review of Economic Doctrines, 1870–1929*, Oxford, 1953. The most useful general book about the period indicated in its title.

Spiegel, *op. cit.*, pp. 443–552, 580–592.

CHAPTER 11

Eugen von Böhm-Bawerk, *The Positive Theory of Capital*, trans. by William Smart, Macmillan, 1891.

J. B. Clark, *The Distribution of Wealth*, Macmillan, 1899.

J. B. Clark, *The Philosophy of Wealth*, Ginn, 1903.

F. Y. Edgeworth, *Mathematical Psychics*, Kegan Paul (London), 1881. A late effort to employ utilitarian psychology.

Irving Fisher, *Mathematical Investigations into the Theory of Value and Price*, Yale, 1892. An early use of indifference curves.

Irving Fisher, *Theory of Interest*, Macmillan, 1930.

Alfred Marshall, *Principles of Economics*, Macmillan, 1920.

Friedrich von Weiser, *Natural Value*, trans. by C. A. Malloch, Macmillan, 1893.

Knut Wicksell, *Lectures on Political Economy*, trans. by E. Classen, Routledge and Kegan Paul (London), 1934.

P. H. Wicksteed, *Common Sense of Political Economy*, Routledge and Kegan Paul (London), 1935. One of the great marginalist syntheses.

J. R. Hicks, *A Revision of Demand Theory*, Oxford, 1956. Chap. I is an excellent selective history of utility doctrine.

Hutchison, *op. cit.*

A. C. Pigou (ed.), *Memorials of Alfred Marshall*, Cambridge, 1925.

J. A. Schumpeter, *Ten Great Economists*, Oxford, 1951. Authoritative sketches.

G. J. Stigler, *Production and Distribution Theories*, Macmillan, 1941. A leading analysis of the theories of the 1880's and 1890's.

CHAPTER 12

Friedrich List, *National System of Political Economy*, Longmans, Green, 1904. Among a good deal else, List advanced most systematically the infant industry argument for the protection of domestic industries.

Wilhelm Roscher, *Principles of Political Economy*, Holt, 1877.

Werner Sombart, *The Jews and Modern Capitalism*, Free Press, 1951. A radical variant of Weber's explanation of capitalism's rise.

Arnold Toynbee, *The Industrial Revolution*, Beacon Press, 1956. The great-uncle of the present Arnold Toynbee, Toynbee invented the term and analyzed the phenomenon.

Max Weber, *The Protestant Ethic and the Spirit of Capitalism*, Pelican, 1937. The title suggests the thesis.

Harris, *op. cit.*, Chap. VI.

Hutchison, *op. cit.*

H. M. Robertson, *Aspects of the Rise of Economic Individualism*, Cambridge, 1935. Still another emphasis on capitalism's beginnings.

Spiegel, *op. cit.*, pp. 342–359.

CHAPTER 13

John R. Commons, *Legal Foundations of Capitalism*, Macmillan, 1924.

W. C. Mitchell, *Business Cycles and Their Causes*, University of California, 1941. PT. III of Mitchell's 1913 study.

W. C. Mitchell, *Business Cycles: The Problem and Its Setting*, National Bureau of Economic Research, 1927.

Spiegel, *op. cit.*, pp. 378–443.

Thorstein Veblen, *Theory of Business Enterprise*, Scribner, 1904.

Thorstein Veblen, *Theory of the Leisure Class*, Modern Library, 1931.

Thorstein Veblen, *Engineers and the Price System*, Huebsch, 1921.

Joseph Dorman, *Thorstein Veblen and His America*, Viking, 1934. A careful account of Veblen's life and a complete summary of his work.

Harris, *op. cit.* Excellent analyses of Veblen and Commons.

CHAPTER 14

J. M. Keynes, *Economic Consequences of the Peace*, Harcourt Brace & Howe, 1920. The polemic which first brought Keynes into public prominence.

J. M. Keynes, *Essays in Biography*, Macmillan, 1933. A collection which displays to best advantage Keynes' gifts as a literary stylist.

J. M. Keynes, *General Theory of Employment, Interest and Money*, Harcourt Brace, 1936. Probably the most influential book on economics of the first half of the twentieth century.

J. M. Keynes, *A Treatise on Money*, Macmillan, 1930.

Seymour Harris (ed.), *The New Economics*, Knopf, 1947. A valuable collection of critical and favorable appraisals of Keynesian economics.

R. H. Harrod, *Life of John Maynard Keynes*, Macmillan, 1951. A complete biography written by an admirer and disciple.

J. K. Johnstone, *The Bloomsbury Group*, Noonday Press, 1954.

CHAPTER 15

Arthur F. Burns, *The Frontiers of Economic Knowledge*, Princeton, 1954. Essays by the most influential proponent of the statistical approach to the comprehension of business cycles.

Gottfried Haberler (ed.), *Readings in Business Cycle Theory*, Blakiston, 1944. A valuable collection of important journal articles.

Simon Kuznets, *Economic Change*, Norton, 1953. Essays by another leading proponent of statistical interpretation of business cycles.

Dennis Robertson, *Banking Policy and the Price Level*, Augustus Kelley, 1949. Emphasizes "real" changes as explanation of business cycles.

Joseph A. Schumpeter, *Business Cycles*, McGraw-Hill, 1939. An encyclopedic treatise which emphasizes the role of the entrepreneur and the innovation.

Gottfried Haberler, *Prosperity and Depression*, United Nations, 1946. The best summary and analysis of contemporary business-cycle theory.

Howard S. Ellis (ed.), *A Survey of Contemporary Economics*, Blakiston, 1948. Chaps. 2, 5, 8, 9.

CHAPTER 16

Edward H. Chamberlin, *Theory of Monopolistic Competition*, Harvard, 1946. With Joan Robinson (see below) the inventor of the modern theory of imperfect competition.

Joel Dean (ed.), *Readings in the Social Control of Industry*, Blakiston, 1942. A valuable collection of important journal articles.

John R. Hicks, *Value and Capital*, Oxford, 1939. Hicks revived indifference curve analysis and extended Walrasian general equilibrium theory. An important theoretical contribution.

Joan Robinson, *Economics of Imperfect Competition*, Macmillan, 1948.

George Stigler (ed.), *Readings in Price Theory*, Irwin, 1952. An important collection of journal articles.

Robert Triffin, *Monopolistic Competition and General Equilibrium Theory*, Harvard, 1940. An extension and criticism of Chamberlin's theory.

CHAPTER 17

John Maurice Clark, *Economic Institutions and Human Welfare*, Knopf, 1957.

Bertrand de Jouvenel, *The Ethics of Redistribution*, Cambridge, 1951. An eloquent statement of the benefits of unequal distribution of income.

Maurice Dobb, *Political Economy and Capitalism*, International Publishers, 1945. Closely reasoned essays based on Marxist opinions.

Ellis, *op. cit.*, Chaps. 12, 13.

Bernard F. Haley (ed.), *A Survey of Contemporary Economics*, Vol. II, Irwin, 1952. Chaps. 1, 3, 4, 10.

Friedrich A. Hayek (ed.), *Collectivist Economic Planning*, Routledge and Kegan Paul (London), 1935. Several sides of the argument about the feasibility of rational allocation of resources under socialism.

John A. Hobson, *Work and Wealth*, Allen & Unwin (London), 1933. An important book of an early welfare economist.

Frank H. Knight, *The Ethics of Competition*, Augustus Kelley, 1951. A series of essays by an influential economist not easily classified as a member of any school.

Oskar Lange and Fred M. Taylor, *On the Economic Theory of Socialism*, Minnesota, 1938.

I. M. D. Little, *A Critique of Welfare Economics*, Oxford, 1950.

A. C. Pigou, *Economics of Welfare*, Macmillan, 1932. A landmark, in the Marshallian tradition, of the theory of economic welfare.

Sir Dennis Robertson, *Utility and All That*, Allen & Unwin, 1952. An urbane and skeptical criticism of contemporary welfare economics.

Joseph A. Schumpeter, *Capitalism, Socialism and Democracy*, Harper, 1950. A reluctant forecast, by an admirer, of capitalism's demise.

Melvin W. Reder, *Studies in the Theory of Welfare Economics*, Columbia, 1947.

Indexes

Index of Names

Index of Subjects

Catalog

If you are interested in a list of fine Paperback
books, covering a wide range of subjects
and interests, send your name and address,
requesting your free catalog, to:

McGraw-Hill Paperbacks
1221 Avenue of Americas
New York, N.Y. 10020